"The early modern missionary movement was decisively shaped by a number of iconic figures: among the chief of them was Adoniram Judson. This original and incisive study of his piety helps us not only understand his life and what made him tick but also the pattern of missionary piety that came after him. A great study!"

—MICHAEL A. G. HAYKIN
Professor of Church History and Biblical Spirituality,
The Southern Baptist Theological Seminary

"Adoniram and Ann Judson have always been heroes to me for a host of reasons: their courage to obey the Great Commission, to explore biblical truth as it related to baptism, to act on what God showed them even at great personal cost, and to remain faithful in missions though great suffering. E. D. Burns provides insightful analysis of Adoniram Judson's spiritual fortitude that enabled endurance, which I pray will spark a supreme desire to please Him among many readers."

—M. DAVID SILLS
DMiss, Ph.D., A.P. and Faye Stone Chair of Christian Missions and Cultural Anthropology,
The Southern Baptist Theological Seminary

A Supreme Desire to Please Him

Monographs in Baptist History

VOLUME 4

SERIES EDITOR
Michael A. G. Haykin, The Southern Baptist Theological Seminary

EDITORIAL BOARD
Matthew Barrett, California Baptist University
Peter Beck, Charleston Southern University
Anthony L. Chute, California Baptist University
Jason G. Duesing, Midwest Baptist Theological Seminary
Nathan A. Finn, Union University
Crawford Gribben, Queen's University, Belfast
Gordon L. Heath, McMaster Divinity College
Barry Howson, Heritage Theological Seminary
Jason K. Lee, Cedarville University
Thomas J. Nettles, The Southern Baptist Theological Seminary, retired
James A. Patterson, Union University
James M. Renihan, Institute of Reformed Baptist Studies
Jeffrey P. Straub, Central Seminary
Brian R. Talbot, Broughty Ferry Baptist Church, Scotland
Malcolm B. Yarnell III, Southwestern Baptist Theological Seminary

Ours is a day in which not only the gaze of western culture but also increasingly that of Evangelicals is riveted to the present. The past seems to be nowhere in view and hence it is disparagingly dismissed as being of little value for our rapidly changing world. Such historical amnesia is fatal for any culture, but particularly so for Christian communities whose identity is profoundly bound up with their history. The goal of this new series of monographs, Studies in Baptist History, seeks to provide one of these Christian communities, that of evangelical Baptists, with reasons and resources for remembering the past. The editors are deeply convinced that Baptist history contains rich resources of theological reflection, praxis and spirituality that can help Baptists, as well as other Christians, live more Christianly in the present. The monographs in this series will therefore aim at illuminating various aspects of the Baptist tradition and in the process provide Baptists with a usable past.

A Supreme Desire to Please Him

The Spirituality of Adoniram Judson

E. D. Burns

Foreword by Jason Duesing

☙PICKWICK *Publications* · Eugene, Oregon

A SUPREME DESIRE TO PLEASE HIM
The Spirituality of Adoniram Judson

Monographs in Baptist History 4

Copyright © 2016 E. D. Burns. All rights reserved. Except for brief quotations in critical publications or reviews, no part of this book may be reproduced in any manner without prior written permission from the publisher. Write: Permissions, Wipf and Stock Publishers, 199 W. 8th Ave., Suite 3, Eugene, OR 97401.

Pickwick Publications
An Imprint of Wipf and Stock Publishers
199 W. 8th Ave., Suite 3
Eugene, OR 97401

www.wipfandstock.com

PAPERBACK ISBN: 978-1-4982-8025-9
HARDCOVER ISBN: 978-1-4982-8027-3
EBOOK ISBN: 978-1-4982-8026-6

Cataloguing-in-Publication data:

Names: Burns, E. D.

Title: A supreme desire to please him : the spirituality of Adoniram Judson / E. D. Burns.

Description: Eugene, OR: Pickwick Publications, 2016 | Series: Monographs in Baptist History 4 | Includes bibliographical references and index.

Identifiers: ISBN 978-1-4982-8025-9 (paperback) | ISBN 978-1-4982-8027-3 (hardcover) | ISBN 978-1-4982-8026-6 (ebook)

Subjects: LCSH: Judson, Adoniram, 1788–1850. | Spiritual life—Baptists.

Classification: BX6495 B85 2016 (paperback) | BX6495 (ebook)

Manufactured in the U.S.A.   10/05/18

To Kristie,
a beautiful companion and missionary wife,
who humbles me with her hope-filled courage
and devotion to Christ.

> "Resolved to make the desire to please Christ the grand motive of all my actions."
>
> ADONIRAM JUDSON

Contents

Foreword by Jason Duesing | ix
Preface | xi
Acknowledgments | xiii
Abbreviations | xvii

1. Introduction | 1
2. The Life and Context of Adoniram Judson | 18
3. "Yield to the Word of God": Bibliocentric Spirituality | 64
4. "Thy Will Be Ever Done": Ascetic Spirituality | 94
5. "We Reap on Zion's Hill": Heavenly-Minded Spirituality | 143
6. "O, The Love of Christ": Christocentric Spirituality | 171
7. Conclusion | 206

Bibliography | 213
Author Index | 233

Foreword
The Significance of Adoniram Judson

ON THE OCCASION OF the centennial anniversary of Adoniram Judson's first arrival in Burma, W. O. Carver, professor of comparative religion and missions at Southern Baptist Theological Seminary, wrote an article for the seminary's journal, *Review and Expositor*, entitled, "The Significance of Adoniram Judson."[1] Carver set out not to provide a biographical overview of Judson's life, but rather showed how Judson's character and piety served as examples for a generation of missionaries and the formal start of modern missions from the United States.

Even though Carver signals the progressive theological drift from which his seminary would take nearly a century to recover, his article on Judson is appreciative and insightful.[2] While written over one hundred years ago, his conclusions regarding Judson's place in history as well as Judson's significance for the present, still ring true today. In sum, Carver observed that Judson's life had an effect "not only in drawing men into service, but rather more, perhaps, in sustaining men in service."[3] That the study of Judson's life could have this kind of encouraging effect on many in the centuries following his death is what makes his life significant and it is also why I am

---

1. Carver, "The Significance of Adoniram Judson."

2. That Carver would focus too on Judson's evangelistic faithfulness is remarkable as Carver represents one of the early professors in Southern Baptist higher education who "who tried to bridge the gap between religious modernity and Southern Baptist traditionalism." See Smith, Review of *William Owen Carver's Controversies in the Baptist South*. Or, as Wills states in his magisterial institutional biography of the seminary, "The teaching of W. O. Carver was an important source" behind the seminary's growing reputation as a "liberal school" in the early twentieth century. See Wills, *Southern Baptist Seminary*, 255.

3. Carver, "The Significance of Adoniram Judson," 478.

delighted that you hold in your hands a copy of E. D. Burns's *A Supreme Desire to Please Him: The Spirituality of Adoniram Judson*.

The study of Judson's life and thought is fraught with difficulty for so much of what he wrote or recorded he also, at a challenging moment in his life, went to great lengths to destroy. Biographers and researchers in the past have only been able to piece together the facts of Judson's life from those who have gone before but without any single comprehensive or standalone treatment. That changes now with *A Supreme Desire to Please Him*.

First, this book is the first theological synthesis and comprehensive analysis of all known primary and secondary Judson sources. In other words, E. D. Burns has managed to uncover just about every imaginable stone related to Judson and then also rightly classify them.

Second, as W. O. Carver noted, one of the valuable characteristics of Judson's life was his piety. Here, too, Burns capitalizes on perhaps the best possible avenue through which to pursue research related to Judson. By focusing on Judson's spirituality, Burns has done something entirely original and, therefore, all the more helpful for readers.

Third, Burns has successfully moved the bar of knowledge and understanding of Judson and his contribution much higher than was previously the case. Further, his analysis of portions of Judson's life and thought not before considered in depth is key. One example of this includes Burns's exploring and explaining Judson's "dark night" of self-denial following the death of his wife, daughter, and father in light of the influence of Samuel Hopkins's teaching on disinterested benevolence.

This study of the spirituality of Adoniram Judson could not come at a better time in the history of Christianity. As Burns shows, Judson's love for God and the Bible fueled a life marked by self-denial, prayer, joy in Christ, and a desire to see such love and joy proclaimed and multiplied among the nations of the earth. Thus, in our own day, as W. O. Carver noted, the reading of the work of God in the life of Judson can still serve to draw men and women into Gospel ministry as well as sustain those currently laboring in mission fields around the globe. Indeed, the life of Judson and this book by E. D. Burns may be the very best vehicles to call and sustain many to that end. Indeed, may God see fit to bless the nations once again through the significant life of Adoniram Judson.

Jason Duesing
Provost and Associate Professor of Historical Theology
Midwestern Baptist Theological Seminary
Kansas City

Preface

THIS BOOK IS THE denouement of over three years of research. Some initial comments are necessary in terms of stylistic choices made throughout this book: "Judson" will predominantly refer to the subject under consideration, Adoniram Judson Jr. Some authors refer to him as Adoniram, but unless such an author is quoted or unless there might be contextual confusion in relation to his father or other family members, his surname will identify him. All citations and quotes from primary sources retain their original spelling and punctuation. The spelling often varies depending on the author and depending on the era of each piece's publication. However, when not quoting primary sources, "Burma" will be used to refer to the present-day country of Myanmar, and to be consistent, this will be the spelling used for the older spelling, Burmah. "Burman" and "Burmese" are also used interchangeably as they were used in the nineteenth century. In addition, all other original spelling will remain unaltered in quotations. The original emphases will be indicated with italics only. When Judson's nineteenth-century biographers transcribed his journals and letters, they often italicized those words that he underlined once, and they capitalized those words that he underlined twice. In this book, all his emphases are italicized and not capitalized. And all Scripture references are from the King James Version, unless otherwise noted.

Acknowledgments

In 1989 I first sensed the missionary call to spend my life for the glory of Christ among the nations. Along the way, the life and piety of Adoniram Judson has challenged and inspired me to be devoted for life. It was a great honor to study and learn from his inimitable missionary spirituality and make it available to strengthen those missionaries and ministers who have suffered long in the cause of Christ. I am above all else eternally thankful for the sustaining and empowering grace of God the Father, the Son, and the Holy Spirit.

First, this project would not have been possible without the sweet and selfless encouragement of my lovely bride, Kristie. Her genuine enthusiasm for this book has made every sacrifice seem bearable. I hope a historian will someday write her biography and highlight how she has joyfully stood by me and how she has faithfully served her sovereign Lord through untold sacrifice and adversity. She is a treasure that I do not deserve. *The future is as bright as the promises of God.*

Second, I want to thank my father, Dan. All of my life, he has relentlessly stood by me in sickness and adversity. He has earnestly encouraged me to spend and be spent for Christ's gospel. And to my mother, Linda, I am grateful for her tender and strong love. She has been a humble example of how to suffer well. And to my sister, Emily, I am grateful for her endless love and laughter. Both Mike and Mindy have also been so gracious and encouraging, of which I am undeserving. All members of my immediate and extended family have been incredibly supportive. I love you all. *We shall meet in that blessed world where the loved and the parted here below meet ne'er to part again.*

Third, to those who loyally support and stand with us in the gospel, we are forever grateful for your partnership. I am grateful to Pastor Ben Mosier, my longest standing friend, whose loyal friendship and unending admiration throughout my life have been more than I deserve. I am thankful for all those brothers from Moody who were awakened with me in a God-centered flame of missionary zeal, and I am unworthy of those brothers around the world with whom I have served for years. Yet, their biographies will remain unwritten this side of heaven. Let us stay *devoted for life*.

Fourth, I am humbled by the kindness and grace of my mentor, Michael Haykin. His evangelical spirituality and his ardent love for Jesus have been contagious for me. I have felt immensely privileged to know him and to study under his tutelage. His keen eye for detail, his passion for truth, and his bold evangelical scholarship have been so instrumental for this project. I am also thankful to Don Whitney and David Sills, whose biblical teaching and warm friendships have indelibly marked my spirituality and my missiology. And to Greg Wills, I am grateful for his wisdom, encouragement, and scholarly advice for this book. I am thankful for Jason Duesing's scholarship and his valuable feedback.

Fifth, I would like to acknowledge and thank those who have given me advice about resources and materials for this book. I am grateful for those emails and meetings with Judson enthusiasts: Rosalie Hall Hunt, Benjamin Brandenburg, Jack McElroy, William Brackney, Allen Yeh, and Chris Chun. I am also grateful for the hospitality and expertise of the scholars at the American Baptist Historical Society: Jan Ballard, Deborah Van Broekhoven, and Janet Winfield. I am grateful for the assistance of Taffey Hall at the Southern Baptist Historical Society and Archives, for the help of Diana Yount at the Trask Library of Andover Newton Theological School, and for the assistance of Ben Ruppert and Kevin Hall at the Boyce Library. I am also grateful to Joe Harrod for his advice and to Jordan Edwards for his logistical help. I am thankful for Kyle Schwahn's helpful feedback on the original manuscript. I wish to thank Jake Porter for first encouraging me to pursue this project. And, I am grateful to Jim Blumenstock and the rest of the Asia Biblical Theological Seminary faculty for their gracious support during my research and writing. I also want to thank Rob Wiggins and Western Seminary for their kind encouragement and support for my writing.

This project would not be comprehensive if I had not providentially discovered some of Judson's Burmese tracts that no one had ever translated into English. A qualified Burmese translator, April T. T. Aye, was instrumental in translating two of Judson's untranslated tracts: *A Digest of Scripture* and *The Septenary*, and a Burmese biography of Judson, *Sketch of the Life of Dr. Judson*, by Melvin Jameson. I am indebted to her superior translation skills and command of the English language. I am also thankful to my seminary students in Burma and to the Burmese pastors who have shared with me their esteem for Judson and for his translation.

Finally, to my sons, Elijah and Isaiah, I love you. I am so proud of you because of your love for Jesus and your desire to preach the gospel. You both will grow up to be great men of God. *Keep straight forward, and trust in God.*

E. D. Burns
Chiang Mai, Thailand
May 2015

Abbreviations

ABHS American Baptist Historical Society, Atlanta
ABCFM American Board of Commissioners for Foreign Missions
BMS Baptist Missionary Society
SBJME *The Southern Baptist Journal of Missions and Evangelism*

1

Introduction

"IT SEEMS TO BE a divine law that those who bestow roses must feel thorns."[1] These were the words of Edward Judson (1844–1914), describing the thorny sufferings and fragrant legacy of his father, the first American Baptist missionary to Burma, Adoniram Judson Jr. (1788–1850).[2] Judson's life and labor were a paragon of relentless obedience to the missionary call and of humble submission to the sovereignty of God.[3] The

---

1. Edward Judson, *The Life of Adoniram Judson*, 560.

2. Though Judson has popularly claimed the title of the first American missionary, some debate exists. George Liele (c. 1750–1828), born a slave in Virginia, sided with the British in the Revolutionary War and escaped to Jamaica as an indentured servant in 1783. While on the island, he preached the gospel to fellow slaves, baptizing them and overseeing the beginnings of many Baptist churches. By 1814, Jamaica had approximately eight thousand Baptists. Some credit Liele with being the first American missionary. See Neely, "Liele, George." See also Brackney, "Judson, Adoniram," 345–46; Livingstone, "Judson, Adoniram," 282; Mobley, "Judson, Adoniram, Jr.," 337–40; Moyer, "Judson, Adoniram," 219; and Schaff, "Judson, Adoniram," 257–58.

3. The primary sources of letters, journals, sermons, and tracts from which all of Judson's biographical sketches chiefly draw are Judson Letters, Manuscript Collection, American Baptist Historical Society, Atlanta, Georgia; *The Baptist Missionary Magazine* 1–89 (1817–1909); *Southern Baptist Missionary Journal* 1–5 (1851–1846); Papers 1815–1849, Archives and Manuscripts, Microfilm Collection, Southern Baptist Historical Library & Archive, Nashville, Tennessee; and Papers 1811–1888, Manuscripts, Trask Library Special Collections, Andover Newton Theological School, Newton Centre, Massachusetts. Also, there are two letters at Boston University School of Theology Archives, Boston University, Boston, Massachusetts. Manuscripts from the following are on microfilm and are duplicates of what is contained in the American Baptist Historical Society: Papers of Adoniram Judson—Collection 333, Manuscripts, Microfilm, Billy Graham Center Archives, Wheaton College, Wheaton, Illinois; American Baptist Foreign Mission Society records, #4424, Division of Rare and Manuscript Collections, Cornell University Library, Ithaca, New York; and Papers, 1815–1849, Microfilm, New

diamond of his piety glistens upon the dark cloth of God's inscrutable providences.

In an era of great American folk heroes such as Daniel Boone (1734–1820) and Davy Crockett (1786–1836), and legendary ventures such as the Lewis and Clark Expedition (1804–1806), many hailed Judson as an exemplar even before his death.[4] Not long after his death he was endowed with the honor of "the Christian hero of the nineteenth century."[5] Today,

---

York State Historical Documents, Albany, New York. The following also have helpful manuscripts for Judson-related research: American Board of Commissioners for Foreign Missions Archives, 1810–1961 (ABC 1–91), Houghton Library, Harvard University, Cambridge, Massachusetts; Baptist Collection, University Archives, John Hay Library, Brown University, Providence, Rhode Island; and Special Collections, University Archives, John Hay Library, Brown University, Providence, Rhode Island. There are four prominent biographies by contemporaries of Judson, whose extractions from journals, letters, and sermons occasionally overlap; these biographies are Middleditch, *Burmah's Great Missionary*; Knowles, *Memoir of Mrs. Ann H. Judson*; Wayland, *Memoir*, 1–2; and Edward Judson, *The Life of Adoniram Judson*. Furthermore, drawing content from the aforementioned nineteenth-century biographies, the landmark biography of the twentieth century was Anderson, *To the Golden Shore*. And five other significant historical treatments in the twentieth century of Judson's life were Warburton, *Eastward*; Hull, *Judson the Pioneer*; Torbet, *Venture of Faith*; James, *My Heart in His Hands*; and Brumberg, *Mission for Life*. In the twenty-first century, the prominent biography that gathered quotes from the previous authoritative biographies in addition to original research on the Judson legacy is Hunt, *Bless God and Take Courage*. And a twenty-first-century study of his life and thought is Duesing, *Adoniram Judson*.

4. For instance, a contemporary described the adulatory welcome of Judson's homecoming in Boston on October 16, 1845, one day after Judson's arrival: "The arrival of this devoted missionary in his native land, has produces a thrill of emotion in a multitude of hearts, which may be imagined, but cannot be described. His appearance among us was like life from the dead . . . When it was known that he had arrived in the city, thousands were eager to look upon the face of a man whom God had so highly honored as the messenger of his grace to the heathen. To gratify this desire, intelligence was circulated on Friday, verbally, in order to avoid all publicity, that the friends of missions would meet in the Bowdoin Square church, in the evening, to see and welcome him. The house was densely filled. The pastors of the churches in the city and vicinity were present, and a more affecting meeting we never before attended. We never before saw so large a congregation all moved by so deep and mighty an impulse. Language could not give vent to emotions which struggled in every bosom." Crowell, "Reception at Boston," 236–37. Brackney's observation is apt: "During his own lifetime, Adoniram Judson became a mythic figure, but even more so in his death. Tall and handsome, he had the profile of an American frontiersman. His struggles with Burmese officials and exploits during the Anglo-Burmese War marked him as a rugged religious individualist in the mold of Davy Crockett (1786–1836) or Andrew Jackson (1767–1845), his contemporaries back home in the United States." Brackney, "The Legacy of Adoniram Judson," 125.

5. One biographer said, "[Judson] more than any other man of his age, may justly claim the title of *The Christian Hero of the Nineteenth Century*! I know of no man in modern times, whose life has been a more eventful one, and which bears a stronger

and unquestionably in his own day, Judson has been venerated as an icon of missionary fortitude—indeed "a sort of Christian Paladin."[6] According to one early biographer, Judson's religious biography, made available to the evangelical multitudes through the printing press, "has done more efficient service in quickening spiritual life and promoting Christian usefulness. No man has fulfilled his course in latter times with whose life it could be more profitable for the churches of Christ to have a familiar knowledge,"[7] than that of Judson. Admirers thrust him into "celebrity status."[8] Judson was "among the most courageous of the religious adventurers of the nineteenth century."[9] His contemporaries considered him to be among men who,

> do not represent the spirit of their age, or the opinions of a people; they are prophets of the future; they represent *ideas* which, struggling for mastery, become the property of succeeding times. They identify their fortunes with the success of a principle; they enshrine in their hearts some great truth, unwelcome to their generation, and feel themselves impelled to go forth as its heralds, to conquer as its champions, or die as its martyrs. Among the men of this higher order, as far as the elements of character are concerned, Adoniram Judson holds a distinguished place.[10]

---

resemblance to the character and sufferings of the Apostle Paul, than that of Adoniram Judson." Gray, *The Christian Hero of the Nineteenth Century*, 2; emphasis in original.

6. Conant, *The Earnest Man*, 470; see also Brumberg, *Mission for Life*, 1. One biographer who knew Judson described him as "Adoniram Judson, D.D., the apostle and champion of American Missionaries among the heathen. That man of men—that missionary of missionaries—that noble representative of American enterprise, intelligence, and virtue, as they were developed in his life and death." Gillette, *A Sketch of the Labors*, 10. For further evidence of the great influence of Judson's life on so many in his day and thereafter, see his son's reflections on Judson's legacy: "Posthumus Influence," in Edward Judson, *The Life of Adoniram Judson*, 568–80. Also, for hagiographical descriptions of Judson's inimitable labors by his contemporaries, see Dowling, *The Judson Offering*, iii.

7. Middleditch, *Burmah's Great Missionary*, iii. Brumberg suggests that Judson's raw sincerity is what made his biographies so interesting and inoffensive to the secularists of the mid-nineteenth century. Brumberg, *Mission for Life*, 11.

8. James, *My Heart in His Hands*, 14. William Owen Carver (1868–1954), the Southern Baptist missiologist, commented that many famous missionaries had purposefully kept diaries and recorded events for the sake of making "incidents that would be commonplace to other men" seem to be "dramatic and heroic." In contrast, he said that Judson sought to destroy his letters and records when he heard they could "make him out a great hero" and be "used to lionize him." Carver, "The Significance of Adoniram Judson," 476.

9. Butler et al., *Religion in American Life*, 306.

10. Hague, *The Life and Character of Adoniram Judson*, 6; emphasis in original.

Judson's "seraphic zeal"[11] inspired those of his own generation and those to follow. One hundred years after his birth, many biographies, indeed hagiographies, had "made the name of 'Judson' a household word throughout the length and breadth of Christendom."[12]

Though eminent in his home country, Judson was also renowned in and around Burma as "Jesus Christ's man" who published writings, telling of the eternal God:

> Others come from the frontiers of Kathay, a hundred miles north of Ava—"Sir, we have seen a writing that tells about an eternal God. Are you the man that gives away such writings? If so, pray give us one, for we want to know the truth before we die." Others come from the interior of the country, where the name of Jesus Christ is a little known—"*Are you Jesus Christ's man?* Give us a writing that tells about Jesus Christ."[13]

Judson's reputation in Burma as a disciple of Christ accordingly spread to the United States where his supporters likewise recognized him as such a man. He arrived back in the United States in the fall of 1845, and while he was attending a special meeting of the Triennial Convention in New York, "The mover of the resolutions . . . presented [Judson] to Dr. [Francis] Wayland with the expressive and well-understood words: 'I present to you *Jesus Christ's man*.'"[14] This apropos title exemplifies the Christ-centered spirituality of Adoniram Judson.

Status Quaestionis

Although the story of Adoniram Judson has become legendary, there has never been a systematic synthesis and study of his spirituality. The attraction of Judson's life is evident in the dramatic ways in which his biographers highlight the tragedy, romance, and triumph of his story; undoubtedly, the numerous times his biography has been rewritten using the same sources and sketching the same events reveals the allure of his life's story.[15] Yet,

---

11. Richards, *The Apostle of Burma*, vii.

12. Ibid., vi.

13. Adoniram Judson, "Mr. Judson's Letter to Rev. Mr. Grow," 31–32; and Middleditch, *Burmah's Great Missionary*, 273; emphasis in original.

14. Dowling, *The Judson Offering*, 249; emphasis in original.

15. Levens insightfully comments, "Context, genre, audience, and voice are the four key issues to consider when reading these resources." Levens, "Reading the Judsons," 41. For an excellent article discussing the editorial purposes and contexts of these periodical and biographical publications, and the primary sources and literary works of

no work has comprehensively synthesized those aspects of his piety that grounded and sustained him amid his illustrious labors and sufferings. Judson's story is peculiar in the history of evangelical missions and in the history of the life and thought of the American church. Yet, Judson's influence upon missions and the American church has not been merely missiological; his influence, as his biographers have attested, has been evangelical and motivational. Because of the significant effect of his piety upon evangelical spirituality and missions, the contours of his piety deserve examination. The missionary spirituality that courses through the sundry accounts of Judson's life has been effective "not only in drawing men into service, but rather more, perhaps, in sustaining men in service . . . By his heroic persistence in well-doing under almost unsuperable difficulties and unbearable hardships have they learned to endure and persevere."[16] More than the incredible tragedy and adventure of his account, truly his enduring piety has made his story seem so other-worldly, inimitable, and worthy of retelling.

The nineteenth century witnessed the publication of biographies, which had accessed volumes of primary source material. Of these, the biography that stands at the headwaters is the two-volume work by the president of Brown University and Baptist pastor, Francis Wayland (1796–1865).[17] Wayland had access to all of Judson's remaining letters and journals in the

the Judsons, see ibid., 37–73.

16. Carver, "The Significance of Adoniram Judson," 478.

17. Wayland, *Memoir*, 1–2. For an early example of a typical enthusiastic review of Wayland's memoir of Judson, see "Adoniram Judson" (1853), 158. One biographer well observed that "Wayland paid little attention to the human side of Judson, his social qualities, his cultural interest, his informal friendliness, his attractive pleasantries." Warburton, *Eastward*, 196. In spite of this critique, Wayland does indeed discuss, at the end of his second volume, Judson's intensity, humor, and playfulness; Wayland also highlights Judson's peculiar affection for each of his wives, friendly devotion to his children, excessive neatness, his nurse-like sympathy for the afflicted, and his reserved manner except in the presence of his family. For Wayland's full description of Judson's unique personality, see Wayland, *Memoir*, 2:373–404. One of Emily's biographers also described Judson well in his home life and within the context of relationships and family. For very warm descriptions of Judson's joyful temperament, smiling face, tenderness with people, and buoyancy of spirit, see Kendrick, *The Life and Letters of Mrs. Emily C. Judson*, 141–215. For Hague's descriptions of Judson's happy temperament and smiling countenance, see Wayland, *Memoir*, 2:359. Also, for an account from Emily about Judson's regular romantic, spontaneous, and playful personality, see Edward Judson, *The Life of Adoniram Judson*, 322–23. John Marshman (1794–1877), son of Joshua Marshman (1768–1837) of the Serampore Trio, described Judson's affection as a family man and cheerful disposition, in Wayland, *Memoir*, 2:359–60. Another of Judson's colleagues described his tender disposition toward children, his remarkable memory of songs, verses, and stories, his ability to skim books and remember everything he read, his interesting and intellectual conversational topics, and his humble aversion to talking of himself and his past experiences. See Stevens, *A Half-Century in Burma*, 12–17.

possession of the American Baptist Missionary Union and the American Board of Commissioners for Foreign Missions.[18] Also, Judson's widow, Emily C. Judson (1817–1854), furnished Wayland with family letters and reminiscences that he considered of significant interest. Wayland's biography is noteworthy because he personally knew Judson, he was an educator, he had access to all of Judson's known correspondence and journals, and he had Emily's enthusiastic assistance. Wayland wrote to promote the cause of missions to which Judson was peculiarly devoted.[19]

Published within a year of Wayland's biography, Robert T. Middleditch's (1825–1907) biographical account liberally quoted many of the same primary source extracts used by Wayland.[20] And yet, Middleditch's biography does not contain nearly as much biographical narrative as Wayland's, which probably explains why it is only one volume. Middleditch sought to write a biography that would be a middle ground between short popular narratives and Wayland's exhaustive two-volume work. The controlling aim of Middleditch's biography was to promote Judson's life in order to arouse spiritual vitality and encourage Christian activism.[21] Middleditch certainly highlights those trials in Judson's life where his piety shone brightest.

Asserting that Wayland's biography had gone out of print and that there was a need for recollecting Judson's unique personal traits for new readers, Judson's son, Baptist pastor and professor, Edward Judson, compiled a consecutive story of Judson's life, using original journals and letters that were available to Wayland.[22] Edward's biography uniquely includes some of Judson's sermons and tracts to which Wayland only referred partially.

Though not a biography on Judson himself, James D. Knowles's (1798–1838) biography of Judson's first wife, Ann Hasseltine (1789–1826), provides much insight into Judson's spirituality.[23] In addition to Wayland's biography and Edward Judson's biography, Knowles's biography of Ann has

---

18. Wayland said, "I have read every thing that could be collected of Dr. Judson's writings, both in print and in manuscript... I have withheld nothing of any importance which I have found among his papers. The evidence is therefore before the world, and let the world judge of it." Wayland, *Memoir*, 2:386.

19. Ibid., 1:6.

20. Middleditch, *Burmah's Great Missionary*. Edward H. Fletcher (b. 1823), the publisher, originally took credit for Middleditch's biography, since Middleditch initially published it anonymously. Fletcher sought to publish this biography before Wayland's eminent biography. See Fletcher, *Records of the Life*. See Anderson's discussion of this in *To the Golden Shore*, 512.

21. Middleditch, *Burmah's Great Missionary*, iii.

22. Edward Judson, *The Life of Adoniram Judson*.

23. Knowles, *Memoir of Mrs. Ann H. Judson*.

been expressly valuable for Judson's biographers of the twentieth century.[24] Significant in Ann's biography are records of Judson's early piety and consecration to the missionary call. Hannah Chaplin Conant (1809–1865), likewise, wrote a biography worthy of mention. Unique to her biography is her record of his season of darkness and depression. Judson and her mother, Mrs. Chaplin, wrote letters to one another during that melancholic period.[25]

Other early biographers and writers that deserve mention for their extensive, though not always unique, citations that illustrate Judson's remarkable piety are: Ann H. Judson, J. Clément (1815–1883), A. D. Gillette (1807–1882), James L. Hill (1848–1931), John Dowling (1807–1878), Daniel C. Eddy (1823–1896), William Hague (1808–1887), J. Nelson Lewis (1836–1863), William Carey Richards (1818–1892), Asahel C. Kendrick (1809–1895), and Emily C. Judson.[26] The magisterial biographies of the nineteenth century often used extracts of Judson's journals and letters that illustrate the contours of his piety, which can be found also in *The Baptist Missionary Magazine*.[27]

In the twentieth century, Stacy R. Warburton (1875–1940), seeking to reintroduce the Judson narrative for a new generation, contributed a new biography for the new century.[28] Because of the influx of uncritical hero novels and because Wayland's biography and Edward Judson's biography were out of print, Warburton sought to retell the same story with similar

---

24. See Warburton, *Eastward*, ix; Hulse, *Adoniram Judson*, 5.

25. Conant reported, "For the most part, the materials used in this sketch were already in print; but for one portion of his history—that depicted in Chapter XX.—the writer may claim some special advantages, not open to the public nor to Dr. Judson's other biographers. His interior life, during the painfully interesting period there described, was fully revealed in his letters to my mother, who, in turn, combated his morbid ideas with all the earnestness of honest friendship, and sought to win him back to more cheerful and Christian views. This correspondence was, from motives of delicacy, destroyed; but my own recollection of Dr. Judson's letters is quite fresh and clear, and has served as my clue in portraying this peculiar, and, to many minds, inscrutable phase in the spiritual experience of so great and good a man." Conant, *The Earnest Man*, xxvii.

26. See Ann Hasseltine Judson, *An Account*; Conant, *The Earnest Man*; Clément, *Memoir of Adoniram Judson*; Gillette, *A Sketch of the Labors*; Hill, *The Immortal Seven*; Dowling, *The Judson Offering*; Eddy, *A Sketch of Adoniram Judson*; Hague, *The Life and Character of Adoniram Judson*; Lewis, *Judson Centennial Services*; Richards, *The Apostle of Burma*; Kendrick, *The Life and Letters of Mrs. Emily C. Judson*; Forester, *Memoir of Sarah B. Judson*; Emily Chubbuck Judson, *The Kathayan Slave*; Tooze, *The Life and Letters of Emily Chubbuck Judson*.

27. For instance, Wayland claimed that his sources "consisted chiefly of [Judson's] official correspondence, much of which had been published in missionary periodicals." Wayland, *Memoir*, 1:3–4. See also *The Baptist Missionary Magazine* 1–89 (1817–1909).

28. Warburton, *Eastward*, ix.

attention to Judson's life and character.[29] Though not delineating Judson's piety in any unique way, Warburton did contribute to the study of Judson by compiling the most up-to-date research on Judson at that time.[30] He also offered succinct remarks and analyses of significant aspects of the Judson drama.

Later in the twentieth century, Courtney Anderson (1906–2001) published a momentous biography on Judson, often viewed as the definitive one aside from Wayland's biography.[31] Anderson uniquely told the Judson story by bringing together short salient extracts from journals and letters and by couching them in a dynamic narrative that seems more like a novel than a historical record. In his foreword, Anderson quoted the Great Commission from Matthew 28:18–20 and then remarked that Judson obeyed it. In response, he essentially stated his driving research question: "Why?"[32] Throughout his gripping narrative Anderson tied together many factors that contributed to Judson's piety, including his father's intense influence and Hopkinsian disinterested benevolence; but the predominant motive that Anderson seemed to highlight in order to answer his aforementioned question was that Judson wished to please God with all his might and to love Jesus above all.[33]

Anderson's biography tends to blend uncited direct quotes from primary sources with creative narration that might leave the reader wondering which details are historically verifiable and which details are Anderson's imaginative story-telling. If the reader had previously read Wayland's biography or any of the early popular biographies with substantial extracts, discerning between actual events and extracts and Anderson's interpretive narrations would not be too difficult. Though a masterful story-teller and biographer, he offered little commentary on Judson's theology and spirituality. Regarding the sources, Anderson predominantly used biographies by Wayland, Edward Judson, and Warburton. From his vantage point, all the biographers have used essentially the same sources.[34]

---

29. Warburton said, "No serious study of Judson's life has appeared since Edward Judson published his *Life of Adoniram Judson* more than fifty years ago. That and Wayland's original *Memoir* are out of print. A number of brief biographies have appeared, but have been incomplete, popular in form, and quite uncritical in treatment . . . A new biography is greatly needed." Ibid., ix.

30. Ibid., ix–xi.

31. Anderson, *To the Golden Shore*.

32. Ibid., iii.

33. For examples, see ibid., 50, 85.

34. Anderson agreed with Wayland's comments about the scope and limit of primary sources: "My materials, therefore, consisted chiefly of his official correspondence,

A twentieth-century book about Ann, written by Sharon James, is also worthy of mention: *My Heart in His Hands: Ann Judson of Burma*.[35] This book contains many of the letters and journals included in the authoritative biographies by Wayland, Knowles, and Edward Judson, and it also includes some excerpts from Ann's book, *An Account of the American Baptist Mission*.[36] Additionally, James cites six of Ann's unpublished letters.[37] And for a new generation, this book sheds light once again on the bright missionary ardor of Ann and Adoniram.

In the early twenty-first century, Rosalie Hall Hunt has retold the Judson narrative once again for the rising generation.[38] Hunt's biography contains the most updated biographical and archaeological information, along with pictures of recent archaeological findings. Seeking to retrace the steps of Judson and his legacy, Hunt, like Anderson, liberally weaves together extracts from letters and journals with riveting creative narrations. In Hunt's biography, the controlling themes relevant to Judson's piety are his love to God and courage.[39]

Furthermore, in the twenty-first century, surrounding the Judson bicentennial celebrations, a group of theologians and missiologists contributed to a volume, edited by Baptist theologian, Jason G. Duesing, seeking to interpret and retell Judson's story from a critical and balanced approach.[40] The aim of the volume's contributors is not only to ignite a renewed enthusiasm for finishing the Great Commission, but also to encourage those in Great Commission work to endure in such a worthy venture.[41] Though all the contributions are quite relevant for understanding his piety, the chapter by church historian, Robert Caldwell, is most explicit in its treatment of

---

much of which had been published in missionary periodicals . . . Enough, however, has been preserved to present his missionary character with remarkable distinctness. His opinions on many subjects can never be recovered, but the record of his deeds is beyond the reach of both fire and flood." See Wayland, *Memoir*, 1:3–4; and see Anderson, *To the Golden Shore*, 509. Also in the twentieth century, Brumberg has helpfully contributed to Judson studies; see Brumberg, *Mission for Life*.

35. James, *My Heart in His Hands*.

36. Ann Hasseltine Judson, *An Account of the American Baptist Mission*.

37. In James's book there are eight citations of letters unpublished in the previous biographies, but two of those have been published elsewhere; see Ann Hasseltine Judson, "Ann Hasseltine Judson's Letters, 1818–1822," 372–75. The six other unpublished letters reside in the Angus Library.

38. Hunt, *Bless God and Take Courage*.

39. Ibid., viii.

40. Duesing, *Adoniram Judson*.

41. Ibid., xxii.

Judson's piety.[42] With evangelical historical scholarship, this volume presents Judson's missionary call, historical background of the modern missions movement, theological and spiritual formation, significant biographical details, missiological principles, and overall exemplary character.

In light of the bicentennial celebrations, church historians, Allen Yeh and Chris Chun, edited a volume on the life and labor of Judson.[43] This volume uniquely looked at the pioneering efforts of both Adoniram Judson and William Carey (1761–1834). The first part discusses Carey, while the second part discusses Judson, and the third highlights the links between the two pioneers. In the chapters devoted to Judson, the contributors outline these aspects: his similarities with Orlando Costas (1942–1987); the similarities between his historical background and contemporary issues; his lasting legacy in Burma; the evangelical relationship between Judson and the Serampore Trio in India; the enduring culture of Baptist missions as inspired by both Judson and Carey; and the foundational role that the wives of Carey and Judson played in supporting their husbands. This volume, unique in its approach, demonstrates the lasting legacy of Judson for Baptists and for missionaries alike. While many of the chapters contribute to the corpus of Judson studies, the chapter by church historian, Michael A. G. Haykin, most specifically relates to Judson's spirituality: "We are Confirmed Baptists."[44]

One final bicentennial book, by self-published Jack McElroy, deserves mention.[45] McElroy has done Judson bibliophiles a great service: he has compiled together four of the most prominent tracts used by Judson, three of which Judson himself wrote. McElroy also supervised the English translation of one of Judson's tracts that had never before been translated, *The Epitome of the Old Testament*.[46] McElroy also included *The Investigator* by Judson's missionary colleague, Jonathan Wade (1798–1872),[47] which Judson revised and used often in tract evangelism, *The Catechism* by Ann Judson,[48]

---

42. Caldwell, "New England's New Divinity," 31–54.

43. Chun and Yeh, *Expect Great Things*.

44. See Haykin, "'We Are Confirmed Baptists': The Judsons and Their Meeting with the Serampore Trio," 103–12. This chapter was also published in an edition of *The Southern Baptist Journal of Missions and Evangelism*, which celebrated the bicentennial anniversary of Judson's departure to the East; see Haykin, "'We Are Confirmed Baptists': The Judsons and Their Meeting with the Serampore Trio in 1812," 14–21. Also, in this issue, another contribution that discusses, albeit indirectly, the spiritual formation of Judson is: Duesing "Breaking the Strong Attachment to Home and Country," 6–13.

45. McElroy, *Adoniram Judson's Soul Winning Secrets Revealed*.

46. Adoniram Judson, *The Epitome of the Old Testament*.

47. Wade, "The Investigator," 239–62.

48. Ann Hasseltine Judson, "The Catechism," 23–30.

The Golden Balance by Adoniram,[49] *A View of the Christian Religion* by Adoniram,[50] and *The Star in the East* by the Scottish theologian and ordained minister of the Church of England, Claudius Buchanan (1766–1815), which was instrumental in birthing Judson's missionary vision.[51] The author has also compiled sixteen selected journal entries over twenty-three years of Judson's life that exhibit his missionary spirituality. This book does not exhaustively contain all of Judson's works, which are scattered throughout numerous resources, but it does compile those of Judson's published works that saliently demonstrate his piety.

Besides the plentiful biographical sketches celebrating Judson's legacy, there have been some academic theses and dissertations written in view of his life and labor, chiefly in relation to his missiological philosophy and translation theory.[52] Of all the dissertations written in reference to Judson, the only one that thoroughly discusses his thought and theology is by Max H. Brown.[53] In this thesis, Brown suggests that Judson's inimitable perseverance in his missionary call directly relates to the Hopkinsian influence of his formative years. Brown essentially outlines the New Divinity theology of Samuel Hopkins (1721–1803), the protégé of the evangelical theologian Jonathan Edwards (1703–1758), and posits that Hopkins's theology of disinterested benevolence is explanatory for Judson's severe asceticism and self-denial. Though there is certainly some direct influence of Hopkinsian theology upon Judson's spiritual formation, Brown does not use the vast corpus of Judson materials. In fact, he makes assertions about Judson, but

---

49. Adoniram Judson, "The Golden Balance," 191–214. See also Adoniram Judson, *The Golden Balance*.

50. Adoniram Judson, "A View of the Christian Religion," in *Tracts*, 1:31–53. See also Adoniram Judson, *A View of the Christian Religion*; also published in Adoniram Judson, *The Septenary*.

51. Buchanan, *The Star in the East*.

52. For a cultural and linguistic study on Judson's translation theory and theological contextualization in translation, see Dingrin, "A Missiological and Theological Critique," 104–235. For a discussion of Judson's keen ability to translate the name of God in a contextually powerful way, see Laisum, "Naming God in Burma Today." For a brief treatment of Judson's evangelistic strategies and translation philosophy, see Vuta, "A Brief History," 118–41, 267–71. For a survey of the many cultural and contextual challenges facing evangelism and conversion of Burmese Buddhists, with some reference to Judson's work, see Khai, "Barriers in Conversion." For a survey of the effect of Baptist missions on the Burmese people, see Mang, "A Chin History," 110–36. For a very brief sketch of Judson's missionary efforts from the perspective of a Christian-Buddhist ecumenicist, see Kam, "Christian Mission to Buddhists in Myanmar," 56–64. For a work that suggests the need for renewal among Karen Baptists and mentions briefly the Judson legacy, see Taw, "A Renewal Strategy," 72–76.

53. Brown, "The New Divinity."

never directly quotes from any of the nineteenth-century biographies, magazines, or from any of Judson's own published works; the only Judson source Brown references is Courtney Anderson's biography, which he does fifteen times. Brown sketches the life and historical context of Judson in the first chapter, and then in the second chapter he outlines the life, historical context, and basic theology of Hopkins. In the third chapter he summarizes three sermons by Hopkins that he posits represent a theological framework that might have undergirded Judson's thought, but he draws no direct correlation. Yet, Brown's conclusions are insightful and helpful.

In light of all the aforementioned biographies, historical studies, and theses/dissertations, no work has synthesized and categorized the spirituality of Adoniram Judson.[54] The wealth of biographies and celebrations of his life reveal the enduring inspiration of his faith and devotion to Christ. His missionary spirituality serves as the magnetic force between the iron of his Calvinistic theology and the steel of his evangelical missiology. In light of all that Judson wrote that is still available today and considering all that was written about him, especially by those who knew him personally, an overall synthesis of his spirituality would be most beneficial to the ongoing study of Judson's life and thought for both contemporary missions and theology. As in his own day, Judson's piety would be useful today for stirring aspiring ministers and missionaries to count the cost, to awaken a desire to please Christ, and to trust him in his mysterious providences.

Thesis

The purpose of this book is to answer the following question: in what ways and to what extent did Adoniram Judson's spirituality affect the endurance and effect of his missionary labor? In answering the primary research question, this book will address the following related questions: first, in what ways did the Bible dominate Judson's missionary spirituality? Second, how did Judson's self-denying submission to God's providence buttress his spiritual life? Third, to what extent did the promises of heaven pervade Judson's piety? Fourth, what were the roles of Judson's affection for Christ and consecration to Christ's commission in his spirituality? In sum, this book will argue that the center of Adoniram Judson's spirituality was

---

54. One biographer briefly highlights what he proposes to be categories of Judson's foundational doctrines: the gospel of salvation, credobaptism, the means of grace (i.e., preaching, church-planting, disciple-making, and prayer), the doctrines of grace, the doctrine of sanctification, Postmillennialism, and the role of missionary societies. Hulse, *Adoniram Judson*, 45–53.

a heavenly-minded, self-denying submission to the sovereign will of God, motivated by an affectionate desire to please Christ through obedience to his final command revealed in Scripture. Moreover, this book will demonstrate that Judson's unique ascetic spirituality went beyond the classic categories of evangelical piety.

Methodology

The primary methodology for this book is an inductive synthesis and analysis of primary-source materials by Adoniram Judson and by those who knew him. During his lifetime, various circumstances led to the destruction of most of his early letters and journals.[55] Yet many letters, journals, tracts, and sermons survived and were published.[56] Not long after his death, numerous memoirs of his life and labor went to publication, most of which copiously highlighted relevant extracts from his letters, journals, and some writings of his wives.[57] There are hundreds of journals, letters, tracts, and sermons in his memoirs and in *The Baptist Missionary Magazine*.[58]

Though Judson never wrote for the academy or for a popular American audience, he spent much of his ministry, along with Bible translation, in writing tracts in a language/culture that had never had Christian translations. Judson's tracts and related published works include, (1) *The Epitome of the Old Testament*; (2) *The Golden Balance: The Christian and Buddhist*

---

55. In his definitive biography, Wayland described the loss of many of Judson's letters and journals: "When . . . I undertook to compile the following Memoir, I supposed that a large amount of his correspondence and other writings would be easily accessible. In this respect, however, I was entirely disappointed. From peculiar views of duty, Dr. Judson had caused to be destroyed all his early letters written to his family, together with all his papers of a personal character. Mrs. Ann H. Judson, from prudential reasons, during their captivity in Ava, destroyed all his letters in her possession. Manuscripts were also consumed by the burning of Mr. Steven's house in Maulmain. Dr. Judson's correspondence with Dr. Staughton perished by the shipwreck of a vessel on the passage from Philadelphia to Washington. Last of all, his letters to his missionary brethren in Burmah were lost by the foundering of the ship which was conveying them to this country." Wayland, *Memoir*, 1:3–5.

56. Despite the original materials that perished due to fire, flood, or intention, Wayland identified how and where he accessed the original manuscripts for his two-volume biography; see ibid., 1:4–6.

57. As mentioned previously, there are four eminent biographies by contemporaries of Judson, whose extractions from journals, letters, and sermons occasionally overlap; these biographies are Middleditch, *Burmah's Great Missionary*; Knowles, *Memoir of Mrs. Ann H. Judson*; Wayland, *Memoir*, 1–2; Edward Judson, *The Life of Adoniram Judson*.

58. See *The Baptist Missionary Magazine* 1–89 (1817–1909).

Systems Contrasted; (3) *A View of the Christian Religion*; (4) *A Digest of Scripture*; (5) *Septenary, Seven Manuals*; (6) *The Threefold Cord*; (7) *Christian Baptism*; and (8) *An Account of Meh Shway-ee, a Burman Slave Girl*.[59] His tracts are rich resources of his spirituality. In addition to his tracts, he also wrote a few hymns as well.[60] They are a mixture of his foundational theology and his ardent piety. He wrote them for the discipleship of his baptized converts and for the evangelization of Burmese Buddhists. Overall, his writings abundantly exhibit his evangelical devotion and missionary motivation. Moreover, his preserved letters, journals (and those of his friends and family), and sermons, paint a picture of Judson's striking spirituality.

Judson's correspondence mixes thoughts about practical matters related to the complexities of life in Burma, matters related to ministry plans and records of activities, occasional words of reflection, and brief expressions of piety. Those sections of his correspondence that are more spiritually reflective were extracted and published in *The Baptist Missionary Magazine*, and his early nineteenth-century biographies often cite those same extracts.[61] His letters are excellent sources for accessing his spirituality because in them he shows how he interprets the providences of God in his life for supporters in the United States.

Judson's journals, similar to his correspondence, demonstrate his spiritual reflection on his trials and translation efforts. Unlike his letters which

---

59. Adoniram Judson, *The Epitome of the Old Testament*; also published in McElroy, *Adoniram Judson's Soul Winning Secrets*, 59–106. Adoniram Judson, *The Golden Balance*; also published in McElroy, *Adoniram Judson's Soul Winning Secrets*, 43–57. Adoniram Judson, *A View of the Christian Religion*; also published in McElroy, *Adoniram Judson's Soul Winning Secrets*, 23–31. Adoniram Judson, *The Threefold Cord*; also published in Edward Judson, *The Life of Adoniram Judson*, 571–77. Adoniram Judson, *Christian Baptism*. Adoniram Judson, *An Account of Meh Shway-ee*. Adoniram Judson, *A Digest of Scripture*. Adoniram Judson, *The Septenary*. In *The Septenary*, Judson included a short manual he had already written, called, *Public Service Hand-Book for Pastors*; see Adoniram Judson, *Public Service Hand-Book*. Also, his other published works are Adoniram Judson, *The Elements of English Grammar*; Adoniram Judson, *The Young Lady's Arithmetic*; Adoniram Judson, *Letter to the Female Members*; Adoniram Judson, *Grammatical Notices*; Adoniram Judson, *Burmese Bible*. For this book's research, in partnership with a Burmese translator, April T. T. Aye, the author supervised the project of translating both *The Septenary* and *A Digest of Scripture* into English for the first time. Also, for this book, April T. T. Aye translated into English a Burmese biography of Adoniram Judson: Jameson, *Sketch of the Life of Dr. Judson*.

60. See Adoniram Judson, "Come, Holy Spirit, Dove Divine," 586. Judson is also credited with writing the following hymns: "Our Father God, Who Art in Heaven" and "Our Saviour Bowed Beneath the Wave" in Julian, *A Dictionary of Hymnology*, 609. For praise of Judson's unmatched ability to write hymns and poetry in accord with the complexities of the Burmese language, see Stevens, *A Half-Century in Burma*, 12.

61. Wayland, *Memoir*, 1:4.

were often addressed to specific individuals pertaining to particular situations, his journals are often not directed to any single individual, and they tend to be more contemplative of God's providences in his life and ministry.

Like Judson, his coworkers corresponded and recorded in journals about their experiences. Though their correspondence and journals are significant for understanding the history surrounding the mission, only some describe Judson and his spirituality. Of those secondary sources that reflect upon Judson's spirituality, his three wives biographically recorded most accounts, and others who knew him personally recorded some supplementary elements.[62]

Judson's few known sermons are excellent sources of his spirituality. Though he desired to preach more often, he was compelled to expend himself for the translation of the Burmese Bible and for the development of the Burmese-English dictionary.[63] According to Baptist missionaries, while in India, Judson preached an impressive sermon on baptism.[64] And, Judson preached only one sermon in English, an ordination sermon, in Burma.[65] His other sermons survived because he transcribed them for others to read on his behalf due to his failing voice, which he suffered during a brief visit to the United States in 1845.[66] During his brief visit to the United States, his sermons were especially poignant, likely because he would have only one opportunity, through the preached word, to personally plead with the churches in America. Because his opportunities to preach in English were rare, his sermons earnestly display the dominance of his Christ-enamored piety. These sermons of his later years contain sage-like exhortations from his hearty piety and lifelong missionary devotion.

---

62. See Gouger, *A Personal Narrative*; Edward Judson, *The Life of Adoniram Judson*; Kendrick, *The Life and Letters of Mrs. Emily C. Judson*; Forester, *Memoir of Sarah B. Judson*; Emily Chubbuck Judson, *The Kathayan Slave*; Tooze, *The Life and Letters of Emily Chubbuck Judson*; Ann Hasseltine Judson, *An Account*; Conant, *The Earnest Man*; Clément, *Memoir of Adoniram Judson*; Gillette, *A Sketch of the Labors*; Hill, *The Immortal Seven*; Dowling, *The Judson Offering*; Eddy, *A Sketch of Adoniram Judson*; Hague, *The Life and Character of Adoniram Judson*.

63. Adoniram Judson, *Burmese Bible*; Adoniram Judson, *A Dictionary*. Because of the burdensome translation needs, his opportunities to preach were limited; see Wayland, *Memoir*, 2:355.

64. Carey, "Letter of Dr. Carey," 149–50; see also Knowles, *Memoir of Mrs. Ann H. Judson*, 66.

65. Wayland: *Memoir*, 2:486–94.

66. To read his sermons, see Edward Judson, *The Life of Adoniram Judson*, 445–47, 460–61, 469–74, 577–79; Wayland, *Memoir*, 2:38–41, 199–200, 227–38, 254–58, 284–88, 486–99; and Middleditch, *Burmah's Great Missionary*, 322–44, 362–98, 460–61.

Various presuppositions have influenced this book. First, evangelical spirituality and evangelical theology ought not to be divorced from each other, for they are friends. Second, evangelical spirituality includes evangelical activism as a key subset. And the study of the history of Christian missionary activism should include the influence of evangelical spirituality. Third, Adoniram Judson's missionary spirituality illustrates an example of a life wholly consecrated to Christ and the proclamation of his gospel in light of relentless hardships and hazards. The character of Judson's self-denying submission to the will of God in his pursuit of Christ's glory is a high standard from which evangelicals can learn.

Summary of Contents

This introductory chapter principally establishes the import of the book, states the research question, thesis, and methodology for the study, and describes the relevance of studying Judson's spirituality for theology and missions today.

Chapter 2 situates Judson within the historical context of the eighteenth century, and especially within the theological movements and missionary zeal that established the context for his spiritual formation. This chapter also includes an overview of his life and ministry.

Chapter 3 demonstrates the all-consuming centrality of the Word of God in Judson's life. His devotion to keeping the Word, translating the Word, preaching the Word, and using the Word in evangelism and discipleship all establish his bibliocentricism.

Chapter 4 illustrates Judson's relentless submission to obeying his missionary call. It considers the role of duty, self-denial, and asceticism in Judson's missionary spirituality. This chapter looks at Judson's submissive piety in the face of severe suffering as he sought to trust in God's mysterious will and to glorify God for his infinite wisdom.

Chapter 5 shows how Judson's vision of heaven pervaded his spiritual senses. It displays how hoping in heavenly rest gave Judson the perseverance to stay the course, and it shows how the optimistic vision of eternal reward and millennial glory drove him to spend himself and be spent for the glory of Christ.

Chapter 6 establishes that the unifying feature of Judson's spirituality was an affectionate desire to please the Lord Christ. It considers the role of Christ's Great Commission in his spiritual formation. This chapter shows Judson's love to commune with Christ and pray earnestly for Christ's coming glory to spread through the success of the gospel in the salvation of sinners. Many themes of the previous chapters tie into the controlling theme of his love for Christ.

Chapter 7, the conclusion, summarizes answers given to the research question and related questions. It contains an evaluation of Judson's spirituality and an application of its usefulness for modern evangelicals, and especially for ministers and missionaries.

2

The Life and Context of Adoniram Judson

THE ACCOUNT OF ADONIRAM Judson is worthy of his numerous biographies. His story is truly captivating with drama, adventure, and tragedy. In order to understand his renowned courage and endurance, this chapter will consider the historical context of his evangelical missionary compulsion, and the theological roots of his spiritual formation. A short biographical sketch of his life will underscore these factors.

The Eighteenth Century

Adoniram Judson came of age and commenced his missionary venture in the last third of the "long" eighteenth century (1688–1837).[1] During the early period of Great Britain's rise to world dominance, the world witnessed King Louis XIV (1638–1715) of France's declaration of war on England (1689), William of Orange's (1650–1702) confirmation as king over Charles II (1630–1685), and King George II's (1683–1760) ascension to the throne in 1727. This was an era when the English, Welsh, and Scottish assimilated into a common identity as British. Two of the chief features in this collective sense of being British were a desire for the prominence of the British Empire

---

1. See Marshall, *The Oxford History of the British Empire*, 1. This era beheld the zenith of the Age of Reason, under the influence of thinkers, activists, and philosophers such as Thomas Paine (1737–1809), John Locke (1632–1704), David Hume (1711–1776), Rousseau (1712–1778), Voltaire (1694–1778), Isaac Newton (1643–1727), Benjamin Franklin (1706–1790), and Thomas Jefferson (1743–1826). This surge of enlightened humanism and individualism played a major role in the American Revolution (1765–1783), the American Declaration of Independence (1776), and the United States Bill of Rights (1791). For two books about this era and its influences, see Cragg, *The Church and the Age of Reason*; and Vidler, *The Church in an Age of Revolution*.

and a shared inheritance from the Reformation of Protestantism.[2] The three Protestant ethnicities also galvanized their British identity in opposition to France, their threatening Catholic foe. This empire spread through a dominant Royal Navy and an ever-increasing merchant fleet, and concurrently English-speaking missionaries were establishing Christ's empire. In the latter half the eighteenth century, Evangelicals from Europe and North America rose to the challenge of extending Christianity's reach into Africa, Asia, and Australasia. According to the church historian, Michael Haykin, this explosion of missionary activism and globalization of the Christians faith "must be regarded as the most salient event in the history of Western churches since the Reformation."[3]

Many Christians saw the expansion of the British Empire during this century as the providential working of God to spread around the world the gospel discovered in the Reformation.[4] For instance, Andrew Fuller (1754–1815), the Particular Baptist pastor in Kettering and mobilizer for the Baptist Missionary Society, said that the providential aim behind Britain's vast Empire was "for the very purpose of introducing the gospel."[5] And just as Rome's conquests paved a way for the gospel to travel to Britain, he said, so "those of Britain may make way for its general introduction in the East."[6] Like the Roman roads of the first and second centuries, the British Empire made international inroads on which the gospel could travel.

Evangelicalism Emerges

David W. Bebbington, Professor of History at the University of Stirling in Scotland, has argued that since 1734 the English-speaking world has seen the unparalleled rise of evangelicalism, influenced by European Continental Pietism, the Great Awakening in America, and the Evangelical Revival in Britain in the eighteenth century. Bebbington demonstrates that eighteenth-century evangelicalism contained four components: conversionism,

---

2. See Colley, *Britons*, 10–58, 387–89.

3. Haykin, "Just before Judson," 9–10.

4. Stanley, "Christianity and Civilization," 169–97; see also Stanley, *The Bible and the Flag*.

5. Fuller, "An Apology for the Late Christian Missions to India," 771–72.

6. Ibid., 769. Though Fuller said the above, he also demonstrated greater concern for the glory of God over the British Empire: "[The] eternal hereafter . . . must be of infinitely greater moment, both to governors and governed, than all the affairs of the greatest empire on earth." Ibid.

biblicism, crucicentrism, and activism.[7] The "Bebbington quadrilateral"[8] provides valuable descriptions of historical evangelical spirituality; it has become the standard grid through which to understand the evangelical spirituality of the eighteenth and nineteenth centuries.[9]

Bebbington distinguishes evangelicalism from Puritanism in that the latter lacked the activism of the former, which he traces to Puritanism's underdeveloped doctrine of assurance.[10] He argues that evangelicalism saw assurance as the ordinary experience of every believer,[11] and he traces this to the empiricism of the Enlightenment era of the eighteenth century. Evangelicals valued empirical evidence; and, divine encounters became grounds for evidential assurance of conversion.[12] Conversely, Haykin maintains that in the Great Awakening of 1740–1742, Jonathan Edwards reconsidered the doctrine of assurance because many in his congregation had false ideas of

---

7. Bebbington, *Evangelicalism in Modern Britain*, 20. Gillett also supplements assurance, prayer, and holiness to Bebbington's fourfold filter; see Gillett, *Trust and Obey*, 34–39. Sheldrake also contends that evangelical spirituality has been historically comprised of communion with God, practical Christianity, and theology; see Sheldrake, *Spirituality and History*, 52, quoted also in Randall, *What a Friend*, 20. McGrath proposes, more broadly, four features of Christian spirituality: "[First,] knowing God and not just knowing about God; [second,] experiencing God to the full; [third,] a transformation of existence based on the Christian faith; and [fourth,] attaining Christian authenticity in life and thought." McGrath, *Christian Spirituality*, 4. McGrath also aptly defines Christian spirituality as concerned with the "quest for a fulfilled and authentic Christian existence, involving the bringing together of the fundamental ideas of Christianity and the whole experience of living on the basis of and within the scope of the Christian faith." McGrath, *Christian Spirituality*, 2.

8. Larsen, "The Reception Given," 25.

9. Bebbington's quadrilateral "is now receiving the ultimate compliment of being cited without acknowledgement, as if it is not one scholar's opinion but simply the truth we all know." Ibid., 29. More narrowly, Brackney traces evangelical piety and thought within the Baptist tradition, of which Judson would become both a beneficiary and a benefactor. Brackney proposes the genes of Baptist thought in order of predominance: the authority of Christ, the priority of Scripture, Christian experience, a modified Reformed theological tradition, church membership, evangelical nature, and religious liberty. See Brackney, *A Genetic History of Baptist Thought*, 528–36.

10. Bebbington, *Evangelicalism in Modern Britain*, 43, quoted in Haykin, "Evangelicalism and the Enlightenment," 50. For a thorough argument that the Puritans truly upheld a strong missionary vision, see Rooy, *The Theology of Missions*.

11. Bebbington, *Evangelicalism in Modern Britain*, 45, quoted in Haykin, "Evangelicalism and the Enlightenment," 51.

12. Bebbington, *Evangelicalism in Modern Britain*, 47–50, quoted in Haykin, "Evangelicalism and the Enlightenment," 51. In an enlightening essay, so to speak, in response to Bebbington's notion of evangelicalism being closely linked to the Enlightenment, Stanley seeks to clarify and modify the direct relationship between Enlightenment ideology and evangelicalism. See Stanley, "Christian Missions and the Enlightenment," 8–16.

how to discern true conversion. An undue focus on experience and impressions eclipsed what Edwards called "fruits of grace." Like the Puritans, Edwards claimed that perseverance was the ground for assurance.[13] In other words, evangelical activism and the doctrine of assurance are more similar to Puritan spirituality than Bebbington claims,[14] and significant continuity exists between Puritan and evangelical spirituality.

In *The Devoted Life*, Randall C. Gleason and Kelly M. Kapic broadly define Christian spirituality as seeking "a deeper awareness of God's presence as defined by the Christian faith according to the Bible."[15] Yet, they delineate seven unique elements of Puritan spirituality.[16] First, it was a "movement of spirituality."[17] Church historian, Richard Lovelace, terms it "a Reformed holiness movement."[18] Contemporary evangelicalism commonly uses phrases like "having a quiet time" or "doing devotions" to describe drawing near to God through biblical meditation, which eighteenth-century evangelicalism often called "enjoying" or "practicing religion." Puritanism would call a similar spiritual practice "communion with Christ."[19] Gleason and Kapic identify this Puritan notion of communion with Christ as fitting well in the category of Christian spirituality because it also emphasizes Spirit-guidance and Bible-saturation.[20] Puritanism was essentially the foremost model of Reformed sanctification. Certainly, it valued conversion;[21] but the truly converted soul ventures on a pilgrimage of progressive holiness.[22] Second, in conjunction with the first point, the Puritans emphasized communion with God as the affectionate response to the mind's vision of Christ-centered truth.[23] Third, to them Scripture was the food that strengthened the affections of their heart and the health of their souls.[24] Describing the Bible-

---

13. Haykin, "Evangelicalism and the Enlightenment," 56.
14. See ibid., 55–60.
15. Kapic and Gleason, "Who Were the Puritans?," 24.
16. Ibid., 24–30.
17. Ibid.," 24.
18. Lovelace, "Afterword," 301.
19. Kapic and Gleason, "Who Were the Puritans?," 24.
20. Ibid.
21. Packer describes Puritan Spirituality as "Bible-based, Christ-centered, conversionistic, and church-oriented." Packer, "Puritan Spirituality," 702.
22. Kapic and Gleason identify John Bunyan's *Pilgrim's Progress* as an illustration of the Puritan pilgrimage unto personal holiness. See Kapic and Gleason, *The Devoted Life*, 25.
23. Ibid.
24. In his classic work on meditation, Edmund Calamy (1600–1666) gloried in the fruit of biblical meditation: "*Meditation*, while it is in the understanding *chews* upon

saturated writings of the Puritan preacher John Bunyan (1628–1688), the Victorian preacher, Charles Spurgeon (1834–1892) famously said, "Why, this man is a living Bible! Prick him anywhere—his blood is Bibline, the very essence of the Bible flows from him."[25] Truly, they were a people of the Word.[26] Fourth, they were chiefly Augustinian in the weight they placed upon the pervasive depravity of man and the absoluteness of God's sovereign grace.[27] Due to man's inability and unwillingness to do good, the Puritans stressed their desperation for God's gracious justifying and sanctifying work. It is by the Holy Spirit alone that God empowers the regenerate to live in obedience. Fifth, the Puritans greatly emphasized the necessity of the Spirit for their pursuit of holiness and their communion with God. Sixth, they passionately disagreed with Roman Catholic sacramentalism and the similar sacramental spirituality they observed in the Anglican Church. And seventh, Puritanism was essentially a "Protestant and Reformed holiness and renewal movement."[28] J. I. Packer sees evidence of this in their constant use of terms such as "reformation" and "reform" to encourage heart transformation, their call for personal revival in their devotional writings, and the fact that God brought revival through the Puritan pastors' ministry.[29]

---

the things of God, and of Christ, and of Heaven, but when the understanding hath chewed these things, it must not devour all these things it self [sic], but it must convey the meat it hath chewed (as meant the meat is conveyed from the stomach into the liver, and then into the heart, and then into all the other parts of the body) into the *heart*, and into the will, and into the affections, and into the conversation." Calamy, *The Art of Divine Meditation*, 26.

25. Spurgeon, *Autobiography*, 159.

26. Beeke observes, "The Puritans never tired of saying that biblical meditation involves thinking upon the Triune God and His Word. By anchoring meditation in the living Word, Jesus Christ, and God's written Word, the Bible, the Puritans distanced themselves from every kind of counterfeit spirituality or mysticism that stresses . . . flights of the imagination at the expense of biblical content." Beeke, "Puritan Meditation," 75–76.

27. Consider the evangelical impulse of Augustine's conversion: "During all those years [of rebellion], where was my free will? What was the hidden, secret place from which it was summoned in a moment, so that I might bend my neck to your easy yoke? . . . How sweet all at once it was for me to be rid of those fruitless joys which I had once feared to lose! . . . You drove them from me, you who are the true, the sovereign joy. You drove them from me and took their place, you who are sweeter than all pleasure, though not to flesh and blood, you who outshine all light, yet are hidden deeper than any secret in our hearts, you who surpass all honor, though not in the eyes of men who see all honor in themselves . . . O Lord my God, my Light, my Wealth, and my Salvation." Augustine, *Confessions* 9.1 (trans. Coffin, 181).

28. Packer, "Puritan Spirituality," 702.

29. Packer, *A Quest for Godliness*, 36–37, quoted in Kapic and Gleason, "Who Were the Puritans?," 30.

In *The Devoted Life*, Richard Lovelace sets up the discussion for how evangelical spirituality organically developed out of Puritan spirituality. He says that the Puritans referred to the "half-reformation" of the sixteenth century. He explains, "not that the Reformation itself was at fault, but it needed the church to follow through on its teaching." Some of the Puritans said, "We have reformed our doctrines, but not our lives."[30] They sought to cultivate the garden of their souls and fan into flame their holy affections for the Triune God. Since Puritanism was essentially a Reformed holiness movement and sanctification is borne out of decisive regeneration, Lovelace suggests that Puritanism was first a "born again" movement, and thus the forerunner to evangelicalism.[31]

In his book, *Evangelical Spirituality,* James M. Gordon acknowledges the usefulness of the aforementioned Bebbington quadrilateral: "The experience of conversion in response to the divine grace, the centrality of the cross, the primary authority of the Bible and the imperative to service for Christ's sake are hallmarks of the Evangelical spiritual tradition."[32] However, Gordon does not limit himself to this standard fourfold filter. As he comments, "Rather than attempt a tidy definition of 'spirituality,' I have tried to show that, whatever definition is used, it must include the impact of doctrine on experience and moral practice."[33] He argues that the litmus test for true soul renovation and any spiritual experience "is how far it contributes to growth in love."[34] Equally, Lovelace claims that love to God and love to people must be the fruit of any evangelical spiritual experience.

> The goal of authentic spirituality is a life which escapes from the closed circle of spiritual self-indulgence, or even self-improvement, to become absorbed in the love of God and other persons. For the essence of spiritual renewal is "the love of God... poured out within our hearts through the Holy Spirit" (Rom 5:5 NASB). "My love," said Augustine, "is my weight." The substance of real spirituality is love.[35]

---

30. Lovelace, "Afterword," 300.
31. Ibid., 301.
32. Gordon, *Evangelical Spirituality*, 329.
33. Ibid., viii.
34. Ibid., 28.
35. Lovelace, *Renewal as a Way of Life*, 18.

Similar to the Puritan spirit of Edwards's affectionate pursuit of God as the greatest treasure in every good gift and spiritual experience,[36] Gordon contends that evangelical spirituality loves God for himself.[37]

Much like the Puritan emphasis on communion with Christ, Gordon observes that inherent to evangelical spirituality has been a robust Christocentric inclination.[38] "Lived doctrine centred on Christ, growth towards maturity measured by Christ, and moral renewal after the image of Christ provide the goals of the Christian spiritual life."[39] John Stott (1921–2011), the great bulwark of evangelical spirituality, whose writing exemplified Christocentric piety said,

> God has given us both [Scripture and sacrament] in order to display Christ before the eyes of our heart, to attract our attention to Him and to draw out our faith in him. Scripture and sacrament alike are Christ-conscious, not self-conscious . . . They are binoculars for the magnification of Jesus Christ . . . Our gaze is to be on Christ.[40]

Stott's evangelical spirituality truly captures the Christ-enamored heart religion of eighteenth-century evangelical spirituality.

---

36. Jonathan Edwards himself said it best: "God himself is the great good which [the redeemed] are brought to the possession and enjoyment of by redemption. He is the highest good, and the sum of all that good which Christ purchased. God is the inheritance of the saints; he is the portion of their souls. God is their wealth and treasure, their food, their life, their dwelling-place, their ornament and diadem, and their everlasting honour and glory. They have none in heaven but God; he is the great good which the redeemed are received to at death, and which they are to rise to at the end of the world. The Lord God is the light of the heavenly Jerusalem; and is the 'river of the water of life' that runs, and 'the tree of life that grows, in the midst of the paradise of God.' The glorious excellencies and beauty of God will be what will for ever [sic] entertain the minds of the saints, and the love of God will be their everlasting feast." Edwards, "God Glorified in Man's Dependence," 5.

37. Gordon, *Evangelical Spirituality*, 321.

38. The ministry of Robert Murray McCheyne helpfully illustrates how Puritan spirituality and eighteenth-century evangelical spirituality shared continuity: "McCheyne brought into the pulpit all the reverence for Scripture of the Reformation period; all the honour for the headship of Christ of the Covenanter struggle; all the freeness of the gospel offer of the Marrow theology; all the bright imagery of Samuel Rutherford; all the delight of the Erskines in the fulness of Christ." Blaikie, *Preachers of Scotland*, 294, quoted in Gordon, *Evangelical Spirituality*, 145. Also, Gordon says, "McCheyne measures his spiritual vitality by the enjoyment and help he gained from regular reading of Scripture . . . It is the assimilation of the truth of God that enables the believer . . . to know the love of God." Gordon, *Evangelical Spirituality*, 140.

39. Gordon, *Evangelical Spirituality*, 4.

40. Stott, *Christ the Controversialist*, 103.

Furthermore, such Christ-pursuing evangelicalism organically grew out of Puritanism. Though Bebbington sees eighteenth-century evangelical spirituality emerging out of the Enlightenment with its emphasis on assurance based on spiritual encounter, both Puritan and evangelical spirituality followed the same Christ-centered compass. Yet, the path and personality of each was unique. Like Puritanism, evangelicalism was a genuine "outpouring of the Spirit of God."[41] It is significant that eighteenth-century evangelicalism, like its Puritan antecedent, demonstrated its inherent value of communion with Christ by the Spirit through the Bible unto personal holiness and mission.[42] Moreover, the Christ-enamored, activistic impulse of the evangelical spirituality of the eighteenth and nineteenth centuries prominently rose in the form of the modern missionary movement.

Roots of the Modern Missionary Movement

Despite "the hampering effects of the Enlightenment Era," Protestants rallied for foreign missions in a milieu freed from the "the limitations of medieval Christianity, once they had caught the vision of a world in need."[43] The genesis of the modern missionary movement has been popularly associated with the Baptist missionary to India, William Carey, the "Father of Modern Missions."[44] Yet, there would have been no William Carey if there had not been an Andrew Fuller. Fuller, a humble autodidact and pastor of a small Particular Baptist church in Kettering, was the thinker, mobilizer, organizer, and rope-holder of the first advance of the modern missionary

---

41. Haykin, "Evangelicalism and the Enlightenment," 60.

42. Adam proposes harmony within the tension of evangelical and Reformed (or Puritan) spirituality: "Evangelical spirituality tends towards an intense personal relationship with God, is naturally egalitarian, and is suspicious of formality. Reformed spirituality is more concerned with our state before God than our relationship with him, depends more on the authorized minister, and tends to be more formal in style. Spirituality that is both Evangelical and Reformed can avoid the weakness and gain the strengths of both . . . Biblical spirituality can be genuinely Evangelical and Reformed in its ethos." Adam, *Hearing God's Words*, 37–38.

43. Torbet, *Venture of Faith*, 4.

44. Smith, *The Life of William Carey*, 315. However, considering the hagiographical accounts of Carey's missionary career, Neill said, "This was not the beginning of modern missions, not even the beginning of Protestant missions . . . [It meant that] the immense forces of Anglo-Saxon Christianity would now be released for missionary service; this was significance enough." Neill, *A History of Christianity in India*, 503–4. Torbet also explained that, "for more than two centuries prior to Carey's time, Protestants had conducted missions among non-Christians. Chief among these Protestants were the Moravian Brethren, or *Unitas Fratrum*, who traced their spiritual descent from John Huss and possibly from Peter Waldo." Torbet, *Venture of Faith*, 3.

movement.[45] He contended against the cheap grace of Sandemanianism,[46] and in response to the cold-heartedness of Hyper Calvinism, his groundbreaking treatise, *The Gospel Worthy of All Acceptation*,[47] fanned into flame evangelical Calvinism.[48] As Brian Stanley has noted, "[Fuller's] book was of prime importance in preparing the ground for Baptist missionary endeavor, precisely because it enabled Particular Baptists to restore concepts of moral obligation and human responsibility to the very centre of their theology of salvation."[49] Fuller's influence was largely due to the timeliness of his work, which hit a nerve among others who were asking the same questions and searching for an alternative to hyper-Calvinism.[50] Regarding his indelible

---

45. For an introductory synopsis of the birth and growth of the Baptist Missionary Society, see Stanley, *The History of the Baptist Missionary Society*, 1–35. For a very significant treatment of the historical, theological, and evangelical context in which the Judsons volunteered for missions, see Leonard, "'Wild and Romantic in the Extreme,'" 74–95.

46. See Fuller, "Strictures on Sandemanianism," 561–646.

47. Fuller, "The Gospel Worthy of All Acceptation," 328–416. Fuller's theology was robustly atonement-centered. In this monumental work, Fuller surveyed the Scriptures and argued from many passages that the prophets, psalmist, apostles, and Jesus himself frequently called unbelievers to repentance and faith. Fuller fought tenaciously against hyper-Calvinist beliefs that said the elect will be saved and therefore evangelism is unnecessary and even cruel for those non-elect, and he battled the hyper-Calvinist notion that someone needed to discern a warrant of faith that they are truly elect before they can believe and be born again. Fuller argued from Scripture that there are numerous examples of the indiscriminate command to believe and repent, and out of such a universal gospel call, the elect are awakened to faith in Christ by the Spirit. Fuller's thesis, simply put, was that the duty of the minister is to preach the gospel indiscriminately because the duty of all is to believe and repent.

48. This evangelical Calvinism became termed "Fullerism," which seemed to combine the doctrines of grace and evangelical conversionism and activism. Morden further describes Fullerism as the Particular Baptists' premier manifestation of "Edwardsean Evangelical Calvinism." Morden, *Offering Christ to the World*, 5. Fuller well-contextualized this Edwardsean brand of Evangelical Calvinism into his Particular Baptist milieu. Chris Chun explains, "Fuller was not simply replicating Edwards . . . Fuller's main contribution was to expand, implicate and apply Edwardsean ideas in his own historical setting. Fuller fully absorbed Edwardsean concepts and made them his own, later applying them in his polemical debates. In the course of these he often cast new light on the ideas of Edwards by implicating the corresponding positive as well as the negative." Chun, "'Sense of the Heart,'" 127.

49. Stanley, *The History of the Baptist Missionary Society*, 5–6

50. Brewster quotes E. F. Clipsham from "Andrew Fuller and Fullerism," 269. "At the very time when Fuller was working out and propagating his doctrine, others including a group of young ministers of outstanding ability and growing influence were thinking along lines similar to his own . . . In other words, *Fuller provided a theology such as thinking men were seeking.*" Brewster, *Andrew Fuller*, 98. Quoting the identical citation from E. F. Clipsham, Mauldin draws a similar conclusion that "the time was right for

influence as a pastor-theologian, Paul Brewster well-summarizes Fuller's impact among evangelical Baptists: "His concern for the souls of those who would hear him preach illustrates Fuller's greatest legacy among Baptists: to support missionary-oriented theology that helped foster deep concern for the salvation of the lost."[51]

Fuller's atonement-centered system of theology predominantly drove his ministry praxis as a preacher, as secretary for the Baptist Missionary Society (BMS), and as an apologist. As a preacher, Fuller's concern for souls compelled him. Employing as many means as possible, Fuller pressed for decisions, pursued young and old, far and near, and he practiced prayer as the requirement for Spirit-empowered evangelism. In conjunction with William Carey's focused devotion to world missions, Fuller's soteriological convictions and theological articulation birthed the BMS, which would later consume Fuller's life as a rope-holder through fund-raising, administration, and writing in defense of missions.[52]

It was from Carey's friendship with Fuller and their shared evangelical piety that Carey called for the use of means in converting the heathen. Out of this evangelical Calvinism, Carey wrote *An Enquiry into the Obligations to Use Means for the Conversion of the Heathen*.[53] On par with the Reformer, Martin Luther's (1483–1546) ninety-five theses, this treatise by Carey may well go down in church history as one of the most influential theological/missiological paradigm shifts in history. It is indeed "the Magna Carta of the Protestant missionary movement."[54]

In addition to the unmatched influence of Fuller, Carey's ideas developed through a juxtaposition of Puritanism, Moravianism, and Pietism.[55] According to historian Stephen Neill (1900–1984), Carey's missions strategy can be summarized in five points: indiscriminate preaching of the gospel by any method possible, widespread publication and distribution of the translated Scriptures, planting a church as soon as possible, studying the culture and worldview of the target people, and training up indigenous

---

the success of Fullerism." Mauldin, *Fullerism as Opposed to Calvinism*, 65.

51. Brewster, *Andrew Fuller*, 106.

52. "Fuller's apologetic skills were also much needed throughout his years of service to the BMS. His ability to engage important officials in word and print regarding the mission's validity proved invaluable. In this way, Fuller was a great defender for the cause of missions and, in particular, the BMS throughout his lifetime." Mauldin, *Fullerism as Opposed to Calvinism*, 52–53.

53. Carey, *An Enquiry*.

54. Mulholland, "From Luther to Carey," 88.

55. For an in-depth article on the influence of the Moravians, Puritans, and Pietists, see Mulholland, "Moravians, Puritans," 221–32.

pastors and leaders.[56] Carey's five strategies of missions are significant because Judson's missionary strategies are nearly identical. They are, nevertheless, not original to either Carey or Judson. But these five strategies have largely characterized the philosophy and methodology of the evangelical missions movement.

Judson's missiological convictions and practices were: the importance of personal faith and believer's baptism, evangelism and contextualization, linguistic and cultural acquisition, and the establishment of self-supporting indigenous churches.[57] Or stated another way, Judson's methods were learning the language and culture proficiently, publicly preaching the gospel, translating the Bible and distributing tracts, planting churches, and training indigenous pastors.[58] "Literate and civilized as they were,"[59] the Burmese were ready for the written Word of God, thought Judson initially. Though their literacy was high compared to other parts of Asia, because their literacy level was insufficient for reading the Scriptures, he "opened a school for teaching adults to read."[60] He later said it was his "intention to place [three Karen] men in the adult school, and qualify them to read and interpret the Scriptures to their countrymen."[61]

---

56. Neill, *A History of Christian Missions*, 224.

57. See Eitel, "The Enduring Legacy," 129–48. Similarly, in articles of agreement adopted by Judson and two other missionary companions, Judson briefly described the means of evangelization by which he was convicted: "We agree in the opinion that our sole object on earth is to introduce the religion of Jesus Christ into the empire of Burmah; and that the means by which we hope to effect this are, translating, printing, and distributing the Holy Scriptures, preaching the gospel, circulating religious tracts, and promoting the instruction of native children." Wayland, *Memoir*, 1:184; Middleditch, *Burmah's Great Missionary*, 121.

58. One biographer points out that one main area of difference between Carey and Judson was that Carey emphasized establishing schools in order to educate young people with a broad education, whereas Judson was more single-minded in his approach to evangelism, translation, discipleship, church-planting, and instructing young people more narrowly with the Bible. For a brief and interesting discussion about the differences between the methods of Carey and Judson, see Hulse, *Adoniram Judson*, 47. For another similar summary of Judson's missionary methods, see Neill, *A History of Christian Missions*, 249; see also Conant, *The Earnest Man*, 290–302.

59. Anderson, *To the Golden Shore*, 56.

60. Adoniram Judson, journal, August 17, 1831 to October 23, 1831, Box No. AJ 4, Folder 5 and Microfilm Roll 1, Judson Letters, ABHS; see also Adoniram Judson, "Mr. Judson's Journal, Maulmein, Aug. 14th, 1831 [to Dec. 29th, 1831]," 322; and see Wayland, *Memoir*, 2:11.

61. Adoniram Judson, journal, August 17, 1831 to October 23, 1831, Box No. AJ 4, Folder 5 and Microfilm Roll 1, Judson Letters, ABHS; see also Adoniram Judson, "Mr. Judson's Journal, Maulmein, Aug. 14th, 1831 [to Dec. 29th, 1831]," 322–25; and see Wayland, *Memoir*, 2:12.

Carey's missionary inspiration and strategies were not original to him. Carey immersed himself in the Puritans, especially the writings Jonathan Edwards,[62] David Brainerd (1718–1747), and John Eliot (1604–1690).[63]

> Puritan missions gave William Carey a workable strategy, an inspirational model, and a conceptual framework for his own missionary endeavors . . . Eliot provided a model for Carey: preacher, translator, agriculturalist, reformer, organizer of churches, humanitarian. It was from him that William Carey drew his missionary strategy.[64]

Just as Eliot modeled a missionary strategy, Brainerd inspired Carey that missions were worth whatever the cost. "Carey read [Brainerd's] diary almost daily. The covenant he and other missionaries drew up as a basis for their lives together in India said, 'Let us often look at Brainerd in the woods of America, pouring out his very soul before God for the people.'"[65] Similarly, Judson read of the Moravian missionary, Christian Scwhartz (1726–1798), who worked in the Tamil language in India, and who inspired him greatly. Accounts of John Eliot and David Brainerd also left their evangelical impact on Judson's soul.[66]

What is more, Judson, Carey, and Fuller were all aware of the labors of Pietist missionaries, such as the Moravian Brethren, an eighteenth-century renewal movement that emerged from German Pietism.[67] The Moravians launched a wave of international evangelical missions through the inspiration and leadership of Count Nicholas Ludwig von Zinzendorf (1700–1760).

---

62. For Carey's reference to Edwards on prayer, see Carey, *An Enquiry*, 11.

63. For Carey's numerous references to both Brainerd and Eliot, see Carey, *An Enquiry*, 36, 69, 70, 71, 87. Regarding the influence of Eliot and Brainerd on Protestant missions, see Carpenter, "New England Puritans," 519–32.

64. Mulholland, "Moravians, Puritans," 227–28.

65. Ibid., 231. Mulholland also says, "What influenced Carey most was Brainerd's radical single-mindedness, his passion for souls, his desire to do God's will regardless of the cost. And the extent that Brainerd's thoughts became Carey's thoughts can be seen in many of Carey's writings." Ibid.

66. Hulse, *Adoniram Judson*, 12. See also Brumberg, *Mission for Life*, 25; and see Neill, *A History of Christian Missions*, 198–99.

67. See Carey, *An Enquiry*, 11, 71. See also Hulse, *Adoniram Judson*, 12. Three general characteristics were common to all of Pietism's manifestations: first, a mystical element that emphasized emotional experience and heartfelt expression existed especially in the context of personal Bible study; second, the practice of holy living and active compassion developed out of this emphasis on experience; third, because of this orientation towards active compassion, Pietists concerned themselves with the unevangelized heathen. See Spener, *Pia Desideria*. See also Schattschneider, "William Carey, Modern Missions," 8–10; and see Schattschneider, "Pioneers in Mission," 63–67.

The Moravian missionaries came from Moravia in present-day Germany. Moravia was essentially a refugee region for persecuted non-Catholics. On August 13, 1727, the Moravian refugees experienced a tremendous revival, from which emerged a great evangelical missionary movement.[68]

Zinzendorf received his formational training and pietistic ideas at the University of Halle, under the leadership of the activistic Pietist, August Hermann Francke (1663–1727).[69] The Pietist leader, Philip Jakob Spener (1635–1705), founded the University of Halle; his famous *Pia Desideria* ignited Pietistic passion among young men and issued an evangelical renewal movement among scholastic Lutherans.[70]

Numerous Pietistic missionaries came out of Halle. Yet the Germans did not want to send missionaries because of the University of Wittenberg's negative view on the extremes of Halle-brand Pietism. Nevertheless, Frederick IV (1671–1730), the king of Denmark, sought to send out missionaries from Denmark, yet he could not find any in Denmark. So, he inquired in Germany and found the Pietists. Denmark actually sent out two German

---

68. Mullholland aptly explains, "Moravian history predates the Reformation. Originally known as the *Unitas Fratrum*, the Unity of the Brethren, these Czech Christians were the followers of the martyred John Hus, a Reformer before the Reformation . . . After Hus's death (July 6, 1415), his followers, who were sometimes called Hussites, and sometimes Bohemian Brethren, experienced a resurgence . . . Then in the wake of the religious wars of the 1600s, Bohemia came under a Roman Catholic king, who unleashed a fiery persecution against these Moravians . . . Years later, in 1722, a small band of these refugees was searching for some place where they could be secure. When they crossed into Germany, they heard about a place called Herrnhut, which was a small parcel of land on the estate of Nicholas Ludwig von Zinzendorf." Mulholland, "Moravians, Puritans," 222–23.

69. After studying at Halle, Zinzendorf then studied at the University of Wittenberg, the great Lutheran bastion of scholasticism, which stood against error and mixture. Where Wittenberg was the center of rigid scholarship, Halle was the center of pietistic activism. For further analysis of Zinzendorf's piety and influence, see Burns, "Moravian Missionary Piety and the Influence of Count Zinzendorf."

70. In his *Pia Desideria*, Spener called for six things: (1) pastors should preach from the whole Bible and the church should be broken up into small groups to study the Bible for spiritual formation, not theological debate; (2) the priesthood of all believers needs to be revived, and lay people should be encouraged to be active in the church, as opposed to depending only on the highly educated clergy; (3) more focus on heart issues such as the spiritual life and love for humankind is needed over against theological dogma; (4) the fruit of a true Christian is evidenced by good deeds, witness, and moral living, over against theological precision; (5) Christian leaders should be trained through Bible studies and prayer groups where one's devotional life could be cultivated; (6) sermons are not occasions for showing off one's education but for rousing the saints to love and good deeds. Mulholland, "From Luther to Carey," 90–92. See also Neill, *A History of Christian Missions*, 194.

Pietist missionaries, Bartholomew Ziegenbalg (1682–1719) and Heinrich Plutschau (1677–1752), to India to work among the colonies of Denmark.[71]

Ziegenbalg and Plutschau were the first Protestant missionaries in India. Within the first week in India, they started learning the Tamil language, and after three years they had translated the New Testament into Tamil, which is still used today by Tamil-speakers. After serving in India for nine years (1705–1714), Ziegenbalg and Plutschau returned to Denmark and trained many more Pietist missionaries. In fact, while Zinzendorf was at Halle, Ziegenbalg steadily mentored him. Ziegenbalg proposed these five mission strategies: (1) educate people to read so that they can read the Bible; (2) translate the Bible in the native tongue; (3) learn the culture and the worldview of the people; (4) preach for the personal conversion of the heathen; (5) establish local churches and promote congregational indigenization.[72] The five missions strategies that both Carey and Judson promoted were essentially these five points proposed by Ziegenbalg. Clearly, these Pietists influenced the missions strategies of Carey and Judson, which have deeply affected the succeeding missionary movement for generations. Fifty years before the BMS sent Carey to India, the Moravian Church had pioneered the way into pagan countries both by principle and example. The Moravians took the missionary instinct of Pietism and created a missionary culture.

The missionary movement was an activistic fruit of the evangelical eighteenth century. Against all rational explanation, the evangelical aftershocks of the long eighteenth century still continue in the twenty-first century. Stephen Neill said, "The cool and rational eighteenth century was hardly a seed-bed for Christian growth; but out of it came a greater outburst of Christian missionary enterprise than had been seen in all the centuries before."[73]

---

71. See Aberly, "Bartholomew Ziegenbalg," 39–65.

72. Neill, *A History of Christian Missions*, 195–96. Zinzendorf adapted and promoted Ziegenbalg's five principles for the Moravian missionaries: "(1) The plain, simple, believing, and consolatory preaching of the gospel; (2) To neglect no opportunity of bearing testimony in other places concerning Jesus as the only way to life; (3) An object of primary concern to promote the printing of various useful and edifying works; (4) They considered how they might be useful to . . . those of other persuasions. (5) They deliberated also upon providing schools for the education of children in a christian-like [sic] manner." Spangenberg, *The Life of Count Zinzendorf*, 445.

73. Neill, *A History of Christian Missions*, 477.

The New Divinity of New England

Adoniram Judson was not the son of an international missionary, but he was the son of a missions-minded Congregationalist pastor. Adoniram Judson, Sr. (1752–1826) was born at Woodbury, Connecticut, the son of William Judson, an immigrant from Yorkshire. Judson, Sr. ministered in three parishes before assuming the pastorate in Plymouth. Prior to going to Plymouth, Judson, Sr. served as a Congregationalist home missionary to Vermont.[74]

When Adoniram Judson, Jr. was fourteen years old, living in Plymouth, his father preached a message from 2 Corinthians 6:17, which says, "Come out from among them, and be ye separate, saith the Lord, and touch not the unclean thing; and I will receive you." Judson, Sr. illustrated how to obey this text by drawing upon the example of their Puritan forbearers who "discovered a remarkable spirit of self-denial, boldness, and perseverance in the cause of religion,"[75] and "who left England and came to America. Probably they understood the meaning of the words, as well as many other passages of Scripture of a like import, which might give them courage and strength, through all their trials, in the discharge of duty."[76] He called his congregants to flee the Babylonian system that Scripture uses "to represent all the sin and moral evil in this world of apostasy."[77] However, his call was not to "a separation of any particular society or family, or forsaking all intercourse with the world; but a separation from all moral evil, and faithful discharge of all Christian duty . . . And to return to God, to love him supremely, and to delight in his service."[78] For, "true faith, in the system of grace or truth, will produce Christian practice."[79]

In Judson, Sr.'s mind, there was in recent history no greater example of obedience to this text than the Puritans who sailed to the New World. He said that the Puritans were different than most because they esteemed the "gospel system of grace," and they upheld the doctrines of the Trinity, total depravity, regeneration, Christ's divinity and atonement, the need for repentance and faith, the perseverance of the saints, heaven and hell, and he exclaimed, "O how evident is their belief in the providence of God!" He went on to say they beseeched the throne of grace and honored God

---

74. Barnes, *Pioneers of Light*, 9.
75. Adoniram Judson, Sr., *A Sermon Preached in the New Meeting House*, 5.
76. Ibid., 8.
77. Ibid., 12.
78. Ibid., 13.
79. Ibid., 11.

for delivering them by "his sovereign goodness."[80] According to the elder Judson, God has acted for his name's sake throughout history, and he is progressively advancing the kingdom of his beloved Son and expelling the darkness through the gospel. Judson, Sr. said that "in acting for his own glory, [God] has spread the knowledge of his name among those who sat in darkness and the shadow of death . . . And he is now succeeding the missionary cause, in spreading truth and knowledge." Judson, Sr. went on to discuss his optimism in the fact that Christianity was more widespread than in any other time in history.[81]

This homily demonstrates the robust Puritan and Edwardsean spirituality of Judson's father. Its tenor exhibits a strong adherence to Calvinistic doctrine, a devotion to holiness, and a consecration to costly obedience. Judson's father loved "the example of primitive Christians."[82] Joan Jacobs Brumberg comments that Judson, Sr. admired the apostolic model of pioneer missionaries, such as John Eliot and David Brainerd. She maintains that Eliot's successful translation of the Bible into Mohawk amazed Judson, Sr., just as it had astounded Cotton Mather (1663–1728).[83] The evangelical piety of Judson, Sr. was not an anomaly in his day in New England; he was a New Divinity man.

The New Divinity movement of New England arose during the latter half of the eighteenth century. Leaders of the movement, such as Congregationalist ministers Samuel Hopkins and Joseph Bellamy (1719–1790), studied under the tutelage of Jonathan Edwards, and they sought to uphold and advance Edwardsean revival theology. They accomplished this primarily through a pastoral training network called the "school of the prophets." After graduating from divinity school, newly trained ministers would move into the parsonages of Hopkins or Bellamy for a year-long mentorship; they mastered the heart of Edwardsean theology, and they learned the skills of their ministerial trade. In fact, Bellamy mentored Adoniram Judson Sr. for gospel ministry after Judson Sr.'s graduation from Yale (1775) before assuming the pulpit in Malden, where Judson Jr. was born.[84]

80. Ibid., 9–11.
81. Ibid., 21.
82. Ibid., 14.

83. Brumberg, *Mission for Life*, 24. Mather wrote about John Eliot's labors: "Behold, ye Americans, the greatest honor that ever you were partakers of. The Bible was printed here at our Cambridge, and is the only Bible that ever was printed in all America, from the very foundation of the world." Mather, *Magnalia Christi Americana*, 564, quoted in Brumberg, *Mission for Life*, 24.

84. Conforti, *Samuel Hopkins and the New Divinity Movement*, 230; Anderson, *To the Golden Shore*, 5, 13. For helpful resources on the New Divinity theology and

Providentially, the congregations of New Divinity ministers witnessed the revivals of New England that launched the Second Great Awakening (1790s). These revivals, conversely, were not of the same "new measures"[85] that the "father of modern revivalism,"[86] Charles G. Finney (1792–1875), promoted for effecting revival. Finney's methods were confrontational, motivational, direct, and he used the means of special music, revival meetings, and imploring sinners to the anxious bench "to demonstrate that sinners really did possess natural ability."[87] In their own Hopkinsian revivalistic *ethos*, the New Divinity men employed the theological intricacies of Jonathan Edwards, which included his differentiation between the sinner's moral inability and natural ability. They also upheld his doctrine of disinterested benevolence, which was, as Robert Caldwell has said, "the basis for an exclusive Edwardsean spirituality that motivated a radical self-denial among America's early missionaries. This mixture of Edwardsean theology with traditional Calvinism resulted in a unique theological school in the Reformed tradition."[88]

Edwards published *Freedom of the Will* in 1754 in order to correct Arminian objections to Calvinism.[89] He argued that divine sovereignty and

---

Edwardsean influence of Bellamy and Hopkins, see Foster, *A Genetic History*; Kling, *A Field of Divine Wonders*; Conforti, *Jonathan Edwards*; Conforti, *Samuel Hopkins and the New Divinity Movement*; Rowe, *History of Andover*; Woods, *Memoirs of American Missionaries*; Whittemore, *The Transformation of the New England Theology*.

85. These New Measures were innovative means of motivation. They "included allowing women to testify (though not to preach) in church, nightly meetings for praise and preaching, and the 'anxious bench,' a place set aside near the front of the meeting house where sinners could give their lives to Christ." Butler et al., *Religion in American Life*, 178.

86. Hankins, *The Second Great Awakening and the Transcendentalists*, 137.

87. Sweeney and Guelzo, *The New England Theology*, 228.

88. Caldwell, "New England's New Divinity," 31. Historically, the five points of Calvinism have been a system summarized in the acronym, TULIP: Total Depravity, Unconditional Election, Limited Atonement, Irresistible Grace, and Perseverance of the Saints. To see how the classic five points of Calvinism compares to the tenets of New Divinity theology, see an extract of Hannah Adams's (1755–1831) "The View of Religions," in Woods, *History of the Andover*, 32–34. At the end of her ten-point summary of Hopkinsianism, Adams states, "The Hopkinsians warmly advanced the doctrine of Divine decrees, the doctrine of particular election, the doctrine of total depravity, the doctrine of the special influences of the Spirit of God in regeneration, the doctrine of justification by faith alone, the final perseverance of the saints, and the consistency between entire freedom and absolute dependence; and therefore claim it as their just due—to be called Hopkinsian Calvinists." Adams, "A View of Religions," 33–34. For a succinct synthesis of how the doctrines of grace permeated Judson's missionary theology, see Nettles, *By His Grace and for His Glory*, 148–54.

89. Edwards, "Freedom of the Will," 3–89.

human responsibility are not at odds, and his distinction between natural and moral ability became a hallmark doctrine for New Divinity theology.[90] In the legacy of Edwards, the New Divinity men contended that sinful men can indeed repent, but they do not want to repent. Their desires are corrupt, though their natural abilities to comprehend the reasonableness of the gospel are intact. Sinners' volitions act according to the prevailing motives of their hearts. Edwards said, "It is that motive, which, as it stands in the view of the mind, is the strongest, that determines the Will."[91] Freedom of the will is not the power of contrary choice, but rather, it is the freedom to do as one pleases according to the strongest disposition of the heart.

Edwards and the New Divinity men taught that sinners choose according to their strongest inclinations, and they have the freedom to do as they please according to their hearts' desires. Therefore, they are accountable and culpable for the actions of their free will. Only through God's sovereign work of grace to overcome man's sinful heart can a sinner's will be set free to desire and delight in God. Thus, divine sovereignty, moral necessity, freedom, and moral accountability are not inconsistent. Since all have the natural ability to repent, New Divinity ministers would make indiscriminate calls to believe the gospel. This call for immediate repentance was in opposition to the Old Calvinist view that said conversion was a gradual process in which God would cause regeneration while sinners were appropriating the means of grace. In Puritan fashion, such means would include: prayer, listening to preaching, reading the Bible, and seeking God. This would result in a long struggle of guilt, anxiety, and introspection.[92] In reality, the differentiation between the Old Calvinist view and the New Divinity view was a matter of emphasis; the New Divinity emphasized an immediate application of the means of grace, and the Old Calvinists emphasized a long, drawn out struggle while applying the means of grace. If someone were to ask a New Divinity minister how to repent immediately, the minister's answer would be similar to that of an Old Calvinist: employ the means of grace and seek God, and he would perhaps create new affections to predispose the sinner to repent and trust in Christ alone. Slowly the New Divinity men moved

---

90. For Edwards's distinction between natural and moral ability, see ibid., 8–11.

91. Ibid., 5.

92. Caldwell states, "The problem New Divinity ministers saw with this approach is that it sometimes became an excuse for spiritual lethargy (i.e., 'I'm not ready; God has not begun His work in me yet'). They reacted strongly against such an attitude. 'You indeed are ready; you *can* if you *will*,' they said. 'You possess the natural capacity to comply with the claims of the gospel. The only thing keeping you from Christ is your stubborn, sinful will! Repent immediately!'" Caldwell, "New England's New Divinity," 46; emphasis in original.

away from an emphasis on revival to an emphasis on self-examination and inclinations of the heart for or against Christ.[93]

In addition, Edwards influenced the New Divinity men to seek the good of God and of others over their own interests. This other-centered "disinterested benevolence" emerged from Edwards's *A Treatise Concerning Religious Affections*[94] and *A Dissertation on the Nature of True Virtue*.[95] Edwards said,

> Virtue, as I have observed, consists in the cordial consent or union of being to being in general. And that frame of mind, whereby it is disposed to *relish* and be *pleased* with the view of this, is benevolence, or union of heart, to being in general; or it is an universally benevolent frame of mind. Because, he whose temper is to love being in general, must therein have a disposition to approve and be pleased with love to being in general.[96]

For Edwards, self-forgetfulness was a sign of regeneration. Self-disinterest indicated that a person had become so joyfully enamored with God that he did not feel the need to be assured of his salvation. Self-disinterest naturally leads to disinterested love for God and others, which manifests itself in acts of sacrifice for the good of others and the glory of God. Once the Holy Spirit enlightens the heart to see and love God's glory and beauty at conversion, the Holy Spirit then grants new desires that manifest universal benevolence. The true believer then has a passion for the glory of Christ and affectionately esteems a life lived under the cross. The love and preoccupation with self is severed and the believer discovers his greatest joy in God. Central to the spirituality of Edwards was this benevolent spirit.[97]

At the headwaters of the New Divinity movement were Joseph Bellamy and Samuel Hopkins; these disciples of Jonathan Edwards "personified the New Divinity."[98] They "both vigorously sought to advance their mentor's

---

93. Conforti helpfully explains that "love of God and neighbor and not the saving of one's soul became the core of Hopkinsianism. The true Christian must lose himself in a cause higher than his own salvation—namely, the temporal and eternal well-being of others." Conforti, *Samuel Hopkins and the New Divinity Movement*, 121.

94. Edwards, "A Treatise Concerning Religious Affections," 234–343.

95. Edwards, "A Dissertation on the Nature of True Virtue," 122–42. Edwards's biography of David Brainerd was his famous illustration of true piety and disinterested benevolence; see Edwards, "Life and Diary of the Rev. David Brainerd," 313–458.

96. Edwards, "A Dissertation on the Nature of True Virtue," 141; emphasis in original.

97. Caldwell, "New England's New Divinity," 47.

98. Brown, "The New Divinity," 6.

revivalistic, pietistic, and ecclesiastical vision."[99] Bellamy, a rural pastor in Bethlehem, Connecticut, wrote many theological treatises, of which his renowned works are *True Religion Delineated*[100] and *The Wisdom of God in the Permission of Sin*.[101] "Bellamy was . . . a thoroughgoing Edwardean as far as the theory of virtue is concerned. Like Edwards, he was also in general upon the plane of the old Calvinism. In many things his positions will be found to be identical with those of Edwards."[102] Bellamy argued against the notion that God foreordains sin; God merely permits sin, which manifests "the heart and character of God as it could not otherwise have been revealed, to give his creatures a true specimen of themselves, and thus to advance his own glory and their good. For the greatest thing we can possibly have is an increased knowledge of God and of ourselves."[103] The American Church historian, E. Brooks Holifield, says that Bellamy emulated Edwards in emphasizing that "the heart of true religion and true virtue consisted in the love of God for God's own intrinsic excellence."[104]

Samuel Hopkins was, more than Bellamy, the theologian for the New Divinity movement. His *System of Doctrines* became the first American systematic theology.[105] Holifield says that Hopkins's "writing achieved such influence that for many the New Divinity became synonymous with 'Hopkinsianism.'" Holifield goes on to say that Hopkins's conversion influenced the rest of his life and ministry. Hopkins was "a melancholy man who remained doubtful of his own salvation."[106] Prior to his conversion, Hopkins had read the biography of Brainerd, which caused him to fear that he had

99. Caldwell, "New England's New Divinity," 36.

100. Bellamy, "True Religion Delineated," 3–363. Foster said, "The *True Religion Delineated* discusses the nature of religion, and gives two answers, apparently different, but in the end coalescing in one, viz., that it consists in a conformity to the law of God, and a compliance with the gospel of Christ. These two answers determine the two parts of the treatise. The first treats the law, which it finds perfectly fulfilled in the one exercise of love. The second then considers the gospel, and is thus led to the successive topics of the ruin of man, the atonement, and the application of that atonement through faith, together with the reward of everlasting life promised to the believer." Foster, *A Genetic History*, 108.

101. Bellamy, "The Wisdom of God in the Permission of Sin," 3–270.

102. Foster, *A Genetic History*, 109.

103. Ibid., 119–20.

104. Holifield, *Theology in America*, 137.

105. Caldwell, "New England's New Divinity," 37. Hopkins, *The System of Doctrines*. He also wrote the first biography of Edwards; see Hopkins, *The Life and Character of the Late Reverend*.

106. Holifield, *Theology in America*, 136.

never been born of the Spirit.[107] He sought to discern the state of his soul and the presence of the Holy Spirit in his life.

After graduating from Yale, Hopkins went to live with and be mentored by Jonathan Edwards. While Hopkins lived with Jonathan and Sarah Edwards, he edited for publication some of Edwards's works, including *The Nature of True Virtue*[108] and *The History of Redemption*.[109] From Edwards, Hopkins learned that the genuinely converted minister must "personify the practical piety and self-sacrificing zeal that were among the distinguishing marks of conversion."[110] Edwards also taught him that he was "'not to expect outward ease, pleasure and plenty.' . . . A minister could not even 'depend upon the friendship and respect of men; but should prepare to endure hardness, as one that is going forth as a soldier to war.'"[111] When Hopkins entered the ministry, he surrendered his life to the cause of Christ as a frontier preacher. Years after he had renounced the world and had committed to a life of self-denial, Hopkins outlined theologically the self-sacrificing, missionary spirituality that supported him in Housatonic.[112] Hopkins lived a life of austerity, living out the Edwardsean vision of self-sacrificing piety, ready and willing to be accursed for the glory of God.

Hopkins established God's disposition to be one of disinterested benevolence.[113] For the people of God, Christ is the model of which this piety seeks to apply itself:

> A Christocentric formulation of that disposition is the imperative to love God and love the neighbor as Jesus demonstrated in his life and teaching . . . Moreover, true holiness provides a view of experience in which suffering is transformed and interpreted as a participation in a Christological benevolence.[114]

---

107. Conforti, *Samuel Hopkins and the New Divinity Movement*, 30.

108. See Edwards, "A Dissertation on the Nature of True Virtue," 122–42.

109. Whittemore, *The Transformation of the New England Theology*, 78; see also Edwards, "A History of the Work of Redemption," 532–619.

110. Conforti, *Samuel Hopkins and the New Divinity Movement*, 47.

111. Ibid., 47, quoting Edwards, "The True Excellency of a Gospel Minister," 955–60.

112. See Conforti, *Samuel Hopkins and the New Divinity Movement*, 48.

113. New Divinity theology continued to develop and, later under the influence of Edwards Amasa Park (1808–1900) at Andover Theological Seminary, New Divinity articulated that "the love of God is thus [its] determining principle." Foster, *A Genetic History*, 491.

114. Brown, "The New Divinity," 40.

Edwards's notion of "true virtue" influenced Hopkinsian "true holiness" and Bellamy's "true religion."[115] Edwards illustrated signs of true virtue in the regenerate believer: "a love of Christ, an acceptance of Christian truth, a concern for eternal salvation, a sense of one's odiousness and smallness."[116] "Where Edwards saw true virtue as essentially a matter of right affections, Hopkins viewed it as right actions."[117] Furthermore, Hopkins contended that true conversion proved itself in a willingness to be damned for the glory of God; and, in imitation of Christ, the true convert manifested an "unconditional surrender to the sovereign will of God."[118]

Hopkins sought to improve upon some of Edwards's theological views. A primary improvement he made was in his understanding of sin and self-love. For Edwards, sin was "*any other* elective preference than that of the good of being in general."[119] Hopkins expounded upon this, which many of his successors adopted: self-love is enmity with God; self-love blinds the heart to moral excellence; from self-love originates irreverence and godlessness; and, "the opposition between holiness and selfishness is that between a wholly disinterested affection and a wholly interested affection."[120] Just as disinterested benevolence assists in a life of holiness, self-interest assists in a life of sin.

Moreover, the governmental theory of atonement,[121] propounded by the New Divinity in response to the Universalist claim that "the doctrine of

---

115. Ibid., 47.

116. Conforti, *Samuel Hopkins and the New Divinity Movement*, 28, quoting Edwards, "Distinguishing Marks of a Work of the Spirit of God," 257–77.

117. Conforti, *Samuel Hopkins and the New Divinity Movement*, 121.

118. Rowe, *History of Andover*, 8. See also Hopkins, "A Dialogue between a Calvinist and a Semi-Calvinist," 143–57.

119. Foster, *A Genetic History*, 153.

120. Ibid., 154.

121. The governmental theory of the New Divinity said, "Christ died not to redeem a debt but to preserve the dignity of the divine government. Having promulgated a moral law, God could not permit its subversion without allowing the destruction of the moral order itself. When Christ died to vindicate the honor of the law, he made it possible for God to forgive sinful rebels without upsetting the moral order." Holifield, *Theology in America*, 132–33. Regarding Bellamy and Hopkins, Holifield explains, "Both Bellamy and Hopkins retained older Calvinistic views of atonement even as they said that Christ died to secure God's moral government. But their use of governmental metaphors and their rejection of a limited atonement opened the door for a more explicit governmental theory." Ibid., 147. For a systematic definition of the governmental theory, see Grudem, *Systematic Theology*, 582. As Nicole helpfully explained, "It must be at once apparent that a fundamental flaw afflicts this view. How can the suffering and death of Christ be an expression of divine justice unless he is seen as burdened with sin, with real, not hypothetical, sin? Under the conditions stated, the death of Christ

universal salvation followed logically the doctrine of universal atonement,"[122] influenced the New Divinity *ethos* of self-denial. In God's government, he permitted moral evil, indeed even willed it, for the greater good and happiness of the whole. Hopkins contended that the world was "much better" because sin prompted the "full display of God's redemptive love and grace in salvation and allowed God's 'power and wrath' to be manifested in the judgment . . . of sinners."[123]

Hopkins said it best in his preface to "Three Sermons from Romans 3:5–8." He argued that all the sin and pain in the world is "for the general good of the whole." He claimed that believing this truth is essential for "a true and cheerful submission to God's will as it is manifested in what he does and what he permits." If a person submits to God's will, such a person sees God's will "as *wise* and *good*." Because God permits sin and misery in the world, it must work for a good end; otherwise, God's will would not be wise and good, and it would not be worthy of submission. As the believer grows in "true benevolence," he passionately "seeks the good" of all. He is also, then, "conformed to God . . . in true holiness." Hopkins went on to contend, "If Christians, therefore, tamely give up this truth, where will they go for support and comfort in dark and evil times?"[124] When God's greatest aim is to manifest his glory and worthiness, then "the purpose of life is not happiness, but holiness. Life is not a state of ease and enjoyment, but a state of trial, in which God will try humanity, proving them, that he might know what is in their hearts."[125] Because God is absolutely sovereign and just, he deserves the unwavering trust and hope of the elect. This submission to God's holy justice and infallible, sovereign wisdom is the foundation for the theology of self-denial and suffering that pervaded the New Divinity. This New Divinity theology and the spirit of religious renewal converged at the great bastion of orthodoxy and missionary mobilization: Andover Theological Seminary.

---

appears as an act of flagrant injustice. How can justice be manifested where it is not exercised? If Christ is indeed seen as the substitute of the sinner, he may be charged with the full burden of the sinner's guilt and therefore be struck with God's own wrath as an act of justice. But unless this substitution takes place, there is no way for the Lord's suffering to be an expression of divine justice. The governmental view fails precisely at the point it had been thought to validate." Nicole, "Post Script on Penal Substitution," 450–51.

122. Holifield, *Theology in America*, 147.

123. Jauhiainen, "Samuel Hopkins and Hopkinsianism," 108; emphasis in original. See also Hopkins, "Sin, through Divine Interposition," 503–8, 527–28.

124. Hopkins, "Sin, through Divine Interposition," 493–94; emphasis in original.

125. Brown, "The New Divinity," 51.

Andover Theological Seminary

When Henry Ware, Sr. (1765–1845), a Unitarian minister, assumed the Hollis Professorship of Divinity at Harvard and replaced biblical Hebrew with French, orthodox observers saw this as apostasy. One result was the banding together of faithful New Divinity men to found Andover Theological Seminary in 1807, where they endeavored to stand against the invasion of liberal and Unitarian doctrine. The Andover faculty were to reaffirm a Calvinist creed every five years and confirm their commitment to not only stand against

> Atheists and Infidels, but to Jews, Mahommetans, Arians, Pelagians, Antinomians, Arminians, Socinians, Unitarians, and Universalists, and to all other heresies and errors, ancient or modern, which may be opposed to the Gospel of Christ, or hazardous to the souls of men.[126]

The fires of evangelical Calvinism were still burning bright and hot at Andover when Adoniram Judson enrolled in 1808.

At Andover, the way of life among the faculty was not much different from in the country. They maintained modest lifestyles, hoeing gardens, milking cows, and cutting hay.[127] There were only two professors on faculty when Judson enrolled. Eliphalet Pearson (1752–1826), Professor of Sacred Literature, taught for one year and then was replaced by the young Moses Stuart (1780–1852), "the prince of biblical learning in America."[128] Leonard Woods (1774–1854) served as Abbot Professor of Christian Theology, made possible by a donation of twenty thousand dollars from Samuel Abbot of Andover.[129] Between 1809 and 1811, Edward Dorr Griffin (1770–1837)

---

126. Rowe, *History of Andover*, 14. See also Brumberg, *Mission for Life*, 27.

127. Anderson, *To the Golden Shore*, 49.

128. Rowe, *History of Andover*, 54. "It was [Stuart] who set the standard and fixed the methods of biblical study for the next generation, for he remained at his post in Andover for thirty-eight years until 1848. Men who sat at his feet went to imitate him in their teaching at other seminaries . . . The imprint of Stuart's mind was felt still farther afield, for Miron Winslow [1789–1864], class of 1818, translated the Bible into the Tamil tongue of India and compiled a Tamil-English lexicon, and Samuel Austin Worcester [1798–1859], class of 1823, translated parts of the Bible into the language of the Cherokees in America, setting an example to other missionaries." Ibid., 54–55; see also Winslow, *A Sketch of Missions*. See also Bowden, "Worcester, Samuel Austin," 748.

129. Anderson, *To the Golden Shore*, 47. For a thorough account of the genesis of Andover and its first professors, see Rowe, *History of Andover*, 10–22; and see Woods, *History of the Andover*, 47–62, 145–58. Other professors joined the faculty of Andover in the early days, but Judson's time at Andover did not overlap with them: Austin Phelps (1820–1890), Edwards Amasa Park, Ebenezer Porter (1772–1834). See Rowe, *History*

served on the faculty, but torn between his preaching duties at the prominent Park Street Church in Boston and his professorship, he chose to remain in Boston and leave his post at Andover.[130] Andover provided

> young people of each denomination with a sympathetic host environment for the nurture and maturation of proper religious sentiments. To that end, prospective Congregational clergymen were shaped by Andover's controlled environment, with its regulated pattern of prayer, study, and useful work . . . In addition to the seminary's well-known function as an orthodox arsenal for the war against the liberals, it provided the means for directing youthful evangelism.[131]

Andover became the Hopkinsian bulwark: "Professors were expected to train their guns of orthodoxy against error, whether within or outside the walls of embattled Zion."[132]

The professors at Andover Theological Seminary engaged the students intellectually and spiritually. Leonard Woods recounted the illuminating spiritual *ethos* shared among the faculty and the students of Andover.[133] Not more than a few weeks after the seminary opened, Woods called the faculty and students to a meeting for prayer and religious intercourse, which developed into a regular "Wednesday Evening Conference."[134] Every student was supposed to attend. Woods and Stuart would pray with them and give wise counsel in relation to Christian doctrine and practice.[135] Woods stated, "While we attached high importance to literary acquisitions, we gave a still higher place *to spiritual improvement*. We strove to make the impression

---

of Andover, 40–61.

130. Woods, *History of the Andover*, 147–50.

131. Brumberg, *Mission for Life*, 28–29.

132. Rowe, *History of Andover*, 49. "It is symbolic of Andover's staunch theology that the first book to be drawn from the Seminary library was a volume of the works of Jonathan Edwards. That Professor Woods was loyal to the Hopkinsian principle that one should be willing to be damned for the glory of God, appears when on the occasion of the birth of his fifth child he was in doubt whether he ought to ask God to save all his children. That Calvinistic theology did not breed hardness of heart is plain from the kindness and affection which Woods showed in his domestic life, and his patience and sympathy with his friends and students." Ibid., 49.

133. For a full description of the spiritual life fostered at Andover, see Woods, *History of the Andover*, 159–70.

134. Ibid., 164.

135. Later in life, Stuart said that his "most valuable contribution" to the seminary was the Wednesday evening conferences. Rowe, *History of Andover*, 50.

. . . that spiritual religion and growth in grace should be their paramount object."[136]

During these conferences every Wednesday evening, only the students were invited. It was strictly a time for the faculty to mentor the theological students. The faculty addressed the seminarians on matters of "holy religion, both doctrinal, experimental and practical."[137] They spoke on different subjects for six to seven years, and purposefully did not repeat the same subject at least for three years. Woods's general list of subjects discussed during the three-year rotation of weekly Conferences included

> (1) Intellectual and moral improvement as objects of pursuit in the Seminary—moral improvement the first and highest. (2) Directions for intellectual improvement. (3) Importance of taking care of the health. (4) Right use of time. (5) Duty of repentance as obligatory on Christians. (6) Habitual devotion. (7) Dispensations of Providence, the means of moral discipline. (8) Love to the souls of men as a Christian duty—how to strengthen and manifest it. (9) Revivals of religion—several Conferences touching the nature of genuine revivals—the means of promoting them—cautions to be observed—the work of the Holy Spirit—antecedents and consequences of a revival. (10) Self-examination—treated in several Conferences under the following heads:—importance of the duty—hindrances to the right performance of it—how to conduct it—mistakes to be avoided. (11) Doubts of Christians respecting their own piety—how occasioned and how to be removed. (12) Christian hope, its nature, grounds and influence. (13) Social and secret prayer compared—peculiar advantages of each—both should be united. (14) Different virtues and graces connected—all alike in their nature, and promote each other. (15) Brotherly love—occasion for it among students—its happy effects. (16) Government of the appetites and passions—aids to the duty—need of Divine help. (17) Regard to reputation as a motive to action—when right and when wrong. (18) Conquest of easily-besetting sins. (19) Godly sorrow—its nature and use. (20) Duty of confessing sin, both to God and to man. (21) Danger of little sins, so-called. (22) Special dangers of theological students, as ambition, pride, levity, &c.—remedy for these evils. (23) Eminent holiness to be earnestly sought. (24) Declensions in religion—symptoms—causes—evils consequent. (25) Faith as a principle of the Christian life. (26) Humility. (27) Forgiveness of injuries. (28) Love of

---

136. Woods, *History of the Andover*, 163; emphasis in original.
137. Ibid., 164.

enemies. (29) Reading the Scriptures and other religious books. (30) Strict observance of the Sabbath. (31) Christian conversation and correspondence. (32) Self-denial. (33) Watchfulness. (34) Dependence upon God practically considered. (35) How to treat doubts and difficulties as to the truths of revelation. (36) Living near to God. (37) Good habits. (38) A good conscience. (39) Indwelling sin—its power, deceitfulness and cure. (40) Justification. (41) Importunity in prayer. (42) Grieving the Spirit. (43) Right example.[138]

Woods recorded that the students loved these Wednesday night Conferences, and that they were "indispensable to the highest moral improvement and usefulness of the students."[139]

During every term, the faculty and students would engage in "the Seminary Fast."[140] They would search their hearts, confess sin, and cry out to God for deliverance from temptation and for growth in grace. They spent the morning in personal reflection and devotion, and then by ten o'clock there was a meeting among the students for prayer. At noon the professors would meet together themselves to confess sin, pray for one another, pray for the students, sing hymns, and seek the Lord for grace to persevere in the faith and the sacred work of the ministry. Woods reflected, "If we ever knew the blessedness of fraternal love and fellowship, and the higher blessedness of communion with our God and Saviour, it was at those favored seasons." Then in the afternoons of the day of fasting, Woods said the professors would meet for an hour with the class and exhort them from Scripture to stay faithful to their religious and ministerial duties, "looking unto Jesus, and relying on His all-sufficient grace."[141]

Woods also recorded the books of experimental and practical religion that the professors would often recommend for the students to read for their

---

138. Ibid., 165–66. Also, Woods recorded that, during the summer months, the professors spoke on practical ministerial duties, such as "the nature and importance of the sacred office—qualifications for it—its many and arduous duties—difficulties and discouragements of a minister—also his encouragements and comforts—his duty to doubting, dejected Christians—to offenders and backsliders—to children—to the afflicted, the sick, and the dying—wise distribution of his duties—importance of training up Christians to assist him in his work—intercourse with other ministers—attachment to the cause of Missions—plainness and fidelity in preaching—importance of an affectionate manner—how to treat the thoughtless and those who are under conviction of sin—duty of circumspection—great worth of private character—preparation for death." Ibid., 166.

139. Ibid., 167.

140. Ibid.

141. Ibid., 168.

spiritual good: "Owen *On Spiritual-Mindedness,* and *On the 130th Psalm,* Baxter's *Saints' Rest,* Edwards *On the Affections,* Doddridge's *Rise and Progress, The Life of Brainerd,* and the works of Howe and Leighton." He said that if students did not read books such as these, they would risk losing "their present advancement in holiness, and their future usefulness in the ministry."[142]

From Andover's birth, missionary zeal burned in the hearts of the young evangelicals. With the convergence of the Hopkinsian calls to radical sacrifice for God's glory, the collegiate revivals, and the renewed evangelical Calvinism, Andover Theological Seminary was a seedbed of missions mobilization.[143] Brainerd-like, self-denying missionary spirituality permeated the culture of the institution. "To get through Andover without reading Brainerd was virtually unthinkable."[144] Attending Andover during Judson's time were some young men who sensed a call to missions while studying at Williams College: Samuel Nott (1788–1869), Samuel J. Mills Jr. (1783–1818), Samuel Newell (1784–1821), and James Richards (1784–1822). On a Saturday afternoon in August 1806, they had committed themselves to consider missions under a haystack during a rainstorm, which has been famously called the Haystack Prayer Meeting.[145] They formed the Society of the Brethren at Williams College, and the leaders of the Brethren went various places after graduation. Subsequently, the Society of the Brethren relocated to Andover Seminary and launched on September 14, 1810.[146] Gordon Hall (1784–1826) and Luther Rice (1783–1836) also joined the society at Andover in 1810.[147]

> The spirit of the members was deeply devotional. Every student who joined was required by the constitution to read and pray in order to determine his duty, whether he should spend his life among the heathen. Special devotions were observed on Sunday

142. Ibid., 169.

143. See Kling, "The New Divinity," 791–819.

144. Brumberg, *Mission for Life,* 25.

145. For an account of the famous Haystack Prayer Meeting, see Richards, *The Haystack Prayer Meeting.*

146. Woods compared the society at Williams to the society at Andover: "The objects of the two Societies were in some respects the same. The one at Williams College however, was composed *exclusively* of such as had already devoted their lives to the cause of Missions. Its object was, *to effect a mission to the heathen in the persons of its members.* The Society at Andover, seems to have been planned by the same individuals, for the purpose of exciting inquiry, and enlisting others in the same cause." Woods, *Memoirs of American Missionaries,* 14; emphasis in original.

147. The Society at Andover persisted for sixty years after transferring there from Williams College; see Rowe, *History of Andover,* 112.

mornings and Tuesday evenings, and the second Tuesday in January was kept as a day of fasting and prayer for the missionary cause.[148]

Andover's was the primary society that influenced other seminaries. Andover certainly sent out the most missionaries. Brumberg explains that Andover's youth voluntarism converged with its "new humanitarian Calvinism" and launched a great wave of "youth-initiated evangelicalism."[149]

Biographical Sketch

The following summary of Judson's life and ministry will focus on those people and events that most influenced his spiritual formation. Some biographical facts will remain unmentioned, but in consideration of Judson's spirituality, this sketch will highlight significant details that are helpful for understanding his overall historical and biographical contexts.

Ambition Building (1788–1804)

Adoniram Judson, Jr., the first child of Reverend Adoniram Judson Sr. and Abigail Brown Judson (1759–1842), was born in Malden, Massachusetts on August 9, 1788.[150] Judson's father, a Hopkinsian Congregational minister, whom Joseph Bellamy had mentored, assumed pulpits in Wenham, Braintree, and finally Plymouth. Having grown up under the New Divinity-influenced preaching of his father, Judson breathed the air of evangelical Edwardsean piety. His father raised him with "a heavy dose of orthodoxy and Christian nurture."[151] Described as "grave and quiet, stern in bearing

---

148. Ibid., 112–13. For a succinct historical summary of the beginning phases of the American foreign missionary enterprise, see Warburton, *Eastward*, 23–26.

149. Brumberg, *Mission for Life*, 38. The Second Great Awakening (c. 1790–1840) captured the hearts of many young people, which aroused in them a missionary impulse. Brumberg says, "The moving force behind American foreign missions was a small cadre of zealous young men, students at Williams College and the theological seminary at Andover. The convergence at Andover of Adoniram Judson and Samuel J. Mills provides a striking demonstration of the dynamics of youthful voluntarism." Brumberg, *Mission for Life*, 26. For other accounts of the convergence of Mills, Judson, and other youthful volunteers, see Bendroth, *A School of the Church*, 49–55; see also McBeth, *The Baptist Heritage*, 344–55; and Richards, *Samuel J. Mills*, 60.

150. Judson's younger siblings were Abigail Judson (b. 1791) and Elnathan Judson (1794–1829), and when Judson was eight years old, his seven-month-old sister, Mary (b. February 18, 1796), died. See Anderson, *To the Golden Shore*, 19.

151. Brumberg, *Mission for Life*, 22. For an example of godly parenting, Adoniram

The Life and Context of Adoniram Judson

and strict in family discipline,"[152] Judson's father was a God-enamored man. His God was both benevolent and fearsome. Disobedience to Judson Sr.'s God would have terrible consequences. As Courtney Anderson noted, "Much of the importance of Adoniram's father resided in books, particularly one Book which he used in church, and into which he would look for hours in the parsonage. This was the Bible."[153]

Able to read a chapter from the Bible by age three, Judson also demonstrated a keen facility for math and for languages.[154] He was so gifted in Latin that he was nicknamed Virgil.[155] His father fed his youthful ambition to strive for greatness, assuring him that he would be a great man, and Judson greatly desired to please his father and to be like him.[156] At age four, Judson would often imitate his father and preach to his friends, and the hymn he liked singing the most at that age began with "Go preach my Gospel, saith the Lord."[157] Judson owed much to his father, "his stately courtesy, his dignity of literary style, perhaps his theology, certainly his burning ambition."[158]

At age fourteen (1802), not long after his family moved to Plymouth, Judson became critically ill. After being assured that he would live,

---

Judson Sr. said to parents: "We taught them to remember God their creator. We taught them the fear of God, the law of God, and those things which are essential to inherit the kingdom of God. We endeavored to instruct them in all the principles, doctrines, obligations, and duties, to God and man. We labored to indoctrinate them in the glorious scheme of grace through the Redeemer, and to impress their minds with a conviction of sin, and of an eternity of happiness and misery. And O how affecting, how solemn the thought, if any of your children should miss of [sic] salvation by your neglect! Be persuaded, then, to bring them up for God." Adoniram Judson Sr., *A Sermon Preached in the New Meeting House*, 19–20.

152. Warburton, *Eastward*, 4. From his research, Anderson also described Adoniram Judson Sr. as, "stoical, forbidding, and austere." Anderson, *To the Golden Shore*, 6.

153. Anderson, *To the Golden Shore*, 12–13.

154. Ibid., 20.

155. Edward Judson, *The Life of Adoniram Judson*, xxix; see also Anderson, *To the Golden Shore*, 20; Warburton, *Eastward*, 5.

156. Anderson said, "The person Adoniram feared above all others was his father. It was not only that he was a minister. It was not even that he was Adoniram's father in a day when fathers ruled their children with an iron hand. It was the sheer awesomeness of the man himself. He was nearly incapable of humor. He was just, but with the retributive justice of God Himself. He was stern, austere; and as God did not overlook the sparrow's fall, so Mr. Judson did not overlook trifles." Anderson, *To the Golden Shore*, 19.

157. Ibid., 18. This is the beginning stanza of the hymn, "O Preach My Gospel, Saith the Lord," by Isaac Watts (1674–1748); see Watts and Rippon, *The Psalms and Hymns of Dr. Watts*, 679.

158. Warburton, *Eastward*, 4.

he still had more than one year of convalescence to endure. "Bookish and intellectualized,"[159] he spent much of his recovery "feeding ambition with visions of greatness and glory, such as no mortal had yet won."[160] Though Judson knew that fame, if it were worth anything, must be perpetual, yet he knew there was a contradiction with his ambition for prestige in this life and his desire to enjoy fame in the next. However, he was convinced that being a humble Christian would interfere with his ambitions for greatness. "He was naturally the subject of manifest pride and ambition."[161] He had yet to see that the path to glory was by way of the cross.

From Deism to Hopkinsianism (1804–1810)

Judson entered Rhode Island College at Providence, later Brown University, at sixteen years of age (1804). His entrance examination evidenced that he excelled in Latin, Greek, geography, mathematics, and astronomy. Because of his advanced status, he was able to bypass his first year and enroll as a sophomore. Impressed with his industriousness and sharp intellect, the university president, Asa Messer (1769–1836), wrote a letter to Judson's father, complimenting him for raising a strong-minded son.[162] However, Judson's heart did not exercise the affections for God as his New Divinity father had raised him. While at Brown, in the "height of the wild-fire delusion of infidelity,"[163] Judson, a brilliant mind looking for the next riddle to solve, built an intellectually-stimulating friendship with a skeptic, Jacob Eames (d. 1808). When Judson graduated in 1807, he consequently sought to live as a skeptical Deist.[164] Judson knew that this dabbling with Deism

---

159. Anderson, *To the Golden Shore*, 28.

160. Conant, *The Earnest Man*, 17.

161. An extract of a letter from Leonard Woods to the pastor of the First Baptist Church in Lowell, Massachusetts, Daniel Clarke Eddy, on November 25, 1850; Eddy, *A Sketch of Adoniram Judson*, v.

162. In the letter, Messer said, "This, I can assure you, is not by way of complaint. A uniform propriety of conduct, as well as an intense application of study, distinguishes his character. Your expectations of him, however sanguine, must certainly be gratified. I most heartily congratulate you, my dear sir, on that charming prospect which you have exhibited in this very amiable and promising son; and I most heartily pray that the Father of mercies may make him now, while a youth, a son in his spiritual family and give him an earnest of the inheritance of the saints of light." Edward Judson, *The Life of Adoniram Judson*, 17.

163. Babcock, *God Glorified in His Servants*, 7.

164. The title of his valedictorian address showed his Deistic worldview: "An Oration on Free Enquiry; with the Valedictory Addresses . . . Adoniram Judson." Anderson, *To the Golden Shore*, 35.

would certainly not please his pious father, though he retained a consuming desire to please him. As soon as he received word of earning the honor of valedictorian, he wrote eagerly to his father: "Dear Father, I have got it. Your affectionate son, A. J."[165]

Straight out of college, Judson tried his hand at opening a school: Plymouth Independent Academy. By the summer of 1808, Judson had run the school for approximately a year.[166] From an outward perspective, he seemed successful and satisfied; but inwardly, his wanderlust raged. Then, on his twentieth birthday, he closed the school. With a horse from his father, Judson set out to explore the west. He rode to Sheffield, Massachusetts where his uncle Ephraim pastored. Leaving his horse there, he traveled to New York. Entertaining dreams of writing for the theater in New York, Judson joined some actors who "lived a sort of vagabond life, slept where they could, and not infrequently skipped without paying their bill."[167]

After having his fill of recklessness and revelry, Judson returned to fetch his horse in Sheffield, but his uncle was not home. Yet, staying in his house was a pious young minister whose "conversation was characterized by godly sincerity, a solemn but gentle earnestness, which addressed itself to the heart, and Judson went away deeply impressed."[168]

The next day, Judson's prodigal path came to a full stop when, while staying at a country inn, he endured the wailing of a dying man through the night, just to find out the next morning that the man who died was his infidel-companion from Brown, Jacob Eames. Judson, chilled by the dreadfulness of the death of his Deist friend, experienced a crisis of faith. Not long afterwards, being influenced by reading *The Fourfold State*[169] by Thomas Boston (1676–1732) and being cajoled by a conversation with Moses Stuart

---

165. Warburton, *Eastward*, 9

166. During this time Judson had authored two textbooks: Adoniram Judson, *The Elements of English Grammar*; Adoniram Judson, *The Young Lady's Arithmetic*.

167. Warburton, *Eastward*, 12. Henry Gouger (1799–1861), a fellow prisoner with Judson in Ava, recorded his discussions with Judson about this time in his life. Gouger admonished Wayland's account as far too Pollyannaish in describing this season of carousing (see Wayland, *A Memoir*, 1:23). Gouger said, "I will give the story as I heard it from the actor's own mouth . . . in his words:—'In my early days of wildness, I joined a band of strolling players. We lived a reckless, vagabond life, finding lodgings where we could, and bilking the landlord where we found opportunity—in other words, running up a score, and then decamping without paying the reckoning. Before leaving America, when the enormity of this vicious course rested with a depressing weight on my mind, I made a second tour over the same ground, carefully making amends to all whom I had injured.'" Gouger, *A Personal Narrative*, 179.

168. Wayland, *Memoir*, 1:23–24.

169. See Boston, *Human Nature in Its Fourfold State*.

and Edward Dorr Griffin, Judson enrolled in the newly founded Andover Theological Seminary.

He did not initially feel assurance of his conversion. Wayland recalled a conversation he had with Judson about his gradual conversion. He said that Judson did not have an "overpowering, Bunyan-like" experience, but that he was "prayerful, reflective, and studious of proofs; and gradually faith, trust in God, and finally a hope through the merits of Christ, took possession of his soul."[170] Nevertheless, approximately six weeks after enrolling at Andover, Judson "was enabled to surrender his whole soul to Christ as his atoning Savior."[171] In December 1808, Judson "made a solemn dedication of himself to God,"[172] and in May of 1809, he joined his father's church in Plymouth, the Third Congregational Church. During this time, Judson's piety began to manifest as he sought to make future plans no longer for his own fame, but for "being as best to please God."[173] His correspondence during this period revealed "an earnest striving after holiness, and an enthusiastic consecration of every endowment to the service of Christ."[174]

---

170. Wayland, *Memoir*, 1:37.

171. Ibid., 1:28. There are no documented details of his conversion narrative, but in his autobiographical record, he included the closest description available to the approximate timing of the beginning of his "change of heart." He recorded, "1808, Nov., began to entertain a hope of having received the regenerating influences of the Holy Spirit." See "Autobiographical Record of Dates and Events," in Edward Judson, *The Life of Adoniram Judson*, 562. A Baptist pastor in New Zealand, Frank William Boreham (1871–1959), said in his biography of Judson that he knew of three different descriptions of what he thought were the first signs of Judson's conversion, but none had dates attached to them. See Boreham, *A Temple of Topaz*, 134. From a letter to his brother, Elnathan, on October 24, 1810, it is evident that Judson still sought greater assurance of his conversion. In an excerpt from his letter, he said, "I think I could never say with so much assurance as I can lately, I do love God . . . Brother, you must pray for me, that I may enjoy the presence of God, and have a spirit of prayer." Adoniram Judson to Elnathan Judson, letter, October 24, 1810, Box No. AJ 1, Folder 1 and Microfilm Roll 1, Judson Letters, ABHS. Brumberg explains the significance of the conversion narrative: "Since conversion would determine the future course of the individual and, by implication, the world, evangelical literature was conversion-centered. In fact, there was an intriguing variety of nineteenth-century literature produced by evangelicals, which focused on conversion in one way or another. In addition to spiritual autobiography and conversion narratives, evangelicals wrote books, childrearing literature, memoirs of missionaries and converted heathens, temperance tales, and domestic and sentimental fiction . . . The doctrine of the 'change of heart' would be basic to writing about Judson's life and work." Brumberg, *Mission for Life*, 34–35. For a landmark study on the rise of spiritual autobiographies and their significance in the Evangelical Revival of the eighteenth century, see Hindmarsh, *The Evangelical Conversion Narrative*.

172. Wayland, *Memoir*, 1:28.

173. Ibid., 1:29; see also Anderson, *To the Golden Shore,* 50.

174. Wayland, *Memoir*, 1:29.

In September 1809, exactly one year after his being jolted out of infidelity by the death of Jacob Eames, Judson read Claudius Buchanan's sermon, "The Star in the East."[175] He came to realize that all his worldly determination for greatness could be satisfied in seeking to please Christ alone. "Everything in his life had prepared him for the idea. A career as the first American foreign missionary curiously combined his many conflicting ambitions. Fame, eminence, humility, self-sacrifice, obscurity, adventure, uniqueness, the service of God—it had all of these."[176] Consequently, he read everything he could about the East and missions. Judson even read the British army officer, Michael Symes's (1761–1809) *Embassy to Ava*,[177] not knowing he would serve in Burma. Symes painted Burma as a land where

> its people were civilized. They could read and write, and had an extensive literature . . . What a prospect for a missionary! thought Adoniram as he turned the pages of Symes's book. Surely a people like this needed nothing but the true Word of God. Once it was brought to them, literate and civilized as they were, they would certainly seize on it.[178]

Judson could not attend classes because he was so preoccupied with his missionary burden. Even after the initial excitement waned, he nevertheless carried a deep sense of duty to be a foreign missionary.

In February of 1810, Judson was walking in the woods behind Andover, meditating and praying about the subject. There, impressed upon his mind with force and clarity, the command of Christ to "preach the gospel"[179] compelled him to devote his life as Christ's missionary; he "resolved to obey the command at all events."[180] This resolute conviction of duty and desire to please Christ held Judson firm, not only through difficulty, but also through other good competing prospects.

---

175. Buchanan, *The Star in the East*. Regarding the content of Buchanan's sermon, Duesing suggests that "what might have caught Judson's attention was Buchanan's description of his passion to see the translation of the Scripture into various languages." Duesing, "Breaking the Strong Attachment to Home and Country," 11.

176. Anderson, *To the Golden Shore*, 53. Rufus Babcock (1798–1875) pointed out that initially the burgeoning missionary enterprise was highly unpopular. He extracted lengthy quotes from the *Edinburgh Review* from 1808, and after citing some vitriolic sentiments, Babcock said, "We will not pollute our pages nor pain your ears with the Billingsgate utterances of a coarser and less delicate character . . . To this maligned object the attention of Judson was turned." Babcock, *God Glorified in His Servants*, 11–13.

177. See Symes, *An Account of an Embassy*.

178. Anderson, *To the Golden Shore*, 55–56.

179. See Mark 16:15.

180. Wayland, *Memoir*, 1:52.

One such event presented itself in 1810 when the respected Edward Dorr Griffin of Andover visited Judson at his family's home. Confident of Judson's command of the Scriptures and preaching gift, Griffin asked Judson to be his assistant pastor at the prestigious Park Street Church in Boston. This was the ambitious opportunity Judson's father had been priming him for all his life. Yet, in the presence of his overjoyed family, Judson broke their hearts by declining the flattering prospect and laying bare his soul for the cause of missions. As his biographer, Wayland, put it: "From the time of his self-consecration to the missionary service, he became . . . a man of one idea."[181]

A Missions Movement (1810–1812)

Judson and some seminary companions had started a study group on missions, called the Society of Inquiry Respecting Missions, of which he became "the enthusiastic, intrepid leader."[182] On June 28, 1810, Judson and his companions went to Bradford to present their case for foreign missions to the General Association of Congregational Ministers of Massachusetts. Judson offered himself for missionary service to the General Association of Congregational Ministers of Massachusetts, along with Samuel Newell, Samuel Nott, and Gordon Hall.[183] Judson forcefully made a case for their missionary desire, though his "excess of self-reliance"[184] was not a light irritation to some. The next day Judson received a reprimand for his "impetuousness and self-will"[185] for which he expressed regret and repentance. Yet, the sting of the rebuke did not last long; the Board gave its approval and appointed them as missionaries. Consequently, the American Board of Commissioners for Foreign Missions (ABCFM) was born,[186] and on September 19, 1811, the ABCFM appointed Judson as a missionary.[187]

181. Ibid., 1:39.

182. Rowe, *History of Andover*, 116.

183. Judson subsequently graduated from Andover on September 24, 1810; see Anderson, *To the Golden Shore*, 84–85.

184. Ibid., 100.

185. Ibid., 101.

186. For a thorough account of the development of the ABCFM, see Tracy, *History of the American Board*. For the minutes of the meeting, see "Minutes of the First Annual Meeting of the American Board," 9–10.

187. Prior to this appointment, he had traveled to London in the spring of 1811 to visit the London Missionary Society to solicit missionary funding. Along the way, a French privateer captured his ship and imprisoned him in France for a short time. Nevertheless, after his release, he arrived in London on May 6, 1811. See Edward Judson,

A Consecrated Woman (1810–1812)

Before the afternoon meetings of the aforementioned General Association of Congregational Ministers of Massachusetts, Judson and his colleagues ate lunch at the home of Deacon John Hasseltine (1756–1837) of Bradford. There at Deacon Hasseltine's home, Judson met Ann Hasseltine for the first time.[188] He cultivated an acquaintance with her through letters and visits.[189] Then exactly one month later, he declared his intentions to be her suitor.[190] With Hopkinsian *pathos*, Judson wrote a letter to Ann's father, seeking consent to take his daughter into the face of certain suffering and hardship "for the sake of him who left his heavenly home, and died for her; . . . for the sake of perishing souls; for the sake of Zion, and for the glory of God."[191] Judson and Ann exchanged letters, in which they declared their ardent devotion to Christ and his service. Ann described Judson as a man with a single-minded "love to Jesus, and a desire to manifest it in all its varied forms."[192] As he expressed his spirituality to Ann, the controlling concern of his life was, "Is it pleasing to God?"[193]

On February 6, 1812, the day after his marriage to Ann,[194] Judson received ordination along with Nott, Newell, Rice, and Hall at America's oldest Protestant church, the Tabernacle in Salem.[195] They accepted the commission as America's first foreign missionaries.

The Life of Adoniram Judson, 562; Anderson, *To the Golden Shore*, 87–89.

188. Her other name was Nancy Hasseltine.

189. See Middleditch, *Burmah's Great Missionary*, 38.

190. See Anderson, *To the Golden Shore*, 82–83, and Hunt, *Bless God and Take Courage*, 23–25.

191. Knowles, *The Memoir of Mrs. Ann H. Judson*, 36; also quoted in Wayland, *Memoir*, 1:31.

192. Wayland, *Memoir*, 1:31, quoted also in Anderson, *To the Golden Shore*, 85.

193. Edward Judson, *The Life of Adoniram Judson*, 13; see also Wayland, *Memoir*, 1:32.

194. During their marriage, Ann bore Judson three children, one stillborn and two that died in infancy: Roger Williams Judson (1815–1816) and Maria Elizabeth Butterworth Judson (1825–1827). See Hunt, "The Judson Family Tree," in *Bless God and Take Courage*, 404.

195. Hunt, *Bless God and Take Courage*, 31. Leonard Woods of Andover preached on Psalm 67 at Judson's ordination. For a rich example of the evangelical Hopkinsian piety in which Judson grew spiritually, see Woods, *A Sermon Delivered at the Tabernacle in Salem*.

Leaving and Cleaving to the Call (1812–1814)

Approximately two weeks after their marriage, the Judsons boarded a ship called the *Caravan* and set sail.[196] The ship arrived in Calcutta, India in June 1812.[197] During their voyage, in preparation to associate with the Baptist missionaries in India, Judson studied the credobaptist position, and through much biblical exegesis and prayer, Judson was "was compelled, from a conviction of the truth" of the veracity of credobaptism, "though he paid dear for it."[198] Ann, with equal conviction, agreed. This change of sentiments caused the Judsons to forsake their Congregational association, and to receive believer's baptism in India (September 6, 1812).[199] In India, Judson preached a renowned sermon on Christian baptism, which William Carey said was the best he had ever heard.[200] Luther Rice also received believer's baptism in November of 1812, and the missionaries decided Rice should return to America to elicit financial support from the American Baptists. After returning to America the following year, Rice helped mobilize and unify the early organizational efforts of the American Baptists for missions.[201] In May of 1814, the first national organization of Baptists in America, the Triennial Convention, began in Philadelphia, which witnessed local and regional Baptist societies unite behind the cause of advancing the work of missions.[202]

---

196. Newell, along with his new wife, Harriet Newell (1793–1812) were also onboard the brig. Nott, Hall, and Rice set sail aboard the *Harmony* the next day.

197. On August 8, 1812, Nott, Hall, and Rice arrived at the port in Calcutta in the ship *Harmony*. See Edward Judson, *The Life of Adoniram Judson*, 562.

198. Middleditch, *Burmah's Great Missionary*, 52–53; Wayland, *Memoir*, 1:108; Knowles, *The Memoir of Mrs. Ann H. Judson*, 62–63.

199. See Wayland, *Memoir*, 1:95–109. William Ward (1769–1823) of the Serampore Trio baptized the Judsons. On November 1, 1812, Luther Rice also received baptism because of his change of sentiments. See Taylor, *Memoir of Reverend Luther Rice*, 116.

200. Knowles, *Memoir of Mrs. Ann H. Judson*, 66. See also Adoniram Judson, *Christian Baptism*.

201. For a testimony of Rice's zeal and ability to stir up missionary devotion, see Lincoln and Wayland, *A Memoir of the Life*, 53–55. For examples of Rice's letters and journals, see Rice, *Dispensations of Providence*. For an account of his life, see Taylor, *Memoir of Reverend Luther Rice*.

202. For a thorough synopsis of the genesis of the Triennial Convention and its legacy, see McBeth, *The Baptist Heritage*, 343–92. The Triennial Convention was a landmark event for Baptist history. Torbet said, "The organization of the Triennial Convention in 1814 was a triumph of the principle of national co-operation in the foreign missionary enterprise . . . In many respects Luther Rice was a fortunate choice as promotional agent of the Board, for he combined vision, untiring energy, and a knowledge of the foreign field. He, therefore, was instrumental in developing financial support." Torbet, *A History of the Baptists*, 331. Brackney also observes that Judson's

Judson and Ann left India by decree of the British East India Company for fear that foreign missionary work would interfere with trading, and because of the British's suspicion of Americans due to the raging Anglo-American War of 1812.[203] In July of 1813, they arrived in Rangoon, the port of the despotic country of Burma.[204] William Carey's son, Felix Carey (b. 1794),[205] had been already serving in Burma for four years, and he aided the Judsons in their initial transition. There was no team or ministry for the Judsons to join.

---

mission work inspired "a sense of national denominational identity and purpose" for the American Baptists. Brackney, "The Legacy of Adoniram Judson," 124. Baptist historian Leonard states, "The willingness to use the word *denomination* to describe this new society was an important step for Baptists in the new nation. It brought together various associations, individuals, and churches concerned about the foreign missionary task." Leonard, *Baptist Ways*, 165. The new mission organization adopted the name, The General Missionary Convention of the Baptist Denomination in the United States of America for Foreign Missions. The American Baptist Board of Foreign Missions was often called the American Baptist Board. Then in 1845, they readopted the name, American Baptist Missionary Union; see Wayland, *Memoir*, 1:126–27. Judson rejoiced at the formation of the American Baptist Board; see his journal entry in Ann Hasseltine Judson, *An Account of the American Baptist Mission*, 53–54.

203. For a helpful explanation of the historical context surrounding the charter and its effect on the missionaries, see Middleditch, *Burmah's Great Missionary*, 47–50.

204. Anderson recorded that work in Burma seemed hopeless. The Judsons had "put Burma out of their thoughts, for about that country they had learned a good deal more that was unpromising . . . In Burma they would be under both a king and local governors who were absolute despots and that governmental corruption was unbelievable.—And the laws were the bloodiest on earth: the commonest punishments were beheading, crucifixion, and 'pouring melted lead in small quantities down the throat,' and these were inflicted for such minor offenses as chewing opium or drinking spirits." Anderson, *To the Golden Shore*, 139–40. Though Burma was on Judson's heart, they were obliged to leave India as soon as possible without a definite destination. They sailed to the Isle of France, met with their American co-laborer, Samuel Newell. Then they discovered that his wife, Harriet, had gone into premature labor, lost the baby, and died herself of tuberculosis. The Judsons decided to try moving to Penang, but they had to stop first in Madras, India. Judson urgently looked for a ship to go anywhere because they did not want to be deported to England and because Ann's baby was due in weeks. The only ship available, the *Georgiana*, was bound for Burma. Just as the ship set sail, Ann's hired European delivery nurse fell dead, and while on the voyage to Burma, Ann gave birth to a stillborn son. Rosalie Hall Hunt describes their voyage as "mingled with horror and sadness," and "Rangoon was a wretched-looking place . . . scarcely better than a neglected swamp." Hunt, *Bless God and Take Courage*, 49–50.

205. Felix Carey and his wife and two children left for Ava in August of 1814, and their boat capsized, leaving only Felix alive. He later seceded from the mission. See Edward Judson, *The Life of Adoniram Judson*, 563; Hunt, *Bless God and Take Courage*, 60.

Translating and Preaching (1814–1821)

While in Burma, Judson devoted himself to the study of Burmese language and culture. His ambition surged because the Scriptures remained untranslated into Burmese. Judson wanted to be the first missionary to pioneer the translation of the first Bible for Burma.[206] He would earn the reputation "as the man who gave the Bible to the Burmese."[207] He learned Pali, the scriptural language of Burmese Buddhism, and in July 1816, he finished the *Grammatical Notices of the Burmese Language*.[208] A week later, Judson wrote the first introduction of Christianity into the Burmese language, which revealed his optimistic postmillennialism: *A View of the Christian Religion, in Three Parts, Historic, Didactic, and Preceptive*.[209] Of all the tracts he disseminated, he called it "the staple commodity."[210] The following year, in May of 1817, he completed the translation of the Gospel of Matthew. Two days later, he began compiling a Burmese dictionary, which took him most of his life to finish.[211]

---

206. See Anderson, *To the Golden Shore*, 147. Knowles recorded a letter from Ann saying, "[Burma] presents a very extensive field for usefulness . . . and the Scriptures have never been translated into their language. This is a very strong inducement to Mr. Judson to go there as there is no other place where he could be equally useful in translating. But the privations and dangers would be great." Knowles, *Memoir of Mrs. Ann H. Judson*, 61.

207. Brumberg, *Mission for Life*, 67.

208. Adoniram Judson, *Grammatical Notices*.

209. Adoniram Judson, *A View of the Christian Religion*; also published in Adoniram Judson, *The Septenary*. Not long after completing *A View of the Christian Religion* (completed on July 20, 1816), Judson's mission printer, George H. Hough (1757–1830) and his wife Phebe, arrived in Burma on October 15, 1816. Also, during his time of tract writing, Judson's seven-month-old son, Roger Williams Judson, died on May 4, 1816. This was his first tract; the day it was finished, Judson initially called it *Summary of Christian Doctrines*, but then once Hough printed it later that October, Judson changed it to *A View of the Christian Religion*. Sometimes, it was even called *The Way to Heaven*, but that can be confusing because one of Judson's coworkers, Grover Smith Comstock (1808–1844), later wrote a tract by the same name; see Comstock, "The Way to Heaven," 55–77. See Edward Judson, *The Life of Adoniram Judson*, 563–64.

210. In a letter to the printer, Cephas Bennett (1804–1885), on February 7, 1831; Wayland, *Memoir*, 1:517.

211. During this time, in September 1818, missionaries James Colman (1794–1822), and his wife Elizabeth (Lucy) Colman (b. 1794), and Edward Willard Wheelock (1796–1819) and his wife Eliza Harriet Newman Wheelock (b. 1798) arrived to join the mission. After Colman's death, Elizabeth married Amos Sutton (1802–1854), an English General Baptist missionary in Orissa, India. See Collier, *Colman and Wheelock*; and see Anderson, "Amos Sutton," 652. See Edward Judson, *The Life of Adoniram Judson*, 563–65.

In April 1819, Judson started hosting public worship gatherings in Burmese. Judson constructed his own *zayat*, which was a place for public meetings, in order preach the gospel to passersby and disseminate tracts.[212] Judson built the *zayat* on a main thoroughfare to the Buddhist holy site, the Shway Dagon Pagoda. Judson said its purpose was "to be a Christian meeting house, the first erected in this land of atheists, for the worship of God. . . to adore the majesty of heaven, and to sing with hearts of devotion the praises of the incarnate Saviour."[213]

In June of 1819, Judson baptized the first Burmese convert, Moung Nau (b. 1784),[214] which Judson hoped was "the beginning of a series of baptisms in the Burman empire . . . in uninterrupted succession to the end of time."[215] Moreover, a week later, Moung Nau became the first Burmese to commune at the Lord's Table, which Judson had long waited to administer.[216] Because of the pressure of the government, Judson traveled for over a month to Ava to petition to king for religious freedom. In January of 1820, the king denied liberty to Judson and his fellow missionaries to propagate Christianity unfettered in his kingdom. Nevertheless, within six months, Judson had

212. Middleditch cited Edward Wheelock's description of a *zayat* for those in the West who had never seen one before. Wheelock wrote about the one to which Judson refers. Middleditch recorded Wheelock as saying, "A *zayat* somewhat resembles an American shed, and is made of bamboos. The one now building [*sic*] will be much cooler, and better than the generality of *zayats*. It is to be made partly of bamboos, the top only covered with leaves." Then Middleditch went on to explain the *zayat* further: "It was divided in three parts. The first division, which was one third of the whole, was open to the road, and set apart for occupancy by Mr. Judson, for conversation with passers-by. The more central division was made entirely of boards, being intended for worship on the Sabbath, and for a school conducted by Mrs. Judson during the week. The third division was a sort of entry-way to the mission-house, situated in the rear and facing on another road." Middleditch, *Burmah's Great Missionary*, 122.

213. Wayland, *Memoir*, 1:212.

214. "Moung" is a title used to designate a young or middle-aged man; see Middleditch, *Burmah's Great Missionary*, 125.

215. Wayland, *Memoir*, 1:224.

216. Ibid., 1:224. During this time of great celebration of the first Burmese convert, sadness came over the missionary community. Edward Wheelock, who had arrived the year prior, was very ill with tuberculosis and became severely depressed. Also, his wife, Eliza, could not emotionally handle her husband's terrible illness, and she began imagining that people in the mission were trying to slowly kill him. She decided they both needed to flee Rangoon in order to survive. In August 1819, he and his wife, Eliza, set sail for Bengal. However, two weeks later on the voyage, in a depressed, delirious fit, he threw himself overboard and died. Judson never heard from Eliza again either. She chose to remain in India, where she married "a Mr. Jones of Calcutta." See Anderson, *To the Golden Shore*, 215–31, 269. For a grievous account of Edward Wheelock's battle with deep melancholy and his tragic death, see Collier, *Colman and Wheelock*, 73–75.

baptized ten converts. This was a great season of excitement, even though the journey thus far had met many disappointments and challenges.

Darkening Clouds of Providence (1821–1830)

Eight years after landing in Rangoon, Ann became very ill, and in August 1821, she embarked for the United States and did not return to Rangoon till December 1823.[217] During her absence, Judson finished translating the Burmese New Testament in July 1823 (though it underwent two subsequent revisions in 1829 and 1837), and he compiled a tract called *The Epitome of the Old Testament*.[218] Judson upheld evangelism, translation, tract distribution, and the equipping of indigenous church leaders as superior for the spread of the gospel over against establishing schools, hospitals, and civilizing the locals with Western culture.

Eight days after Ann arrived back in Rangoon from her voyage to America, they moved to Ava, the imperial capital, and arrived in January 1824. Five months later, Judson was arrested on suspicion of being a British spy during the first Anglo-Burmese War.[219] During his imprisonment in Ava, Ann gave birth to Maria Elizabeth Butterworth Judson in January of 1825. Then in May 1825, Judson relocated from the king's prison in Ava to the vicious prison in Oung-pen-la, where he suffered unremitting torture.[220] During more than twenty months of imprisonment and torture, his wife, though sickly herself, cared for him and pleaded with the Burmese officials for his release. Concurrently, Ann was caring for her newborn daughter, Maria. The prison released Judson in December 1825, and they moved to Amherst, a new British settlement, seven months later. At thirty-seven years old, Ann died in October of 1826, while Judson was working for the British embassy as an interpreter in Ava. Heartbroken, he mourned, "notwithstanding the consolations of the gospel, grief claims its right, and tears their

217. Not long after Ann left, in December 1821, Jonathan Price (d. 1828) and his wife, Hope Price (d. 1822), arrived in Burma. Hope Price subsequently died in May 1822. She was buried next to Roger Judson. See Edward Judson, *The Life of Adoniram Judson*, 564–65; Anderson, *To the Golden Shore*, 274–75.

218. Adoniram Judson, *The New Testament*. Adoniram Judson, *The Epitome of the Old Testament*.

219. Both Jonathan Price and George H. Hough went to prison in Ava along with Judson. In order to save them from starvation, Ann daily brought food and cared for their needs. See Anderson, *To the Golden Shore*, 324–31.

220. Wayland insightfully elucidated the reality of imprisonment in Burma: "Imprisonment, among a semi-barbarous people, is something very different from confinement. It is confinement imbittered [sic] by every device of malicious and brutal cruelty." Wayland, *Memoir*, 1:329.

course."[221] He returned in January of 1827 to Amherst. With great sorrow, Judson also suffered the loss of two-year-old Maria in April of 1827.[222] To add to his despair, he received word three months later that his father had died in November of 1826.

Judson slipped into deep darkness in the aftermath of such suffering. In May 1828, he renounced the title of D.D., which Brown University had awarded him in 1823, and he gave away his property to the American Baptist Board. In October 1828, he isolated himself to a hermitage where he applied himself to the ascetical spiritualities of Madame Guyon (1648–1717),[223] Thomas à Kempis (1380–1471),[224] and François Fénelon (1651–1715),[225] which was odd because these writers were Roman Catholic mystics and Judson's spiritual roots were in the New Divinity.[226] During this time, in February 1829, Judson wrote *The Threefold Cord* to outline his views of discipleship, which resemble a combination of austere disinterested benevolence and ascetical mysticism.[227] In March of 1829, he also wrote *The Golden Balance* to compare and contrast the Christian system over against the Buddhist system.[228] In November 1829, he finished the *Septenary, or Seven Manuals* to train the Burmese pastors in ministering to the churches; the manuals consisted of his *View of the Christian Religion*, Ann's catechism, and guides for conducting public worship, funerals, weddings,

---

221. Ibid., 1:416.

222. One week before Maria's death, George (1801–1831) and Sarah Boardman (1803–1845) arrived in Amherst on April 17, 1827. See Edward Judson, *The Life of Adoniram Judson*, 565.

223. Madame Jeann Guyon, a French mystic, was an advocate of Quietism, which the Roman Catholic Church considered heretical. She published *A Short and Easy Method of Prayer*, for which the Roman Catholic Church imprisoned her (1695–1703). Quietism was the practice of contemplation and interior passivity in order to grow spiritually and attain union with God. See Guyon, *A Short and Easy Method of Prayer*.

224. Thomas à Kempis was a German Canon Regular, who lived as a priest under the Rule of St. Augustine. He is best known for his widely read *The Imitation of Christ*. See à Kempis, *Imitation of Christ*.

225. Fénelon was a French Roman Catholic archbishop of Cambrai who met Madame Guyon in 1688 and admired her piety. He was best known for his didactic French novel, *The Adventures of Telemachus*. See Fénelon, *The Adventures of Telemachus*.

226. See Anderson, *To the Golden Shore*, 386–89.

227. Adoniram Judson, *The Threefold Cord*; also published in Edward Judson, *The Life of Adoniram Judson*, 571–77; and Wayland, *Memoir*, 2:459–66. Wayland charitably commented on some of Judson's extreme methods of sanctification and asceticism, in Wayland, *Memoir*, 2:382–87.

228. Adoniram Judson, *The Golden Balance*.

and baptisms.[229] Around this time, he wrote the well-known hymn, "Come, Holy Spirit, Dove Divine."[230]

Toward the end of that dark period, in December 1829, Judson heard of the death of his brother, Elnathan, in Washington D. C. seven months prior.[231] Before leaving for Burma, Judson had pleaded with Elnathan and prayed for his conversion to Christ, but Elnathan had refused. Yet when Judson heard of Elnathan's death, he also discovered that Elnathan had trusted in Christ about ten minutes before dying.[232] This good news caused his heart to rejoice, and it marked the termination of the darkness that had weighed him down for so long.[233]

Fruit-Bearing in All Seasons (1830–1850)

This was a season of abundance and anticipation; the mission in Burma baptized many new believers, received many new missionaries, and printed many new tracts.[234] In 1830 and 1831, Judson undertook many evangelistic

---

229. Adoniram Judson, *The Septenary*. In this publication, Judson included a short manual he had previously compiled, called, *Public Service Hand-Book for Pastors*. See Adoniram Judson, *Public Service Hand-Book*.

230. Adoniram Judson, "Come, Holy Spirit, Dove Divine," 586. It is possible that Judson began to write parts of this hymn before 1829; for instance, in his journal from September 11, 1819, Judson concluded thus: "Come, Holy Spirit, heavenly Dove!" Wayland, *Memoir*, 2:234; Edward Judson, *The Life of Adoniram Judson*, 137; Conant, *The Earnest Man*, 215.

231. One month after getting word of Judson's brother's death, Cephas Bennett, his wife, Stella Kneeland Bennett (1808–1891), and their two children, Elsina and Mary, arrived in Maulmain in January 1830. See Ranney, *A Sketch of the Lives and Missionary Work*. See also Bennett, *Vocabulary and Phrase Book*.

232. Wayland, *Memoir*, 1:474–75. For another example of Judson's prayers for his family, see a letter on December 13, 1827 to his mother and sister following his father's death; in it Judson prayed for them to enjoy the "divine presence" in spite of "the repeated strokes of our heavenly Father's hand" in their anticipation of "the high enjoyment of everlasting life," in ibid., 1:443–44.

233. See Anderson, *To the Golden Shore*, 391–92.

234. By 1830, the missionaries were printing a number of pieces of literature. They printed two non-religious educational catechisms called, "A Catechism of Astronomy" and "A Catechism of Geography." Warburton credited Judson with writing these, though there are no direct references in his known writings of him being the actual author; see Warburton, *Eastward*, 159. They are generally associated with him because in his journal he listed them in the middle of some tracts he and his colleagues had written, translated, and printed; see Adoniram Judson, journal, November 29, 1829, Box No. AJ 4, Folder 2 and Microfilm Roll 1, Judson Letters, ABHS; Adoniram Judson, "Mr. Judson's Journal, Nov. 29th, 1829," 245–46; Middleditch, *Burmah's Great Missionary*, 252. It is possible Jonathan Price wrote the tracts. In an extract of a journal on May 18, 1826,

tours into Rangoon, Prome, and among the Karen people in the jungles. In January of 1834, he completed the first Burmese translation of the Old Testament.

In April 1834, Judson married Sarah Boardman, widow of George Boardman, missionaries to the Karen people.[235] The year before Adoniram and Sarah's marriage, the mission celebrated the baptism of the one hundredth Karen convert north of Maulmain. In December , 1834, Jonathan and Deborah Wade (1801–1868), Sewall M. Osgood (1807–1875), a printer, and his wife, Elhira B. Osgood (d. 1837), and other missionaries arrived in Maulmain.[236] On the same ship, the *Cashmere*, Sarah's son, George Dana Boardman (1828–1903) returned to America for health concerns. Then in November 1835, Judson baptized the one hundredth member of the Burmese church in Maulmain. Later in February 1836, Howard Malcom (1799–1873) from the American Baptist Board arrived, along with several new American missionaries.[237]

During this time, Judson preached his only sermon in English in Burma. It was the ordination sermon for S. M. Osgood, in May 1836.[238] Judson's central Christ-enamored theme emerged in this sermon. He observed that Christ was controlled "by a supreme regard to his Father's will, . . . love to

---

George Dana Boardman noted, "[Price] proposes to open a school for teaching several branches of useful learning, such as, Geography, Astronomy, Chemistry, &c. and he thinks, that in a few years . . . the whole system of Burman religion, founded as it is, on false Astronomy and Geography, may be completely undermined and subverted." See Boardman, "Extracts from Mr. Boardman's Journal," 44. Also, for an example of how Price's astronomy, geography, and science courses challenged the Buddhist worldview of the Burmese students, see Knowles, *Memoir of Ann H. Judson*, 256–57. Years later, Grover Smith Comstock would find great success in evangelism using the catechisms on geography and astronomy; see Comstock, "Journal of Mr. Comstock," 69. Judson also wrote a tract in 1836, after his revision of the Old Testament, called, "The Life of Christ," which Sarah B. Judson translated into Peguan. See Adoniram Judson to Dr. Lucius Bolles, letter, Box No. AJ 2, Folder 2 and Microfilm Roll 1, Judson Letters, ABHS; Adoniram Judson, "Letter of Mr. Judson, Dated Maulmein, Dec. 21, 1837," 300–301; Wayland, *Memoir*, 2:118; Wayland dated the letter as December 31, 1837 instead of the December 21, 1837. See also Starr, *A Baptist Bibliography*, 12:220. For a record of other writings by the missionary team, see Warburton, *Eastward*, 158–61; see also Bennett, *Tracts, In Burmese*, 1.

235. George Boardman died on February 11, 1831. See Edward Judson, *The Life of Adoniram Judson*, 566. See also King, *Memoir of George Dana Boardman*, 293–309.

236. For a biographical account of S. M. Osgood, see Smith, *Sewall Mason Osgood*.

237. See Edward Judson, *The Life of Adoniram Judson*, 565–66; Anderson, *To the Golden Shore*, 400–427. Malcom, the pastor of Federal Street Church in Boston, was eager to meet the legendary Judson; Malcom said Judson was "the most interesting man alive." Mild, *Howard Malcom*, 44.

238. See Wayland, *Memoir*, 2:486–94.

the Father, and desire to please him. The true pastor, and, indeed, every true Christian, must be influenced by the same principle."[239] The following year, 1837, Judson finished a tract called *A Digest of Scripture: Consisting of Extracts from the Old and New Testaments; On the Plan of "Brown's Selection of Scripture Passages,"*[240] which outlined the basic systems of Christian doctrine, similar to a confession of faith. He also revised the New Testament that year, and the whole Bible in 1840.[241]

During this abovementioned period of fruitfulness, Sarah bore Judson eight children, three of whom died young: Abby Ann Judson (1835–1902), Adoniram Brown Judson (1837–1916), Elnathan Judson (1838–1896), Henry Judson (1839–1841), Luther Judson (stillborn on March 8, 1841), Henry Hall Judson (1842–1918), Charles Judson (1843–1845), and Edward Judson.[242] Because of dysentery, Sarah was obliged to take a voyage back to the United States. Judson, Sarah, and their three elder children left in April of 1845. A week later, Sarah died and was buried at the port of St. Helena. Still grieving Sarah's death, Judson and his children arrived in Boston in October of 1845 and received a hero's homecoming. Judson traveled to many churches and universities where he spoke of his desire to please the Savior and to obey his commission.[243] Yet, because of his failing voice due to sickness, others had to read aloud many of his sermons in his presence. Many of his messages implored for ardent love to Christ. To truly love Jesus was to fully obey his final commission, he emphasized, and the missionary call was to be a lifelong venture.

Judson met Emily Chubbuck, a novelist, in December 1845,[244] and he asked her to write a biography of Sarah Judson, a task that led to their being married in June 1846. They straightaway set sail for Burma five weeks later and arrived in November 1846.[245] The following June 1847, Emily had

239. Ibid., 2:491–92.

240. Adoniram Judson, *A Digest of Scripture*.

241. Adoniram Judson, *The Holy Bible*. During this season, he also wrote on practical matters, such as female dress; see Adoniram Judson, *Judson's Letter on Dress*.

242. During this season, on August 29, 1842, Judson heard of his mother's death on January 31, 1842. See Edward Judson, *The Life of Adoniram Judson*, 566–67; Hunt, *Bless God and Take Courage*, 402–4.

243. See Wayland, *Memoir*, 2:368–70.

244. Before Judson even met Emily, he had left Adoniram and Elnathan in Worcester to study, and he had sent Abby Ann to Plymouth on November 13, 1845. Two weeks later, on November 28, 1845, he received word that Charlie had died in Maulmain on August 5, 1845. See Hunt, *Bless God and Take Courage*, 402–4; Edward Judson, *The Life of Adoniram Judson*, 566–67; Anderson, *To the Golden Shore*, 442–65.

245. Before Judson and his new bride left for Burma, he took leave of Adoniram, Elnathan, and George Dana Boardman on July 4, 1846 and Abby Ann on July 9, 1846. See

finished the biography of Sarah. Emily bore him two children, one of whom died at birth.[246] In January 1849, Judson finished the dictionary.[247] Due to illness, he went on a sea voyage to recover his health, but died at sea on April 12, 1850. God had granted his fervent prayers, as his third wife, Emily, put it, "for a long life of labor and self-denial."[248]

Edward Judson, *The Life of Adoniram Judson*, 567.

246. Emily Frances Judson (1847–1911) was born in Maulmain on December 24, 1847; Charlie Judson (1850) was stillborn on April 23, 1850, ten days after his father's death on April 12, 1850. Four years later, Emily Chubbuck Judson died on June 1, 1854. See Hunt, *Bless God and Take Courage*, 403; Anderson, *To the Golden Shore*, 506.

247. The dictionary subsequently underwent publication in 1852. See Adoniram Judson, *A Dictionary*. E. A. Stevens (Edward Abiel Stevens [1814–1886]) should not be confused with his son E. O. Stevens (Edward Oliver Stevens [1838–1910]). Edward Abiel completed Judson's nearly finished dictionary after his death; see Stevens, *A Half-Century in Burma*, 17. Edward Oliver expanded the work years later; see Stevens, *A Vocabulary, English and Peguan*.

248. Wayland, *Memoir*, 2:366–68.

3

"Yield to the Word of God": Bibliocentric Spirituality

THE FOUNDATIONAL SOURCE OF Adoniram Judson's forty-year-long perseverance was the supreme and sufficient Word. The sacred Scriptures so arrested Judson's mind and heart that he yearned to do nothing but go proclaim the Word. This chapter will seek to demonstrate that Judson's bibliocentric spirituality was evident in his allegiance to keeping the Word, making disciples with the Word, and evangelizing with the Word. The work of sowing gospel seed was slow and not as socially acceptable as other humanitarian efforts, but Judson was certain that the written Word required proclamation through publication and preaching. He was not depressed when there were no signs of life or when growth was slow, for the overriding purpose of his Bible-proclamation was for the glory of God. He was ever hesitant to grant assurance to new "professing believers" until they had showed a degree of submission to Scripture. Judson's strong bibliocentrism was the ground of his Reformed theology and missionary labor. The Bible established his vision of God and stimulated his desire to please Christ by keeping and proclaiming it.

Keeping the Word

Since the beginning of Judson's missionary impulse, the Word of God gripped his conscience and affection. Judson evidenced a high loyalty to the commands of Christ from the moment that God had called him to be a missionary and from when he discovered Scripture's teaching on baptism.

It was the Scripture that impressed upon his mind the urgency of the missionary task and finally compelled him to devote himself to foreign missions. During a walk in the woods behind Andover Theological Seminary, while Judson was meditating and praying, he later recalled, "that the command of Christ, 'Go into all the world, and preach the gospel to every creature,' was presented to my mind with such clearness and power, that I came to a full decision, and though great difficulties appeared in my way, resolved to obey the command at all events."[1] In a sermon later in his ministry, Judson would recall this momentous walk in the woods. Someone had asked him if faith or love influenced him to reach the heathen in foreign lands. After thinking about the question, he concluded that neither influenced him very much. Then he rehearsed the experience in the woods behind Andover Seminary. Feeling discouraged that no one had gone before and no way was open to him to engage in foreign missions, he felt quite alone in his ambition. "The field was far distant, and in an unhealthy climate. I knew not what to do. All at once that 'last command' seemed to come to my heart directly from heaven. I could doubt no longer, but determined on the spot to obey it at all hazards, for the sake of pleasing the Lord Jesus Christ."[2]

While on voyage to Asia and upon his arrival in Serampore, Adoniram Judson embraced the doctrine of credobaptism. He knew that the Serampore Trio were Baptists, and he had wanted to be able to defend infant-baptism from the Scriptures. Accordingly, he set himself to study the Bible in order to defend his position.[3] Judson's wife, Ann, recorded her thoughts on the transition from paedobaptist convictions to credobaptist convictions.[4] She highlighted Judson's dogged commitment to biblical exegesis over denominational tradition. She said in a letter to her parents in February 1813 that Judson was "determined to read candidly and prayerfully, and to hold fast, or embrace the truth, however mortifying, however great the sacrifice."[5] She

---

1. Middleditch, *Burmah's Great Missionary*, 22. See also Wayland, *Memoir*, 1:51–52; and Conant, *The Earnest Man*, 42–44.

2. Edward Judson, *The Life of Adoniram Judson*, 473–74. See also Wayland, *Memoir*, 2:234–35.

3. For an apt analysis of Judson's shift from Congregationalist to Baptist, see Wills, "From Congregationalist to Baptist," 149–63.

4. A few more extracts from her journals during that time portray how Judson's devotion to searching the Scriptures influenced Ann's own pursuit of the biblical teaching on baptism. Knowles includes Ann's journal entries from August 10 and 23, and September 1 and 5, 1812. These journals show how the Judsons wrestled with the issue of baptism, sought to obey Scripture, and took the risk of losing the security found in their mission society. See Knowles, *Memoir of Mrs. Ann H. Judson*, 63–64.

5. Edward Judson, *The Life of Adoniram Judson*, 40. In a letter to her parents, the day after her baptism, Ann made a very similar statement: "Mr. Judson resolved to

was anxious that he would become a Baptist, and in an earlier letter to her parents in September 1812, the day after their baptism,[6] she recalled that she "frequently urged the unhappy consequences if he should." But, in spite of his new bride's fretfulness, Judson retorted "that his duty compelled him to examine the subject, and he hoped he should have a disposition to embrace the truth, though he paid dear for it." Ann would try to persuade him to stay in agreement with paedobaptism, but he assiduously studied both sides of the debate, reading the authoritative theologians of both perspectives. She said that "after having examined and re-examined the subject, in every way possible, and comparing the sentiments of both Baptists[7] and pedobaptists[8] with the Scriptures, he was compelled from a conviction of the truth, to embrace the former." Then, after devoting herself as well to the Scriptures, trying to vindicate her long-held paedobaptist beliefs, Ann also came to agree with the Baptist position. She told her parents that they became Baptists "not because we wished to be, but because truth compelled us to be." Furthermore, they were both well aware of the dilemma they faced by changing their sentiments on baptism; she told her parents that "a renunciation of our former sentiments has caused us more pain than any thing which ever happened to us through our lives."[9]

If Judson were to follow his newfound credobaptist convictions, his connection with the Congregationalist missionary society in America would inevitably be broken. Knowing the certain adversity they would face

---

examine it candidly and prayerfully, let the result be what it would." Wayland, *Memoir*, 1:108.

6. On the same day (September 7, 1812) as this letter to her parents, Ann wrote a letter to a friend that sounds very similar; the contents of the two letters easily blur together. See Edward Judson, *The Life of Adoniram Judson*, 38–40; and also Wayland, *Memoir*, 1:105–6.

7. See Adoniram Judson, *Christian Baptism*. In the preface, Judson indicated that he predominantly consulted *Paedobaptism Examined* by Abraham Booth (1734–1806). See Booth, *Paedobaptism Examined*. Judson also cited the Baptist theologians Henry Danvers (c. 1622–1687), John Gill (1697–1771), and Joseph Stennett I (1663–1713); see Adoniram Judson, *Christian Baptism*, 74–75, 84–85. See also Danvers, *A Treatise of Baptism*; Rippon, *A Brief Memoir of the Life*; Stennett, *An Answer to Mr. David Russen's Book*. See also, Stennett, *The Works*.

8. Judson primarily utilized paedobaptist theologians Samuel Worcester (1770–1821), Samuel Austin (1760–1830), and Peter Edwards, which Ann identified in a letter to her parents on February 14, 1813. See Wayland, *Memoir*, 1:107. For Judson's citations of these writers, see Adoniram Judson, *Christian Baptism*, 6, 15, 36, 41, 45, 47, 60, 66, 91. See Worcester, *Two Discourses*; Austin, *A View of the Economy of the Church of God*; and Edwards, *Candid Reasons*.

9. Wayland, *Memoir*, 1:108. See also Middleditch, *Burmah's Great Missionary*, 52–53.

in breaking ties with the Congregationalists, Judson wrote a letter to the Third Church in Plymouth where he had been a member and shared his newfound biblical convictions. Judson reflected on how painful it would be to "forsake" his parents, his church, the missionary society, and his companions. He was grieved that he would "forfeit the good opinion" of his friends, causing some grief, and "provoking others to anger." He feared that his close friends would chastise him "as a weak, despicable Baptist."[10] Such demoralizing prospects were daunting, but he concluded, "it is better to be guided by the opinion of Christ, who is the Truth, than by the opinion of men." Regardless of their good intentions, Judson could not agree with those whom he believed to be in error under the scrutiny of the Scriptures. He resolved, "The praise of Christ is better than the praise of men. Let me cleave to Christ at all events, and prefer his favor above my chief joy."[11] Both he and Ann, "after much laborious research and painful trial,"[12] decided to become Baptists, forsaking their Congregational association. It was a great step of faith to leave the missionary society that initially sent them out, since they were unsure as to whether a Baptist society would adopt them and support them as missionaries. This risk, which Judson singularly initiated, demonstrated his unswerving allegiance to the Scriptures and his commitment to obey every command.[13]

In September 1812, at Lal Bazaar Church in Calcutta, William Ward, a teammate of William Carey and one of the Serampore Trio, baptized Adoniram and Ann "in obedience to [Christ's] sacred commands."[14] In a subse-

---

10. At this time in history, Baptists were second-class citizens and despised. For Judson to forsake his status in the Congregational church to become a confessional Baptist demonstrated his allegiance to the Word in the face of hostility and cultural ridicule. William Owen Carver (1868–1954), the Southern Baptist missiologist, commented that "by no means were Baptists universally respected by Christians of other communions, however deserving of respect they may have been." Carver, "The Significance of Adoniram Judson," 482.

11. Middleditch, *Burmah's Great Missionary*, 54. See also Wayland, *Memoir*, 1:102.

12. In a letter written to the Serampore Trio in India, on August 27, 1812, these were the words Judson used to describe the process of coming to the conviction of believer's baptism. See Middleditch, *Burmah's Great Missionary*, 54. Judson also wrote a very similar sounding letter to Lucius Bolles (1779–1844) of Salem, Massachusets on September 1, 1812. See Wayland, *Memoir*, 1:111.

13. Leonard, Baptist scholar and church historian, insightfully explains: "For the Judsons, the resolute Biblicism of their duty to embark on an international mission was not limited to Calvinism. It led them to revisit the biblical basis for Christian baptism, and with that a decision to move toward the Baptists, deserting the Congregational support system they had worked so diligently to build and secure." Leonard, "'Wild and Romantic in the Extreme,'" 88.

14. See the letter written to the Serampore Trio in India, on August 27, 1812, in

quent sermon at Lal Bazaar Baptist church, Judson contended for believer's baptism. His argument was so theologically articulate and textually faithful that Carey, the great missionary-theologian and linguist, said in a letter that it was the best sermon on believer's baptism that he had ever heard. He wrote that Judson's convictions changed because, according to Judson, paedobaptism "has no foundation in the word of God."[15]

Biblical Truth and Baptism

In his *Christian Baptism*, Judson's Word-centered devotion is manifestly on display. He started by unfolding Matthew 28:19 and asked the questions: "what is baptism? and, To whom is baptism to be administered?"[16] Judson scrutinized the Greek text of Matthew 28:19, and masterfully demonstrated why "baptism" should translate as "immersion." He proceeded to discuss the etymology and semantic range of the Greek words, *baptō* and *baptizō*, in both the New Testament and the Septuagint. His research consisted of looking at every instance in which these words occurred and then considered them in light of the surrounding literary context and in light of the cultural and historical contexts. With copious footnotes, theological acumen, and abundant citations of sundry theologians throughout church history, Judson magisterially handled the Old and New Testaments.

At the conclusion of his sermon on baptism, Judson cited the command to be baptized, "He that believeth and is baptized, shall be saved; but he that believeth not, shall be damned" (Mark 16:16). Then he asserted that "to believe in Christ is necessary to salvation; and to be baptized is the instituted method of professing our belief." He argued that whether one believes in Christ is not the only question worth considering as he said, "but it is also a very important question to all Christians, whether they have been baptized." He then went on to plead with his brethren to "diligently use the means of discovering truth. Put yourselves in the way of evidence. Indulge free examination." He said that just as a person who hides in a cave cannot enjoy the rays of sunlight, so is a person who refuses to explore Scriptural truth. He charged that the degree of one's love for truth would determine the degree of labor spent in search of it. God will thus leave in error those who are indifferent to truth. Lastly, Judson appealed to his hearers:

Middleditch, *Burmah's Great Missionary*, 54.

15. From a letter written by Carey to William Staughton (1770–1829) on October 20, 1812. Knowles, *Memoir of Mrs. Ann H. Judson*, 66. This letter was also reprinted thirty years later in Carey, "Miscellany:—Messrs. Judson and Rice," 149.

16. Adoniram Judson, *Christian Baptism*, 1.

In order, therefore, to stimulate your minds to candid and energetic research, prize truth above all other things. Be impressed with the conviction, that nothing can compensate you, for the loss of truth. "She is more precious than rubies, and all the things thou canst desire are not to be compared unto her [Prov 3:15]." She will keep you in the right way, the way of duty, of usefulness, of happiness. She will lead you to heaven. Seek her, therefore, as silver, and search for her, as for hid treasures. Finally, *If any man desire to do the will of God, "he shall know of the doctrine, whether it be of God."*[17]

For Judson, baptism was a matter of fidelity to the Scriptures, and it was worth the risk of becoming a Baptist. In a letter to his home church, the Third Church in Plymouth, Judson charitably and courageously defended his conviction in this regard. He was aware that his change of sentiments "would give much pain" to many whom he respected and cherished, including his father, the pastor. He hoped to demonstrate how persuasive were "the potency of those arguments which constrained" him to become a Baptist. He wanted them to know that he was not merely making a hasty, unfounded decision. He did not want them to perceive his change of conviction as spiteful. Judson insisted that his change of sentiments was "from a single regard to truth and duty."[18]

So arresting were Judson's exegetical articulation and persuasion for truth that his father actually became convinced of credobaptism years later and resigned his pastorate in Plymouth. At the Second Baptist Church of Boston, Thomas Baldwin (1753–1825) baptized the elder Judson and his wife, Abigail Brown, and daughter, Abigail, on the last day of August 1817.[19]

---

17. See ibid., 93–94; Scripture quotation from John 7:17; emphasis in original.

18. Adoniram Judson, *A Letter to the Rev. Adoniram Judson, Sen.*, 23–24. Despite Judson's attempt to clearly articulate his conviction from Scripture in a humble, winsome manner, the Congregationalist, Enoch Pond (1791–1882), claimed that Judson's change of sentiments was "one of the most mysterious and unaccountable events which has ever occurred in the Christian world." Pond could not comprehend why Judson would have renounced paedobaptism other than because of "resentment" toward the board that commissioned Judson. See Pond, *A Treatise on the Mode and Subjects of Christian Baptism*, 5–8. See also, Nott, *A Letter Addressed to Rev. Enoch Pond*.

19. See Anderson, *To the Golden Shore*, 202–3; Hunt, *Bless God and Take Courage*, 268–69. See also Chessman, *Memoir of Rev. Thomas Baldwin*.

Baptistic Conversionism

Judson's newly-developed theology of baptism greatly influenced his view of Christian conversion. His passion for the conversion of the heathen was not satisfied with mere tract distribution or immediate professions of faith. Judson recorded that when a Buddhist would begin considering Christianity, all his relatives and acquaintances would rise up to prevent him. So, because of the shameful stigma of forsaking one's cultural and familial identity, Judson said that "to get a new convert is like pulling out the eye tooth of a tiger."[20] It would have been tempting to soften the exclusivity of the gospel and thus promote religious multi-perspectivalism and ecumenical dialogue, but Judson's adherence to biblical convictions prevented him from settling for inoffensive and socially acceptable theological minimalism. In a journal entry in February 1820, Judson recorded a conversation he had with the Buddhist teacher, Moung Shwa-gnong, which illustrates his convictions. Moung Shwa-gnong insisted that he held to the fundamentals of the Christian religion, but Judson was not convinced that he was a genuine convert. Moung Shwa-gnong said, "I believe in the eternal God, in his Son Jesus Christ, in the atonement which Christ has made, and in the writings of the apostles, as the true and only word of God." Yet, he claimed he tried avoiding persecution by going along with people to the pagoda for worship so that he did not look out of place, but he was sincerely not in agreement with his former ways of worship. Judson observed that Moung Shwa-gnong was progressing in the direction of discipleship, but he contended that Moung Shwa-gnong still lacked full devotion to Christ's commands. Judson said, "Teacher, you may be a disciple of Christ in heart, but you are not a full disciple. You have not faith and resolution enough to keep all the commands of Christ, particularly that which requires you to be baptized, though in the face of persecution and death."[21] Moung Shwa-gnong consequently left without pursuing baptism any further. But in July 1820, Moung Shwa-gnong found Judson and confessed his desire to be baptized. Not wanting to grant false assurance to Moung Shwa-gnong, Judson interviewed him one more time. Judson asked him,

> Do you believe. . .that none but the disciples of Christ will be saved from sin and hell? . . . How then can you remain without taking the oath of allegiance to Jesus Christ [in public baptism], and becoming his full disciple in body and soul?[22]

---

20. Wayland, *Memoir*, 2:13.
21. Ibid., 1:263.
22. Ibid., 1:281.

Moung Shwa-gnong then convinced Judson of his submission to Christ's command to be baptized and corresponding marks of spiritual life.

The evidence of transference from the kingdom of darkness to light was the public profession of faith and allegiance to Christ at baptism. Judson's desire for a pure, set-apart Burmese church drove his effort to discern the authenticity of their conversion, since baptism would mark their entry into the heavenly citizenship with the people of God. Judson looked for certain signs of life in each professing Christian before administering the ordinance. He contended that the soul of a genuine disciple of Christ must be morally transformed. Vital signs of this change are

> a deep and universal sorrow for the sins of his past life, an entire renunciation of all hope of salvation by any merits of his own, an unreserved surrender of himself to Christ, relying on him alone for pardon and acceptance with God, and an earnest desire to live henceforth in obedience to all the requirements of the gospel; and that these spiritual exercises terminate in a radical change of moral character, leading to a pure and holy life.[23]

Therefore, Judson held that a professing believer's candidacy for baptism and essentially for church membership must be evidenced through such signs of moral and spiritual change, and native Christians must likewise affirm the authenticity of these signs in the person. "This new creation must comprehend not only a change in practice, but a change in motives, and in all the moral affections."[24]

In his "Burman Liturgy," Judson wrote out the provisions for native pastors in baptizing new members. He maintained that new converts could only be baptized with the consent of other members who knew the candidates. If they were unwilling, based on external knowledge of a candidate's lack of spiritual fitness for membership, then baptism was not permissible.[25] In the same liturgy, Judson suggested that each church partake of the Lord's Table at the beginning of each season or at the beginning of each month. If a person persisted in unrepentant violation of the commands of Christ, Judson said that such a person should be disallowed from taking the elements.

---

23. Ibid., 2:9.

24. Ibid. For an example of Judson employing church discipline and excommunication, see Adoniram Judson, *The Christian Index*, 4. Also, for another description of the excommunication process, which Judson called a "solemn and *dreaded* infliction," see Wayland, *Memoir*, 2:127–28; emphasis in original.

25. Wayland, *Memoir*, 2:471.

And, if that person were to remain unrepentant after a year, they were to be excommunicated from the church.[26]

In one of his practical tracts for church order and discipleship, *The Septenary*, Judson suggested this prayer as part of the closing liturgy for the baptism service:

> Prayer to be said before baptism ... O almighty and everlasting God, who has great compassion; previously I/we had worshiped and followed the wrong god and have transgressed against our Saviour and have sinned. By your grace I/we repent and confess my/our sins. Referring to the fact that those who believe in Jesus Christ and took baptism will be saved, with faith I/we ask to be baptized. As body filth is washed off by water may my/our conscience be washed off by the blood of the lord Jesus Christ. Like the dead body of flesh is buried in the ground through baptism, die as son of the world and in coming out of the water help me/us to resurrect as new person of heaven. The person who takes baptism must discard wrong religion and worship the Father, the Son and the Holy Spirit till the end of days. Rejecting own preference, bear the cross and follow Jesus Christ. I/we promise to try and put into effect all the principles a believer should follow. Grant upon me/us the Holy Spirit so that I/we do not break my/our promise and abide with the principles all the days of my/our life/lives. I/we reverently pray that when I/we pass away from this world let me/us be at thy foot together with the saints enjoying the never-ending heavenly riches, through Jesus Christ our lord. Amen.[27]

Evident in this prayer is that baptism was a public divorce from the futile ways of this world. Judson's baptism prayer was the final step to the giving of assurance of salvation.

Slow Assurance

In keeping with Judson's theology of baptistic conversionism, he was slow to grant early assurance of salvation. Regarding the first Burmese Christian, Moung Nau, Judson recorded in his journal (April and May of 1819) the process of Moung Nau's conversion. In brief prayerful journal entries over this period, he revealed his theology of man's depravity, God's sovereignty, regeneration, and post-conversion spiritual affections for Christ. Judson's

26. Ibid., 2:472.
27. Adoniram Judson, *The Septenary*, 66–67.

journals reveal that he was slow to declare assurance of salvation, indicating his high view of the necessity of signs of the Spirit's indwelling presence for assurance.[28]

On April 25, he sat down to teach the Bible in the *zayat* and the young Burman man, Moung Nau, inquired deeply about Judson's teachings.[29] Moung Nau continued to show significant interest in Judson's teaching so that by May 5 Judson was hopeful that Moung Nau was near regeneration. Facing the temptation to hastily announce that he had introduced the first Burman to Christ in order to impress his supporters, Judson was nonetheless hesitant to claim that Moung Nau had been truly converted, even though

> [Moung Nau] expresses sentiments of repentance for his sins, and faith in the Saviour. The substance of his profession is, that from the darknesses, and uncleannesses, and sins of his whole life, he has found no other Saviour but Jesus Christ—nowhere else can he look for salvation; and therefore he proposes to adhere to Christ, and worship him all his life long.[30]

Even after evidencing more signs of regeneration the following day, Judson still prayed that Moung Nau's blinded mind would be enlightened by the truth and that he would "cleave inviolably to the blessed Saviour."[31] It was not until May 15, after ten more days of intensely conversing with Judson and after all the other members of the mission were convinced of Moung Nau's newborn faith, that Judson finally admitted that Moung Nau had been born again. One of the final conversations with Moung Nau that convinced Judson of his conversion was that after being warned from the Scripture of certain persecution and possible death for professing Christ, Maung Nau claimed that he would rather die for Christ and enter paradise than live comfortably here and be in hell forever. This final conversation in addition to all the other discussions persuaded Judson of the genuineness of the first

---

28. Though this was Judson's normal conviction, there were times when Burmans were on their deathbed, and Judson was glad to assure them of their salvation upon hearing of their confession of sins and of their love for and trust in Jesus. For example, see Adoniram Judson, *An Account of Meh Shway-ee*. Also, another example of this is his journal entry on March 11, 1832 when he wrote about baptizing an old man without hearing a testimony of the old man's Christian conduct, which was not Judson's normal practice; see Adoniram Judson, journal, February 29, 1832 to June 25, 1832, Box No. AJ 4, Folder 8 and Microfilm Roll 1, Judson Letters, ABHS; Adoniram Judson, "Mr. Judson's Journal, Feb. 29th, 1832 [to May 16, 1832]," 41–45. See also Middleditch, *Burmah's Great Missionary*, 294; and Wayland, *Memoir*, 2:44–45.

29. Middleditch, *Burmah's Great Missionary*, 125.

30. Conant, *The Earnest Man*, 194–95, quoted also in Wayland, *Memoir*, 1:216–17; emphasis in original.

31. Wayland, *Memoir*, 1:217.

Burman conversion.[32] On June 27, 1819, Moung Nau was duly baptized as the first Burman Christian, and on July 4, Judson "had the pleasure of sitting down, for the first time, to the Lord's table with a converted Burman."[33] In many letters, he referred to his converts as his *baptized* converts.[34] Judson's joy over these converts was not only that they were converted to the Redeemer's kingdom but that they could also partake with him and other baptized believers at the Lord's Table. Baptism was the door that opened the banquet hall of the King and his covenant people.

Disciple-Making with the Word

Judson sought to train up the church through the regular teaching of the Word. If he was not translating, then he was teaching and training.[35] Just as he saw the dictionary as indispensable for the ongoing propagation of the Scriptures, he also viewed Bible-based discipleship as the vehicle for the ongoing sustenance and maturity of the indigenous church. Two main works he wrote illustrate his ability to synthesize doctrine for the sake of discipleship: "A Burman Liturgy"[36] and *A Digest of Scripture*.[37]

32. Ibid., 1:219.

33. Adoniram Judson, journal, July 3, 1827 to October 20, 1827, Box No. AJ 4, Folder 4 and Microfilm Roll 1, Judson Letters, ABHS. See also Middleditch, *Burmah's Great Missionary*, 125–27.

34. For example, see Wayland, *Memoir*, 1:283, 415, 444–60, 520.

35. Judson developed biblical/theological education for the Burmese ministers-in-training. The Bible courses covered both the Old and New Testaments, but the teachers prioritized the New Testament, teaching "verse by verse, with comparison of parallel passages made in the recitation room. It was the constant aim of the teacher not only to unfold the sense of the Scriptures, but also to show the pupils practically how to make the bible [*sic*] its own interpreter." See "Intelligence from the Missions," 8. See also Adoniram Judson, Burman Theological Seminary Report, July 10, 1840, Box No. AJ 3, Folder 2 and Microfilm Roll 1, Judson Letters, ABHS. For a brief discussion on Judson's unique approach to discipleship that blended his conversionistic impulse and his desire to train and educate for the work of the ministry, see Carver, "The Significance of Adoniram Judson," 481–82.

36. See Wayland, *Memoir*, 2:467–75.

37. Adoniram Judson, *A Digest of Scripture*. In the *Baptist Missionary Magazine*, Judson briefly described his purpose and method of writing *A Digest of Scripture*: "My principal work in the study, beside correcting a part of the Old Testament, has been 'A Digest of Scripture, consisting of extracts from the Old and New Testaments, partly taken from Brown's selection.' . . . Upon this I have spent nearly four months, intending, according to the best of my ability, to make it an elaborate work, containing the most important passages of scripture, arranged under successive heads, beginning with 'The Scripture of Truth,' and ending with 'The Retributions of Eternity.' I trust this book will be . . . useful as a book of reference." Adoniram Judson, "Letter of Mr. Judson, Dated

Judson's "A Burman Liturgy" provided doctrines useful for discipleship. Judson prepared this liturgy in 1829 for new missionaries who had not yet learned the language and for his Burmese assistants whom he trained for ministry. Judson commenced the liturgy with worship given to the Trinity, and in response to God's self-revelation, he then outlined the fundamental biblical commands: the commands of righteousness, which require loving God and loving others, and the commands of grace, which require repentance of sin and faith in the Lord Jesus Christ. He then proposed six short "formulas of worship," which set the congregants' gaze upon the sovereign God who governs all things for his pleasure and the eternal happiness of his people. After this summary of theology proper, Judson outlined a basic Christology in twelve articles. His Calvinistic doctrine of particular redemption is obvious here. His atonement-centered theology is explicit, and it does not indicate any adherence to the governmental theory of atonement common among the New Divinity tradition. Thus, Judson said in the fifth article that "the Son of God, according to his engagement to save the elect . . . laid down his life for man, in the severest agonies of crucifixion, by which he made an atonement for all who are willing to believe."[38]

Judson's doctrines of regeneration, union, justification, and perseverance informed his views of discipleship and spiritual formation. In articles seven through nine, it was stated:

> Art. VII. In order to obtain salvation, we must believe in the Lord Jesus Christ, and become his disciples, receiving a change of nature, through regeneration, by the power of the Spirit. Art. VIII. Those who become disciples obtain the pardon of their sins through the cross of Christ; and being united to him by faith, his righteousness is imputed to them, and they become entitled to the eternal happiness of heaven. Art. IX. Disciples, therefore, though they may not in this world be perfectly free from the old nature, do not completely fall away; but through the sustaining grace of the Spirit, they persevere until death in spiritual advancement, and in endeavors to keep the divine commands.[39]

After the articles on these basic doctrines, he listed formulae for administering baptism, the Lord's Supper, and for appointing evangelists, missionaries, elders and pastors, deacons, and itinerant preachers. He concluded

---

Maulmein, Dec. 21, 1837," 300.

38. Wayland, *Memoir*, 2:469.

39. Ibid.

this section of formulae with more detailed instructions on administering baptism, the Lord's Supper, and on practicing church discipline.[40]

The final section of the liturgy contained "Thirty Precepts, being a Digest of Christian Law," which illustrated those primary spiritual qualities that Judson saw in Scripture as essential for the true disciple. Judson's copious devotion to detail influenced his commitment to systematize the biblical commands for the sake of obeying Scripture rightly. His thirty biblical laws for Christians include:

> (1) Love God with all the soul . . . (2) Love others as thyself . . . (3) Repent of thy sins . . . (4) Believe in the Lord Jesus Christ . . . (5) Set not thy heart on worldly good, but keep in view the happiness of heaven . . . (6) Avoid idleness, and be diligent in thy calling . . . (7) Covet not the property of others . . . (8) Do no violence . . . (9) Steal not . . . (10) Defraud not . . . (11) Lie not . . . (12) Bear not false witness . . . (13) Murder not; and let the murderer die . . . (14) Be not drunk . . . (15) Commit not adultery . . . (16) Besides thine own wife or husband, lust after none . . . (17) Subdue pride, and cultivate a meek and humble spirit . . . (18) Bear with the faults of others; return not evil for evil; love thine enemies, and do them good . . . (19) Be charitable to the poor . . . (20) Honor and support thy parents . . . (21) Honor ministers of religion, and cheerfully contribute to their support . . . (22) In regard to rulers, whether disciples or not, honor them; pray for them; obey their orders, not involving sin against God . . . (23) As thou hast opportunity, do good unto all men . . . (24) In performing worship, avoid idolatry . . . (25) Pray to God always . . . (26) In all things deny thyself, and seek the will of God . . . (27) On the first day of the week, assemble with others to worship God and hear the word . . . (28) Profess the religion of the Lord Jesus Christ by receiving baptism . . . (29) Afterwards receive the Lord's supper, in remembrance of the divine love . . . (30) Go into all the world, and preach the gospel to every creature.[41]

More extensive than his liturgy, Judson's *A Digest of Scripture* is a compendium of doctrinal assertions using the language of Scripture in order to teach the basic doctrines of the Bible. Judson did not write a thorough systematic theology textbook, but he compiled the Scriptural evidence necessary for producing such a larger work. Grounded in the infallibility and

---

40. Ibid., 2:470–72.

41. Ibid., 2:473–75. Judson cited multiple Scripture references for each of the thirty precepts. For the sake of brevity, the above citation does not include the corresponding Scriptures.

sufficiency of the Bible, Judson sought to use the Bible's own language to explain its doctrine. *A Digest of Scripture* exemplifies his conviction of the perspicuity of Scripture and its power to convert and revive the soul. In nearly two hundred pages of biblical text upon text, Judson outlined what he saw as the whole of Scriptural doctrine for the sake of training the church to think and live biblically. The table of contents, not including each chapter's subsections, includes chapters on topics such as bibliology, the being and attributes of God, the Trinity, the state of man, the Lord Jesus Christ, salvation bestowed, salvation accepted, the evidences of faith, the benefits of faith, duty to God, duty to men, duty to oneself, prayer, the church, the extension of the gospel, and the affliction of believers.[42]

Proclaiming the Word

Judson contended that gospel proclamation is not comprised only of oral communication, though proclamation is certainly not less than oral communication. Proclamation, moreover, essentially involves distribution of the Scriptures. Judson scolded those who were indifferent to the universal dissemination of the Bible. At the ninth annual meeting of the American and Foreign Bible Society, held May 15, 1846, in New York, Judson gave an address[43] that portrays his theology of gospel proclamation and his Word-centered piety. He said that the modern usage of the English word *preach* is "too specific for the original." He went on to say that the Greek word certainly suggests "oral communication," yet that is "not the exclusive meaning of the original word." Judson believed that the word *proclaim* is a more suitable translation of the meaning of the original Greek. He argued that *proclaim* has the idea of oral preaching and literature distribution, just as a king's ambassador could proclaim a pardon to the inhabitants of a city through both oral declaration and printed publication, and just as Paul could equally proclaim the gospel through both preaching in the synagogues and publishing gospel truth through his Epistles. Judson's intention

---

42. See Adoniram Judson, *A Digest of Scripture*, i–iv.

43. In November 1845, when Judson arrived in America, his voice was faltering, so he requested that someone else read aloud his addresses in his presence. Later in the spring of 1846, his voice was stronger, and he gave more addresses without assistance. See Edward Judson, *The Life of Adoniram Judson*, 468–76. On the back of the last page of Judson's original manuscript for the above address are the hand-written words of S. S. Cutting (1835–1882): "Dr. Judson's remarks before the American and Foreign Bible Society, New York, in his own hand writing." Adoniram Judson to the American and Foreign Bible Society, address, May 15, 1846, Papers, 1811–1888, Trask Library Special Collections, Newton Centre, Massachusetts.

was not to demote the power of preaching, but to promote the efficacy of the text of the Scriptures. His explanation demonstrates his bibliocentric piety and his conviction that the Word of God is alive and active.

Judson further explained that when a missionary first goes to a heathen people, the missionary's communication is largely oral; however, "he will have very imperfectly fulfilled his commission if he leaves them without the written Word." Judson maintained that such neglect results in the kind of "mischievous consequences" that are evident in mission stations "conducted by the Man of Sin," that is, Roman Catholic missions.[44] He went on to caution that among some Protestant mission stations, there had recently been "a tendency to promote the oral communication of the Gospel, not, indeed, to an undue pre-eminence, but in such a manner as to throw a shade over the written communication by means of tracts and Scriptures." He went on to explain that though the initial indiscriminate, evangelistic preaching of the gospel and tract distribution might initially seem more successful, "all missionary operations, to be permanently successful, must be based on the written Word. Where that Word is most regarded and honored, there will be the most pure and permanent success." He said that the written "Word of God is the golden lamp hung out of heaven to enlighten the nations that sit in darkness, and to show them the path that leads from the confines of hell to the gates of paradise." Judson upheld the Bible, in its original languages, as comprehensively containing all existing revelation from God to the world. The written Word is "just *the book*, the one book, which Infinite Wisdom saw best adapted to answer the end of a written revelation." It is not another grandiose achievement of human reason; it surpasses all other works of philosophy and logic. It is paradoxically complex and clear, profound and transcendent, "perfect and unique." He charged the church to remember the holy responsibility that God had given to her. He said that God entrusted his perfect Word as "the sacred deposit in the hands of the church." Judson issued woes to those who deny others to partake in such a treasure and to those who seek to snuff out the light of the gospel of heaven. He praised God for those who were working hard at distributing the Bible around the world. He wished to see the Bible translated and broadcast in every language and to be "deposited in every palace, and house, and hut inhabited by man."[45]

---

44. The Protestant Reformers commonly identified the Roman Catholic Church as the Antichrist. See Froom, *The Prophetic Faith of Our Fathers*, 148–58.

45. Adoniram Judson to the American and Foreign Bible Society, address, May 15, 1846, Papers, 1811–1888, Trask Library Special Collections, Newton Centre, Massachusetts. See also Wayland, *Memoir*, 2:235–38, and Middleditch, *Burmah's Great Missionary*, 388–91; emphasis in original. For similar sentiments in another letter, see Wayland, *Memoir*, 2:126–27; and Middleditch, *Burmah's Great Missionary*, 318–19;

Eight years earlier, he had uttered similar sentiments in a letter to the American Baptist Board. He said that he had hoped to complete the Bible and deposit it in every village and township across Burma. Though it would require great endurance and much expenditure, once Bibles were positioned in the places of influence and prominence in each town, the seed sown "would spring up in abundant fruit to his [God's] glory." Judson observed that the townspeople would often gather at the houses of the educated leader, whether it be a priest or principal, in each village for the purpose of listening to the leader read from a religious book. Consequently, he said that he sought to introduce and leave the Bible at the chief location in every town in order that the light of the gospel would efficaciously pervade the dark corners of the Burman empire where no missionary could reside.[46]

In the letter, he went on to say that Protestant missions of his era differed from Roman Catholic missions by "honoring and sounding out the Word of God." He asserted that those missionaries who esteem the proclamation of Scripture higher than any other charitable venture would "be most owned of God, and blessed with the influence of the Holy Spirit." He then referred to an analogy he used for contextualization in evangelism.[47] He likened the Bible to "only one golden lamp which God has suspended from heaven" to guide sinners to heaven. He warned that missionaries dare not obscure its light by preventing its indiscriminate and universal circulation. He cautioned against perceiving this goal as somehow demoting the role of gospel preaching, because preaching is "the grand means instituted by Christ for the conversion of the world."[48] However, he explained that all evangelism and discipleship "must be based on the written Word." Even if the preacher were to depart from a village, the gospel witness would not go with him, since "the inspired Word may still remain to convert and to edify." From his bibliocentric perspective, preaching the gospel and the written

---

emphasis in original.

46. See Edward Judson, *The Life of Adoniram Judson*, 410–11.

47. Though some missionaries thought he was merely "eccentric" in his cultural adaptation, Judson sought to contextualize and dress in priestly garments as a "religion-propagating teacher." For descriptions of his contextualization, see Wayland, *Memoir*, 2:383–85.

48. Two years earlier on February 8, 1836, in a letter to Amariah Joy (1809–1899) in Waterville, Maine, Judson similarly said, "The grand means of converting the heathen world is to preach the glorious gospel of our great God and Saviour Jesus Christ, in the vernacular language of the people . . . resolving, in a word, with the great apostle of the Gentiles, to know nothing but Jesus Christ and him crucified." Ibid., 2:108. In a letter on January 16, 1840, to his fellow missionary, Francis Mason (1799–1874), Judson asserted, "I rather think it is a sound principle in missions, that the degree of success is proportionate to the quantity of gospel preached." Ibid., 2:154.

Word were inseparable. Together they are, he said, "the two arms which are to pull down the kingdom of darkness, and build up the Redeemer's. Let us not cut off one of these arms, for the other will by itself be comparatively powerless." He was convinced that the history of the church testified to the fact that one of these arms alone is impotent without the other.[49]

Judson's argument that gospel proclamation comprises both Bible distribution and oral preaching explains why he exclusively focused on translation and preaching. In articles of agreement adopted by Judson and his missionary companion, George H. Hough, Judson thus briefly described the means of evangelization that he promoted. He said that the chief means by which "to introduce the religion of Jesus Christ" to the Burmese would be "translating, printing, and distributing the Holy Scriptures, preaching the gospel, circulating religious tracts, and promoting the instruction of native children."[50]

Publishing the Word

Two very important events marked the year 1816: the arrival of a printing press, which was a gift from the Serampore missionaries, and the appointment of a professional printer from Philadelphia, George H. Hough, to operate the press. Judson was overjoyed at the prospects of printing the Bible in the Burmese language. Judson subsequently wrote a letter to the Board of Managers to solicit funds for the management of the printing press. In this letter he discussed taking the press from Rangoon to Ava, about which he said, "such a measure would doubtless tend to the furtherance of the cause, and to the introduction of religion into the very heart of the empire, where Satan's seat is." Being the engine of the Reformation, Judson hoped the printing press would ubiquitously broadcast the Word of God in Burma. Judson believed that, through a long labor of love, the supernal light revealed from the Word would finally dawn, and other nations would "participate in the same glorious light." Many disappointments would surely assail the faith of the missionaries and the missionary societies, but, he urged, "let patience have her perfect work; let us not be weary of well-doing; for in due time we shall reap, if we faint not."[51]

---

49. Edward Judson, *The Life of Adoniram Judson*, 410–11. See also Middleditch, *Burmah's Great Missionary*, 318–20; and Wayland, *Memoir*, 2:126–27.

50. Adoniram Judson and Hough, "Articles of Agreement," 183–84. See also Wayland, *Memoir*, 1:184; and Middleditch, *Burmah's Great Missionary*, 121.

51. Adoniram Judson and Hough, "Communication from Rev. Messrs. Judson and Hough," 182–83. See also Wayland, *Memoir*, 1:183–84; and Conant, *The Earnest Man*,

For Judson, the work of translation, Bible distribution, and proclamation were *the* work of missions, and if a door were shut in one region, he did not agree with employing some other politically and socially acceptable platform for the purpose of staying in the region. Rather, he contended that the missionary ought to continue trying to enter other locations in order to broadcast the Bible to as many people in as many nations as the Lord wills.

Regarding the possibility of expanding translation and literature distribution into China after he had finished his Bible translation, for example, Judson wrote to the president of the Triennial Convention, Spencer H. Cone (1785–1855). Judson spoke of his passion to see the Bible dispensed in other languages for the conversion of the nations, and he described his concocted strategies for introducing the Bible to China and beyond. From his activistic evangelical perspective, there was no other alternative to such missionary work. Because of the indomitability of the proclaimed Word, he said his duty was to scatter gospel seed, letting the Scripture do all the work. He charged,

> But we must all go forward, preaching the Gospel, and distributing bibles and tracts in every possible way, and in every language under heaven. If one door is shut up, we must push in at another. Victory, we are sure, will be ours at last.[52]

In 1832, after reading the manuscript of a presentation at the Triennial Convention about the need for a mission in France, by a Board member, Howard Malcom,[53] Judson responded to Malcom because of one sentence that caught Judson's activist temper: "The sentence, 'Evangelized France, teeming with religious books, would furnish reading to all the intelligent classes in Europe,' contains a volume. O that the people of the United States would read it well, and rise at the call!" Judson even said that though he felt called to reach Burma, he would gladly give a very large portion of his missionary supplies to "rescue perishing France." Judson then asked Malcom what could be so significant in the United States that would hold him from giving himself to France. Then he listed other gospel-less areas of the world that burdened his soul. Judson prayed for Malcom and his colleagues to awaken and to devote themselves more to the opportunities God had offered to the American church.[54]

173–75. For similar convictions, see Adoniram Judson, "Address of Dr. Judson," 268.

52. Letter to Spencer H. Cone, February 4, 1836 in Middleditch, *Burmah's Great Missionary*, 312.

53. Howard Malcom was the pastor of Federal Street Church in Boston. To read of Malcom's admiration of Judson, see Mild, *Howard Malcom*, 44.

54. Middleditch, *Burmah's Great Missionary*, 308. With similar concern for the

Translating the Word

Judson admitted that he had a different translation philosophy than many missionaries.[55] The labor of many missionaries, he said, had been "dreadfully misdirected." He said that it was the duty of a man to spend his whole life to produce "a *really good* translation,"[56] and this required working "*slow and sure,* and to see to it that whatever we do, in regard to the inspired word, is *well done.*"[57] Emily described him as "very strenuous about his Burmese

---

nations at large, Judson issued a famous appeal for the many villages, cities, and nations surrounding Burma who had yet to receive one gospel witness; see Dowling, *The Judson Offering*, 175–81. Also, by 1838, the church in Burma had begun to slow in numerical growth. Judson was not content with fewer conversions. His heart yearned for more faith to see more converted. He directly challenged the complacency of the Christians even in Burma to not settle for evangelism fatigue; he said that God allowed such a small number as twelve converts in that one year due to their "scanty faith." Wayland, *Memoir*, 2:122–23. See also Middleditch, *Burmah's Great Missionary*, 327.

55. In a letter to Daniel Sharp (1783-1853) in June 1833, Judson explained his translation philosophy and why he made "such a tedious work of translating, when some persons dispatch the whole New Testament, and perhaps part of the Old, within a year or two after entering their field of labor. There are two ways of translating—the one original, the other second hand." Wayland, *Memoir*, 2:55. In a letter to Solomon Peck (1800-1874) in July 1839, Judson also addressed the issue of translation philosophy, and said he agreed with the American Baptist Board's resolution that all Bible translators ought to "endeavor, by earnest prayer and diligent study, to ascertain the exact meaning of *the original text*, and to express that meaning as exactly as the nature of the language into which they shall translate." Adoniram Judson to Rev. Solomon Peck, letter, July 12, 1839, Box No. AJ 3, Folder 2 and Microfilm Roll 1, Judson Letters, ABHS. See also Wayland, *Memoir*, 2:146; emphasis in original. What is more, a colonial administrator in Calcutta, Charles Edward Trevelyan (1807-1886), promoted Romanizing the languages of the East so that they had the same script as Europe; Judson opposed the plan and wrote to Lucius Bolles of the American Baptist Board and argued for translating the Bible into the "native character." Judson strongly disagreed with Trevelyan who promoted translating into the "Roman letter," which Judson called "Trevelyanism." He said the plan to Romanize the Burmese language was "yet in embryo" and "an untried enterprise," which he called "highly chimerical." To read all of his reasoning, see Adoniram Judson to Lucius Bolles, letter, October 3, 1834, Box No. AJ 2, Folder 2 and Microfilm Roll 1, Judson Letters, ABHS; see also Wayland, *Memoir*, 1:84–87; Trevelyan, *The Application of the Roman Alphabet*.

56. For a cultural and linguistic study on Judson's translation theory and theological contextualization in translation from the perspective of an ecumenical scholar, see Dingrin, "A Missiological and Theological Critique." For a more focused treatment of Judson's theological contextualization, see Laisum, "Naming God in Burma Today."

57. Edward Judson, *The Life of Adoniram Judson*, 405–6; emphasis in original. As early as 1816, in a letter to William Staughton, Judson reported that he felt "dispirited" because of the slow and arduous nature of language study. Yet he wanted to finish what he had set out to do. He said that he did not believe the gift of tongues was available in this age and that the missionary must learn the language in order to translate and preach the Scriptures. Because of the monotony of language study, the early romance

version, and would no doubt have persevered in his translation if the whole world had been against him."[58]

Regarding his work ethic and duty of translation, Judson read volumes of theological and critical resources from both Germany and America.[59] He also read copiously from Burmese literature and various other genres in order to familiarize himself with the unique nuances of the language.[60] He wanted to express the biblical meaning in a way so accurate and understandable that his translation would need little revision in the future.[61] Wayland claimed that he mastered the Burmese language "to a degree never before attained by a foreigner."[62] Though he availed himself to the best of exegetical commentaries and scholarship, he would not let the publications of scholars do the work for him. He ever insisted on going to the original biblical texts themselves and only using the critical commentaries as references. Thus, he would not canonize an interpreted verse until he was certain of its meaning

---

of missionary life that he had originally felt at Andover had subsided; but, though his views of missionary work were different from six years prior, he said "it does not always happen that a closer acquaintance with an object diminishes our attachment and preference. We sometimes discover beauties, as well as deformities, which were overlooked on a superficial view; when some attractions lose their force, others more permanent are exerted . . . So it has been with me, I hope, in regard to the work of missions." Wayland, *Memoir*, 1:178. Twenty-three years later, in a letter to Solomon Peck on January 5, 1839, Judson alluded to his early change of view of missionary work. He said he "warded off the translation of the Bible, thinking it would fall to Boardman, or Jones, or some other: but the providence of God, at length, laid it upon me." And so, he said, "I now feel that it is one main duty of the remnant of my life to study and labor *to perfect the Burmese translation of the Bible*." Wayland, *Memoir*, 2:128–29; emphasis in original. Also, for Judson's comments to Cephas Bennett in 1831 about the usefulness of dying to self in learning the language for the sake of becoming more holy and for becoming more actively useful in the language, see Wayland, *Memoir*, 1:522.

58. Edward Judson, *The Life of Adoniram Judson*, 408.

59. For Judson's letters requesting specific books to assist his translation work, see Adoniram Judson to Lucius Bolles, letter, December 20, 1830, Box No. AJ 2, Folder 2 and Microfilm Roll 1, ABHS; Adoniram Judson to Lucius Bolles, correspondence, February 5, 1831, Box No. AJ 2, Folder 2 and Microfilm Roll 1, ABHS; Adoniram Judson, "Mission Books," correspondence, January 31, 1835, Box No. AJ 2, Folder 1 and Microfilm Roll 1, ABHS; Adoniram Judson to Lucius Bolles, letter, August 29, 1836, Box No. AJ 2, Folder 1 and Microfilm Roll 1, ABHS; Adoniram Judson to Solomon Peck, letter, January 21, 1839, Box No. AJ 3, Folder 1 and Microfilm Roll 1, ABHS; and Adoniram Judson to Solomon Peck, correspondence, December 22, 1839, Box No. AJ 3, Folder 2 and Microfilm Roll 1, ABHS.

60. Wayland, *Memoir*, 2:166.

61. Ibid., 2:165. Wayland said that he remembered "stripping" his library of the best books and sending them to Judson. Ibid.

62. Ibid.

in the original language and in the Burmese language.[63] Wayland recorded that an eminent linguist in India who was an expert in Burmese said of Judson's translation, "We honor Wickliffe and Luther for their labors in their respective mother tongues; but what meed [sic] of praise is due to Judson for a translation of the Bible, *perfect as a literary work*, in a language so foreign to him as the Burmese?"[64]

Preaching the Word

Judson and his first wife, Ann, were at times tempted to despair for lack of noticeable "success" in their proclamation and translation efforts. In his biography of Adoniram Judson, Francis Wayland established how Adoniram and Ann valued the preaching of the gospel in missions as opposed to doing other "fruitful" ministries, albeit good ones, which seemed to bring in more immediate "fruit." Wayland said that the letters of the Judsons never suggested regrets or doubts about the seeming fruitlessness of their labor. They did, however, indicate their concern that their friends in the States would grow weary of their lack of success. Wayland said that their letters expressed "entire certainty" about the ultimate success of their work, though they might only see it in glory. As he commented:

> Their confidence rested solely and exclusively on the word of God. They believed that he had promised; they, doing, as they

---

63. Adoniram Judson to Solomon Peck, correspondence, December 28, 1840, Box No. AJ 3, Folder 3 and Microfilm Roll 1, ABHS. See also Wayland, *Memoir*, 2:161–63.

64. Wayland, *Memoir*, 2:167; emphasis in original. Approximately one hundred years after Judson's death, the Burma Christian Council invited the Prime Minister of Burma, U Nu (1907–1965), to attend a tea. The Christian leaders were discussing whether to publish a new Burmese Bible translation. U Nu, though a devout Buddhist, was quite familiar with the Christian Scriptures (i.e., Judson's translation), and he retorted, "Oh, no, a new translation of the Bible is not necessary. Judson's translation captures the language and idiom of Burmese perfectly and is very clear and understandable." Brown, "The Life and Work of Adoniram Judson," 24. For another discussion of Judson's timeless translation, see Hunt, *Bless God and Take Courage*, 254–55. John Marshman, son of Joshua Marshman, described Judson's dedication to mastering the Burmese language. He said of Judson, "His views were always elevated and comprehensive; his powers of observation very acute; and his knowledge and appreciation of character, more especially of the Burmese language and literature was more complete than that of any other foreigner." Wayland, *Memoir*, 2:359. After studying and synthesizing all of Judson's letters and other works, Wayland concluded, "The powers of Dr. Judson seem rather to have belonged to the logical than the imaginative . . . I do not remember an ambiguous sentence, or one that does not express precisely what he evidently intended, in all that he has written. The almost entire absence of figurative language is remarkable, especially in a man of so strong and various impulses." Wayland, *Memoir*, 2:374.

believed, his will, accepted the promise as addressed to themselves personally . . . By faith, through many long years of discouragement, they endured, as seeing Him who is invisible; relying not at all on what they could do, but wholly on what God had promised to do for them.[65]

Though famous for his labor of love in translation, Judson was a preacher at heart. His desire to see the gospel preached drove him to translate the Bible from which the missionary must preach. For Judson, preaching the gospel was ultimately "the great business of his life."[66] He gave himself to translation because he believed God's providence ordained such a responsibility to him and because the American Baptist Board requested it.[67] Wayland recorded that whenever Judson's translation work intermitted, he would go to the *zayat* and preach heartily.[68] Justus Vinton (1806–1858),[69] who labored with Judson, said of Judson's earnest preaching:

> True, he preached in Burman; but though I did not know the meaning of a single sentence he uttered, still my attention was never more closely riveted on any sermon I ever heard. Were I to fix upon any one characteristic of the preacher which, perhaps, more than any other, rendered his discourse interesting and impressive, I should say it was earnestness of manner. It was impossible for any one [sic] to escape the conviction that his whole soul was in the work. Every tone, every look, every sentence, spoke out in the most emphatic language, to tell us

---

65. Wayland, *Memoir*, 1:205–6. See also Wayland's comments about Judson's unwavering trust in God to redeem Burma through the proclaimed gospel, in ibid., 2:380–81.

66. Ibid., 2:97. For an example of Judson's notable preaching gift, see Mary Hasseltine's (b. 1784) reminiscences of Judson's command in preaching in ibid., 1:30–31. See also ibid., 1:39.

67. For an example of how Judson viewed God's providence guiding through the requests of the Board, see his letter on March 12, 1838, to the American Baptist Board. He said that he would know that God gave him the task of "poring [sic] over manuscripts and proof sheets" if the American Baptist Board "expressly ordered it" because he believed that "*vox senatus vox Dei*." Ibid., 2:122.

68. See ibid., 2:97. For a fellow missionary's description of Judson's "constant desire to be preaching," see ibid., 2:355. For another firsthand missionary account of Judson's desire to preach and his indefatigable preaching efforts, see Stevens, "Extracts from Letters of Mrs. Stevens," 83–85.

69. Vinton became a very powerful preacher and revivalist among the Karen people. He labored for twenty-five years. He arrived in Burma on December 7, 1834 on the same ship with Sewall M. Osgood and his wife, Elhira B. Osgood. See Luther, *The Vintons and the Karens*.

that the man was seriously in earnest, and himself believed the truths he uttered.[70]

At the close of 1827, Judson's journal entries describe the mission's proclamation efforts under his leadership. He recorded a few means "for the spread of truth." First, they met for public worship every Sunday at 10:30 in the morning, and the assembly numbered between twenty and seventy. Attendees included the missionaries, Buddhist scholars, native converts, truth-seekers, and occasional travelers. During the public meeting, they would sing songs of adoration and praise, followed by a casual extemporaneous homily, which depended upon the nature of those gathered each time. Then the assembly would finally close in prayer. Though some would leave right afterwards, many would remain and engage in religious discussions for a significant amount of time.

Second, they would practice regular evening worship. This was more of a gathering for the mission families, the scholars, and the local Christians. Approximately twenty people gathered for the daily evening worship. They would begin by reading Scripture, and an explanation and exhortation would follow. After concluding in prayer, Judson would spend the remainder of the evening with the new converts and host "instructive and profitable" conversations based on the Scripture. The next day he would reason from the Scriptures in the *zayat* with any truth-seekers who had attended the night before.[71]

The Infallible Word

For Judson, the Word of God was the supreme and the sufficient source of truth for salvation in Christ. He was also convinced that the Bible, whether printed or preached, was an infallible evangelist. As such, he believed that the most faithful missionary spirituality had to pattern itself after the model of the apostles in Acts who went about scattering the seed of the Word. In order to see the power of God in missionary activity, the missionary must heed this pattern. Consequently, Judson sought to seize every opportunity in conversations with individuals to implore them to be reconciled to God in light of the love of Christ.[72] Since God blessed the apostles' obedience to

---

70. Wayland, *Memoir*, 2:388–89.
71. Middleditch, *Burmah's Great Missionary*, 240–41.
72. See Wayland, *Memoir*, 1:206–7.

Christ's final command, Judson devoted himself to keep the proclamation of the Word central to his missionary activity.[73]

Many missionaries considered the Burmese men too difficult to reach with the gospel, so they opened schools for the native children in order to educate them from a civilized Western worldview.[74] They started with proclaiming the gospel, but after many setbacks, they opted for more humanitarian ministries and social work.[75] Judson, however, spent himself to evangelize instead of using other reputable social and educational platforms because he believed in the transforming power of the Word. Moreover, Judson was adamantly "opposed to large missionary stations"[76] because he believed they became self-absorbed and unfruitful. Mission stations would distract missionaries from their devotion to God's work. If missionaries would not keep their activistic piety centered on evangelizing with the Word, they would inevitably spend themselves on "indirect, subsidiary, and questionable modes of effort, such as indoor labor, school teaching, English preaching, bookmaking—things in themselves good, but not distinctively missionary."[77] Even in his last year of life, Judson's commitment remained to preaching the gospel instead of educating natives in English schools and teaching English civility. In a letter to the Corresponding Secretary of the American Baptist Board, Solomon Peck, Judson said that he was increasingly convinced of the truth that *"English preaching, English teaching,* and *English periodicals* are the bane of missions at the East." He argued that English schools could never convert all the unreached peoples. Such schools, he said, "are very pretty things to amuse English visitors with, and make interesting reports for people at a distance, who cannot enter into the merits of the case."[78]

---

73. See ibid., 2:167.

74. For a thorough discussion of the missionary methods of civilization through education versus cultural contextualization and proclamation, see Case, *An Unpredictable Gospel*, 19–47.

75. See Wayland's account of Judson's gospel-preaching philosophy contrasted with the teaching and civilizing methods of English missionaries and of other mission stations in Wayland, *Memoir*, 1:205–8.

76. Ibid., 2:96.

77. Ibid., 2:96–97. Often, missionaries would engage in social work because their theology drove their methodology. In one of her early letters in August 1817, to a friend named Mary, Ann Judson described the depravity of the Burman hearts and illustrated how the Judsons viewed human depravity, which led them to the conviction that gospel proclamation is fundamental for conversion. See Ann Hasseltine Judson, *An Account of the American Baptist Mission*, 97–102. For a short extract, see Middleditch, *Burmah's Great Missionary*, 89.

78. Adoniram Judson to Solomon Peck, correspondence, March 16, 1849, Box No.

Judson was not so naïve to think that the New Testament contained a static formula for missionary success. However, he did trust in the Scripture's prescribed means of gospel proclamation. Ultimately, the joy of his missionary piety was not in immediate fruit, but rather, in his expectancy that it all depends upon the will of Christ to make his Word run and triumph. After building the first *zayat* in Rangoon for the purpose of proclaiming the Bible, Judson enthusiastically described this new approach in a letter to Lucius Bolles.[79] He signed off with a hope-filled prayer to Christ that he alone would breathe the miracle of new life into the dry bones of Burma. "On thee, Jesus, all our hopes depend. In thee all power is vested, even power to make sinful creatures instrumental in enlightening the heathen."[80] With seeming undiminished evangelistic eagerness three years later, Judson wrote a letter to his friend and missions mobilizer, Luther Rice,[81] in September 1822. Judson expressed his enduring dependence for the work of Christ's Spirit alone to fill the missionaries in their proclamation efforts and make them "a burning and shining light" in that land of overwhelming darkness. He called on Rice to pray earnestly that the day of God's favor for Burma would come quickly.[82] And two months later in November 1822, in a letter to Daniel Sharp,[83] Judson expressed hope to establish a legal residence in the Burmese capital in order to publish and preach the Scriptures. He imagined that if he could live in such a center of influence and concurrently "enjoy an

---

AJ 4, Folder 2 and Microfilm Roll 1, Judson Letters, ABHS; emphasis in original. For a short extract of this letter, see Wayland, *Memoir*, 2:317–19. Solomon Peck had been the professor of Latin at Amherst College (1825–1832) prior to assuming the position of Secretary of the Baptist Board of Foreign Missions; see Hitchcock, *Reminiscences of Amherst College*, 30.

79. At the time, Lucius Bolles was the Corresponding Secretary of the Board and the pastor of First Baptist Church of Salem. During his change of sentiments on the way to India, Judson wrote to Bolles for financial support, and Bolles commenced a fundraising effort. Bolles was a graduate of Brown University (1801) and a theology student under the pastor of the First Baptist Church of Boston, Samuel Stillman (1737–1807). Bolles was a founding member of the Newton Theological Institution and the pastor of First Baptist Church of Salem, Massachusetts. See Stillman, *A Sermon, Preached January 9, 1805*; Sharp, *Christian Mourning*.

80. Adoniram Judson, "Extract of a Letter from Mr. Judson, to One of the Editors, Rangoon, Feb. 20, 1819," 215.

81. For a description of Rice's mobilization success, see Lincoln and Wayland, *A Memoir of the Life*, 53–55; and see Torbet, *A History of the Baptists*, 331.

82. Middleditch, *Burmah's Great Missionary*, 171.

83. Sharp was the pastor of Charles Street Baptist Church in Boston (1812–1853) and one of the founders of the Newton Theological Institution (1825). He published *Recognition of Friends in Heaven*. See also Sharp, *Services at the Fortieth Anniversary*.

ordinary measure of the Holy Spirit, the Christian religion will be gradually introduced—at least, that some precious souls will be rescued and saved."[84]

Slow Gospel Growth

While Judson knew that Scripture dissemination was slow work, he was equally certain that the disseminated Word would bear fruit in time, though it be "after trying the faith and sincerity of his servants, some fifteen or twenty years."[85] Sensing dissatisfaction among people back home because of how prolonged the mission work seemed, he wrote to Luther Rice in August of 1816. Judson recounted his hard work and sense of duty for the conversion of the Burmans. He defended the slow growth of Word-sowing, that it was not his work to manipulate, but it was God's work to operate. He said there were many instances in other fields where the seemingly fruitlessness of proclaiming the Word "began to be a shame to the cause of missions." He said to Rice, "if they ask again, what prospect of ultimate success is there?—tell them, as much as there is an Almighty and faithful God who will perform his promises, and no more." He went on to criticize those whose confidence rested in anything but God's supreme and sufficient Word. Judson admitted the hard ground in Burma was a "filthy, wretched place" with no comfort. But, he was so hopeful of God's promises that even if he could live in the world's choicest place instead, he would prefer to die. Expressing his evangelical piety, he concluded, "If we desert it, the blood of the Burmans will be required of us."[86]

---

84. Middleditch, *Burmah's Great Missionary*, 172. In a letter to the missionary printer, Cephas Bennett, in November 1830, Judson expressed similar conviction that the Scriptures are essential for the salvation of souls, see Adoniram Judson, "Baptist Foreign Mission," 279. Then Judson wrote another letter to Bennett in March of 1831 to update him about the progress of Judson's tract distribution. See Wayland, *Memoir*, 1:520–21.

85. Adoniram Judson, "Extract of a Letter from Rev. Mr. Judson, to Dr. Baldwin, Dated Rangoon, August 5, 1816," 99. From his own experience, Judson understood that the influence of Scripture did not always produce immediate results. Though he grew up under a passionate father (Adoniram Judson Sr.), who was a pastor trained under the New Divinity Men, Judson did not become a Christian until 1808, after he had graduated as a Deist from Brown University. However, from a very young age the Bible had influenced him: "At three years of age, Judson, taught to read by his mother, read a chapter in the Bible to his father. At four years of age he gathered the neighboring children and preached to them." Gifford, *Adoniram Judson*, 5.

86. Adoniram Judson, "Extract of a Letter from Mr. Judson to Mr. Rice, Rangoon, August 3d, 1816," 184; emphasis in original.

With equal conviction, a few weeks later Judson wrote to Thomas Baldwin. With no exciting news to share, he persevered in his duty to study and to translate, knowing that a Burmese Bible would be the best missionary. He exclaimed,

> I have no doubt that God is preparing the way for the conversion of Burmah to his Son. Nor have I any doubt that we who are now here are, in some little degree, contributing to this glorious event. This thought fills me with joy. I know not that I shall live to see a single convert: but, notwithstanding, I feel that I would not leave my present situation to be made a king.[87]

Apologetics and Evangelism

Judson resolutely upheld the Bible as the supreme fountain of truth in evangelism and discipleship. A Buddhist teacher, Moung Shwa-gnong, was debating with Judson about the validity of the Christian gospel, and he told Judson that he could not adhere to a religion whose king would allow his son to undergo such humiliation. Judson's account of the controversy exemplifies his unswerving allegiance to the Bible, and it illustrates his own evangelistic method of Bible-based apologetics.[88] After much debate over some tracts and the Gospel of Matthew, Judson said in direct terms that he was not a true disciple of Christ. He reasoned, "A true disciple inquires not whether a fact is agreeable to his own reason, but, whether it is in the book. His pride has yielded to divine testimony. Teacher, your pride is still unbroken. Break down your pride, and yield to the word of God." Subsequently,

---

87. Wayland, *Memoir*, 1:192.

88. Judson's Bible-based evangelistic methods held that the Bible is God's self-revelation, and from that biblical worldview alone can the evangelist authoritatively reason for God. This is not to say that Judson was a strict Presuppositionalist according to the terms of contemporary apologetics (an apologetic theory propounded by Reformed theologian, Cornelius Van Til [1895–1987], in the twentieth century; see Van Til, *A Survey of Christian Epistemology*, 200–210); Judson was, rather, an Edwardsean evangelist. He did indeed employ reason in his apologetic methods. In fact, he often reasoned his case for Christianity in comparison and contrast with Buddhist theology. For a classic example of this, see Adoniram Judson, *The Golden Balance*. The church historian Holifield aptly describes the Edwardsean view on reason and revelation: "The Edwardseans espoused the familiar conviction that the 'best and more sure guide' for the theologian was scriptural revelation. They assumed that reason could demonstrate some religious truths—such as the existence of an omnipotent God—but they continued to believe that revelation stood above reason, offering truths that reason alone could not attain. And they used the common 'evidences' to prove that 'the Scriptures are a revelation inspired of God.'" Holifield, *Theology in America*, 135–36.

the teacher later replied that he saw the error of trusting in his reason alone. He admitted his belief in Christ's crucifixion "because it is contained in the Scripture."[89] To Judson, this was a sign of life because it demonstrated spiritual awakening to the revelation of the Scriptures.

Judson valued the written Word so much that he refused to "waste" tracts by just handing them out without the recipients demonstrating interest.[90] In 1831, after the Shway Dagon festival, in a letter of thanks to James Grow (1769–1859), a pastor in Thompson, Connecticut, who donated fifty dollars to Judson's work,[91] Judson expressed his confidence in the sufficiency of the written Word to convert souls into Christ's kingdom. He said he had given away ten thousand tracts, but only to those who requested them. People traveled for three months from Siam and China and from a hundred miles north of the capitol because they had heard that Judson was the man who gave away writings about how to escape the eternal hell. They asked him, "Are you Jesus Christ's man? Give us a writing that tells about Jesus Christ." He lamented in the letter that he felt so worn out because of how many thousands of individuals from hundreds of miles away were trav-

---

89. Clément, *Memoir of Adoniram Judson*, 83–84, quoted also in Edward Judson, *The Life of Adoniram Judson*, 142; Conant, *The Earnest Man*, 223–24; and Wayland, *Memoir*, 1:241–42. In the *Burma Baptist Chroncile*, Maung Shwe Wa said this about Judson's method and message: "These tracts had served two purposes; they stirred up interest in the new religious teacher [Judson] and brought many people to the *zayat* to hear more. Then the Gospel of Matthew and tracts presenting the basis of the Christian faith served as follow-up for those who had visited the *zayat* and were interested in carrying the subject further. The whole basis of Judson's approach was person-to-person teaching in an informal atmosphere . . . The Gospel he preached was that there is an Eternal God who is not subject to change or decay, whose children we are; that in not recognizing and obeying him, man is guilty of sin; that all men are sinners and as such will suffer in hell in the future life; but that God, being love, sent his son, Jesus Christ, into the world to save sinners, with the result that those who believe on him and follow his commands may lead changed lives and share in his great merit and look forward to a happy life in heaven." Shwe Wa, *Burma Baptist Chronicle*, 39–40.

90. In a letter to Francis Wayland after Judson's death, Emily C. Judson said that he modified his view of Bible distribution later in life because he saw the Old Testament as requiring a teacher so that people could understand clearly the Old Testament's complexities; nevertheless, Judson viewed the gospel accounts as perspicuous and efficacious for evangelistic distribution. She said that he had observed some Burmans who were lazy and did not wish to preach the gospel, so they just gave Bibles to people who would never read them. This grieved him because they wasted valuable literature. He said this was because they were simply lethargic and lacking urgency to expound the gospel. Of all his distributions, Judson saw the most conversions among those who read his translation of Matthew and his tracts, *A View of the Christian Religion* and *The Golden Balance*. For Emily's letter, see Edward Judson, *The Life of Adoniram Judson*, 411–13.

91. See an account of the donation in Bayles, *History of Windham County*, 677.

eling to Ava just to receive literature about the good news of Jesus Christ. Judson believed that the coming glory of Christ's millennial kingdom would increasingly materialize to the extent that he could spread abroad tracts and Bibles.[92]

After being harassed by the Burmese government because of a false rumor that he was a British spy, Judson left for Prome in June of 1830. He reflected upon his arrival at Prome and noted that the inhabitants of Prome, being founded hundreds of years before Christ, had perished without one gospel witness up until the day Judson set foot there. Every day for over three months in the heart of the city, he would preach the gospel in their native tongue. Even though he did not see a great revival of religion, he deeply believed that God "ordered that a missionary of the Cross . . . [would] pour forth Divine truth" for a people languishing in darkness. Thousands had heard the gospel truth, but there were no immediate revivals of religion. Now, the residents of Prome were accountable for the gospel light which Judson had distributed through preaching and tract distribution, which would increase their misery on Judgment Day if they continued in their rebellion. Judson interpreted his seemingly fruitless evangelistic efforts in Prome "with less dissatisfaction" than any period of his ministry until then. Even in his "unsuccessful" evangelism, he was satisfied because he had evangelized for God's glory. Upon reflection, he rejoiced,

> What a wonderful phenomenon must this have been to celestial beings, who gaze upon the works and dispensations of God in this lower world! It was necessary to the accomplishment of the Divine purpose that, after so many centuries of darkness, there should be such an exhibition of light as has been made, and no more. Thousands have heard of God who never, nor their ancestors, heard before.[93]

In time, the local authorities became suspicious of Judson, so they threatened any serious Burmese inquirers and forced Judson to leave Prome.

---

92. Adoniram Judson, "Mr. Judson's Letter to Rev. Mr. Grow," 31–32; and Middleditch, *Burmah's Great Missionary*, 273–74. For his journal entry on March 4, 1831 that corresponded to his exhaustion expressed in this letter, see Adoniram Judson, journal, February 28, 1831 to March 4, 1831, Box No. AJ 4, Folder 2 and Microfilm Roll 1, Judson Letters, ABHS; see also Adoniram Judson, "Extracts from Mr. Judson's Journal, to Rev. Dr. Bolles, Rangoon, Feb. 28, 1831 [to March 4, 1831]," 374. Judson also wrote a letter on that same day to Sarah Boardman, regarding the recent death of her husband, George Boardman. See Edward Judson, *The Life of Adoniram Judson*, 374–75; and King, *Memoir of George Dana Boardman*, 293–309. See also Robbins, *Boardman of Burma*, 144–59.

93. Wayland, *Memoir*, 1:502–3.

Upon his departure, he left knowing that he had done all he could. His soul was satisfied because his evangelism was ultimately for God and he trusted the power of God's Word to convert. He bid Prome farewell and implored the inhabitants to consult the written Word in the absence of his preaching. He departed, saying, "Read the five hundred tracts that I have left with thee. Pray to the God and Saviour that I have told thee of."[94]

Conclusion

This chapter has shown that the written Word of God was the ground in which Adoniram Judson's missionary spirituality grew. The commands he read in the Bible to go proclaim the gospel to all creatures fueled his piety and devotion to pleasing Christ. The supreme and sufficient Word was the burning and shining golden lamp from heaven that guided his evangelical piety. In Judson's spirituality and theology, the Bible was a summons from the King that demanded earnest proclamation through oral preaching, translation, publication, and dissemination. Judson was a preacher at heart, and the evangelical fire that burned in his bones found its release through preaching the translated written Word of God. Allegiance to Christ's command to be baptized was the first step of assurance of genuine conversion. The Scriptures were sufficient for the aim of converting souls to the reign of King Jesus, which was the bibliocentric heart-cry of Adoniram Judson. Seeking to submissively do his duty to God and please Christ, Judson went "forward, preaching the Gospel, and distributing bibles and tracts in every possible way, and in every language under heaven."[95]

---

94. Smith, *Missionary Sketches*, 66–67.
95. Middleditch, *Burmah's Great Missionary*, 312.

4

"Thy Will Be Ever Done": Ascetic Spirituality

JOHN N. MURDOCK (1820–1897), Secretary of the American Baptist Missionary Union (1863–1892), spoke thus at a centennial address (1888) in Adoniram Judson's honor:

> From the day that he accepted Christ as his Saviour, he also accepted the law of service. Having been bought with a price, he belonged henceforth to his Master, and gave himself up to obey His Word and do His will. This sense of loyalty to Christ led to the effort which he made, in company with others, to organize a society for foreign missions . . . This sustained him in the face of difficulties, rendered him superior alike to ridicule and reproach, and held him steadily to the one end he had set before him, as at once the guide and inspiration of his life . . . He stood, as a soldier of Christ, on a forlorn hope, not counting his life dear unto himself, that he might finish the ministry he had received of the Lord Jesus, to testify the gospel of the grace of God to the heathen.[1]

As Murdock maintained, under the weight of incredible affliction, grief, and despair, Judson's staying power was *sui generis*. Judson, in his dying moments, reflected on his long endurance in the hardships of his missionary service, and fittingly cried, "Oh, how few there are who suffer such great torment—who die so hard!"[2] This chapter contends for an all-consuming

---

1. Murdock, "Memorial Address," 15. Murdock was famous for a sermon he gave regarding the American Civil War (1861–1865). See Murdock, *Our Civil War*.

2. Middleditch, *Burmah's Great Missionary*, 428. See also Wayland, *Memoir*, 2:352.

vision of God's sovereignty in Judson's piety. In order to understand his uncommon resilience, it is necessary to consider how Judson's submission to God's sovereign will formed his view of suffering, his consecration to duty, and the centrality of self-denial and asceticism in his spirituality. His ambition to please the infinitely wise God led him to renounce all things for the duty to which he was devoted.

Submitting to the Sovereign Will of God

Adoniram Judson's spiritual formation had its roots in the Calvinism of New Divinity theology. His was an evangelical Calvinism, which was manifest in the Edwardsean *ethos* of Judson's New Divinity father and in the Hopkinsian *pathos* of his New Divinity training at Andover Theological Seminary. God-centeredness pervaded Judson's life, and through it he interpreted every experience, whether in pain or in pleasure, as redounding to the glory of God. Judson humbly submitted to God in risk, affliction, grief, and death. He claimed no rights over God; his chief plea before God was "Thy will be done."

Judson's God-Centered God

From early in his spirituality, Judson had an Edwardsean vision of how enjoyment of God would be ever increasing. Because God is effulgent and infinite in himself, his glory is limitless and therefore the Christian's happiness in God's glory is limitless.[3] In a letter in October of 1810 to Abigail Hasseltine (b. 1788), the sister of his first wife, Ann Hasseltine, Judson sketched his meditations of what it means to be a "lover of Jesus." He said that "love to Jesus" partakes in the genuine spiritual blessings both now and in eternity, and it describes superlative happiness. There is no greater happiness than in loving Jesus because Jesus has supreme control over everything. He said that Jesus has promised happiness to his friends, and his happiness will fill them to capacity; it will be neither partial, nor temporal. With eager expectation of eternal joy, Judson went on to propose:

> Nor does he intend a happiness eternally stationary. It will be eternally increasing ... As their capacities will be eternally enlarging, the quantity of happiness they enjoy will be eternally

---

3. Judson's descriptions of heaven and rewards sound reminiscent to Jonathan Edwards's treatment of heaven and eternal happiness in God. See Edwards, *Works*, 2:243–46.

increasing; and not merely eternally increasing in the same ratio, but eternally increasing in an eternally accelerated ratio. So that there will unquestionably arrive a moment in the ages of eternity when the additional happiness, that instant superadded to the happiness already enjoyed by each glorified spirit, will almost infinitely outweigh the whole sum of human happiness enjoyed in this world. To all this may he aspire who is a lover of Jesus. Blessed Jesus, thou art no "niggard provider." When thou givest, thou givest like a God.[4]

Throughout his life, Judson maintained a prominent God-centered piety. In May 1836, for the ordination of S. M. Osgood, Judson preached from John 10:1-18. His sermon illustrated that God was the all-consuming center of his piety and devotion to ministry. Judson discussed the pastoral duties required in imitation to Christ's obedience to the Father. He outlined briefly his enthrallment with God's God-centeredness. He said that it is useless to compare creatures to their Creator, because God is infinite, eternal, perfect, and that God enjoys in every moment more happiness than all creatures can enjoy for all eternity. Judson went on to argue that God is uppermost in his own affections:

> God loves himself, and ought to love himself, infinitely more than he can love, or ought to love, all creatures which have existed or will exist forever . . . What luminaries suspended in the eternity that is past will burst upon our vision when we quit the prison house in which we are now confined; and what new glories we shall see kindling up at each stage of our future happy existence—glories beaming from the divine face, the uncreated sun, the eternal source of all light and glory, forever unveiling to the view of holy beings, yet never, never to be completely unveiled! How infinitely happy must God be in himself, all his infinite attributes ever known and ever enjoyed to full perfection! Herein eminently consists the happiness of God. What is the collective happiness of all creatures in comparison with the happiness of God?[5]

---

4. Wayland, *Memoir*, 1:35-36.

5. Ibid., 2:486-94. This part of his sermon comprises much of his sermon's fourth point. The year after this ordination sermon, in a letter to S. M. Osgood after his wife's three-year battle with a pulmonary illness and eventual death on October 5, 1837, Judson upheld the absolute sovereignty of God in immense pain. See evidence of Judson's unchanging God-centered theology in Adoniram Judson, "Obituary of Mrs. Osgood, Maulmein, Oct. 6, 1837," 119; see also Edward Judson, *The Life of Adoniram Judson*, 521. See also Wayland, *Memoir*, 2:228.

"Thy Will Be Ever Done": Ascetic Spirituality   97

Judson's first tract, *A View of the Christian Religion*, makes clear this vision of God. He contextually delineated a basic doctrine of God for Buddhists, defining God as the true and only eternal One who never tires, ails, or dies. He explained God's Trinitarian nature and divine attributes, and Judson concluded this section expounding on God's eternal joy. Judson wrote, "He is pure and good, and possessed of everlasting felicity. Before this world was made, God remained happy, surrounded by the pure and incorporeal sons of heaven."[6]

Submitting to God in Risk

Appointed as a missionary in 1812, Adoniram Judson prepared to depart for the mission field. Having met Ann in 1810 at the General Association at Bradford when he presented his letter of inquiry for missions,[7] he subsequently cultivated a relationship with her through visits and letters. In preparation for his departure, he sought the approval of Deacon John Hasseltine of Bradford, Ann's father, for his daughter's hand in marriage. Judson's letter to John Hasseltine reveals an unwavering submission to God's providence, even in the face of unknown risk. Judson asked Ann's father to allow Judson to take her overseas, never to see her again, and to endure great hardships, hazards, disease, poverty, anguish, humiliation, persecution, and even a fierce death. He further asked, "Can you consent to all this, for the sake of Him who left his heavenly home, and died for her and for you; for the sake of perishing immortal souls; for the sake of Zion, and the glory of God?" Then he concluded his appeal to her father by rehearsing the prospects of Ann's eternal reward in the joy of bringing many heathen to the Savior, saving them from eternal torment.[8] Judson and Ann were married at Bradford, on February 5, 1812, and left for the mission field a week later.

---

6. Adoniram Judson, *A View of the Christian Religion*, 1. See also McElroy, *Adoniram Judson's Soul Winning Secrets Revealed*, 23. Judson's basic Theology Proper was outlined in *A Digest of Scripture*. In this tract he cited numerous scriptural proof texts. The sections in his chapter, "The Being and Attributes of God," are: (1) He is a Spirit; (2) He is Eternal and Unchangeable; (3) He Dwells in Heaven, and is also Omnipresent; (4) He is Omniscient; (5) He is Omnipotent; (6) He is Glorious; (7) He is Ever Blessed; (8) He is Righteous and Holy; (9) He is Benevolent; (10) He is the Creator of All Things; (11) He is the Sovereign Controller of All Things; (12) He is the Just Dispenser of Rewards and Punishment; (13) He is Merciful and Forgiving; (14) He is Incomprehensible. See Adoniram Judson, *A Digest of Scripture*, 8–21.

7. To read Judson's letter of inquiry and the minutes of the assembly, see Worcester, "Minutes of the General Association," 86–90.

8. Clement, *Memoir of Adoniram Judson*, 25; Edward Judson, *The Life of Adoniram Judson*, 20; Middleditch, *Burmah's Great Missionary*, 38. Though not from the journal

One major event in Judson's ministry thoroughly demonstrates his submission to God in risk; this was when he personally beseeched the despotic king of Burma. The reason that this singular episode is so illustrative is that Judson wrote many journal entries and letters during this time. Unlike other trying cases, the legal longevity of his mission in Burma was at stake. Judson's anxiety was high. After the transition of monarchs at the end of 1819, the missionaries feared that the newly instated king, a zealous Buddhist, would revive religious persecution for all those non-Buddhists. Burma, already a despotic empire, did not take long to follow the ruthless devotion to Buddhism of its new monarch. It became illegal to promote or adhere to any religion besides Buddhism. Aware of impending persecution and intolerance, Judson wrote to Thomas Baldwin, in December of 1819.[9] He was contemplating a visit in the New Year to the monarch to plead for toleration. Judson wrote that he felt like Esther approaching Ahasuerus,[10] and if the king were to deny religious toleration, the mission's hopes would be lost. He said, "O what a trying case! None can know or experience the uncertainties and anxieties of our present situation. But we sometimes rest on the Saviour, and derive sweet consolation from the assurance that our Jesus will do all things well."[11]

---

of Judson himself, Ann's journal entry indeed represents their common agreement about the reality of pain and their like-minded trust in God's providence. In a journal entry from April 16, 1815, Ann wrote, "We feel more and more convinced, that the gospel must be introduced into this country, through many trials and difficulties; through much self-denial and earnest prayer . . . But all things are possible with God, and he is our only hope and confidence." Ann Hasseltine Judson, *An Account of the American Baptist Mission*, 28; see also Wayland, *Memoir*, 1:169–70. In the following year, 1816, the Judsons suffered the loss of their young son, Roger. Ann's reflection on God's wise providence in suffering reveals the submissive spirituality of the grief-stricken Judsons: "Eight months we enjoyed the precious little gift . . . But God has taught us by afflictions what we would not learn by mercies—that our hearts are his exclusive property, and that whatever rival intrudes, he will tear it away." Knowles, *Memoir of Mrs. Ann H. Judson*, 122. See also Middleditch, *Burmah's Great Missionary*, 108–9.

9. Thomas Baldwin of the Second Baptist church in Boston baptized Judson's colleague, James Colman in 1805. See Collier, *Colman and Wheelock*, 11. See also Chessman, *Memoir of Rev. Thomas Baldwin*, 10–12. See Anderson, *To the Golden Shore*, 202–3; and Hunt, *Bless God and Take Courage*, 268–69. Judson and Colman subsequently left Rangoon on December 21, 1819 for Ava to see the king; see Edward Judson, *The Life of Adoniram Judson*, 564.

10. See Esth 4:16.

11. Adoniram Judson to the Rev. Thomas Baldwin, letter, December 9, 1819, Box No. AJ 1, Folder 2 and Microfilm Roll 1, Judson Letters, ABHS; see also Adoniram Judson, "Letter from the Rev. Adoniram Judson, Jun. to Dr. Baldwin, Dated Rangoon, December 9, 1819," 379–80; Middleditch, *Burmah's Great Missionary*, 134.

After the new monarch took power, Judson resolved to go to his throne and plead for favor for the missionaries to continue their work without interruption and trouble. He had not yet experienced persecution, but the Burmans were afraid to listen to Judson's words because of the possible vengeance of the king. Judson described his trust in God's sovereign purposes in the risk he was taking:

> If the Lord has other purposes, it becomes us meekly to acquiesce, and willingly to sacrifice our dearest hopes to the Divine will. We rest assured that, in either case, the perfections of God will be displayed, and desire to be thankful that we are allowed to be in any way instrumental in contributing to that display.[12]

In January of 1820, Judson and his missionary companion, James Colman, arrived at the emperor's palace. The night before approaching the monarch, Judson recorded his quiet trust and humble submission to God's sovereign will despite his anxiety. He wrote in his journal that he was sleepless throughout the night, and the only comfort he knew was surrendering his missionary labor into his heavenly Father's hands. With a spirit of disinterested benevolence, Judson conceded:

> The work is his, not ours; that the heart of the monarch before whom we are to appear, is under the control of Omnipotence; and that the event will be ordered in the manner most conducive to the divine glory and the greatest good. God may, for the wisest purposes, suffer our hopes to be disappointed; and if so, why should short-sighted, mortal man repine? Thy will, O God, be ever done; for thy will is inevitably the wisest and the best.[13]

The monarch did not grant them their request, yet Judson still refused to give up his work. In his journal in February of 1820, he wrestled with whether it would be wise to leave their post or to stay and risk persecution, whether to leave the Burmese disciples or to stay and risk them being thrown in prison and tortured or be tortured himself. He stood firm, saying that he knew God would gather his elect, even through the most severe trials. He described his hope in God as "the angry gleam of lightning around, discloses the black magazines of heaven's artillery, and threatens death to the unwary gazer."[14]

---

12. Middleditch, *Burmah's Great Missionary*, 134–37. See also Wayland, *Memoir*, 1:244.

13. Conant, *The Earnest Man*, 240. See also Wayland, *Memoir*, 1:253.

14. Middleditch, *Burmah's Great Missionary*, 145–46. See also Wayland, *Memoir*, 1:264–65.

Submitting to God in Affliction

Judson viewed his accumulated afflictions with solemnity. Nothing was by coincidence, and there were no accidents. He believed that God was in control of everything, and furthermore, God had purposes for Judson's usefulness and God's glory.

No other time in Judson's life was more physically excruciating than when he was in prison for 21 months (June 8, 1824—December 30, 1825). Surveying this season of imprisonment and torture reveals to what degree he truly trusted in God and surrendered to his sovereign will. Having been bound and tortured in horrific conditions, Judson wrote to the Corresponding Secretary of the American Baptist Board, Lucius Bolles, about how he trusted that his sufferings would work for his good. He said that his sufferings "have been unavailing to answer any valuable missionary purpose, unless so far as they may have been silently blessed to our spiritual improvement and capacity for future usefulness."[15]

While in prison, he suffered in the company of an Anglo-Indian merchant, Henry Gouger. In his narrative of their imprisonment, Gouger recorded Judson's submission to God's painful providences. He said Judson was mentally distraught for Ann's situation. Despite her own sickness, Ann cared for Judson, and concurrently little Maria was ill. The gravity of this tribulation pushed the Judson family to despair.[16] Gouger also recalled that Judson's "painful sensitiveness to anything gross or uncleanly . . . made him live a life of constant martyrdom." He described Judson as deeply religious. For Gouger the evidence of Judson's profound spirituality was the fact that he constantly "referred every trial and suffering to the will of God, and in exercising a perfect resignation to His dispensations." Gouger mentioned that Judson greatly admired the "calm and placid spirit" of Madame Guyon. Judson often quoted some of her simple verses, Gouger said, with a deep longing "to attain the spirit of them." Judson would often repeat these lines:

> No bliss I seek, but to fulfil
> In life, in death, Thy lovely will;
> No succour in my woes I want,

---

15. Wayland, *Memoir*, 2:420; Middleditch, *Burmah's Great Missionary*, 209. For a similar statement he made in a letter to the missionaries in Maulmain on January 25, 1831, see Wayland, *Memoir*, 1:516.

16. Recording her own submission to the sovereignty of God, Ann wrote, "Had it not been for the consolations of religion, and an assured conviction that every additional trial was ordered by infinite love and mercy, I must have sunk under my accumulated sufferings." Knowles, *The Memoir of Mrs. Ann H. Judson*, 250–51. See also Wayland, *Memoir*, 1:361.

> Except what Thou art pleased to grant.
> Our days are number'd—let us spare
> Our anxious hearts a needless care;
> 'Tis Thine to number out our days,
> And ours to give them to Thy praise.[17]

More than anything, Gouger remembered Judson's self-denying, submissive piety to God's will. Judson's words during those tortuous months revealed what was in his heart. In his frequent recitations of Guyon's writings, the major inspiration of Judson's ascetic spirituality began to materialize.[18]

In addition to Judson's prison narrative, it is revealing to see his perspective on affliction later in life. A couple of years after his imprisonment, Judson had been suffering with severe illnesses. Writing to Thomas Baldwin in February of 1828, Judson recounted these in light of God's inscrutable ways. While he resided in Ava, he was plagued with fever and ague. He moved, therefore, to Rangoon to get away from the climate of Ava, hoping it would help. He explored every medical solution available, and though he wanted to finish the New Testament and see a church planted in Ava, he conceded, "the ways of God are not as the ways of man. He does all things well. Glory be to his holy name forevermore."[19]

After his death, Judson's widow, Emily, wrote some anecdotes and sketches of his piety and missionary devotion. It is helpful to read her narration of his unscripted, unplanned responses to situations and conversations that he never wrote down. She rehearsed Judson's consecrated submission to God's divine right to use a minister at his pleasure and his divine right to end the minister's labor whenever he saw fit. Judson admitted that some people would think it bizarre that God would not let him live to finish the dictionary. Yet, he retorted that it would be actually peculiar if God were to permit him to finish it. Judson explained that all men leave some work unfinished that they or others consider critically important. He said, God does this in order to show us "what really worthless creatures we are, and how altogether unnecessary, as active agents, in the working out of his plans."[20]

---

17. Guyon, *Poems*, 50.
18. See Gouger, *A Personal Narrative*, 174–75.
19. Middleditch, *Burmah's Great Missionary*, 178. See also Wayland, *Memoir*, 1:324. Judson still maintained the same trust in God's meticulous providence nineteen years later. On January 28, 1847, in a letter to his third wife, Emily C. Judson. He said, "God orders all things well—the comforts and the discomforts, the bitter and the sweet, of this short, flitting life . . . If we give up all to God, he will take care of us, and bring light out of darkness, and good out of evil, I do believe; and we shall praise him forever, that he led us through some dark ways in his blessed service." Wayland, *Memoir*, 2:275–76.
20. Wayland, *Memoir*, 2:366.

Emily also recorded a short story of some women who were talking about the sailors being superstitious about transporting missionaries. They believed that God took extra special care of his clergymen, so they saw the missionaries as good luck. One lady said to Judson that she herself believed that God favorably "exercises peculiar care over his people," to which Judson remarked,

> True; so "though he slay me, yet will I trust in him [Job 13:15];" not because I have wrought myself into an unwarrantable belief that he will carry me over smooth waters. He may cast us in a burning fiery furnace, or precipitate us to the lowest depths of the sea, but his care, his tenderness, his love, are still the same.[21]

Emily went on to illustrate Judson's God-centered submissive piety by describing a story of Judson's response to the loss of some missionaries onboard a ship to their missionary destination. He had recruited them during his time back in the United States, and he felt a warm affection for them. Emily said he wept upon hearing the news. He refused to speak of the sad event as though God were unwise or impotent. Someone said that this tragedy would demotivate many from supporting missions. Though Judson initially rejected such a possibility, after a few moments he acknowledged that such a deflated reaction among supporters were possible. Emily said that Judson turned away and was quiet for a few moments. And then he rejoined with a spirit of disinterested benevolence:

> O, when will Christians learn . . . that their puny, polluted offerings of works are not necessary to God? He permits them to work, as a favor, in order to do them good, personally, because he loves them, and desires to honor them, not because he needs them.

He went on to uphold that God would have lost nothing if he sovereignly removed one of his workers, even his best worker, from the harvest field. He said Christians are distraught when the absolutely sovereign God, who has innumerable resources for his disposal, removes one tool. Judson said that God deals with his servants for their own spiritual improvement, and his final purpose is to prepare them individually for eternity. God takes his servants home when he has sufficiently fashioned them for the position that he has formed them to fulfill in eternity.[22]

Emily recalled that Judson never spoke of serving God as a right or something of which he was worthy. Conversely, he spoke tenderly of his

---

21. Ibid.
22. Ibid., 2:366–68.

unworthiness in Christ's service and the kindness of Christ having permitted him to do even a small thing for Christ's name. Judson not only deeply felt his unworthiness of salvation, but he also knew how undeserving he was to bear the gospel to the nations. She said he passionately prayed that he would be faithful to devote his whole life to labor and self-denial.[23]

Submitting to God in Grief

In order to understand how Judson's spirituality functioned in his grief, it is very illuminating to survey his reflections on occasions of great disappointment, and seasons of grave sorrow. More than his physical afflictions, the most pernicious trials he experienced were unbearable sorrows and disappointments.

Judson trusted in God's wisdom and providential hand in every kind of ministry setback and disappointment. Emily noted that he asserted,

> Our obedience was not to be yielded grudgingly; that it must be a cheerful acquiescence in all that God had done, and a sincere, careful study of the indications of his providence afterwards, without any suspicion that our ways were hedged by any thing harder or thornier than his love and mercy.[24]

For instance, during the aforementioned event of beseeching the Burman monarch for religious toleration, in January of 1820, the king looked at Judson's Bible translation, read his gospel tract,[25] and then blatantly rejected Judson's wishes, dismissing him without any hope of future governmental toleration. The next day as he headed home, Judson recorded his trust in God's purposes. Though he experienced the grief of disappointment, he still rested in God's sovereign wisdom. In his journal he rehearsed these lines from the English poet, John Milton (1608–1674):

> Some natural tears we dropped, but wiped them soon;
> The world was all before us, where to choose
> Our place of rest, and Providence our guide.[26]

After traveling for three days, eight miles each day, in the oppressive heat, in his journal he scribbled out all the things that were grievous and

---

23. Ibid., 2:368.

24. Emily wrote this in a note to Wayland, not intending for him to publish it, though he said that he took responsibility for choosing to do so. See ibid., 2:303.

25. Adoniram Judson, *A View of the Christian Religion*.

26. These are the closing lines of Book XII in Milton, *Paradise Lost*, 317.

burdensome about taking such a risk and traveling so far. After listing out what was so discouraging to him, he stopped abruptly in the middle of his sentence, and instead of ending with a final complaint, he said the outcome of such toil had been,

> —the wisest and best possible; a result which if we could see the end from the beginning, would call forth our highest praise. O, slow of heart to believe and trust in the constant presence and overruling agency of our own almighty Saviour.[27]

He concluded his litany of laments by yielding to God's wise and perfect will. In light of this setback, in March of 1820, he concluded a letter explaining the weary situation to Thomas Baldwin:

> We are fully confident that the events which have lately happened to us will turn out to the furtherance of the Gospel. The ways of God are not like the ways of man. It becomes us, not only to acquiesce, but to rejoice evermore.[28]

Having returned to Burma from America, in March of 1847, Judson and Emily were traveling to another city. While they were gone, their house

---

27. Conant, *The Earnest Man*, 240–41; Wayland, *Memoir*, 1:258–59.

28. Middleditch, *Burmah's Great Missionary*, 148. In response the monarch's religious intolerance, Ann likewise well illustrated their mutual submission to God's will: "We wish to leave it all with God, who has so often appeared for us, when we had given up all hope from every other quarter. If he has a work for us to do here, he will provide ways and means for our continuance ... We feel it good to trust in him, endeavoring to perform present duty, and leaving it with him to provide for the future. In our present situation we often feel the preciousness of this passage: 'Commit thy way unto the Lord; trust also in him; and he shall bring it to pass [Ps 37:5].' We are enabled to commit our ways to him, and claim his promises to direct us. If we know anything of our hearts, we have but one prevailing wish—to live and die among the Burmans, either here or elsewhere; and we feel no affliction in this world could equal that of being denied this privilege." Ibid., 149. Ten years later the Burmese government began to think Judson was a spy for the British, and those to whom he had long been preaching and teaching kept avoiding him on account of this rumor. Under the great discouragement of so many abandoning his *zayat*-preaching ministry, he submitted to God's wise providence in hope that some would still be saved. In July of 1830, he wrote that he felt "extremely dejected" and he said that he had never wanted to enter his heavenly rest more than at that moment. Yet in spite of his melancholy and despondency, he said that he was still willing to spend himself and be spent for "the Lord Jesus Christ, to do and to suffer whatever he shall appoint." He hoped that through his distress some would find "the way of salvation through a crucified Saviour." Ibid., 259. See also Wayland, *Memoir*, 1:495. Wayland recorded, "He built a *zayat* by the wayside, and proclaimed these truths to every passer by [sic]. No one paid any attention to his message; but Christ had commanded him to preach the gospel to every creature, and therefore he continued preaching. The more discouraging his prospects became, the more earnestly he fasted and prayed for the coming of the Holy Spirit." Wayland, *Memoir*, 2:387.

in Maulmain burned down, destroying all of their best clothing, books, letters, journals, gifts from America, and many of his manuscripts; the exception was the New Testament. He wrote a letter to E. A. Stevens, the fellow missionary who helped Judson edit and revise the Burmese Bible. In the letter, Judson did not accuse God of cruelty, callousness, or capriciousness; rather, he surrendered to God's infinite wisdom and love in the loss of all his earthly belongings, save the clothes on his back and the New Testament manuscripts. He asked the obvious questions of why God would permit Judson's time to be lost, his property to burn up, and his missionary colleagues who had such a command of the Burmese language to have died beforehand so that now he would not be able to access their learned knowledge. To these questions he swiftly asserted with the *pathos* of disinterested benevolence:

> Because infinite wisdom and love would have it so. Because it is best for us and best for them and best for the cause and best for the interests of eternity that it should be so. And blessed be God—we know it and are thankful and rejoice in it. Glory to God.[29]

Then, three days later, in a letter to the treasurer of the General Convention, Heman Lincoln (1821–1887), Judson said that "all our best clothes and valuables gone. But it is doubtless for the best." He affirmed that

> *God is great.* He sitteth on the heavens, he setteth his foot on the earth, and the inhabitants are as grasshoppers before him. He dwelleth also in the humble and contrite soul; and the rays of indwelling glory appear more resplendent, gleaming through the chinks of the humble tenement. O for that humility and contrition, O for that simplicity of faith, which will secure the indwelling glory! . . . God is not only "great," but good. God is love.[30]

---

29. Adoniram Judson to E. A. Stevens, letter, March 11, 1847, Papers, 1811–1888, Trask Library Special Collections, Newton Centre, Massachusetts. In an earlier letter to E. A. Stevens on March 2, 1847 after hearing of the fire, Judson quoted Job 1:21, which says, "The Lord gave and the Lord hath taken away; blessed be the name of the Lord." And then he said, "My heart overflows with gratitude, and my eyes with tears, as I pen these precious inspired words." He went on to say that the truths of the following poem were more precious than any earthly possession. He said, "Blessed be God for all, For all things here below; For every loss and every cross, To my advantage grow." Adoniram Judson to E. A. Stevens, letter, March 2, 1847, Papers, 1811–1888, Trask Library Special Collections, Newton Centre, Massachusetts. See also Wayland, *Memoir*, 2:278. For a brief account of this fire and its surrounding events, see Edward Judson, *The Life of Adoniram Judson*, 502–4. See also Wayland, *Memoir*, 2:277–81. For another account, see Stevens, *A Half-Century in Burma*, 15–16.

30. Adoniram Judson to Heman Lincoln, letter, March 14, 1847, Papers, 1811–1888,

In addition to his submission to God in the disappointments of ministry, the loss of loved ones, especially his first wife, Ann, uncovered the substance of Judson's faith. After Ann's death (on October 24, 1826), Judson visited the physician who attended her in her dying moments. Discovering the pervasiveness of her pain and the quality of her faith in her dying hours, Judson wrote to Ann's mother, Rebecca Barton Hasseltine (1761–1846). His surrender to the wise providence of God was manifest in this letter. He recounted his wife's "long-protracted sufferings." She endured them with "meekness, and patience, and magnanimity, and Christian fortitude." Then he said he would not have wished her sufferings to be less lest she lose the eternal enjoyment of her rest and reward for her sufferings. He admitted that God took her when she was most useful in Christ's service and most needed for her husband and her child. However, Judson professed his trust that "infinite wisdom and love have presided, as ever, in this most afflicting dispensation. Faith decides that it is all right, and the decision of faith eternity will soon confirm."[31] Judson's own experience of trusting God's sovereignty in his grief helped him counsel others. In 1833, he wrote a letter to comfort the inconsolable Stella Bennett, whose husband and children set sail for America. He composed a short poem:

> Sovereign love appoints the measure
> And number of our pains,
> And is pleased when we take pleasure
> In the trials he ordains.[32]

Almost twenty years after Ann's death, Judson's second wife, Sarah Boardman Judson, became terribly ill. He would again know the sorrow of a departed helpmate. Receiving advice to set sail to a northern climate to recover, Judson felt compelled to attend her voyage, nurse her, and be there in her death. Yet, the greater trial came with deciding what to do with their children during the long voyage. He decided to leave his three youngest children in Burma, not knowing if they would ever see each other again this side of eternity,[33] and he also decided to bring his three eldest children

---

Trask Library Special Collections, Newton Centre, Massachusetts; see also Wayland, *Memoir*, 2:282–83; emphasis in original.

31. Middleditch, *Burmah's Great Missionary*, 227; Wayland, *Memoir*, 1:422–23.

32. Adoniram Judson to Mrs. Bennett, letter, 1833, Box No. AJ 5, Folder 1 and Microfilm Roll 2, ABHS; see also Wayland, *Memoir*, 2:57.

33. Judson's son, Charles, remained in Burma; he died in August 1845, one month before Sarah died in St. Helena. In a touching letter from Judson to his daughter Abby Ann in November 1848, he addressed his submission to God's will in Charley's death; see Adoniram Judson, "Adoniram Judson's Letter to His Daughter Abby Ann," 14. See Edward Judson, *The Life of Adoniram Judson*, 567. Judson made similar comments

back to the United States to leave them with family so they could go to school.[34] Judson noted that "it was so ordered by divine Providence" that on the voyage back to America the ship docked in the port of St. Helena and Sarah died there in September of 1845. After Sarah's death at the port in St. Helena, a minister[35] boarded the ship to console Judson and his children. He described Judson not as speaking in rough dutiful terms to his children, as though they should compose themselves and feel no emotion in light of God's severe providence. Rather, the minister described the grieving Judson as sobbing himself and speaking to his distressed children "in the most consoling language a Christian father's lips could utter."[36]

In one of the last letters he ever wrote, in the final year of his life, Judson maintained a strong God-centered piety in loss. Judson wrote to S. M. Osgood in October 1849, regarding a bereavement in Osgood's life. Judson upheld the meticulous sovereignty of God in that harsh trial, and yet it was the sovereignty of God that gave him hope that such a trial would work for the good of the believer. Judson said that God's purposes, though dark and blurred, would prove bright and clear. Judson commiserated: "We have both

---

about the death of his son, Henry; see Wayland, *Memoir*, 2:177. For another account of Henry's death, see also Adoniram Judson, "Death of His Child, Serampore, June 27, 1841," 54–55.

34. In light of his grave sorrow in leaving behind small children in Burma, he said he sought to esteem Christ above all others and "to face and welcome all [Christ's] appointments." Adoniram Judson to the Rev. Solomon Peck, correspondence, April 13, 1845, Box No. AJ 3, Folder 2 and Microfilm Roll 1, Judson Letters, ABHS; and Adoniram Judson, "Letter of Mr. Judson, Maulmain, April 13, 1845: Sickness of Mrs. Judson," 247–48. See also Middleditch, *Burmah's Great Missionary*, 341–42; and Wayland, *Memoir*, 2:197–98. Judson wrote to Peck again that following September 1845, after Sarah's death (September 1, 1845) in St. Helena. With single-minded devotion to his duty, he did not want to risk his poor health unnecessarily by traveling north in the winter lest he never finish the dictionary. He said, "And though I refuse not to die, I have so much desire, in submission to the will of God, to finish my work in Burmah, that I must confess I am unwilling to expose my poor life, though in other respects of no worth, to any unnecessary hazard." Adoniram Judson to the Rev. Solomon Peck, correspondence, September 1, 1845, Box No. AJ 3, Folder 2 and Microfilm Roll 1, Judson Letters, ABHS. See also Wayland, *Memoir*, 2:202.

35. The Scot, James M'Gregor Bertram (b.1806), previously a pastor in Bristol and a minister with the Ebenezer Christian Missionary Society, became a missionary to the Cape of Good Hope in 1845. For Bertram's moving account of meeting Judson in St. Helena during Sarah's sickness and eventual death, see Hatfield, *St. Helena and The Cape of Good Hope*, 191–96.

36. Ibid., 192. See also Middleditch, *Burmah's Great Missionary*, 349–50; and see Clemént, *Memoir of Adoniram Judson*, 260–62. For a heart-warming poem reflecting on Judson's great endurance amid such loss, see Washburn, "Judson Longing for His Burman Home," 293–94. Washburn also wrote a poem commemorating Sarah Judson; see Washburn, "The Burial at St. Helena," 228–29.

tasted of these bitter cups once and again; we have found them bitter, and we have found them sweet too. Every cup stirred by the finger of God becomes sweet to the humble believer."[37]

Submitting to God in Death

Judson's long life of self-denial and labor ended in a hard death. From the time he set sail in 1812 until his death in 1850, he rarely knew reprieve, recreation, or rest. His dying days reveal the unwavering quality of his God-centered submission. Emily stood by Judson as he suffered during his last days, and when a convalescence voyage proved to be indispensable, Judson, compelled against his wishes, embarked on the voyage. In a letter to the Missionary Union in February of 1850, Judson wrote of his sickness and hopeful recovery. He signed off and entrusted himself to God's wisdom, saying, "May God direct in the path of duty."[38]

During that time, Emily wrote letters and carefully detailed her interaction with him in the few days prior to his final voyage. His hands were too weak to write, so she recorded his words. She noted that he candidly mourned, "This is almost more than I can bear! Was there ever suffering like our suffering?" Judson's health quickly started to decline. He was anxious to get out to sea before it was too late to reverse his illness. The pain was so great that he hardly talked, but Emily said that in those last days he would look at her with a smile and rejoice aloud in Christ's love. As she cared for him day and night, one night he turned to her and said, "This will never do. You are killing yourself for me, and I will not permit it. You must have someone to relieve you. If I had not been made selfish by suffering, I should have insisted upon it long ago." Judson went on to say to her, "I think I know why this illness has been sent upon me; I needed it; I feel that it has done me good; and it is my impression that I shall now recover, and be a better and more useful man." To which Emily asked if he wished to recover. Judson replied that if God would permit, he would like to finish the dictionary because of how much time he had labored on it. He said that he felt like God had brought him through his whole life and labor to this point just to prepare him to be useful. Though at this juncture he realized that he might not finish the dictionary, which meant he would never get to preach as much as he had wished, yet he still hoped in God. Emily then told him that many

---

37. Wayland, *Memoir*, 2:328; see also Edward Judson, *The Life of Adoniram Judson*, 521.

38. Edward Judson, *The Life of Adoniram Judson*, 527. See also Middleditch, *Burmah's Great Missionary*, 421–22; and Wayland, *Memoir*, 2:334.

thought he would not recover. Judson responded to the plain reality that his life was slipping away; he said in tears that he was ready for whatever God ordered according to his perfect will. Emily recorded his words:

> Death will never take me by surprise—do not be afraid of that— I feel so strong in Christ. He has not led me so tenderly thus far to forsake me at the very gate of heaven. No, no; I am willing to live a few years longer if it should be so ordered; and if otherwise, I am willing and glad to die now. I leave myself entirely in the hands of God, to be disposed of according to his holy will.

The next day, when given the option to stay in Burma instead of going to sea, Emily said that Judson did not wish to stay for he would surely die. Not wanting to be a self-made martyr or commit the error of self-murder, he said, that it would be "criminal" to stay back and not try to recover.[39] On the voyage in 1850, after leaving Emily behind, Thomas Ranney (1810–1868), recorded Judson's surrender to the will of God in his dying. Judson said to Ranney that he knew Christ was upholding him. Judson uttered, "*It is all right there*, I believe he gives me just so much pain and suffering as is necessary to fit me to die—to make me submissive to his will." After days of fevers, severe vomiting, and fierce coughing, Judson lamented to Ranney that so few died such a terrible death. On the day of his death, April 12, the fever of death had set in, and Judson whispered, "It is done; I am going."[40]

---

39. Emily Chubbuck Judson, "Closing Scenes in Dr. Judson's Life, Maulmain," 37–39. See also Wayland, *Memoir*, 2:343–46; and see Middleditch, *Burmah's Great Missionary*, 425. Similarly, when on the voyage, Judson did not want to succumb to deterministic fatalism. He wished to try every appropriate prescription in order to make sure that nothing could aid him. After the captain had given Judson several medications to no avail, Judson said to his missionary friend and superintendent of the printing press in Maulmein, Thomas Ranney: "It is of little consequence. I do not wish anyone to think I died because all was not done that could be done for me. Medicine is of no use. The disease will take its course." Edward Judson, *The Life of Adoniram Judson*, 544–45.

40. Middleditch, *Burmah's Great Missionary*, 427–28. See also Wayland, *Memoir*, 2:350–52. After Judson set sail to get well, Emily continued to write to him without any news in return; her last letter to him was on August 2, 1850. By August 19, 1850, she had heard that he died on April 12, 1850. She became so sick with worry during those summer months of waiting that she could barely pick herself up off the couch. For her many heart-wrenching letters during that long time of silence, see Tooze, *The Life and Letters of Emily Chubbuck Judson*, 4:322–86. For a biographical sketch of those months in her life, see Kendrick, *The Life and Letters of Mrs. Emily C. Judson*, 323–41. See also Emily Chubbuck Judson to Solomon Peck, letter, August 21, 1850, Box No. AJ 12, Folder 1 and Microfilm Roll 2, Judson Letters, ABHS; and Emily Chubbuck Judson to Dr Solomon Peck, letter, September 22, 1850, Box No. AJ 12, Folder 1 and Microfilm Roll 2, Judson Letters, ABHS.

The Path of Duty

Grounded in his all-consuming vision of God's comprehensive sovereignty, Adoniram Judson set out on the path of duty, in obedience to his missionary call. His duty to Christ manifested itself in many ways, most noticeably in his resolve to stand for his convictions and his resilience to stay the course and complete what God had called him to do.[41] In his *A Digest on Scripture*, Judson heavily cited Scripture references to delineate what he believed to be the basic biblical duties that the Christian owed to God and to men. With pages of texts cited, Judson said that the Christian's duty to God is to love him supremely through reverence, trust, and obedience.[42] Also, with pages of biblical citations, he outlined the Christian's duty to men, which included themes such as brotherly love, indiscriminate kindness, forbearance, honor, purity of speech, and integrity in relationships.[43]

Standing on the Gospel

During his last year of theological study at Andover Seminary, Adoniram Judson began to sense a call to the mission field. His experience began as many missionary calls do, with a combination of a burden for the unreached peoples, anticipation of the journey, and a sense of duty to God and the Scripture.[44] In a letter in December of 1837, to Stephen Chapin

---

41. At a centennial (1888) address in Judson's honor, his son Adoniram Brown Judson wrote a letter to the editor of the *Judson Centennial Services*, J. Nelson Lewis, to be included in the celebration's records. His closing lines expressed admiration for his missionary father. He said, "As a son of the missionary whose birth we celebrate, I could say but little, except to express a longing, in common with my Christian brethren, for divine help in renewed efforts to imitate the devotion to duty which marked my father's life." Adoniram Brown Judson, "Letter to Rev. J. Nelson Lewis," 56. At the same centennial celebration, John N. Murdock likewise mentioned the role of duty in Judson's commitment to God: "He accomplished the great results of his life . . . from an overmastering and all-comprehending sense of *Duty*. From the day he accepted Christ as his Saviour, he also accepted the law of service. Having been bought with a price, he belonged henceforth to his Master, and gave himself up to obey His Word and do His will." Murdock, "Memorial Address," 15; emphasis in original.

42. Adoniram Judson, *A Digest of Scripture*, 72–78.

43. Ibid., 79–107.

44. Wayland included some letters that reveal Judson's early piety and missionary devotion. Wayland recorded Mary Hasseltine, sister of Ann, describing Judson as "solemn, impassioned, logical, and highly scriptural, without much of the hortatory, with no far-fetched figure or studied ornament of phrase. [She said] I can see his erect, commanding figure in the sacred desk, his manly countenance glowing with celestial fire, laboring intensely to excite in his hearers an interest in those high and holy themes that

(1778–1845), the president of Columbian College, Washington,[45] Judson recounted those days when he sensed God's Spirit calling him to missions. Initially, the romance of the missionary venture excited him, but its thrill soon faded; a strong sense of duty then compelled him. He admitted that his emotions were "extravagant." Yet, he maintained that God, in his wisdom, needed to grant him such a "state of excitement" in order to enable him initially "to break the strong attachment" to his family and homeland and abandon his worldly ambitions. Nevertheless, he said, "That excitement soon passed away; but it left a strong desire to prosecute my inquiries, and ascertain the path of duty." In the letter he confessed that God's sovereignty clearly brought together all his companions from their various backgrounds to Andover.[46] He said that they "came to a mutual understanding on the ground of *foreign* missions and *missions for life*." The gravity of this high calling impressed upon their souls with "awful solemnity," binding them together for that great cause of advancing the kingdom of Christ.[47] When Leonard Woods, professor of Christian Theology at Andover Seminary (1808–1846), recalled the early missionary fervor of Judson and his colleagues at Andover, he noted that it was not "extravagant romantic ideas" that motivated him, but "with very sober scriptural views," Judson and his colleagues "engaged in the enterprise as a serious Christian duty,—a work of benevolence, self-denial, and piety."[48]

---

so fill his own vision . . . He was then in all the ardor of his first love. It may literally be said, that he was a man of one idea, and that was, love to Jesus, and a desire to manifest it in all its varied forms. Yet he was by nature ardent, impetuous, and ambitious, with the most unshaken confidence in his own judgment, irrespective of the advice of his seniors. Of these propensities he was fully conscious, and against them continually warred." Wayland, *Memoir*, 1:30–31. Also, Wayland recorded Ann describing his early spirituality in a letter to her sisters: "She says, 'I feel that there is not a better man on the globe than my husband; not one who labors more strenuously to overcome every unhallowed emotion of his spirit.' She further adds, 'I have known him to spend whole days in fasting and prayer, taking no nourishment but a little fruit in the morning, passing the day at the *zayat*, and returning in the evening languid and pale.'" Ibid., 1:31–32.

45. See Duncan, *A History of Baptists in Missouri*, 418.

46. His missions-minded friends were Samuel J. Mills Jr., Ezra Fisk (1785–1833), James Richards, John Seward (1784–1873), Luther Rice, Gordon Hall, Samuel Newell, and Samuel Nott. See Woods, *Memoirs of American Missionaries*, 14. See also Bendroth, *A School of the Church*, 49–55; and see McBeth, *The Baptist Heritage*, 344–55.

47. Conant, *The Earnest Man*, 42–44, 49–50. See also Middleditch, *Burmah's Great Missionary*, 22–26; and Wayland, *Memoir*, 1:51–53; emphasis in original.

48. Eddy, *A Sketch of Adoniram Judson*, v. For examples of Judson's Christian duty to Scripture, see Knowles, *Memoir of Mrs. Ann H. Judson*, 62–63; Wayland, *Memoir*, 1:108, 111–12; and Middleditch, *Burmah's Great Missionary*, 42–43, 52–56.

Later in life, in retrospect, Emily C. Judson sketched some anecdotes of her marriage to Judson. She recorded his dutiful devotion to preaching the gospel as a missionary and his refusal to entertain people with stories of his labors, as if he were some kind of Christian celebrity.[49] He devoted himself to preaching the gospel not only on the mission field, but at home in his sending churches too. Emily recalled that when visiting her home church,[50] after the sermon, Judson spoke for approximately fifteen minutes "with singular simplicity, and, as I thought, with touching pathos, of the 'precious Saviour,' what he has done for us, and what we owe to him."[51] Afterwards, Emily said that it was evident that the congregation was disappointed that he had not shared any captivating stories of a man coming from the antipodes. Speaking to Emily later, Judson retorted that he preached to the best of his ability on the most remarkable subject, and he was glad that the church could say that even an adventurer like himself "had nothing better to tell than the wondrous story of Jesus' dying love. My business is to preach the gospel of Christ, and when I can speak at all, I dare not trifle with my commission." He went on to say that his duty compelled him to stand for the truth of Christ and Christ's love over indulging them with "amusing stories, however decently strung together on a thread of religion." He said, such ear-tickling "is not what Christ meant by preaching the gospel." Emily recorded that he feared entertaining them with his own escapades only to stand before Christ on the day of judgment and regret wasting an opportunity to preach Christ crucified. Emily recollected that Judson admitted that spreading awareness of missions and missionary work was important; nonetheless, he argued that "the good of the cause of missions did not require a lowering of the standard of gospel preaching; and that whatever was done for missions at the expense of spirituality in the American churches, was lost on the world."[52]

Standing amid the Unknown

Judson's fresh devotion to this duty would undergo testing not long after he vowed himself to obey the missionary call no matter the cost. In the winter of 1810, Edward Dorr Griffin,[53] pastor of the distinguished Park Street

---

49. One account of Judson described him as strongly unwilling to talk of himself and his notable experiences. See Stevens, *A Half-Century in Burma*, 12.
50. This was in Eaton, New York.
51. Wayland, *Memoir*, 2:369.
52. Ibid., 2:370.
53. See Woods, *History of the Andover*, 147–50.

Church in Boston, visited Judson and his family, and Griffin proposed that Judson become his assistant pastor. Judson's family was elated. His ambitions had finally led him to a place of prestige and prominence in the Lord's service that Judson's father had never achieved. His mother was so happy that he could be immediately useful for the Lord and so close to home. Nevertheless, knowing he would break the heart of his mother and knowing that he would risk displeasing his ambition-fueling father, he said, "No . . . I shall never live in Boston. I have much further than that to go."[54] Then he unfolded his plans to please Christ by obeying his call, devoting himself to preaching the gospel to the heathen.[55]

Judson sought approval and consent for the creation of American missions, and he presented a letter in June 1810 to Samuel Spring (1746–1819) of Newburyport[56] and Samuel Worcester of Salem.[57] In spite of Judson's impetuousness and duty-mindedness, of which he was cognizant, he was indeed malleable. Knowing that none of the older gentlemen had been foreign missionaries before, in the letter Judson still humbly inquired of any advice that they could give the enthusiastic seminarians. Though he would

54. Middleditch, *Burmah's Great Missionary*, 26. See also Wayland, *Memoir*, 1:53; and Conant, *The Earnest Man*, 46.

55. One biographer said about this incident, "It seems from the foregoing incident, that his talents for the pulpit had already made a strong impression on his instructors. We know that he possessed, to a very uncommon degree, the qualities which form an effective popular preacher. His mind was at once logical and impassioned, his voice powerful, and his delivery full of life and fire. His sister-in-law, Miss Mary Hasseltine, describes 'his eloquence and oratory' as 'a transcript of Dr. Griffin's.' Should we not, be very likely, even at this day, to consider such peculiar gifts for usefulness at home, as in a great measure thrown away on a missionary to the heathen? Would not many be ready to exclaim: 'To what purpose is this waste!' With such thoughts might vanity and ambition, under the mask of duty, have deluded his own heart, had not a voice—the voice of One whom he loved better than father and mother, yea than his own life or honor—whispered in the depths of his soul: 'I will send thee far hence unto the Gentiles!' The event has proved how narrow and short-sighted is the policy, which would withhold such gifts, as too precious, from the missionary cause." See Conant, *The Earnest Man*, 46.

56. Samuel Spring, a chaplain in the American Revolutionary War and a Congregationalist minister, studied under Nathan Webb (1705–1772), a Congregationalist minister, and at New Jersey College (Princeton University). His father-in-law, Samuel Hopkins, also mentored him. Spring was one of the founding members of Andover Seminary (1808). See McGinnley, "Samuel Spring," 15–28; see also Spring, *A Sermon*; Spring, *Moral Disquisitions*.

57. Samuel Worcester graduated from Dartmouth College in 1795, and he became pastor at the Tabernacle Church in Salem in 1803. He also became the Corresponding Secretary for the ABCFM in 1810. See Worcester, *A Correction of Erroneous Statements*. He strongly engaged in controversy with Unitarianism. See Worcester, *A Third Letter to the Rev. William E. Channing*.

have to pioneer a foreign mission field, Judson assumed the duty, along with his companions, to be "devoted to this work for life" according to God's providential guidance.[58]

The Duty to Stay

Judson constantly faced the temptation to retreat from the fray of missionary service. In order to persevere on the path of duty, he had to make hard choices throughout life that would assist him in his lifelong missionary devotion.

In order to stay on the path of duty, Judson sought to set a useful trajectory. After making plain his devotion to foreign missions for life, Edward Griffin expressed concern that Judson's health was too weak and his constitution too delicate. Judson realized that, if he were to stay his course for a long-term investment, he would have to do his best to improve and sustain a strong constitution. So, he studied physiology, and he created daily habits of exercise and health in order to prolong his life, for he believed that his future usefulness greatly depended on exercising and good health. He walked every morning and evening throughout his life, during which he used the time to pray and meditate.[59]

In the early years of his missionary preparations, Judson wrote letters to Ann Hasseltine. In a letter in January of 1811, Judson demonstrated his early consecration for missionary duty and how he sought to prepare himself to stay the course and finish it. He said that his prayer was that Ann would grow in the "spirit of Christ" and ascend above worldly desires to "be willing to be disposed of in this world just as God shall please." He went on to say that he wished that as the year went on that she would grow "nearer to God," and be ready for whatever the future held, even affliction, anguish, isolation, and death. Considering the great risks of living in the East, Judson presumed that they could be "exceeding [sic] sorrowful, even unto death." Quoting a stanza from a poem by the English poet, Alexander

---

58. Wayland, *Memoir*, 1:55. See also Middleditch, *Burmah's Great Missionary*, 29–30. Judson, Samuel Nott, Samuel J. Mills, and Samuel Newell all signed this letter.

59. See Wayland, *Memoir*, 1:39. For a succinct description of Judson's open-air praying, meditating, and rapid walking, see Warburton, *Eastward*, 119–20. Wayland's comments on Judson's early methods of preparation for long-term service are also appropriate: "From the time of his self-consecration to the missionary service, he became, in the highest sense, a man of one idea. He offered himself up a living sacrifice on the altar, and seemed to look forward with pleasure to suffering and affliction, if it were to be endured in the path of Christian duty." Wayland, *Memoir*, 1:39.

Pope (1688–1744), about dying in a foreign land,[60] Judson summoned Ann to pray earnestly with him for "an overcoming faith" in order to stand firm and stay long.[61]

Approximately two months before the aforementioned letter to Ann, Judson wrote a letter to Ann's older sister, Abigail Hasseltine.[62] In the letter, Judson illustrated the underlying convictions beneath why he would stay so long and suffer so well. He exclaimed that he wished for Christians, including himself, to realize that one moment of torment in eternity would "almost infinitely outweigh all the pain ever suffered in this world." He contended that Christians would then not be "agitated by the trifles which daily occur"; they would not be "impatient under their light afflictions"; and they would not "be unwilling to bear all the hardships and sufferings which Jesus lays upon us in this world."[63] Meditating on eternal torment would prove foundational for Judson's staying power through adversity.

Judson's ability to stay through difficulty was due to his diligence to improve every moment, whether comfortable or inconvenient, for spiritual usefulness. His time-orientation and desire to invest in every opportunity for personal holiness and for Christ's service dictated how he would spend life's dull moments and how proactive he would be at all times. For instance, not long after Judson and Ann departed for Calcutta, they fell hard to seasickness, and the smells of refuse and waste were particularly nauseating. Yet, even in the initial adversity of travel, Judson sought to make the most of

60. See Pope, *The Works of Alexander Pope*, 2:213.

61. Wayland, *Memoir*, 1:34–35; quoted also in Conant, *The Earnest Man*, 82–83.

62. Searching for the dates and identities of Ann's family members was challenging. Having recently researched Ann's siblings herself, Rosalie Hall Hunt said this about locating their information: "The descendants of Ann Hasseltine Judson's siblings proved . . . difficult to locate. Biographies of the Judsons gave no clues, and books of genealogy seemed to have lost the trail of Ann's brothers and sisters after one generation, or two at the most . . . Ann had had three sisters and three brothers. Two brothers had died young, one at six months old, the other at age twenty. Only one of her three sisters had married, Rebecca (Becky) Hasseltine, who married Joseph Emerson. They had two sons, who in turn had children, but those children did not leave descendants, so the line ended there. The other Hasseltine sisters, Polly (always called Mary) and Abigail, never married." Hunt, *Bless God and Take Courage*, 307. Hunt reported that, according to the Hasseltine genealogy, which "is probably the most thorough record available, John Hasseltine was born November 8, 1756 in Chester, New Hampshire, and died May 24, 1837. Rebecca Barton Hasseltine was born in 1761 in Bradford (no month or day) and died Jan. 11, 1846. Both are buried in the old cemetery in Bradford. Polly [Mary] was born April 3, 1784. Abigail was born March 15, 1788. Both were born in Bradford. Ann's brother Joseph Hall Hasseltine was born August 13, 1791, and married Chloe Whipple. Joseph was the only sibling who had children that gave Ann nieces and nephews." Hunt, email message to author, September 17, 2014.

63. Wayland, *Memoir*, 1:35–36.

every opportunity that he might endure in usefulness for the Lord. He wrote a letter from the Bay of Bengal in June 1812, to his colleagues from Andover to exhort them not to waste time and convenience, but to improve every moment for the Lord. Even onboard the ship, Judson said that he sought to be useful for the Lord. Because of his earlier commitment to preserving his physical health through exercise, he learned how to jump rope, which he said was the "best kind of exercise" he had ever found. As soon as he stopped exercising for a few days, his health would fail, so he exercised in order to improve every day for spiritual duties. He wrote to his friends saying that it would be foolish for a passenger to relax on his voyage and not spend his passing time well. He said if a missionary were not to be diligent, even in spite of his seasickness, then the missionary might "acquire habits of indolence and disregard of time which will attach to him through life." No hour on sea, he said, is less valuable for spiritual improvement than an hour in the comforts of land. Judson even recommended that a traveling missionary should start his voyage with "a definite plan of study, for diligent improvement of several months of voyage, as well as for, improvement for several months after his first arrival at his station." And, he closed his letter by warning his friends not to let their comforts become a distraction as, he claimed with a touch of sarcasm, his comforts on the ship had become a distraction for him.[64]

In order to remain on the path of duty, Judson allowed no special privileges to distract him. After serving in Burma for a number of years, an external factor threatened Judson's devotion to his lifelong duty. In 1819, when the war between Britain and Burma was escalating, which led to the banishment of the English missionaries, the American missionaries were also anxious about the looming possibility that they could likewise receive maltreatment and deportation. Facing the reality of inevitable opposition and persecution by the Burmese government, many missionaries were compelled to pull out and commence work in a more tolerant, peaceful environment. Enduring the scrutiny of such a repressive government, Judson's devotion to his call remained firm. Judson determined to wait until the government actually forced him to forego his missionary work through imprisonment or deportation. Christ's example of perseverance motivated him. In a letter to William Staughton[65] of Philadelphia, he wrote that the king, on a whim, could banish the missionaries, which would include confiscation of

---

64. Adoniram Judson to Bros. Mills, Richards, Warren, &c., letter, June 12, 1812, Papers, 1811–1888, Trask Library Special Collections, Newton Centre, Massachusetts.

65. Staughton became the first president of Columbian College (1821–1827). For a brief treatment of Staughton's role in encouraging the missionaries, see Lynd, *Memoir of the Rev. William Staughton*, 174–91.

all their property and even deadly cruelty. Judson's conviction to fulfill his duty and stay came from the fact that he surrendered his American religious freedom by becoming a missionary. He said that most people in history have cowered under some form of despotism with very little provisions of life, liberty, and property. He said, in imitation of Christ who became a man and lived under "the most unprincipled and cruel despot that ever reigned," Christ's disciples, then should not decline serving Christ under tyranny. Later in his letter, he called himself "the most unsuccessful of all missionaries" and asked prayer "for grace to strengthen faith, to animate hope, to elevate affection, to embolden the soul, to enable us to look danger and death in the face."[66]

Moreover, Judson needed not only to withstand the temptation to retreat in the face of adversity, he needed also to stand firm and stay in the face of opportunity. After leaving the prison in Ava, Judson faced many new prospects in different provinces in which to commence a new work, presumably because they were easier and more promising. He was even encouraged to forego his missionary work to become an interpreter for the British government, which would have provided a more stable occupation than the hazards of their previous post. After much prayer, Judson, along with his wife, Ann, concluded it would render them useless in their mission because of how much time it would demand. In a letter to Lucius Bolles in March 1826, Judson's response to this affable opportunity was single-minded. He said he endeavored to know nothing but Christ crucified. He said that because of the "comparative worthlessness of all earthly things," his desire was "to avoid every *secular* occupation, and all literary and scientific pursuits, and devote the remainder of my days to simple declaration of the precious truths of the Gospel."[67] Just as sixteen years earlier when Judson turned down a rare opportunity to preach in Boston with the respected Edward Griffin before departing for India, so at this stage in his life, he was equally resolute.[68]

---

66. Conant, *The Earnest Man*, 184. See also Middleditch, *Burmah's Great Missionary*, 117; and Wayland, *Memoir*, 1:197–98.

67. Middleditch, *Burmah's Great Missionary*, 215. See also Wayland, *Memoir*, 2:421; emphasis in original. In a letter to her sisters, Ann reveals a similar view of their devotion to God's call: "So you see, my sisters, if we had a wish to accumulate property, what an opportunity we have had . . . There is a much greater call for entire and exclusively devoted missionaries than for money. Our friends, we doubt not, will supply all our necessary wants, while we shall be able to spend our strength and our energies for the spiritual good of the Burmans, and avoid those temptations attached to a public situation in the world." Middleditch, *Burmah's Great Missionary*, 215.

68. See Wayland, *Memoir*, 1:53. See also Middleditch, *Burmah's Great Missionary*, 26; and Conant, *The Earnest Man*, 46. By this point, he knew the harsh realities and dry

Judson knew translation was hard work to which he must apply himself rigorously, but he also knew it was the Holy Spirit's work, in which he trusted for illumination and help. Such reliance on the Spirit's empowerment in congruence with his hard work was a key to Judson's perseverance.[69] In a journal entry in June 1832, Judson demonstrated his assiduous resolve to fulfill his duty and finish his course. He said he had calculated that he could finish the whole Bible in two years from that point. But, that was upon the condition that he would restrain himself to that work alone. He could offer no other duties, otherwise the work would drag on for four years. In his journal, he expressed deep yearning for people to pray for him in his isolated state so that he would "enjoy the presence of the Saviour, and that special aid in translating the inspired Word." He said such prayers would be granted if they were offered with humility and fervency.[70]

Even though his fellow missionaries were not directly engaged in his translation work alongside him, they felt the seriousness of Judson's self-denying seclusion. That he was rarely to be seen told them that he was working as hard or harder than anyone else was. The newly married missionary couple, Catherine Sears Webb (b. 1806) and Abner Webb (d. 1891), had just arrived in Burma in 1833, and Catherine Webb witnessed Judson intently studying and translating. She wrote to her parents (Ebenezer [1776–1847] and Frances Pamela Watson [1778–1842]) and highlighted Judson's dutiful labors. She did not describe him as impatient or severe, but rather that her conversation with him was "of a very pleasing nature," and she was happy even to slightly assist him by blunting "the edge of his loneliness." She described him as "uniformly seriously cheerful." He secluded himself day and night, except for exercise twice a day, two meals a day, and occasional social conversation in the evenings. "His petitions for a long life, to labor among

---

discouragements of missionary life, and he could have escaped it all for an honorable vocation. Nevertheless, he went straightforward, trusting in God. Emily recorded that Judson would often say, "If God has designed a work for us to do, he will arrange all the little particulars, and we have only to trust in him." Wayland, *Memoir*, 2:372.

69. Wayland said, "United with all this that was intellectual, there was, in his case, a mind deeply impressed with its own fallibility, and turning with unutterable longing to the Holy Spirit for guidance and illumination." Wayland, *Memoir*, 2:163–67.

70. Adoniram Judson, journal, February 29, 1832 to June 25, 1832, Box No. AJ 4, Folder 8 and Microfilm Roll 1, Judson Letters, ABHS. See also Middleditch, *Burmah's Great Missionary*, 300–301; and Wayland, *Memoir*, 2:50. To read of Ann's description of the intensity with which Judson studied in his early years of language acquisition, see Ann Hasseltine Judson, *An Account of the American Baptist Mission*, 43. For a thorough description of Judson's rigorous language study habits and his passion to see the Bible translated into an easily understandable script for the end goal of preaching it to the common person, see Warburton, *Eastward*, 64–66.

the heathen, mingled as they are with panting aspirations after heaven" all inspired her greatly.[71]

Serving as a fellow missionary with Judson, L. Ingalls (d. 1856) recorded Judson's consuming desire to do his duty to finish the dictionary. Ingalls said,

> He possessed, in an eminent degree, the missionary spirit. This I ascertained, not from his writings, but personal observation ... If I wished to see him, I always knew where to find him—in the study ... It was a great self-denial to be shut up in his study, and he anticipated, with exulting feelings, the completion of the Burmese Bible. He sighed bitterly when he was required to compile a Burmese dictionary.[72]

Another contemporary of Judson also described his sedulous labor in translation and editing, temporarily putting on hold his desire to preach the gospel: "Mr. Judson has been so engrossed with revising the translation of the whole Old Testament, and proof reading, for several years, as to be wholly prevented from laboring publicly either in the *zayat*, or from house to house."[73]

Having tirelessly toiled for the translation of the Burmese Bible, Judson finally finished it in January of 1834. In a distant echo of what he wrote to please his father upon attaining his high academic ambitions at Brown University,[74] Judson wrote joyfully of attaining his God-centered ambition in this postscript of a letter on January 31, 1834:

---

71. Edward Judson, *The Life of Adoniram Judson*, 399. See also Middleditch, *Burmah's Great Missionary*, 302. Abner and Mary Webb arrived in Burma in 1833, and six years later, because of her failing health, they returned to America, never to go back to Burma. That year, their firstborn son died one-day old (December 16, 1833). See American Baptist Missionary Union, *Seventy-Seventh Annual Report*, 13. For Judson's letter to Abner Webb two weeks after the death of their son, see Adoniram Judson to the Rev. Abner P Webb, letter, January 1, 1834, Box No. AJ 5, Folder 1 and Microfilm Roll 2, Judson Letters, ABHS.

72. Dated May 18, 1852, L. Ingalls wrote to Francis Wayland; see Wayland, *Memoir*, 2:355. After his death, Emily recorded conversations she had with Judson about his dutiful work in the dictionary: "I remarked that during this year his literary labor, which he had never liked, and upon which he had entered unwillingly and from a feeling of necessity, was growing daily more irksome to him; and he always spoke of it as his 'heavy work,' his 'tedious work,' 'that wearisome dictionary,' &c., though this feeling led to no relaxation of effort. He longed, however, to find some more spiritual employment, to be engaged in what he considered more legitimate missionary labor, and drew delightful pictures of the future, when his whole business would be but to preach and pray." Ibid., 2:263. See also Middleditch, *Burmah's Great Missionary*, 403.

73. Malcom, "Journal of Mr. Malcom," 55.

74. Wayland recorded Judson's words to his father on April 30, 1807: "When he

P.S.—Thanks be to God, I can *now* say I have attained. I have knelt down before him, with the last leaf in my hand, and imploring his forgiveness for all the sins which have polluted my labors in this department, and his aid in future efforts to remove the errors and imperfections which necessarily cleave to the work, I have commended it to his mercy and grace; I have dedicated it to his glory. *May he make his own inspired Word . . . now complete in the Burman tongue, the grand instrument of filling all Burmah with songs of praise to our great God and Saviour, Jesus Christ. Amen.*[75]

After finishing the Bible translation, Judson temporarily recommenced his work of preaching in Burma, which he loved above all other endeavors. However, Judson's voice started failing, which rendered him useless in preaching. Though saddened by the prospect of never being able to preach again, Judson sought to fulfill his duty by completing a Burmese dictionary.[76] He remained committed to ensuring that its words and meaning were intelligible and that future English-speaking missionaries could access the Burmese text. He resumed to stay the course that God had set out for him in submission to God's will.[77]

A motivating theme in Judson's letters and journals, which compelled his staying power, was the brevity of life. He felt such unction to finish

---

received the highest appointment in the commencement exercises [at Brown University], his delight knew no bounds. He hurried to his room, and wrote, 'Dear father, I have got it. Your affectionate son, A. J.'" Wayland, *Memoir*, 1:22.

75. Adoniram Judson to Bennett, Kincaid & Mason, circular letter, February 3, 1834, Box No. AJ 2, Folder 1 and Microfilm Roll 1, Judson Letters, ABHS; see also Adoniram Judson, "Report of the Board: Missions in Asia," 236–37. See also Wayland, *Memoir*, 2:75–76; and Middleditch, *Burmah's Great Missionary*, 305; emphasis in original. In describing the momentous occasion of Judson's completion of the Burmese Bible translation, the pastor of Madison Avenue Baptist Church, William Hague, said the following: "If in a coming age some Allston should wish to employ his pencil in picturing forth a single action that should express at once the great aim, the chosen means, and the true spirit of the modern missionary enterprise, he could scarcely select a more fitting scene than that which heaven witnessed with a smile, when Adoniram Judson was seen kneeling by the side of that table . . . holding in his hand the last leaf of the Burman Bible, with his eyes uplifted, and with a countenance radiant with joy, thanking God that his life had been spared to achieve this work, and imploring the Divine Spirit to make the silent page a messenger of life to many." Hague, *The Life and Character of Adoniram Judson*, 30–31; see also Middleditch, *Burmah's Great Missionary*, 305–6.

76. Adoniram Judson, *A Dictionary*. For an astute portrayal of the juxtaposition of Judson's earnestness, devotion, linguistic expertise, and intellectual abilities, see Adamson, "Address," 72. For a nearly word-for-word copy of the same address, see also Adamson, "The Baptist Mission and Burma," 15.

77. Wayland, *Memoir*, 2:96–97.

strong, and yet Judson admittedly said that his besetting sin was "a lust for finishing."[78] For instance, in a letter in June 1841, he encouraged his missionary coworker, G. S. Comstock,[79] to keep active in propagating the Scripture and to not get distracted with "knotty questions in biblical criticism." Judson said, "Life is short, and every one [sic] ought to contribute all he can to *ascertain* and *promulgate* the precious truths of the inspired word."[80]

In his journal from June 1832, Judson said that he was urgently working to finish the whole Bible translation because of the "uncertainty of life."[81] Even seventeen years later, his urgency still had not diminished. In a letter to Solomon Peck in August 1849, he said that in light of "the uncertainty of life" and the deteriorating state of the manuscripts, it was his duty to refuse any other opportunities for service or travel "in order to drive forward the heavy work of the dictionary in the most satisfactory manner."[82] Similarly, in another letter two months later in October 1849, to Abram Dunn Gillette,[83] Judson wrote that he was still working hard on the dictionary, which would take him at least another year. Then he referred again to his uncertainty of life.[84] He went on to explain that working for Christ, the greatest Master, was what made his anxiety of the uncertainty of life, his perpetual loneliness, and his heavy burden to finish his duty so tolerable.[85]

Judson had much advice for missionary duty. In 1845, Judson visited Brown University, and there he addressed the students about surrendering to and obeying the call of God in their lives. His lecture was manifestly serious in calling young people to seek out the path of duty to which God might call them. He demonstrated many of the convictions beneath his staying power, which were a juxtaposition of discerning one's unique path

---

78. Edward Judson, *The Life of Adoniram Judson*, 409.

79. See Comstock, "Journal of Mr. Comstock," 69. See also Warburton, *Eastward*, 152.

80. Wayland, *Memoir*, 2:170; emphasis in original.

81. Adoniram Judson, journal, February 29, 1832 to June 25, 1832, Box No. AJ 4, Folder 8 and Microfilm Roll 1, Judson Letters, ABHS; see also Middleditch, *Burmah's Great Missionary*, 300–301.

82. Adoniram Judson to Solomon Peck, correspondence, August 20, 1849, Box No. AJ 4, Folder 1 and Microfilm Roll 1, Judson Letters, ABHS. See also Middleditch, *Burmah's Great Missionary*, 418–19; and Wayland, *Memoir*, 2:326–27.

83. Gillette was the pastor at First Baptist Church in Philadelphia and the manager of the American Baptist publication society. For a famous sermon of Gillette's, see Gillette, *God Seen above All National Calamities*. Moreover, he contributed well to the Judson corpus; see Gillette, *A Sketch of the Labors*.

84. Judson would die six months later in April 1850.

85. See Gillette, *A Sketch of the Labors*, 156–57; and see Middleditch, *Burmah's Great Missionary*, 419.

of duty, submitting to the Scripture, and seeking a conviction of steady duty to Christ. Judson proposed, "There is one, and only one, right path for every man—for each one of you to follow, in order to insure the full approbation of God, and the greatest success in your efforts to do good and glorify him." He went on to say that there would certainly be other good paths, but those paths would not be as fruitful as the one path. Judson directed, "Seek that one path." He said go "straight forward," turning neither to the right nor to the left. Judson said that in order to discern that one path, they must seek it diligently by bringing "the unerring Word of God" to bear upon their plans. He warned, "Reject, at once, whatever has not a firm basis there" in the Scriptures. In terms contextualized for Burma, he said the Bible was the "golden lamp of heaven" that would guide them "along the pathway of duty." He further warned them not to turn their backs on the Scriptures. Nevertheless, he said discerning one's duty requires considering the working of God's providences in each one's character and life situation.[86] He suggested that they seek the counsel of wise men and that they should pray fervently for wisdom.

Judson began a long conclusion by warning not to follow enthusiasm, impressions, and emotions, for Satan often counterfeits truth with such feelings. However, he instructed them to seek to follow "a deep and abiding conviction of duty" that essentially cries, "Woe is me if I preach not the Gospel to the heathen." Judson said this sense of duty alone would "sustain a man under the severe trials and labors of the missionary life," and no man would stay the course without such a settled conviction of duty that is "constrained by the love of Christ," in order to "lead many more, to love him." He concluded by saying,

> But with the assurance that, having humbly submitted himself to the Divine teaching, he has the approval of Christ, he is prepared for any event. With this he can labor; by this he can die. If brought into difficulties, from which there seems no escape, he feels that he has gone thus far in obedience to his Lord's command; that he is doing his Master's work; and that, whatever befalls him, all is well: it is the will of Christ.[87]

With similar solemnity, Judson wrote years earlier, in June of 1832, to the Foreign Missionary Association of the Hamilton Literary and

---

86. Compare this counsel with Emily's description of Judson's strong trust in God to guide and reveal his will to Judson in his praying and watching; see Wayland *Memoir*, 2:372.

87. Middleditch, *Burmah's Great Missionary*, 362–64. See also Wayland, *Memoir*, 2:227–28.

Theological Institution of New York. He wrote to advise missionary candidates to count the cost in order to fulfill their duty. His first few points of advice discussed his conviction that the missionary calling is for life. In order to fulfill one's duty for life, a man should choose a capable companion. Judson cautioned the would-be missionaries to come with realistic expectations of the natives and other Christians. He said that a large reason for missionary repatriation was the missionaries' disappointments with the native customs, language-learning challenges, and frustrations with other Christians. He advised them to count the cost of all these things for the sake of their duty. He observed that most missionaries died within their first five years in the East, so he soberly warned, "Walk softly, therefore; death is narrowly watching your steps."[88] Six months later Judson wrote to the American Baptist Board expressing frustrations about missionaries who would come with short-term commitments.[89] "They are all good for nothing," he noted. They might be "brilliant" preachers in America, but they are "incompetent to any real missionary work." He complained that they come only for a few years in order to acquire "a stock of credit on which they may vegetate the rest of their days" in the ease of America. Instead of making it easier for missionaries when they first arrive to the field, Judson argued that "*missionaries need more trials on their first setting out, instead of less. The motto of every missionary, whether preacher, printer, or schoolmaster, ought to be, 'Devoted for life.'*" Judson unilaterally condemned short-term missions, saying that if they were to become increasingly popular, "it will be the death blow of missions, and retard the conversion of the world a hundred years."[90]

During his furlough, after his visit to Philadelphia in late December 1845, Judson traveled south and stopped in Washington. In a short message, G. W. Samson (1819–1896),[91] the pastor of E. Street Baptist Church in Washington, D. C., honored Judson for his service; and Judson spoke afterward. An anonymous person recorded the piety expressed in Judson's response. Judson advised that missionaries, in order to stay through

---

88. Adoniram Judson "Advice to Missionary Candidates," 577–79. See also Wayland, *Memoir*, 2:38–41.

89. In a letter on February 8, 1836, to Amariah Joy, in Waterville, Maine, Judson said that a young missionary could master the language well enough within two years in order to labor effectively. A short-term commitment of two years would have been useless. See Wayland, *Memoir*, 2:108.

90. Ibid., 2:62–63; emphasis in original.

91. George Whitefield Samson became the fifth president of Columbian College (1859–1871). For one of Samson's many well-known works, see Samson, *The Atonement Viewed as Assumed Divine Responsibility*.

affliction and grief, needed the missions-minded support and sacrifice of the American churches. This account of Judson shows that he believed partnerships of churches with missionaries were essential for long-term sustainability. Without this partnership, fulfillment of the missionary's duty would become rare. This anonymous person recorded Judson saying that though the average missionary only lives for five years on the field, despite such a sacrifice, the churches should still partner with the missionaries in executing their duty to lay their lives down as servants of the Cross.[92]

Self-Denial

The role of self-denial is fundamental for understanding Judson's ascetic spirituality in light of the providence of God. In a letter to the missionaries in Maulmain, Judson discouraged practicing self-denial through "self-inflicted austerities," but in contrast, he commended "evangelical self-denial," which he said "eminently consists in bearing patiently and gratefully all the inconveniences and pain which God in his providence brings upon us." He went on to say that the missionaries should not "attempt to remove them, unless destructive of life or health, or, in one word, capacity for usefulness."[93] In Hopkinsian fashion, Adoniram Judson saw self-love as the essence of sin, and self-denial in the path of love to God and people as the essence of virtue. The passion and methods of the mystics inspired him, yet their teachings were not the foundation of his self-denial. Judson suffered immense darkness and confusion for a season; and, his theological influences, his sufferings, and his writings all need consideration in order to understand the dominance of self-denial in his spirituality.[94]

At Judson's ordination in 1812, Leonard Woods promoted the cost of self-denial as essential to disinterested benevolence. Woods's opening charge is illustrative of the self-sacrificing spirituality that affected Judson during his days at Andover. Woods said that out of "holy affection reigning" in the heart of the devoted Christian, he "counts it a privilege to do and suffer any thing for the advancement of his cause." Woods said that nothing ultimately could deter such a Christian. The prospects of losing all earthly comforts and even undergoing extreme persecution and torture are more to be desired than any earthly pleasure. Woods said that such a devoted Christian "is as steady to his purpose, as resolute, active, and patient in pursuit, as the restless miser, or the ambitious conqueror." Woods went

---

92. Middleditch, *Burmah's Great Missionary*, 377–78.
93. Wayland, *Memoir*, 1:516.
94. See Wayland's synthesis of Judson's self-denying piety, in ibid., 2:379–80.

on to say that just as such a miser or conqueror lusts for wealth and booty, so the true Christian dreams of spreading the gospel and eternal happiness. With increase in conversions comes increase in desire for more. He said that the benevolence of the true Christian's heart is ever expanding with the expanding of Christ's kingdom. There is no neutral option in the kingdom of Christ. Until every tribe, tongue, and nation submits to Christ, "the enlightened, fervent Christian cannot rest." Woods contended that such is "the true spirit of our holy religion." He likewise said this holy affection controls and fuels the true church of Christ.[95]

The Context of Judson's Dark Night and Self-Denial

In order to understand Judson's spirituality of self-denial in light of the absolute sovereignty of God, briefly reviewing Samuel Hopkins's teaching on disinterested benevolence is helpful.[96] Considering Judson's exposure to Madame Guyon's writings and methods is additionally helpful.[97] Admittedly, the following descriptions of Hopkinsianism and Guyonism are very truncated, and the influences of both New Divinity theology and Roman Catholic asceticism in Judson's piety deserve fuller development. But this is beyond the scope of this book.

Hopkinsian Disinterested Benevolence

In Hopkins's famous piece, "A Dialogue Between a Calvinist and a Semi-Calvinist," he suggested that a true Christian should be willing to be damned forever for the glory of God.[98] Hopkins argued that the Christian who truly loves his neighbor as himself should be willing to give himself over to pain in order to save others from greater degrees of suffering. According to E. Brooks Holifield, Hopkins "defined holiness as disinterested benevolence . . . One either loved God above self or one loved self above God."[99] In relation to Romans 9:3, Hopkins noted that the truly benevolent Christian could say, like Paul, that he would willing to be damned if it meant that

---

95. Woods, *A Sermon Delivered at the Tabernacle in Salem*, 10–11; emphasis in original.

96. For in-depth explications of New Divinity and Hopkinsian theology, see Conforti, *Samuel Hopkins and the New Divinity Movement*.

97. For an example of what Judson read, see Guyon, *A Short and Easy Method of Prayer*.

98. See Hopkins, *Works of Samuel Hopkins*, 3:143.

99. Holifield, *Theology in America*, 140.

some sinners might be saved.[100] Moreover, Hopkins applied this difficult doctrine as a test of truly regenerate Godward affections. In terms strikingly similar to Judson's self-denying submission to God and desire to please him, Hopkins said it was impossible that a man would love himself more than God and not be damned. Yet, he maintained that the man "who loves God supremely, and desires his glory above all things," such a man would necessarily be willing to be damned if it were most glorifying to God. Hopkins further said that if a man cannot say, "Let God be glorified, let what will become of me," then it is because he loves himself more than God's glory; thus, "he is not a true friend, but an enemy, to God."[101]

Madame Guyon's Devotion

In relation to the developed doctrine of disinterested benevolence, Edwards Amasa Park, in his *Memoir* of Hopkins, interestingly observed, "There is a striking resemblance between the feelings of Dr. Hopkins and the feelings of Fenelon, Madame Guion, and many other mystics, with regard to the endurance of pain for the divine glory." Park went on to comment on how "unnatural" it is to ascend to such lofty ideas of "sentiment and reasoning." Surely, such a man must hold "an ideality far above that of the masses."[102] It is no coincidence that Judson prepared for ministry in a fertile Hopkinsian environment and that he also gravitated to the self-denying devotion of a mystic like Guyon.[103] Judson read Guyon's writings as a means of awakening a greater longing for the knowledge of God and for finding inspiration for pursuing holiness. The combination of his eccentric personality, the demanding New Divinity training at Andover, and his self-imposed Roman Catholic asceticism was a potent mixture.[104]

The Dark Hour

Judson was released from prison in December 1825, and ten months later, Ann died. His two-year old daughter, Maria, died in April 1827, and he

100. See Hopkins, *Works of Samuel Hopkins*, 3:145–46. See Rom 9:3.
101. Hopkins, *Works of Samuel Hopkins*, 3:147.
102. Park, *Memoir of the Life and Character of Samuel Hopkins*, 211.
103. As in the aforementioned account of Judson's imprisonment and torture (June 8, 1824 to December 30, 1825), one of his cellmates, Henry Gouger, recorded Judson's admiration for Madame Guyon's devotion. See Gouger, *A Personal Narrative*, 174–75.
104. See Warburton, *Eastward*, 118–19. See also Edward Judson, *The Life of Adoniram Judson*, 303–4; and Wayland, *Memoir*, 1:473–74.

heard of the death of his father, Adoniram Judson Sr. (on November 25, 1826) that July. After hearing of his father's death, Judson fell into deep despair. News of his father's death awakened in him many memories of his father inspiring him to greatness. His father's well-intended ambitions for his son had developed into worldly ambitions in Judson's mind, to which Judson still felt fettered. Courtney Anderson perceptively interpreted the collision of God's ways with Judson's self-made ambition:

> [Judson] began to suspect that his real motive in becoming a missionary had been not genuine humility and self-abnegation but ambition—ambition to be the *first* American foreign missionary; the *first* missionary to Burma; the *first* translator of the Bible into Burmese: *first* in his own eyes and the eyes of men. He had a lust to excel . . . He had always known that his forwardness, self-pride and desire to stand out were serious flaws in his nature. Now he began to suspect that they were more than flaws. They made his entire missionary career up to now a kind of monstrous hypocrisy, a method of securing prominence and praise without admitting it to himself. He had deluded himself. But he had not deluded God. Perhaps here was the intention in all these deaths: to teach him true humility . . . For Adoniram's mission, God had approval; for Adoniram and his self-love, a harsh lesson.[105]

Therefore, in desperation to rid himself of his perceived self-love, in May of 1828, he renounced the title of Doctor of Divinity, conferred on him by Brown University a few years earlier. He also gave away all his private property (amounting to approximately six thousand dollars) to the American Baptist Board. He chose to give up one twentieth of his missionary support and opted to reduce his support by one quarter. He also wrote to his sister, Abigail in Plymouth, and requested that she destroy all his old letters and writings. She wrote him to confirm that she had done according to his wishes.[106]

---

105. Anderson, *To the Golden Shore*, 382–83; emphasis in original. Also, Wayland helpfully summarized Judson's natural strengths that God sanctified throughout his life: intense desire for prominence, indomitable perseverance, steadiness, self-confidence, ambition, well ordered, and a strong preference for privacy and anonymity. These qualities were evident in Judson's early life, and with spiritual maturity, Wayland said, Judson's piety steered his personality. Wayland described Judson's piety as heavenly-minded, self-denying, prayerful, and unshaken in his confidence in God and God's promises. For Wayland's full synthesis of Judson's early personality and seasoned piety, see Wayland, *Memoir*, 2:373–404.

106. See Abigail Judson to the Rev. Adoniram Judson, letter, May 22, 1830, Box No. AJ 8, Folder 2 and Microfilm Roll 2, Judson Letters, ABHS.

Still sensing the conviction of his self-love, he moved to a little hut he had made, which he called "the Hermitage." He moved on the second anniversary of Ann's death (October 24, 1828), and that night he wrote to Mary Hasseltine and Abigail Hasseltine. He lamented the loss of Ann and the corresponding "loathsome sepulcher of [his] own heart." He said that he viewed Ann's grave and the stormy evening in which he wrote the letter as analogies of his sinful heart. The combination of his grief and self-loathing was incalculable.[107] While at the Hermitage, he could not free himself of the guilty feelings that much of his suffering corresponded directly to his inner corruption. Consequently, he dug a grave and sat by it for days, imagining his body decaying in the ground. However, this did not last long; he gave up the grave-contemplation and went back to his work. Though he lived in the Hermitage, he still committed himself to writing and translation. During this time, he wrote the *Three-fold Cord*.[108]

After extreme efforts of self-denial, it seemed as if his self-denial was not working sufficiently to subdue his sin, so he decided to try solitude. He left the Hermitage with his Bible and spent forty days in an overgrown pagoda in the wild jungle. There he sought after God but could feel no divine nearness. On the third anniversary of Ann's death, he wrote to her sisters, Mary and Abigail Hasseltine, and inquired, "Have either of you learned the art of real communion with God, and can you teach me the first principles? God is to me the Great Unknown. I believe in him, but I find him not."[109] To express his utter melancholy, Judson wrote a long poem to Ann's mother, Rebecca Barton Hasseltine, called "The Solitary's Lament." These extracted stanzas of the poem reflected his despondency; furthermore, they manifested his trust in Christ:

> The vale of death, so dark and drear,
> Where all things are forgot;
> Where like they whom I loved so dear;
> I call—they answer not.
>
> O, bitter cup which God has given!
> Where can relief be found?
> Anon I lift my eyes to heaven,
> Anon in tears they're drowned.
>
> Yet He who conquered death and hell
> Our Friend at last will stand;

---

107. Anderson, *To the Golden Shore*, 388.
108. Adoniram Judson, *The Threefold Cord*.
109. Wayland, *Memoir*, 1:473.

And all whom He befriends shall dwell
In Canaan's happy land—

Such promise throws a rainbow bright
Death's darkest storm above,
And bids us catch the heaven-born light,
And praise the God of love.[110]

Judson's spirituality was such that even though he could not feel the presence of God in his melancholy, that is, in the same terms described in some of Guyon's writings, he nevertheless trusted in the promise of Christ's final victory over sin, death, and suffering.

Judson's Self-Denial in Perspective

In his biography of his father, Edward Judson said, in relation to this dark period, that his asceticism was "the outcome of a transient and superficial mood rather than his real and underlying character," which was precipitated by twenty-one months of physical torture, the deaths of his loved ones, and his self-imposed solitude.[111] Judson's son further observed that "it was his intense piety that carried him into these extremes of self-denial. His was a great religious nature, wrestling for Christ-likeness."[112] He did not adhere to the Roman Catholic theology of Madame Guyon,[113] but he desired to

---

110. Edward Judson, *The Life of Adoniram Judson*, 307–9.

111. Ibid., 305. Hunt, in her well-researched account of the Judson history and legacy, says this period is "out of character with the whole of who he was." She warns that Honoré Morrow, in Morrow's biographical novel, *Splendor of God*, had so "fictionalized" the account that genuine facts had been smothered in historical inaccuracies to the point of being pagan. Hunt condemns Morrow's imaginative rendering of this dark season in Judson's life, and calls it "pure fiction, somewhat like a colony of termites in the timber of Judson history." Hunt, *Bless God and Take Courage*, 345. See even more unreserved condemnation of Morrow's fictional account in Hanna, "What Price Missions?," 811. See also Morrow, *Splendor God*, 291–321.

112. Edward Judson, *The Life of Adoniram Judson*, 310.

113. Hulse well observed that "Madame Guyon and the mystics she represented laid great stress upon the inner life and union of the soul with God. They taught that our wills may be completely lost in the divine will, that we should strive after a disinterested love for him, and that entire sanctification is possible in this world. The aim of every believer is to be entirely at rest in God. Roman Catholic theology is destitute of exposition on union with Christ let alone the experimental side of that central truth . . . It is not surprising then that interest has been shown in those who have been prepared to explore the experimental aspect of this truth. This interest in experience arose out of Judson's genuine spiritual needs . . . Judson regarded Roman Catholicism as a system hopelessly given to idolatry." Hulse, "Adoniram Judson: Devoted for Life," 149–50.

consecrate himself with mystic-like ardor for the sake of attaining the holiness without which no one will see God.[114] If Roman Catholics could deny themselves and aggressively pursue holiness with a flawed doctrinal foundation, surely by observing an Edwardsean tradition, he could do the same.

Regarding the influence of Madame Guyon's writings and monastic solitude, Emily Judson said in retrospect that she did not believe Judson erred in his heart. She said his mental state was "driven by suffering on suffering, by such bereavement . . . and intensity of devotion, to a morbid development. A mind of less strength or a heart of less truthfulness and sincerity would have been wrecked." She suggested that "his sound judgment and elevated piety always carried him through triumphantly."[115]

Even so, Max H. Brown, in his thesis, "The New Divinity: The Theological Context for Adoniram Judson, Jr.," insightfully suggests that in Judson's dark period there was more happening than monastic Quietism. He proposes that Hopkinsian disinterested benevolence mainly influenced Judson, whether consciously or not. Brown says, "It seems that Judson was working out a renewed verification of the presence of grace." He goes on to say that through this raw season of confinement, Judson's faith remained firm, and Judson proved to himself that he was willing to be damned for God's glory. Brown observes that during this time of self-inflicted isolation,

---

114. During his melancholic period of 1829, Judson wrote on March 19, 1829, to his sister and mother, commending the works of Guyon and of the English mystic, William Law (1686–1761); however, he cautioned them to "endeavor to imitate" Guyon's ardor, "so far as she was right." Edward Judson, *The Life of Adoniram Judson*, 303. See also Wayland, *Memoir*, 1:473. Also, during this time in Judson's life, both Wayland and Edward Judson provided a list of seven spiritual practices Judson sought to employ on May 14, 1829. They do not comprise what Judson called his Rules of Life, but they do reflect how the mystics, especially Guyon, influenced his sanctification methods during this season. See Edward Judson, *The Life of Adoniram Judson*, 304; and Wayland, *Memoir*, 1:474.

115. Edward Judson, *The Life of Adoniram Judson*, 305. Another biographer also perceptively discussed the way Judson viewed such mystics' writing: "In the promotion of piety he used some aids which others condemn. Persons who are alarmed at the least approach to popery, view all writings which Roman Catholics extol with suspicion. Nevertheless, Mr. Judson found in the works of Lady Guion, and kindred writers of that communion, productions which gave an insight into the heart, and an impulse to the desire of a holy life, which he could not discover in the generality of human conceptions . . . Mr. Judson did not despise the illustration such works gave of the spiritual life, but cultivated acquaintance with them, doubtless to the benefit of his own soul. His knowledge of the fact that those whose productions he studied had been involved in such fearful delusions, we believe, caused him to exercise a more holy jealousy for truthfulness and reality in his own religion. What in many might be only asceticism, was in him a work of the heart, and his lofty bearing in the vicissitudes through which he was called to pass, manifests how thoroughly his soul was influenced by the highest principles." Middleditch, *Burmah's Great Missionary*, 438–39.

Judson wrote *The Threefold Cord*, which promotes prayer, self-denial, and benevolence. He argues that this is not coincidental, and he says the "synergistic effect" of these three strands of ascetic sanctification "does indicate a rare 'ideality.'" Brown submits, "Judson was just such an enlightened disciple, that he practiced the benevolence that Hopkins described."[116] In addition to Brown's point, though Quietism promoted inaction, Judson was hardly inactive. His evangelical activism ordered his regular routine. Judson may have slipped away to a place of solitude to pray and lament, but he was nevertheless active in writing, translation, and meeting with inquirers; he spent his evenings visiting and ministering to people.[117] Even *The Threefold Cord*, which he wrote during this period, promotes "doing good" as one of the three cords necessary for spiritual vitality. In light of his unceasing missionary labor, Judson evidently did not retreat into Guyon-like escapism. Though Guyon's passion for holiness and pursuit of God inspired Judson, Hopkinsian self-denial controlled him.

Doctrines and Descriptions of Self-Denying Piety

In various forms and on numerous occasions, Judson laid out his practical doctrine of self-denial.[118] He developed this doctrine in many different ways. He wrote his own rules for living, which he sought to daily follow; he

116. Brown, "The New Divinity," 96–97. Some who have read Judson's biography and tertiary sources might surmise that Judson had possibly succumbed to Burmese Buddhist self-denial because of his exposure to Buddhist literature. However, there is no evidence in the totality of the Judson corpus (letters, journals, tracts, sermons, and records from colleagues, friends, and family) that suggests this was ever the case, even in Judson's darkest season. For examples of such a supposition, see Roebuck, "Adoniram Judson," 242; and see Scacewater, "Adoniram Judson's Understanding and Appropriation of Buddhism," 210.

117. See Anderson, *To the Golden Shore*, 390–91. Stacy Warburton helpfully observed that Judson "was never more active in his work . . . While he was engaged in self-mortification for his own spiritual enrichment, he was throwing himself with keen ardor into all the work and fellowship of the mission." Warburton, *Eastward*, 120. Edward Judson also explained that, though Judson "spent many of his waking hours alone in a bamboo hermitage," he was still "directly engaged in missionary work." Edward Judson, *The Life of Adoniram Judson*, 304.

118. In one practical way, in a letter on April 17, 1831, two years after his depression abated, Judson advised Cephas Bennett to persevere in language study and to view it as a death to initial ministry enthusiasm and activism, for it would require much work and self-emptying. This self-denying work of language learning would pay off in the long-term, both in holiness and in the ability to communicate the gospel. Regarding the self-denial of language learning, Judson urged him, "Let us die as soon as possible, and by whatever process God shall appoint. And when we are dead to the world, and nature, and self, we shall begin to live to God." Wayland, *Memoir*, 1:522.

compiled Scripture verses of what he believed to be the biblical teaching on self-denial; and, he wrote instructions of how to employ self-denial in order to grow spiritually.

Rules of Life

He developed his own "Rules of Life," a Benedictine-like daily liturgy, as it were, to guide his decisions, habits, and actions. His rules demonstrate the degree to which Roman Catholic asceticism influenced his spirituality over and above traditional evangelical spirituality.[119] He designed eight rules as daily patterns in order to please Christ in all his actions. He adopted and readopted these eight rules on numerous occasions throughout his life. It was a practice he certainly deemed useful for his spirituality. After language study, he began his public ministry to the Burmans. Upon commencing this new phase of his ministry, he first adopted rules in April of 1819, and then he revised and readopted them five different times in the proceeding eight years. He never explained in his journals or letters the reason why he first started reading Roman Catholic writings, but in his rules that he adopted in 1826, he first mentioned that he was committed to constantly read the Bible and some other devotional book. Moreover, he said he refused to read any books in English that did not have "a devotional tendency," which were likely Roman Catholic writings.[120] By the last reapplication of these rules in 1827, his earnest prayer was, "God grant me grace to keep the above rules, and ever live to His glory, for Jesus Christ's sake."[121] These were his standard eight rules to which he devoted himself much of his life:

---

119. He adopted rules on April 4, 1819, revised and readopted them again on December 9, 1820, April 25, 1821, August 31, 1823, October 29, 1826, and March 11, 1827. Then, fifteen years later on August 9, 1842, he wrote a final set of rules. For five additional rules that he initiated on October 29, 1826, see Edward Judson, *The Life of Adoniram Judson*, 315; Wayland, *Memoir*, 1:322. He also adopted a temporary set of eight rules in 1833 and then a set of four in 1835. See Wayland, *Memoir*, 2:61, 103. The common denominator in these temporary sets of rules and in his other rules in general is his devotion to thrice-daily prayer and living in a constant awareness of God's presence. To read all his Rules of Life, see Edward Judson, *The Life of Adoniram Judson*, 315–16; Wayland, *Memoir*, 1:322–23; Wayland, *Memoir*, 2:61, 103, 190. He also created some miscellaneous resolutions of general goals, which were similar to his rules, such as the observance of secret prayer three times a day, seeking to preach the gospel daily, and seeking to practice brotherly love. He wrote resolutions like these on March 22, 1837, and revised and renewed them on August 6, 1837 and July 12, 1838; see Wayland, *Memoir*, 2:114. See also Edward Judson, *The Life of Adoniram Judson*, 315–16; Wayland, *Memoir*, 1:322–23.

120. See Wayland, *Memoir*, 1:322–23.

121. Edward Judson, *The Life of Adoniram Judson*, 315–16. See also Wayland,

1. Be diligent in secret prayer, every morning and evening.
2. Never spend a moment in mere idleness. *define?*
3. Restrain natural appetites within the bounds of temperance and purity. "Keep thyself pure [1 Tim 5:22]."
4. Suppress every emotion of anger and ill will.
5. Undertake nothing from motives of ambition or love of fame.
6. Never do that which, at the moment, appears to be displeasing to God.
7. Seek opportunities of making some sacrifice for the good of others, especially of believers, provided the sacrifice is not inconsistent with some duty.
8. Endeavor to rejoice in every loss and suffering incurred for Christ's sake and the Gospel's, remembering that though, like death, they are not to be willfully incurred, yet, like death, they are great gain.[122]

Later in his life, he still sought to live daily by a self-imposed pattern of rules. Six years after his last revision of his eight rules, he rewrote the eight rules on January 1, 1833, and then he renewed them thrice that year. They reflected similar sentiments to his abovementioned standard eight rules, though they were shortened. One rule that he added in 1833 was unlike previous rules: "Learn to distinguish and obey the internal impulse of the Holy Spirit."[123]

Two years later, in September of 1835, Judson wrote four rules to help him focus while he finished the revision of the Old Testament. They were similar to his previous rules; they included observing thrice-daily prayer, not reading useless books, heeding his conscience, and seeking to cultivate a constant awareness of God's presence.[124] In August 1842, he wrote a new set of four rules by which to live. This new set essentially abbreviated the original eight rules from 1827. They emphasized secret prayer, avoiding

---

Memoir, 1:322–23.

122. Edward Judson, *The Life of Adoniram Judson*, 315. See also Wayland, *Memoir*, 1:322. It is significant to note that in this eighth point Judson clearly evidenced that he was neither a self-wrought martyr nor was he fatalistic. He saw how suffering and death, though not self-caused, bring great benefits. Adding to his standard eight rules, in October 1826, he supplemented five more rules: "(1) Rise with the sun. (2) Read a certain portion of Burman every day, Sundays excepted. (3) Have the Scriptures and some devotional book in constant reading. (4) Read no book in English that has not a devotional tendency. (5) Suppress every unclean thought and look." Edward Judson, *The Life of Adoniram Judson*, 315; and Wayland, *Memoir*, 1:322.

123. For these eight rules of 1833, see Wayland, *Memoir*, 2:61.

124. Ibid., 2:103.

resentment toward others, benevolence to all, and being kind in mood, expression, and speech in order to please Christ. Judson renewed these four again in December 1842.[125] Judson took his spirituality seriously; he was uncertain of how long he would live,[126] and he knew death could come at any moment.[127]

Judson's extreme rule-keeping was out of sync with classic evangelical spirituality. His ascetic spirituality was unique to him, though inspired by his rigorous training at Andover and by his exposure to Roman Catholic writings. His penchant for order and excellence and his copious self-examination undoubtedly made rule-keeping useful for him. Judson certainly immersed himself regularly in the Bible for the sake of his translation work, and his powerful memory likely aided him in memorizing much of the Scripture that he drew upon during his meditation and prayer times. Yet, it is odd that in all his rule-writing, he never explicitly indicated that Bible intake was supreme and sufficient for sanctification, even though, as previously noted, he regularly promoted the proclamation of Scripture as the necessary means of evangelism and discipleship. Moreover, from his conversion and call to missions at Andover until the end of his life, Judson frequently spoke of the benefit of prayer, especially praying while walking, much more than he ever spoke of the long-standing evangelical practice of Bible meditation.[128] This demonstrates that his own uncommon ascetic spirituality went beyond the Puritan and evangelical piety of his forbearers.

Points of self-denial.

Judson also practiced specific methods of self-denial. He called them "Points of Self-Denial." He sought to deny himself his tidiness, cleanliness, and order, which was a constant struggle for him.[129] Judson sought to deny himself

---

125. Ibid., 2:190. See also Edward Judson, *The Life of Adoniram Judson*, 316.

126. Middleditch, *Burmah's Great Missionary*, 418–19.

127. Edward Judson, *The Life of Adoniram Judson*, 577–79. See also Wayland, *Memoir*, 2:38–41. After he readopted his four condensed rules, he created one final rule that well captured his previous years of zealously pursuing usefulness, and it illustrates the supreme motivation of his dutiful spirituality. This final rule would also be the controlling theme of his piety until his death: "Resolved to make the desire to please Christ the grand motive of all my actions." Wayland, *Memoir*, 2:190. See also Edward Judson, *The Life of Adoniram Judson*, 316.

128. See Wayland, *Memoir*, 1:39; Warburton, *Eastward*, 119–20. See also Wayland, *Memoir*, 2:336–37, 389–91.

129. For example, see Gouger's observations of Judson's neatness in *A Personal Narrative*, 174–75.

his propensity to be irritated with others for inconsequential behaviors and indecorum. He wished to deny himself his avoidance of shame at all cost and his aversion to being wrong. Finally, he tried to deny himself his desire for ease and his disgust for inconvenience.[130]

Judson's self-denial largely targeted excess and indulgence. He did not believe a life of disinterested benevolence and the pursuit of temporal comfort and pleasure were compatible. Judson wrote to Christian women in America to persuade them not to spend their lives accumulating and flaunting costly attire. In a portion of his letter, written in October of 1831, he wrote with emphasis: "*The severest part of self-denial consists in encountering the disapprobation, the envy, the hatred of one's dearest friends*,"[131] and people often misunderstand those who practice self-denial as "concerned about small things." He went on to say that Christ is the commander in this war and he expects each Christian woman to do her duty in accord with his final command. Judson charged them to "go forward," not fearing what others might think of them. To both comfort and confront them, he asserted, "The eye of Christ is upon you." Then he closed with a short jeremiad, admonishing them to fear the One with eyes of fire, "whose irrevocable fiat will fix [them] forever in heaven or hell, and mete out the measure of [their] everlasting pleasures and pains." In light of such eternal prospects, Judson contrasted the futility of "cherishing self-love" with the wisdom of "self-denial." He closed by exhorting them not to wait another moment, but "*do now*" what they will have wished they would have done before that great and awful Day.[132] This letter further reveals that Judson's anticipation of imminent death motivated his self-denial. Moreover, he practiced self-denial because he viewed assurance of salvation and eternal rewards in relation to his disinterested benevolence; and conversely, he viewed eternal condemnation in direct correlation to self-love. His reverence for the supreme Judge drove his self-denial.

Duty to Oneself

Judson's *A Digest of Scripture* serves as a succinct snapshot of the biblical evidence for Judson's doctrine and practice. After the chapters on "Duty to God" and "Duty to Men," Judson outlined the biblical teaching about "Duty

---

130. See the list of Judson's "Points of Self-Denial," in Edward Judson, *The Life of Adoniram Judson*, 315.

131. Emphasis in original.

132. Wayland, *Memoir*, 2:483–85. See also Adoniram Judson, *Judson's Letter on Dress*; emphasis in original.

to Oneself." Citing numerous Scripture references, some examples of what he proposed include themes such as self-examination, self-denial, humility, steadfastness, diligence, contentment, and heavenly-mindedness.[133] This chapter in *A Digest of Scripture* reveals Judson's foundational biblical prooftexts. He did not merely create a doctrine and practice of self-denial based on abstract and philosophical principles. Many of his aforementioned rules of life are indicative of his compilation of biblical verses for teaching the Burmans their Christian duties.

The Born-Again Man.

In *A Digest of Scripture*, Judson underscored three overarching evidences of regeneration: (1) renunciation of all for Christ; (2) perseverance in good works; and (3) peculiar traits of Christian faith.[134] Yet, he mainly developed his practical doctrine of regeneration in his first and most widely published tract (first published in 1816), *A View of the Christian Religion*. In this tract Judson compared and contrasted the signs of the renewed and unrenewed man. It was his attempt to promote genuine assurance.

In Hopkinsian language, he said that the unregenerate man "loves himself supremely," and he loves all the things the world commends as pleasurable and worthy. However, the regenerate man "loves the true God supremely, and desires that the divine glory may be promoted." The regenerate man longs for heaven's everlasting happiness. Furthermore, the born-again man loves others as himself and seeks their good. In very gospel-oriented terms, Judson said that the unregenerate man seeks to merit his salvation, whereas the regenerate man trusts alone in the merits of Christ. Judson reasoned that the ground for avoiding sinful works and doing good works is the meritorious, atoning work of Christ. Greater still, the grand motivation for the desire to refuse evil and promote good is a "supreme love to Jesus Christ, and a desire to do His will." So when the man of God does sin, he quickly repents of offending his "superlatively excellent and lovely Lord," and he puts his trust in Christ's death, asking God for forgiveness. For the born-again man, the best is yet to come.[135]

---

133. Adoniram Judson, *A Digest of Scripture*, 108–23.

134. Ibid., 56–62.

135. Adoniram Judson, *A View of the Christian Religion*, 2.1, 2.2. See also Adoniram Judson, "A View of the Christian Religion." For an easily accessible version, see McElroy, *Adoniram Judson's Soul Winning Secrets Revealed*, 26–28.

Judson's The Threefold Cord.

During his dark time at the Hermitage, in February 1829, Judson penned *The Threefold Cord*.[136] It was a practical treatise on the theme of Ecclesiastes 4:12, which says, "And if one prevail against him, two shall withstand him; and a threefold cord is not quickly broken." The aim of this piece was to help the unsure believer "to grow in grace and attain the perfect love and enjoyment of God." Regarding this "short manual of advice," he urged, "Lay hold of it with the hand of faith, and be assured that it will draw thy soul to God and to heaven." The three cords are secret prayer, self-denial, and doing good.

Judson went on to say that "Secret Prayer" is what gives strength to the other two cords. This portion of his tract suggests that he heavily drew upon Benedictine and monastic daily prayer practices.[137] He upheld, as seen in his rules of life, that prayer should be done morning and evening, and the Christian should arrange his schedule so he can easily pray two to three hours a day in total. Interspersed throughout the day should be approximately seven periods to lift up one's "soul to God in private retirement." The first prayer time in the morning should come after midnight in the silent hours, and then the subsequent times should be at dawn, nine o'clock, noon, three o'clock, six o'clock and nine o'clock in the evening. Expected in this prayer time were both personal reflection and communion with God. Judson urged Christians to let nothing distract from these sacred hours. Practically, he said that prayer should be directed first toward the cross, looking up, "trembling and in tears, to thine incarnate God and Saviour dying on the cross." He instructed prayer for forgiveness of sin, and then supplication for the Holy Spirit to come and guide the ensuing prayer time.

Judson admitted that his second cord, "Self-Denial," had been abused by the Roman Catholic Church and that Protestants consequently had rejected it. However, he charged that self-denial was the one of the three cords that gave "firmness and consistency" to the others. He essentially compared atrophied muscles to a soul that, being unexercised, becomes worthless with self-love and self-gratification. Equally, self-love grows stronger the more it is employed just as a muscle strengthens through use. "The more it is indulged, the stronger it becomes." So, in order to kill self-love, he said, treat it like "a vicious animal," and starve it through self-denial and taking up the cross. In a lengthy discourse calling for renouncing convenience,

---

136. Adoniram Judson, *The Threefold Cord*, 1–6. See also Edward Judson, *The Life of Adoniram Judson*, 571–77; and Wayland, *Memoir*, 2:461–66.

137. For sources on such monastic practices, see Johnson, *Benedictine Daily Prayer*; and Benedict, *RB 1980: The Rule of St. Benedict*.

comfort, entertainment, recreation, and all things pleasant, Judson argued that self-denial was the path on which the true Christian must walk to enter the kingdom of heaven.[138] As an example, he maintained that exposing the mind and heart to any book that did not improve communion with God would in fact disrupt it.[139]

Judson went on to plead for Christians to renounce all things worldly. He called on true Christians to forsake whatever would solicit the contaminations of the lust of the flesh, lust of the eyes, and the pride of life. As he called for renunciation of whatever worldly things gain influence over the soul, he included a footnote that insightfully warned against extreme self-denial. He advised against methods that injure the body and compromise health. He also cautioned against the hypocrisy of dress and appearance that harbors pride. He purposefully sought to lead the reader to despair by suggesting that sin has polluted every good deed, whether done reluctantly or nearly perfectly. He encouraged making the initial sacrifice necessary to enter the hard but rewarding path of self-denial.

Judson said that his third section, "Doing Good," in *The Threefold Cord*, made the previous two sections useful. He said that just as Christ went and did good, so should the follower of Christ.[140] In very Hopkinsian language, he said, "As a true follower of Christ, seek not thine own profit, but the profit

---

138. Judson expounded the verse, "Strait is the gate, and narrow is the way, that leadeth unto life; and few there be that find it" (Matt 7:14).

139. Judson quoted Archbishop Robert Leighton (1611–1684) of Glasgow: "Choose always, to the best of thy skill, what is most to God's honor, and most like unto Christ and his example, and most profitable to thy neighbor, and most against thy own proper will, and least serviceable to thy own praise and exaltation." And again: "Not only be content, but desirous, to be unknown, or, being known, to be contemned [*sic*] and despised of all men, yet without thy faults or deservings, as much as thou canst." See Cheever, *The Select Works of Archbishop Leighton*, 558–63. This book by Leighton was likely required reading at Andover. See Woods, *History of the Andover*, 169. Also, in an original footnote, Judson said, "[S]ee *Rules and Instructions for a Holy Life*, a piece which, though not elaborately finished, contains the very marrow of true religion. Study also Law's *Treatise upon Christian Perfection*, and Kempis's *Imitation of Christ*." Adoniram Judson, *The Threefold Cord*, 3; see also Edward Judson, *The Life of Adoniram Judson*, 574; Wayland, *Memoir*, 2:462. See Law, *A Practical Treatise upon Christian Perfection*; à Kempis, *Imitation of Christ*.

140. Compare this quote to Judson's sermon in Philadelphia on December 24, 1845; he said, "It appears from the inspired writings, that one leading characteristic of Christ was, that 'he went about doing good [Acts 10:38].' To be like him we must go about—not merely stay and do good, but go and do good." Middleditch, *Burmah's Great Missionary*, 375. See also Edward Judson, *The Life of Adoniram Judson*, 469, 475; and Wayland, *Memoir*, 2:464. Adoniram Judson, *The Threefold Cord*, 5; emphasis in original.

of many, that they may be saved."[141] In a helpful summary, Judson explicated how these three cords wrapped together to make one unbreakable cord:

> By practicing self-denial, thou weakenest the debasing principle of inordinate self-love; and by doing good, thou cherishes and strengthenest the heavenly principle of holy benevolence. Let these exercises, then, quickened and sanctified by secret prayer, be the regular work of each day of thy life. Thus I present thee, my brother, with the threefold cold—the three grand means of growing in graces—of gaining the victory over the world, the flesh, and the devil—of drawing the soul from earth to heaven. Means, I say; for I speak not now of faith, the living operative principle within—the hand, with which thou must lay hold of the threefold cord ... Disappoint not the fond hopes of thy longing Saviour. Renounce the world, renounce thyself, and flee into his loving arms, which are open to receive and embrace thee.

He concluded *The Threefold Cord* by encouraging the struggling believer to be hopeful and boldly enter the path of self-denial:

> *Do what thou canst;* stretch out what thou hast, however maimed or withered, and try to lay hold. Try to pray in faith, to practice self-denial, and to do good. And be assured, my brother, that thou wilt quickly find the hand of faith where thou thoughtest it was not.[142]

---

141. Compare this statement to the theology expressed in Hopkins, *Works of Samuel Hopkins*, 3:145–46. See Adoniram Judson, *The Threefold Cord*, 5. See also Edward Judson, *The Life of Adoniram Judson*, 576; and Wayland, *Memoir*, 2:464.

142. Adoniram Judson, *Threefold Cord*, 1–6. See also Edward Judson, *The Life of Adoniram Judson*, 571–77; and Wayland, *Memoir*, 2:461–66; emphasis in original. In a fascinating dissertation about the juxtaposition of Judson's spirituality of self-denial, his translation of the names of God in Burmese, and his ability to contextualize his theology for a Burmese Buddhist culture, Laisum says, "By believing and loving Jesus supremely, the renewed human beings endeavor to avoid evil deeds and to perform good deeds only according to the divine commands, that is, according to Jesus' teaching. This "believing and loving" Jesus in the real lives of the Judsons ... was the internalization of the divine laws or spiritual transformation. Accordingly, instruction for Christians during the Judson era was given in a form known as the "Threefold Cord," that is, secret prayer, self-denial, and doing good. In sum, Judson's understanding and naming God as *Tavara*, or universal principle of existence, enabled Judson to dispute about God rationally ... It also allowed Judson to value the meaning and beauty of Burmese culture and tradition. Thus, the Judsons lived and ate as the Burmese as much as possible ... By naming and addressing God as *Hpaya*, Judson personally preached and practiced self-denial or self-negation as the criterion for true spirituality. However, while refraining from worldly pleasure, fame, self-aggrandizement, etc. for himself, he never failed to envision the well-being of the people. Naming God *Tavara Hpaya*, therefore, is an accurate and intelligible statement about the Christian concept of God in a Burmese

In the final analysis, this tract illustrates the confusion and darkness that had clouded his mind during that painful period. He offered a cord of three strands as a means for sanctification, and none of them promoted the authoritative and sufficient Scriptures as the chief instrument through which the Holy Spirit sanctifies Christians. Ironically, he was concurrently spending himself to translate and teach the Scriptures. Making a similar observation of the absence of the Bible in *The Threefold Cord*, one biographer aptly remarked that "this could not have happened in the earlier or the later periods of Judson's religious life,"[143] because his whole life was immersed in the Scriptures.

The Missionary Model of Self-Denial

Like his teachings about self-denial, whether consciously or unconsciously, Judson exemplified how he practiced self-denial through his missionary piety. Revealing his early consecration to the missionary life, Judson wrote a letter to Ann in 1821 as she was returning to America to recover from illness. His expressions of piety epitomize his duty of renouncing all things to please Christ. He said in the letter that he entertained for a moment how pleasant it would be to find a serene place for rest where he and Ann could enjoy the loveliness of religion together. Then with an about-face, he exclaimed, "But I fled to Jesus, and all such thoughts soon passed away. Life is short. Happiness consists not in outward circumstances." He said that he was burdened by the millions of perishing Burmans who have no other person to tell them the gospel (at that time of writing) than Judson himself. He said he was under obligation "to spend and be spent for Christ." He said that he considered it a great privilege to walk the path of self-denial and suffer for his Lord. He signed off in the letter by calling Ann to join him in prayer for a spirit that grows in indifference to the world's pleasures and empty promises. He said he prayed that their trials would cause their hearts to cleave to heaven's promises and to be enthralled in Jesus, "the uncreated Fountain of all excellence and glory."[144]

Approximately a decade after the above-mentioned letter to Ann, Judson's ascetic spirituality had not decreased. It continued to drive his missionary religion. He wrote in 1832 to the Foreign Missionary Association of the Hamilton Literary and Theological Institution of New York. His

---

context, an analysis, affirmation, and transformation of culture and spirituality theologically." Laisum, "Naming God in Burma Today," 22–24.

143. Conant, *The Earnest Man*, 354.

144. Middleditch, *Burmah's Great Missionary*, 167.

words to would-be missionaries and others in American churches are revealing. In his final points of advice to missionaries, Judson contended for the indispensable role of self-denial for the devoted missionary. He warned that recreation and retreat from the grind of missionary labor are indeed a "disease" to one's "spiritual constitution." Satan loves to tempt Christ's missionaries to pursue more comfortable and opportunistic fields of service, which preclude long-term missionary service. He admonished them to be weary of "the pride of humble men—that secret pride" of being esteemed as "great and good." In order to combat this, he said missionaries should "confess faults" immediately, freely, and publicly. Such self-mortification would aid in subduing pride. He also suggested that the missionaries do not store up money for themselves but to trust in God to provide. As was his habit throughout his life, Judson encouraged bodily exercise for the sake of long-term staying power. And his final point of self-denial was the denial of the "genteel living" of "fashionable European society." Instead, he promoted living in culture like the natives. In sum, Judson encouraged the would-be missionaries to deny themselves whatever personal, sinful, physical, and cultural factors that would impede their usefulness for the Lord's work.[145]

Upon his return to America in 1845, Judson still employed his self-denying model. One writer commented that he arrived in his "refined native home, . . . where no lessons of Divine Truth meet with acceptance unless they are largely seasoned with diversion and pleasantry."[146] He received invitations to preach on many occasions and tell of his sufferings and triumphs. Even at a time when he could slow down and rest from his translation efforts, he did not wish to allow himself relief and relaxation. He pressed on, knowing that life was uncertain and that the dictionary was still incomplete. In a letter to Solomon Peck, before his arrival, he requested that his hosts and supporters allow him to use a quiet room wherever he was staying for his dictionary work. He knew it would be a great sacrifice to shut himself up in a room while back in the land of plenty that he had not enjoyed in over thirty years. Though he would have numerous opportunities to preach in English around the country, he said he would have to refuse many, not only because of his faltering voice, but because preaching in English distracted his concentration in Burmese. Though he loved preaching more than any other spiritual vocation, he said that he had to make a conscious effort from the beginning of his missionary consecration to make choices that would improve his usefulness for whatever task that he believed God had given

---

145. Adoniram Judson, "Advice to Missionary Candidates," 577–79; Wayland, *Memoir*, 2:38–41.

146. Balderston, "Adoniram Judson," 194.

him.[147] This required him to "abjure" his own native language. Regarding denying himself the joy of preaching in English, Judson explained, "When I crossed the river, I burned my ships . . . The burned ships cannot now be reconstructed."[148]

Conclusion

Adoniram Judson, deeply influenced by Hopkinsian disinterested benevolence and inspired by the zeal of Madame Guyon, sought to submit to God's sovereign will no matter the cost. Such a self-denying life of pleasing Christ in the path of missionary duty was his holy ambition. Judson's ascetic piety, though mixed with some controversial practices and notions, established his staying power. His ascetic spirituality was a key theme that distinguished his piety from common evangelical piety. In a life and ministry context of pre-modern medicine, ocean travel, and slow communication, and where death was always nearby and the uncertainty of life was an ongoing concern, Judson's disciplined routine and self-denial seem more reasonable. If he were to die early, the whole Burmese translation project would have disappeared with him. Judson's ascetic missionary spirituality was useful for him in his particular context because it enabled him to complete the task that he believed was his to fulfill. Indeed, the fusion of his New Divinity training, his Roman Catholic ascetic practices, and his peculiar personality may have proven useful for his own sanctification and endurance in ministry; nevertheless, such uncommon features forced the example of his piety to be unattainable for the common evangelical. Furthermore, his belief that God is uppermost in God's affections dominated his vision of life, ministry, happiness, and suffering. All things, whether miniscule or magnificent, whether painful or pleasurable, climaxed in praise to God's infinite wisdom. Judson interpreted all of life through this God-exalted lens. He dutifully submitted to this sovereign God, renouncing all things in risk, affliction, grief, and death. Judson's definitive prayer was, "Thy will, O God, be ever done; for thy will is inevitably the wisest and the best."[149]

---

147. For one example of his wrestling with his duty to translate and compile a dictionary instead of preaching the gospel, see Judson's letter on March 12, 1838, to the American Baptist Board in Wayland, *Memoir*, 2:122.

148. Adoniram Judson to the Rev. Solomon Peck, correspondence, April 13, 1845, Box No. AJ 3, Folder 2 and Microfilm Roll 1, Judson Letters, ABHS. See also Adoniram Judson, "Letter of Mr. Judson, Maulmain, April 13, 1845: Sickness of Mrs. Judson," 247–48. See also Middleditch, *Burmah's Great Missionary*, 342–44; Edward Judson, *The Life of Adoniram Judson*, 445–47; and Wayland, *Memoir*, 2:199–200.

149. Conant, *The Earnest Man*, 240. See also Wayland, *Memoir*, 1:253.

5

"We Reap on Zion's Hill": Heavenly-Minded Spirituality

ADONIRAM JUDSON'S BIOGRAPHER, FRANCIS Wayland, claimed, "In treating of [Judson's] religious character, it would be an omission not to refer to his habitual heavenly mindedness. In his letters, I know of no topic that is so frequently referred to as the nearness of the heavenly glory."[1] Heavenly happiness was Judson's steady comfort in the face of sickness and death; he longingly fixed his eyes to the eternal reward. This chapter will illustrate how Judson's ardent vision of heaven's eternal bliss sustained him through his adversity and self-denial. It will show how his hope for Christ's heavenly glory filling the earth sustained his optimism of the future. Hoping in heavenly happiness gave Judson the perseverance to stay the course, and the prospect of eternal reward motivated him to spend himself and be spent for the glory of Christ.

Heavenly-Mindedness

Judson's spirituality was one of self-denying submission to the sovereign will of God, seeking chiefly to please Christ, his Lord. Pleasing Christ was his motivation, and self-denial was his means of submitting to God's will; and his heavenly-mindedness gave him a hopeful and optimistic perspective. Recording how the promises of the Bible buttressed Judson's heavenward orientation, one anonymous missionary said about Judson that there was "no man in India, or elsewhere, whom I thought riper for heaven. I was

---

1. Wayland, *Memoir*, 2:381–82.

particularly impressed with his firm reliance on the promises of God."[2] Judson interpreted all of God's temporally severe providences through the lens of eternally happy prospects. This hope in future glory comforted him, and he likewise counseled others to endure with their soul's attention fixed on the same happy hope. His anticipation of receiving an eternal reward for his self-denying labors reinforced his spirituality.

A Lifelong Heavenly-Minded Disposition

Judson's heavenly-minded spirituality remained as intense during his last days as it was during his early days. He never vacillated in his patience for heaven's happiness and eternal benefits. In his early years before experiencing the struggles of missionary life, Judson had a heavenward orientation, which he demonstrated in his communications with his fiancée, Ann Hasseltine. Then, by his final year of life, Judson's gaze was still looking heavenward, which his third wife, Emily C. Judson, had recorded. Serving as bookends of his lifelong heavenly-minded disposition are accounts of his eternal perspective expressed to both Ann and Emily.

Judson had an eternal perspective from the beginning. Before Judson and Ann had married, he was beginning to focus his lifelong vision toward heaven. As he considered the unknown risks of the missionary call, he sought to steady his hope in God's good will to reward the faithful in eternity. Though Judson did not know what God held in his temporal future, he nevertheless knew that God had ordained immeasurable happiness for his eternal future. In a letter to Ann in December 1810, Judson pondered the brevity of life and that whatever is done today, "is done to all eternity." He mused on the consequential continuity between one's earthly and eternal existence:

> A life once spent is irrevocable. It will remain to be contemplated through eternity. If it be marked with sins, the marks will be indelible. If it has been a useless life, it can never be improved. Such it will stand forever and ever . . . When it is once past, it is gone forever. All the marks which we put upon it will exhibit forever. It will never become less true that such a day was spent in such a manner. Each day will not only be a witness of our conduct, but will affect our everlasting destiny. No day will lose its share of influence in determining where shall be our seat in heaven. How shall we then wish to see each day marked with usefulness! It will then be too late to mend its appearance. It

2. Ibid., 2:332.

is too late to mend the days that are past. The future is in our power. Let us, then, each morning, resolve to send the day into eternity in such a garb as we shall wish it to wear forever. And at night let us reflect that one more day is irrevocably gone, indelibly marked.[3]

Two years later, on their initial voyage to Asia, Judson and Ann devoted themselves to prayer and studying the Scriptures. Together they pursued the heavenly piety that would sustain them through their tireless labors. While at sea, in April 1812, Ann reflected on Judson's spirituality in a letter. She said he often would dispel her "spiritual darkness" with words of "hope of a happy eternity."[4]

Judson had an eternal perspective to the end. After his death, Judson's widow, Emily, described his orientation toward eternity and how it affected his joyful trust in God and how it quieted her own gloominess. Like the above accounts, Judson's spirituality was oriented to look forward to heavenly glory. Furthermore, by the end of his life, he could look back on a lifetime of the usefulness of a heavenly-minded religion. Emily said he had a very happy disposition, though he could still feel discouraged. Having suffered much, he could carry the burdens of the downcast, but he could equally rejoice with the prosperous. His spirituality habitually grounded its steadiness in God's sovereignty, and she said, though he could be "momentarily disheartened," he was never glum. She said that because he saw all of life's events, "however minute or painful," as ordained by God's infinite wisdom, he was therefore able to "rejoice evermore" that God caused everything to work "to one great and glorious end."[5]

---

3. Edward Judson, *The Life of Adoniram Judson*, 14–15. Even before Judson wrote this letter to Ann, he had already expressed his heavenly-minded conviction to Ann's father in asking him to allow Judson to lead Ann into a life and ministry that would certainly face hazards, pangs, and anguish of all kinds. He pleaded, "Can you consent to all this, in hope of soon meeting your daughter in the world of glory, with a crown of righteousness, brightened by the acclamations of praise which shall redound to her Saviour from heathens saved, through her means, from eternal woe and despair?" Ann Hasseltine Judson, *An Account of the American Baptist Mission*, 36. See also Clemént, *Memoir of Adoniram Judson*, 25; and Middleditch, *Burmah's Great Missionary*, 38.

4. Wayland, *Memoir*, 1:211–12. See also Middleditch, *Burmah's Great Missionary*, 44–45.

5. Emily Chubbuck Judson, "Closing Scenes in Dr. Judson's Life," 35. For a good example of Judson's trust that God works all things for a glorious end, see his letter to Daniel Sharp, on November 30, 1822, about the untimely death of his missionary colleague, James Colman, in, Adoniram Judson, "Letter from Dr. Judson to Mr. Sharp, of Boston, Ava, Nov. 30, 1822," 209–10. For helpful illustrations of Judson's joyful temperament, smiling face, and tenderness with both his family and acquaintances, see Kendrick, *The Life and Letters of Mrs. Emily C. Judson*, 141–215. For William Hague's

After Judson's death, Emily wrote to his sister, Abigail Judson. Emily described Judson's last year, his dying days, and the sweetness of his heavenly-minded piety. She described him as an "uncommonly spiritual Christian . . . It seemed as though the light of the world on which he was entering had been sent to brighten his upward pathway."[6] Looking back on the trials of his life, Judson would often tell Emily that God's kind providence protected and blessed him through his suffering, so that "his joys had far outnumbered his sorrows." During his last months, as he considered the looming reality of his earthly departure, he wished that he and Emily could go together, but such was unlikely. Feeling sad that Emily would have to grieve his death, he encouraged her with his trust that the infinitely wise will of God held their futures firm. Judson said, "He will order all things well, and we can safely trust our future to His hands."[7] In his research on Judson's life, Francis Wayland noted that Judson would often speak of hardships as though soon to be swallowed up in eternal bliss, and he often meditated on that great day for "those who with him had fought the good fight, and were now wearing the crown of victory." Wayland said that Judson's reflection on death was his "solace" in all his life's "troubles."[8]

Heavenly Comfort

Having endured many hardships, when no other earthly consolation sufficed, Judson's steady source of comfort lay in his fixed hope in the promises of heavenly rest.

Judson sought heavenly comfort in insecurity. In a letter to Thomas Baldwin, the pastor at Second Baptist Church in Boston, in February of 1824, Judson expressed his concerns about how the war between Britain and Burma would affect his mission work. Having invested so much into the Burmese mission, nervousness of potential deportments alarmed Judson. In one angry edict, the Burmese monarch could have dissolved all of Judson's sacrifice and labor. He asked Baldwin for intercession to "the throne of grace" on his behalf. And yet, he said, there is a better Intercessor "at the right hand of the Divine Presence in heaven," who is sympathetic, affectionate, and mighty to save. Judson conceded that in his little life experience, he had yet to "taste the sweetness of this precious truth" of having "a greater

---

account of Judson's happy temperament and smiling countenance, see Wayland, *Memoir*, 2:359.

   6. Wayland, *Memoir*, 2:337.
   7. Edward Judson, *The Life of Adoniram Judson*, 534.
   8. Wayland, *Memoir*, 2:382.

Friend" on the throne in heaven. He looked to Baldwin as an example of one who had already walked through much uncertainty and insecurity and had experienced the faithfulness of such a heavenly King. Nonetheless, Judson knew it was a precious promise that would console him in his anxiety. So, in confessing that he still had much improvement yet to make in trusting God's purposes, he asked for Baldwin's prayers. Judson said, "Pray for me, that I may be counted worthy to hold out to the end, and finally meet with you before the throne, and handle a harp of gold in the dear Redeemer's praise."[9] Twenty-two years after his letter to Baldwin, Judson had indeed experienced the precious truth to which he had conceded he knew only partially. After a lifetime of witnessing God deliver him through uncertainty and troublesome anxieties, Judson's security remained in the promises of eternal rest and reward. Before he set sail back to Burma with his newly-wedded wife, Emily, Judson attended a valedictory service in the Baldwin Place Church of Boston in July 1846. Following an address by Baron Stow (1801–1869),[10] Judson told the assembly that though his temporal future was uncertain, not knowing if he would ever again return to America, yet he was certain that they would meet again "in that blessed world where 'the loved and the parted here below meet ne'er to part again.'"[11] He was content knowing that he might die in the near future, to "meet no more on earth" his "dear friends."[12] As his life and labor progressed, Judson beheld the faithfulness of God, and his trust in God's providence and promises of blessings strengthened.

Judson sought heavenly comfort in aloneness. There were many seasons where Judson felt the sadness of separation from his loved ones. A most grievous season of aloneness happened in 1821. Ann became very ill, and the extreme nature of her sickness necessitated a voyage back to America for recovery. Saying goodbye to her, Judson wrestled with the feelings of emptiness and sorrow in her sustained absence. He would not see

---

9. Adoniram Judson to the Rev. Thomas Baldwin, letter, February 19, 1824, Box No. AJ 1, Folder 2 and Microfilm Roll 1, Judson Letters, ABHS; for an extract, see Adoniram Judson, "Letter from Dr. Judson to Rev. Dr. Baldwin, Dated Ava, Feb. 19, 1824," 22–23.

10. Baron Stow was a Baptist minister at the Baldwin Street Baptist Church in Boston (1832–1848), and then later he served as the pastor at the Rowe Street Baptist Church (1848–1867) of Boston. He compiled the Baptist hymnal, *The Psalmist*. See Stow and Smith, *The Psalmist*.

11. This was a reference to a poem written by Judson's second wife, Sarah B. Judson, near the Isle of France right before she died; see Wayland, *Memoir*, 2:211–12.

12. Dowling, *The Judson Offering*, 279. See also Adoniram Judson, "Address of Dr. Judson," 267; Middleditch, *Burmah's Great Missionary*, 396; and Wayland, *Memoir*, 2:254.

her again for over two years.[13] Judson wrote a letter to her in September 1821, a few days after her departure. He described his battle with sin and his dissatisfaction with his state of progressive holiness. He prayed that Ann would know the joy of religion more than he was enjoying it at the time. In his struggle with sin, he rejoiced in how "consoling" it was to surrender their missionary work and their lives "into the faithful hands of Jesus." He said, because "the Lord reigns," he could "safely trust all in his hands, and rejoice in whatever may betide." Suffering with Christ must precede being "glorified with him."[14] Within a few days of writing the aforementioned letter to Ann, Judson wrote in his journal, demonstrating his struggle with melancholy. He mourned that he too often derived "daily comfort and gratification" from the wrong places, which were deceptively empty. His heart's depravity, he said, was so strong that he could not be "satisfied with the pure bread of heaven." Instead, he said he was "continually hankering after the more gross and palatable food of this world—the husks of time and sense." He explained that only when God strips away such counterfeit comforts do Christians realize the source of true satisfaction, and ostensibly, he was referring to the deprivation he felt after Ann's departure. He perceived that his heart was so "ill-disciplined" that even in those happy moments of enjoying "glimpses of heaven," temporal discouragements would "intervene, and swallow up all anticipations of future joy."[15] Then, a few days after this journal entry, Judson wrote to Daniel Sharp regarding his sad struggle with Ann's departure. Judson lamented that not one person could counsel or encourage him. Nevertheless, he asserted that his consolation came from heaven. He said his happiness came from hoping in the saving hands of Christ. The reason he gave for the security of his hope was that Christ was powerful to keep the oppressed from being abandoned and dejected.[16] Judson's spiritual temperament was neither excessive nor emotionless. He could experience real discouragement, and he fought hard to be satisfied with the promises of heaven. Accordingly, he knew the joy of heaven's security.

Eighteen years later, while apart from his second wife, Sarah B. Judson, he wrote a series of letters to her. In a letter in March 1839, he said that he wished they could be together again to enjoy each other's company. He mused that if God allowed "sinful creatures on earth" to enjoy the "exquisite

---

13. Ann left on August 21, 1821 and returned on December 5, 1823. See Edward Judson, *The Life of Adoniram Judson*, 564.

14. Adoniram Judson, "Extracts from Mr. Judson's Letters to His Wife, Rangoon, Sept. 5, 1821," 57.

15. Middleditch, *Burmah's Great Missionary*, 165.

16. Adoniram Judson, "Letter from Mr. Judson to Mr. Sharp, Dated Rangoon, September 17, 1821," 344–45.

delights" of the bond of love as he and Sarah had, then "what must the joys of heaven be? Surely there is not a single lawful pleasure, the loss of which we shall have to regret there."[17]

Judson sought heavenly comfort in death, which, more than any type of event, had a way of revealing the true source of his joy and hope. Feeling the pain of a loved one's death, Judson neither displayed a sulky defeatism nor an indifferent stiffness. His heavenly-minded piety was sorrowful, yet always rejoicing.[18] In a letter to Daniel Sharp in November 1822, Judson discussed his lament over the death of his faithful missionary companion, James Colman. Judson had consented for Colman to visit Calcutta, but while in India, Colman became ill and died. Judson agonized to make sense of the peculiar event, but he trusted that God superintended his decision, "and that in the future world of light we shall see that the great designs of God were furthered by events which appear to us, at present, most disastrous."[19]

Approximately six months after Ann's death, their two-year old daughter Maria died.[20] In a letter to Ann's mother in April of 1827, Judson recounted his "excruciating" grief and his heavenly hope. He said that after experiencing separation for six months, he trusted that "their spirits are rejoicing," though he felt "left alone in the wide world." Instead of despairing of ultimate loss, he rejoiced that it was only temporary, and he thus sought to prepare himself "in readiness to follow the dear departed to that blessed world" under the reign of Christ.[21] In the same year that Maria died, Judson also heard of his father's death.[22] Judson wrote a letter in December of 1827, a year after Ann's death, to her sisters; not many months before penning that letter did he learn of his father's death. In that context of consecutive deaths, he candidly wrestled with the sting of death and yet expressed his hope for heaven in his letter to Ann's sisters.[23] At the outset of the letter, he lamented that "death mocks us, and tramples our dearest hopes and our lives in the

---

17. Wayland, *Memoir*, 2:140.

18. See 2 Cor 6:10.

19. Adoniram Judson, "Letter from Dr. Judson to Mr. Sharp, of Boston, Ava, Nov. 30, 1822," 209–10.

20. See Edward Judson, *The Life of Adoniram Judson*, 565.

21. Adoniram Judson, "Death of Dr. Judson's Child, Letter to Mother Hasseltine, Amherst, April 26, 1827," 131. For a previous letter of equal gravity about Ann's death, see Adoniram Judson to Mother Hasseltine, letter, February 4, 1827, Box No. AJ 7, Folder 3 and Microfilm Roll 2, Judson Letters, ABHS.

22. Judson's father died on November 25, 1826, and Judson heard the news on July 11, 1827. See Edward Judson, *The Life of Adoniram Judson*, 565. Ann died on October 24, 1826, and Judson heard the news of her death on November 24, 1826. See ibid.

23. See Hunt, *Bless God and Take Courage*, 307.

dust." Yet Judson retorted by mocking death, saying, "But go on now and do thy worst. Thy time will come. The last enemy that shall be destroyed is death . . . Thou shalt devour thyself and die." He went on in the letter to say,

> When the crown of life is set on our heads, and we know assuredly that we shall die no more, we shall make heaven's arches ring with songs of praise to Him who hath loved us, and washed us from our sins in his own blood.

He said his comfort came from meditating on Ann enjoying the company of her departed children in the presence of their Deliverer. He derived comfort knowing that someday his union with Christ, together with his loved ones, would be perfectly realized "when we meet in heaven—when all have arrived . . . forever safe" in Christ. He rejoiced in that happy day to "ever praise him who has endured the cross" to bestow such a heavenly reward.[24]

After George Boardman died, Judson married his widow, Sarah, in April of 1834. They were married for eleven years before Sarah's death in 1845.[25] The day after her death, Judson wrote to the Burmese mission. Though he felt crushed under a "desolate" and "dreary" mood, Judson said that he derived "consolation" from the fact that she died "longing to depart and be with Christ." His comfort was rooted in the presence of her heavenly-mindedness in death. He said he was certain that "the love of Christ sustained her to the last," and he said he happily "congratulated her on the prospect of soon beholding the Saviour in all his glory." He believed that she was in heaven resting on Christ's bosom, enjoying heavenly bliss alongside his first wife, Ann. By meditating on the heavenly reward of Ann and Sarah and his other departed companions, he said, "Heaven seems nearer, and eternity sweeter." He concluded his letter with a hope-filled exhortation to "follow those who, through faith, inherit the promises."[26] Judson further described the anguish he felt after burying Sarah. In his "solitude,"

---

24. Middleditch, *Burmah's Great Missionary*, 231–32. After Boardman's death on February 11, 1831, Judson paid him a tribute with glowing expectation of Boardman's heavenly reward. He rejoiced that Boardman had "gone to his eternal rest." He went on to wax eloquent about Boardman's legacy and noble sufferings for Christ's sake. He concluded with a word of hopeful anticipation of Boardman's reward. He said, "Well may we rest assured that a triumphal crown awaits him on the great day, and 'Well done, good and faithful Boardman, enter thou into the joy of thy Lord.'" Wayland, *Memoir*, 1:524. See also Middleditch, *Burmah's Great Missionary*, 271–72.

25. For Judson's personal records and reflections on his decision to marry Sarah, see Adoniram Judson, journal, March 12, 1834 to April 10, 1834, Box No. AJ 4, Folder 4 and Microfilm Roll 1, Judson Letters, ABHS. For a vivid account of Sarah's death, see Adoniram Judson to the Rev. Solomon Peck, letter, September 1, 1845, Box No. AJ 3, Folder 2 and Microfilm Roll 1, Judson Letters, ABHS.

26. Wayland, *Memoir*, 2:203–4.

with his "poor children crying" around him, he said that he felt desolate under the "heart-breaking sorrow." However, in their distress, he said the gospel sustained him: "The promises of the Gospel came to my aid, and faith stretched her view to the bright world of eternal life, and anticipated a happy meeting with those beloved beings whose bodies are moldering at Amherst and St. Helena."[27] Judson's comfort derived not only from the good news of Christ's decisive act of forgiveness and justification on the cross, but it also included the good news of Christ's preserving sanctification and promise of glorification.

Judson sought to communicate heavenly comfort in counseling others; he had a special way with his fellow missionaries who suffered as he did. He could tenderly shepherd their souls to look to Christ, trust him for his sovereign wisdom, and hope eagerly in his promises of rest for labor and reward for service.

To Elizabeth Moore,[28] who lost her child, he commiserated that she felt "anguish never before conceived of" and that her tears would be "O, so bitter!" Affirming that she trusted God had done this "in infinite wisdom and love," he encouraged her to be thankful that her child now occupies heaven. With empathy as one who had lost loved ones, he said, "The warm affections now apparently crushed in the bud will expand and bloom in heavenly glory." Judson encouraged her that her song of praise to God will be ever increasing in "every succeeding age of eternity" because God, "for some special purpose," wisely and lovingly took the child to heaven early.[29]

After George Boardman's death, Judson wrote a note in March of 1831 to console the grieving widow, Sarah Boardman. Judson said he had tasted the "dregs" of the cup she was now drinking, which was "far bitterer" than she expected. He said, though she would endure many months of "heart-rending anguish," his only counsel for her was, "Take the cup with both hands, and sit down quietly to the bitter repast which God has appointed for your sanctification." Judson encouraged her to think of the "diadem which encircles [Boardman's] brow" and the fact that Boardman is now "an immortal saint, a magnificent, majestic king." Due to the present reality of Boardman's reward in heaven, Judson encouraged Sarah to cry "tears of joy." Judson repeated his earlier line, to emphasize what he learned about

---

27. He was referring to Ann, buried at Amherst, and Sarah, buried at St. Helena. Middleditch, *Burmah's Great Missionary*, 352–53.

28. Elizabeth Forbes Moore was married to William Moore in 1847. They subsequently went to Burma as Baptist missionaries. See Phinney, *The Judson Centennial Celebrations in Burma*, 20.

29. Edward Judson, *The Life of Adoniram Judson*, 520–21. See also Wayland, *Memoir*, 2:321.

finding heavenly sweetness through suffering the loss of loved ones; he again advised,

> Yet take the bitter cup with both hands, and sit down to your repast. You will soon learn a secret, that there is sweetness at the bottom. You will find it the sweetest cup that you ever tasted in all your life. You will find heaven coming near to you.

Then he went on to pledge himself "to receive and treat" her little son, George Dana Jr.,[30] as his "own son" and "watch over him" his whole life.[31]

In 1833, Judson sought to console the broken-hearted Stella Bennett, whose husband and children returned to America.[32] He said that "infinite love . . . in the person of the Lord Jesus, is even now looking down upon you, and will smile if you offer him your bleeding, breaking heart." Judson encouraged her that what she would "sow in tears," she would "reap in joy." Then he described "the bright plains of heaven" where she would "hear their celestial songs, sweetened and heightened by [her] present sacrifices and tears."[33] He wrote another letter to Stella Bennett in March 1833, and encouraged her, "Be patient, poor soul! Heaven will be sweeter for all this . . . The dear absent ones will be with you to all eternity."[34]

Feeling the loneliness of being separated from his remaining children once they were old enough to live in America, Judson wrote to his daughter Abby Ann, who was living in Bradford at the old homestead of the Hasseltine family.[35] His words were tender and hope-filled. He implored her to be converted so that she would have the assurance of being in heaven together with the rest of her family someday, since this life was fleeting. He said that he prayed passionately that she and her siblings would convert to Christ and

---

30. He was also known as George Dana.

31. Edward Judson, *The Life of Adoniram Judson*, 374–75. On that same day, Judson wrote both in his journal and another letter to a supporter, James Grow of Thompson, Connecticut. In them he lamented the overwhelming needs and the meager supply of missionaries and materials. See Adoniram Judson, "Mr. Judson's Letter to Rev. Mr. Grow," 31–32; and Middleditch, *Burmah's Great Missionary*, 273–74. See also Adoniram Judson, journal, February 28, 1831 to March 4, 1831, Box No. AJ 4, Folder 2 and Microfilm Roll 1, Judson Letters, ABHS; and Adoniram Judson, "Extracts from Mr. Judson's Journal, to Rev. Dr. Bolles, Rangoon, Feb. 28, 1831 [to March 4, 1831]," 373–74.

32. See Ranney, *A Sketch of the Lives and Missionary Work*.

33. Adoniram Judson to Mrs. Bennett, letter, 1833, Box No. AJ 5, Folder 1 and Microfilm Roll 2, ABHS. See also Wayland, *Memoir*, 2:57–58.

34. Wayland, *Memoir*, 2:65. For more words of encouragement to Stella Bennett revealing Judson's prayerful and Christ-centered piety, see also Judson's next letter to her on May 14, 1833 in ibid., 2:68.

35. Judson took leave of Abby Ann at Bradford on July 9, 1846. See Edward Judson, *The Life of Adoniram Judson*, 567.

thus meet him "at the throne of grace." He pleaded with her: "Meet me in the bosom of Jesus, and we shall live in His blessed presence on high, together with your dear mother, lost to us for a time, but not forever."[36]

In addition to family and close friends, others also were beneficiaries of the influence of Judson's heavenly-minded counsel. For instance, during his last year of life, in a letter to an anonymous missionary in July of 1849, Judson gave words of advice to look away from worldly concerns and look heavenward:

> You must endeavor to look away from all outward things— from the satisfactions and discomforts, the commendations and censures, which are the common lot of man, and find your happiness in your own bosoms, in your work, in communion with God, and in the joyful anticipations of that blessed state, the heavenly Jerusalem, the "happy home" to which we are travelling.[37]

At the end of his life, Emily noted that Judson would often say, "We must look *up* for direction."[38] In one of the last letters Judson ever wrote, in October 1849, he sought to counsel a grieving fellow-missionary, S. M. Osgood.[39] He said that he and Osgood had both experienced the immense pain of losing loved ones, and in light of the severity and sweetness of God's providence, Judson encouraged Osgood to imagine their loved ones in heaven "reposing in the arms of infinite love, who wipes away all their tears with His own hand." He charged Osgood to "travel on and look up." Judson closed by rehearsing the heavenly truth that had been so hope-giving for him; he concluded, "The longer and more tedious the way, the sweeter will be our repose."[40]

---

36. Adoniram Judson, "Adoniram Judson's Letter to His Daughter Abby Ann," 14. See also Edward Judson, *The Life of Adoniram Judson*, 522; and Wayland, *Memoir*, 2:312. In a letter to his sister, Abigail, Judson likewise sought to point her attention to their heavenly reunion where their family would be apart no more. See Wayland, *Memoir*, 2:150.

37. Wayland, *Memoir*, 2:333.

38. Ibid., 2:372; emphasis in original.

39. See Smith, *Sewall Mason Osgood*.

40. Edward Judson, *The Life of Adoniram Judson*, 521–22. See also Wayland, *Memoir*, 2:328–29. Regarding Elhira Osgood's death in 1837, in a letter of condolence, Judson concluded as though he were writing to Elhira Osgood herself about her future glory; he said, "We know that thou sleepest in Jesus, and that when the night of death is passed away, and the resurrection morn appears, thou also wilt again appear, blooming in celestial beauty, and arrayed in thy Saviour's righteousness, a being fitted to love and to be beloved, throughout the ever-revolving hours of an eternal day." Wayland, *Memoir*, 2:118.

Heavenly Longing

For Judson, a heavenly-minded disposition was not merely supplemental to missionary spirituality; it was crucial. Such an upward gaze would indeed provide solace in a myriad of afflictions and anxieties. Moreover, heavenly-mindedness would be supremely useful if it were stronger than a simple awareness of or assent to heavenly realities. Judson demonstrated that a heavenly disposition must be a dominant instinct of true religion, manifesting itself in an expectant longing for the benefits of Christ, anchored in heaven. Judson believed such a longing was fundamental for any missionary and minister of the cross.

Judson saw longing for heaven as useful for the missionary spirit. In an extract from a letter to a friend in October 1818, Judson showed far more concern for the graces of heavenly-mindedness in fellow missionaries than for skill, education, and strength, though he said that the same education and "mental improvement" given to ministers should be expected of missionaries. He desired the heart of the missionary to be heavenward in its affections. He said he was fully convinced that a qualified missionary should habitually enjoy a "closet religion." He maintained that a missionary should be "abstracted from this world, and much occupied in the contemplation of heavenly glories," in addition to exuding various "spiritual graces," which include "humility, patience, meekness, love."[41]

In 1819 after the baptism of the first Burman convert, Moung Nau, Judson was explaining the gospel to another Burman, named Moung Thah-lah. He compared the Christian system with the Buddhist system, saying that though the Buddhist system does not offer a way of pardon, the Christian gospel, however, provides "not only a way of pardon, but a way of enjoying endless happiness in heaven." Upon hearing Judson's explanation of the gospel in terms of a pardon *and* an eternal inheritance, this was most glorious news to Moung Thah-lah; he decided to follow Christ, about which

---

41. Wayland, *Memoir*, 1:211. For one biographer's apt observations of Judson's own missionary spirit, see Middleditch, *Burmah's Great Missionary*, 437. Citing comparable graces though not explicitly mentioning heavenly-mindedness, Judson wrote two years earlier to Luther Rice, in November of 1816. He wrote about the kind of missionaries to send: "In encouraging other young men to come out as missionaries, do use the greatest caution . . . Humble, quiet, persevering men . . . Men of an amiable, yielding temper, willing to take the lowest place, to be the least of all and the servants of all; men who enjoy much closet religion, who live near to God, and are willing to suffer all things for Christ's sake, without being proud of it, these are the men, &c." Adoniram Judson, "Extract of a Letter from Mr. Judson to Mr. Rice, Rangoon, Novem. 14th, 1816," 184–85. See also Wayland, *Memoir*, 1:185–86. Regarding the strategic role Luther Rice played in promoting and mobilizing for the American Baptist Board and in arousing missionary devotion in others, Torbet, *A History of the Baptists*, 331.

Judson instructed him further.[42] This account illustrates the usefulness of heavenly longing in Judson's evangelism.

In an address in 1846, Judson also compared the immediate "manifold blessings" wrought by the gospel "in a world so full of sin" and how the "power" of the gospel "will appear in the world to which we are advancing." There are indeed personal and societal benefits to obeying the gospel in this life, but he said he was discontent with mere social transformation. He said, "It is the Gospel—the Gospel!" that effected blessings throughout Burman society. Considering the promises of heaven, Judson said, "If here, where sin yet reigns, so great a contrast can be wrought, how much greater the contrast between this imperfect state and heaven, free from every defilement!"[43]

Before the Boardman Missionary Society at Waterville College, in 1846, Judson spoke about pleasing the Lord with eternity in view as the foundation of mission work. Judson was speaking to students who were either interested in missions or who were preparing for missions. In light of the trials he had seen, he said he did not want to compel anyone to experience what he had, but he said their compelling sense of duty must come from a heavenly source. He said,

> You have but one life to live in which to prepare for eternity . . . You have only one. Every action of that one life gives coloring to your eternity. How important, then, that you spend that life so as to please the Saviour, the blessed Saviour, who has done everything for you![44]

In October of 1846, on his voyage back to Burma and off the Isle of France, Judson wrote a letter in which he traced his memories of first venturing to Burma with Ann and stopping in Port Louis to visit the "grave of Harriett Newell, the first American missionary who left this world for heaven." Then years later, he buried Sarah on a nearby island. He said he was impressed with the stark reality that a missionary can never "calculate on his final resting place." Though missionaries are "strangers and pilgrims" and

---

42. Middleditch, *Burmah's Great Missionary*, 128.

43. This is from an address at a meeting in Utica, New York in 1846; see Edward Judson, *The Life of Adoniram Judson*, 471–73.

44. Edward Judson, *The Life of Adoniram Judson*, 473–74. See also Wayland, *Memoir*, 2:234–35. In another address, Judson laid out his vision of the continuity of heavenly reality with earthly living. In the context of giving a charge for potential missionary candidates to count the cost of missionary sacrifice, he said, "So far as we are like Christ in this world, so far shall we be like him through eternity. So far as we sustain this cause, which is peculiarly the cause of God, so far we shall be happy through endless ages." Edward Judson, *The Life of Adoniram Judson*, 470. See also Wayland, *Memoir*, 2:233–34; and Middleditch, *Burmah's Great Missionary*, 376.

have "no abiding place on earth," he said that it was from this heavenly longing that they seek "to show the way thither to multitudes" who are "groping in darkness."[45]

Judson saw longing for heaven as useful for loving the brethren. Emily recounted that Judson's heavenly-minded disposition directly motivated his love for people. By contemplating the pervasiveness of brotherly love in heaven, Judson learned to love others for the sake of Christ. Judson would say it is insufficient to be generally pleasant to the people of God; brotherly love requires more than "[abstaining] from evil speaking, and [making] a general mention of them in our prayers." Emily said that his "ardent temperament" made him "subject to strong attachments and aversions," which, she said were difficult for him to bring "under the controlling influence of divine grace." She recorded that he would often say that the Christian's affection for other believers "should be of the most ardent and exalted character: it would be so in heaven, and we lost immeasurably by not beginning now." She recalled that the verse, "'As I have loved you, so ought ye also to love one another [see John 13:34; 15:12],' was a precept continually in his mind."[46] Judson was aware of his easily-irritated nature, and through his rules of life, he sought to daily confront his lack of affection for people.[47] Throughout his life, because of his meditations on death and heaven, his various rules for spiritual maturity in his relationships generally underlined secret prayer, mortifying disaffection for others, showing benevolence to all, and being cordial in all facets of conduct "to please an ever-present Lord."[48]

Furthermore, in January of 1850, four months before his death, Emily recorded that Judson suddenly exclaimed to her his feelings of peace because, from contemplating on his progress of brotherly love for people he knew, he finally concluded that as far as he could know himself, he loved "every one of Christ's redeemed" as would please Christ. He said he loved them "in the same manner, though not probably to the same degree as we shall love one another in heaven." Judson said he would prefer even the lowliest of Christ's elect over himself, which Emily said was an "allusion to the

45. Wayland, *Memoir*, 2:262–63. See also Middleditch, *Burmah's Great Missionary*, 402–3.

46. Wayland, *Memoir*, 2:338. In a letter to Emily in January of 1847, Judson said, "'Trust in God and keep your powder dry,' was Cromwell's word to his soldiers. Trust in God and love one another is, I think, a better watchword. Let us do the duties of religion and of love, and all will be well." Kendrick, *The Life and Letters of Mrs. Emily C. Judson*, 251.

47. See Wayland, *Memoir*, 1:322–23; Wayland, *Memoir*, 2:61, 103, 190; Edward Judson, *The Life of Adoniram Judson*, 315–16.

48. Wayland, *Memoir*, 2:190. See also Edward Judson, *The Life of Adoniram Judson*, 316.

text, 'In honor preferring one another [Rom 12:10],' on which he had frequently dwelt with great emphasis." Judson went on to say that he felt such peace with his conscience, knowing that he was "a miserable sinner in the sight of God, with no hope but in the blessed Saviour's merits." Additionally, he expressed relief that he could not think of any "peculiarly besetting sin" which he had "duty to correct."[49]

Judson saw longing for heaven as useful for self-denying activity. In a letter to his parents in July 1810, in the context of describing his cordial communion with God in Christ, Judson admitted that his temporal future certainly would meet with troubles and uncertainty, yet, he said his "prospects for another life . . . are still brighter." He went on to say that the dreams of this life are empty, and he said,

> O, if we could always realize this, and live above the world,—if we could tread on its trifling vanities, live far from its perplexing cares, and keep an eye fixed on our heavenly inheritance,—how . . . useful we might be![50]

In a journal entry in September 1815, Judson recorded a conversation he had with a Buddhist, named Oo Oungmen, about happiness in heaven. He and Oo Oungmen were talking about someone who had died. Judson said the deceased man was lost because he was not a disciple of Christ, and he explained this by illustrating that one could know if the root of a mango tree is good by looking at its fruit. Judson said that the man who had died did not bear the fruit of a disciple of Christ, to which Oo Oungmen asked if all who are not disciples of Christ are lost. Then, Judson affirmed the exclusivity of Christ. Oungmen declared, "This is hard." Judson responded strongly out of his conviction in an eternal hell and an eternal heaven; he said, "Yes, it is hard indeed; otherwise I should not have come all this way, and left parents and all, to tell you of Christ."[51] Judson then elucidated on how his Christian view of two future eternal realities, one being "miserable" and the other being "happy," compelled him to leave all his earthly comforts and joys in light of heaven's pleasures.[52]

49. Emily Chubbuck Judson, "Closing Scenes in Dr. Judson's Life," 36.

50. Wayland, *Memoir*, 1:58.

51. Similar to this statement about leaving his family for Christ's sake, in a letter to his sister and mother twenty years later on November 1, 1835, Judson said, "Surely, I should have to call myself a most ungrateful son and brother, had I abandoned you forever in this world, as I have done, for any other cause than that of the kingdom of the glorious Redeemer." Ibid., 2:105.

52. Ibid., 1:171–72. After serving as missionaries for nine years, Judson and his first wife, Ann, could have pulled out and retired to a more bearable ministry. The temptation to retreat was especially strong during Ann's illness and consequent two-year

In her recollections of Judson, Emily highlighted how useful Judson's longing for heaven was in relation to his completion of the dictionary. She said that he was so "consecrated" to his work that he found earthly pleasures only in his family. She said, "His thoughts, which were ordinarily fixed with unusual continuity on heaven, seemed to turn thither with a more resistless longing, now that he had accomplished the work which he believed had been appointed to him."[53]

Near the end of his life, Emily told Judson that many people thought he would not recover from his protracted illness. Judson responded to the plain reality that his life was slipping away; he said in tears that he was ready for whatever God ordered according to his perfect will. He said that he was ready because he could not imagine having "more inviting prospects, with brighter hopes." As he lay there on the bed, he said he had unspeakable "views of the loving condescension of Christ, and the glories of heaven." He told Emily that he was willing to stay longer even though his "drawings . . . toward heaven" were beyond comparison. However, he said that he would be willing to spare a few years from his "eternity of bliss" for the sake of the Burmans. He said he was not ready to give up because he knew his reward was very great, and the more he worked, the greater his reward.[54] Nevertheless, Judson said that he was eager to go when Christ so willed, and "when

---

voyage back to America. In a letter in 1821 to Ann, Judson told her how he wished they could find "some quiet resting place on earth" where they could retreat and spend the rest of their days enjoying "the ordinary services of religion." However, he quickly turned from such a thought and drew near to Christ. Judson said that he counted serving Christ and suffering for him "a privilege." He believed that Christ's "heavenly glory" was near, so he said he sought to pour out his life for the Burmans to "show the path to that glory," which he was "anticipating" with great eagerness. He concluded his letter to Ann by pleading with her to join him in prayer to grow in grace and sanctification. Demonstrating how his heavenly longing was useful for self-denial, he said, "Let me pray that the trials which we respectively are called to endure may wean us from the world, and rivet our hearts on things above. Soon we shall be in heaven. O, let us live as we shall then wish we had done. Let us be humble, unaspiring, indifferent equally to worldly comfort and the applause of men, absorbed in Christ." Middleditch, *Burmah's Great Missionary*, 167.

53. Wayland, *Memoir*, 2:163. Wayland said, "[Judson] had a passion for saving souls, and he had reason to believe that, by this labor, many souls were saved who would be his joy and his crown in that heaven for which his whole life was a constant preparation." Ibid., 2:6–7.

54. In a letter to a newly arrived missionary, Lydia Lillybridge Simons, on August 12, 1847, Judson sought to encourage her through the difficult language-learning phase; he said, "We must sow before we reap; and though our whole life should prove to be but sowing time, the harvest of eternity will produce ample returns." Ibid., 2:295.

Christ calls me home I shall go with the gladness of a boy bounding away from his school."[55]

One of the clearest examples of the relationship between Judson's heavenly-minded disposition and his resolve to deny himself the comforts of this world was in a letter in December 1830 to Lucius Bolles. Judson's health had been poor, and the American Baptist Board sent an invitation for him to return home. His heart longed to return to America, he said, to enjoy sweet fellowship with his friends and family and "to witness the wide-spread and daily-increasing glories of Emanuel's kingdom in that land of liberty, blessed of Heaven with temporal and spiritual blessings above all others." Nevertheless, he was willing to postpone such an enjoyable reunion because he was waiting for "a happier meeting, brighter plains, friends the same, but more lovely and beloved." He was convinced that he would soon "enjoy that glory in comparison of which all on earth is but a shadow." Because of such heavenly anticipation, he said, "I content myself, assured that we shall not then regret any instance of self-denial or suffering endured for the Lord of life and glory."[56] After marrying Emily in 1846, Judson said that his hopefulness in the dawn of Christ's heavenly glory led him to welcome all manner of labor, self-denial, and hazards, making his life dissonant with the world's temporal pursuits. He said that he would even spill his "blood like water in such a cause."[57]

That Judson fixated his mind upon and lived in light of heavenly realities is evident. His heavenly-minded disposition carried him from his early impulses of missionary devotion all the way to his final hours. Many trials and afflictions were God's will for his life, but looking heavenward, he sought to do everything to please Christ in order that in heaven his happiness in Christ would be sweeter. His heavenly-minded piety comforted him in aloneness, insecurity, and death. His heavenly-minded instinct helped him to comfort and counsel others in their pain. His longing for the ever-increasing blessings of heaven proved useful for his self-denying missionary activity and his relations with others. He believed that a sustained heavenly longing was essential for true missionary spirituality.

---

55. Emily Chubbuck Judson, "Closing Scenes in Dr. Judson's Life," 38. See also Wilson, *The Lives of Mrs. Ann H. Judson and Mrs. Sarah B. Judson*, 353; and see Wayland, *Memoir*, 2:345–46.

56. Adoniram Judson to Dr. Lucius Bolles, letter, December 20, 1830, Box No. AJ 2, Folder 2 and Microfilm Roll 1, Judson Letters, ABHS; see also Middleditch, *Burmah's Great Missionary*, 271. For some of Judson's comments about bearing up under trials and suffering with Christ in order to reign with him, see Wayland, *Memoir*, 2:295.

57. Wayland, *Memoir*, 2:371.

Postmillennial Hopefulness

Evangelical leaders of the Post-Revolutionary War era (1800–1840) interpreted current events as evidence of the end of the age. For instance, infidelity and indifference to religion in America and political events in Europe all alarmed them that the times were changing. Consequently, preachers arose to issue a solemn plea for repentance, which they believed would effect reformation and revival and eventually the new age of Christ's millennial blessing. Samuel Hopkins, the systematic theologian of the New Divinity, synthesized Jonathan Edwards's millennial doctrine.[58] During the revivals, Edwards's millennial vision grew in popularity, and Hopkins developed Edwards's eschatology in conjunction with an urgent missionary mandate.[59] Much evangelical activism rose to the occasion, creating societies for missions, evangelism, abolition, and theological training, though they believed the actual millennium would be approximately two hundred years in the future.[60] Concerning the millennial optimism of the New Divinity leaders, the American church historian, E. Brooks Holifield, explains that they emphasized both "the benevolence of the Redeemer . . . [and] the ethics of the redeemed." He says that Hopkins taught that the millennium would be an age of triumphant peace where "disinterested benevolence would promote general and cordial friendship." Holifield explains that Edwards's eschatol-

---

58. See Edwards, "An Humble Attempt to Promote Explicit Agreement, &c.," 280–312; see also Edwards, *An Humble Attempt to Promote Explicit Agreement*. For a thorough synthesis of Edwards's eschatology, see McClymond and McDermott, *The Theology of Jonathan Edwards*, 566–79.

59. See Leonard, "'Wild and Romantic in the Extreme,'" 81–86.

60. For a cogent summary of this post-Revolutionary War era and the effects of Edwardsean postmillennialism on the ABCFM and evangelical activism, see De Jong, *As the Waters Cover the Sea*, 227. See also Hutchison, *Errand to the World*, 38–42. Judson completed his first tract, *A View of the Christian Religion*, in 1816. In it he predicted, in very Hopkinsian-sounding language, that within two hundred years from then, the religions of Buddhism, Islam, Roman Catholicism, Hinduism, and all other minor religions "will disappear and be lost, and the religion of Christ will pervade the whole world; all quarrels and wars will cease, and all the tribes of man will be like a band of mutually loving brothers." Adoniram Judson, *A View of the Christian Religion*, 7; see also Bennett, *Tracts, In Burmese*, 34; and Adoniram Judson, *The Septenary*, 17. For an easily accessible version, see McElroy, *Adoniram Judson's Soul Winning Secrets Revealed*, x, 26. Judson believed that the millennium would begin sometime after the year 2000; see Kendrick, *The Life and Letters of Mrs. Emily C. Judson*, 333. Regarding Judson's prediction of the demise of Buddhism under the millennial reign of Christ, Richard Fox Young, Associate Professor of History of Religions at Princeton Theological Seminary, exemplifies a non-evangelical perspective by denouncing it as "a rude eschatological reverie." Young, "Making Comparative Missiology More Comparative," 107, quoted in Dingrin, "A Missiological and Theological Critique," 131.

ogy, alongside "the Edwardean twist on the notion of disinterested benevolence" impelled the various forms of evangelical activism of the nineteenth century.[61]

The initial founding of the ABCFM blossomed out of deep Edwardsean roots of the New Divinity students at Andover Theological Seminary. As historian David Kling has said, the ABCFM "was a New Divinity Creation, rooted in New Divinity theology, inspired by New Divinity revivals, and staffed by a well-established New Divinity social and institutional network."[62] Many of the students at Andover experienced conversion during a season of revival. Yale College witnessed revival during 1801–1802, and the president of Yale, Timothy Dwight (1752–1817), continued to promote revival and millennial hope at other colleges. When Andover first opened, Dwight preached there on the conversion of the Gentile nations as subsequent to the Jews returning to Palestine and converting to Christ.[63] As historian James A. De Jong has explained, many students came to Andover because their "pervasive vision" of the millennium "quickened" their "devotion to missions."[64] The late historian of religion in America, William R. Hutchison (1930–2005), helpfully explained that this era of the rise of postmillennial-driven missions paralleled the rise of American exceptionalism. He said that American mission beliefs "intensified" the "biblical imperatives." Hutchison explained that European Protestants viewed themselves as "exceptional to the point of constituting the only true church," and the Puritan pilgrimage to America "further narrowed and intensified" this exceptional-minded *ethos* "in the crucible of radical Protestantism and within Anglo-Saxon cultural forms."[65] Spiritually formed in the milieu of Edwardsean postmillennialism and Hopkinsian disinterested benevolence, Adoniram Judson devoted himself to foreign missions. He believed that though he might suffer and die, the God of the Bible promised that the glory of the knowledge of Christ would fill the earth as water covers the seas.[66]

---

61. Holifield, *Theology in America*, 149.

62. Kling, "The New Divinity," 13. See also Tracy, *History of the American Board*.

63. Elsbree, *The Rise of the Missionary Spirit in America*, 132.

64. De Jong, *As the Waters Cover the Sea*, 223.

65. Hutchison, *Errand to the World*, 42. In one of Judson's journals, he illustrated this conviction that American Christians should play a significant role in the salvation of the nations; see Adoniram Judson, journal, February 28, 1831 to March 4, 1831, Box No. AJ 4, Folder 2 and Microfilm Roll 1, Judson Letters, ABHS; and see Adoniram Judson, "Extracts from Mr. Judson's Journal, to Rev. Dr. Bolles, Rangoon, Feb. 28, 1831 [to March 4, 1831]," 373–74.

66. See Hab 2:14.

Millennial Glory

Judson believed that Christ's millennial glory would come after the conversion of the heathen and the salvation of the Jews, ushering in an era of heavenly peace and brotherly love. His passion to please Christ as a missionary and his self-denying submission to God's infinitely wise and loving will corresponded to his hope in heavenly happiness and the millennial reign of his Redeemer. With joyful optimism, he kept straightforward because he said that his prospects for the conversion of the heathen were "as bright as the promises of God."[67]

From the beginning of Judson's missionary venture, his ardor for Christ's glory to spread throughout the earth impelled his lifelong missionary devotion.[68] In a letter on December 18, 1837, to Stephen Chapin, the president of Columbian College, Washington, Judson recounted those days when God's Spirit was calling him "with such clearness and power" to "preach the gospel" through the "command of Christ" in the Great Commission. Demonstrating his Trinitarian spirituality as it related to his postmillennial scheme, Judson highlighted how "the providence of God was conspicuously manifested" in gathering young men from all over to launch a foreign missions movement and give themselves to "missions for life." He said it was so obvious that the "Spirit of God" was awakening various individuals in various places in order to enable spiritual "movements" that had "since pervaded the American churches." Such movements of the Spirit, he exclaimed, would "continue to increase until the kingdoms of this world become the kingdoms of our Lord and of his Anointed!"[69] His Christ-enamored spirit manifested itself in his obedience to the Great Commission for the sake of ushering in Christ's millennial reign.

---

67. Wayland, *Memoir*, 2:381. Wayland observed, "It never appeared to him possible for a moment, that God could fail to do precisely as he had said; and he therefore relied on the divine assurance with a confidence that excluded all wavering. He believed Burmah was to be converted to Christ, just as much as he believed that Burmah existed. He believed that he had been sent there to preach the gospel, and he as much believed that the Holy Ghost would make his labors, in some way, or at some time, the means of the salvation of the nation, as he believed that there was a Holy Ghost." Ibid., 2:380–81.

68. One biographer well observed the effect that Judson's ordination and commissioning had upon those gathered. Because of the solemnity and gravity of the commissioning on February 6, 1812, "many who had only looked to their own salvation, or, at the utmost, to the evangelization of their own country, obtained a wider view of the glory of Christ's kingdom, and were led to unite in magnificent plans of mercy, by which multitudes out of every nation, people, and tongue are brought to His throne." Middleditch, *Burmah's Great Missionary*, 41.

69. Conant, *The Earnest Man*, 49–50. See also Wayland, *Memoir*, 1:51–53; and Middleditch, *Burmah's Great Missionary*, 25–26.

In January 1820, as he was traveling to Ava to beseech the king for religious liberty, he went through Pugan, an ancient Burman city. He reflected in his journal on all the generations that Buddhism and atheism had plunged into the dark abyss of despair. His evangelical spirituality was evident in how he expressed his desire for the gospel's advance and for the corresponding reign of Christ to spread. He said that he stood "on the dividing line of the empires of darkness and light." Judson mocked the darkness of the former Buddhist dynasties:

> A voice mightier than mine . . . will ere long sweep away every vestige of thy dominion. The churches of Jesus will soon supplant these idolatrous monuments, and the chanting of the devotees of Buddh will die away before the Christian hymn of praise.[70]

In the spring of 1832, Judson wrote a long appeal to the American Baptist Board for more missionaries. Weighed down in "distress" because of

---

70. Wayland, *Memoir*, 1:251–52. Nearly eight years after becoming a missionary, Judson's desire for Christ's glory to spread had not waned. The new monarch of Burma, a despotic Buddhist, refused religious liberty for the propagation of other religions. Judson resolved to risk his life and beseech the king. In a letter to Thomas Baldwin in December of 1819, he made clear the source of his conviction and courage. Judson said his trust was in Christ's power and purpose to glorify himself: "In approaching the throne, we desire to have a simple dependence on the presence and power of our Saviour, and a single eye to his glory. We have indeed no other ground of hope; we ought to have no other view. We trust that, if the set time to favor Burmah is come, He who is wonderful in counsel, and excellent in working, will open a wide and effectual door for the promulgation of divine truth. But if the Lord has other purposes, it becomes us meekly to acquiesce, and willingly to sacrifice our dearest hopes to the divine will." Wayland, *Memoir*, 1:244. See also Middleditch, *Burmah's Great Missionary*, 136. The next day Judson wrote another letter to Baldwin about the same subject, in which he said that this hazardous endeavor ahead of him consumed his soul. However, he made clear that what was at stake was not the monarch's approval or Judson's own safety, but rather, the "great object" of his concern was "the introduction of the Messiah's kingdom into the empire of Burmah." Adoniram Judson to the Rev. Thomas Baldwin, letter, December 9, 1819, Box No. AJ 1, Folder 2 and Microfilm Roll 1, Judson Letters, ABHS. See also Adoniram Judson, "Letter from the Rev. Adoniram Judson, Jun. to Dr. Baldwin, Dated Rangoon, December 9, 1819," 379–80. Two years after the king refused to grant religious liberty, in February of 1822, with like-minded conviction, Judson wrote to Baldwin that he was still "fully persuaded" that God would soon open the way in Burma "for the introduction and establishment of true religion." He knew he would "encounter the hazards" of public gospel proclamation. Yet, well aware that "difficulties may obstruct, delays may intervene, [and that] the faith of missionaries and their supporters may be severely tried," he was not distraught. He asserted, "but at the right time, the time marked out from all eternity, the Lord will appear in his glory." Adoniram Judson, "Letter from Mr. Judson to Dr. Baldwin, Rangoon, Feb. 6, 1822," 458. See also Middleditch, *Burmah's Great Missionary*, 168.

the "thousands perishing," he penned over nine hundred words, explaining the dire need for more missionaries and his strategy for placing new missionaries in key locations throughout the Southeast Asian region. Then he wrote another five hundred words of intercession for God to "have mercy" on villages and cities alike throughout the region. He concluded with a prayer for mercy on the American churches, that God would "continue and perpetuate the heavenly revivals of religion" and that no American church would be able to enjoy their weekly religious services "without having one of their number to represent them on heathen ground." He prayed for mercy on the seminaries, that half of their ministers-in-training would "be taken by thine Holy Spirit and *driven* into the wilderness, feeling a sweet necessity laid upon them, and the precious love of Christ and of souls constraining them." He prayed that God would heed the monthly concerts of prayer throughout the world and thus "hasten the millennial glory, for which we are all longing and praying and laboring." Judson concluded his lengthy prayer by imploring God to "adorn thy beloved one in her bridal vestments, that she may shine forth in immaculate beauty and celestial splendor. Come, O our bridegroom! Come, Lord Jesus, come quickly."[71] In this letter, he demonstrated the fusion of his postmillennial and evangelical piety. During that spring of 1832 when Judson wrote this letter, pleading and praying for global revival, he was also enthusiastically seeking to raise funds for the establishment of a mission in Palestine to reach the Jews.[72] Twenty years

---

71. Adoniram Judson, "Appeal from the Missionaries, Maulmein, June 4th, 1832," 39–41. See also Wayland, *Memoir*, 2:51–54; emphasis in original. In Wayland's account of this appeal, he recorded the date as March 4, 1832, but *The Baptist Missionary Magazine* recorded the date as June 4, 1832; it is also dated as June 4, 1832 in Dowling, *The Judson Offering*, 175–81. In a letter in 1845, Judson said that "the crowning mercy of [his] life" was attaining his life's highest ambition to become a missionary, and it was a privilege to see eminently pious "successors" pick up the work. More than entrusting his work into their hands, Judson said the mission work was really "in the hands of Christ, who carried it on before we were born, and while we were in arms against him, and will carry it on more gloriously when we repose in the grave and in paradise. Glory be to Him alone." Middleditch, *Burmah's Great Missionary*, 334–35. Judson found great delight in hearing of the news of other missionaries going to parts of Asia previously untouched. In a letter in June 1835, he said, "Happy lot to live in these days! Oh, happy lot to be allowed to bear a part in the glorious work of bringing an apostate world to the feet of Jesus. Glory, glory be to God." Wayland, *Memoir*, 2:101–2. See also Middleditch, *Burmah's Great Missionary*, 326–27.

72. Because Judson believed strongly in the need to reach the Jews in Palestine, he sought to promote a fund of ten thousand dollars to establish missions in Palestine. Though the effort was unsuccessful, a few days before he set sail back to Burma in 1846, Judson received word that a tract, which had detailed his labors and sufferings in Ava, underwent translation in Germany. Some Jews in Germany read it and converted to Christianity. A Jew in Trebizond (present-day Turkey) also translated it for Jews there;

into his missionary venture, he still believed strongly that Christ's millennial reign was imminent, and his missionary activism testified to the reality of his Christ-centered passion.

Before returning to Burma, Judson addressed the Baldwin Place Church of Boston in July of 1846. He started by speaking of his life in third person, explaining how much change he had experienced throughout his life, and at times he would "doubt [his] own personal identity." Yet, "like steersmen in a storm," he felt that he "must keep a steady eye at the compass and a strong arm at the wheel." So many of his early comrades either had moved on in the ministry or had died. He wondered who would carry the banner next after his generation of ministers and missionaries departed. Then, in preparation to begin his full address, he quoted, "Blessed are the dead that die in the Lord. They rest from their labors, and their works do follow them" (Rev 14:13). He quoted this verse again as the final sentences of his address, which served somewhat as a thematic inclusio. Judson recalled the only ground he and those early missionaries had to stand on was "the command and promise of God." Yet by the time of his address in 1846, he said there was much missionary momentum. Referencing his earlier analogy of steersmen in a storm, he called on them to "look forward with the eye of faith" because widespread missionary devotion was advancing and new Bible translations were "illuminating all lands." Encouraging them that the millennial glory was at hand, he said, "See the Sabbath spreading its holy calm over the face of the earth, the churches of Zion assembling, and the praises of Jesus resounding from shore to shore." Even though most of the world still remained in darkness, nevertheless, he said the obstructions of the Holy Spirit's "descent and operations" were falling, so that "the revivals of religion" would become "more constant and more powerful." Though the era of glory was imminent, Judson maintained that "the gracious designs of God" had yet to come to fruition. Zion has "yet to triumph, and become the joy and glory of the whole earth." He exclaimed that it was a "great privilege" and a "precious opportunity" to participate with Christ in the blessing of

---

after reading of his sufferings, they too experienced awakening and requested a missionary to come to them. Judson responded with weeping because of his unbelief that God could use such a weak vessel for the salvation of the Jews. See Wayland, *Memoir*, 2:32–37; and see also "A Sweet Surprise," 174. For letters Judson wrote about raising funds for Palestine, see Adoniram Judson, "Raising Funds," letter, January 1, 1832, Box No. AJ 5, Folder 2 and Microfilm Roll 2, Judson Letters, ABHS; Adoniram Judson to Dr Lucius Bolles, letter, May 8, 1832, Box No. AJ 2, Folder 4 and Microfilm Roll 1, Judson Letters, ABHS; Adoniram Judson to Mr. Patison, letter, February 20, 1832, Box No. AJ 5, Folder 1 and Microfilm Roll 2, Judson Letters, ABHS; Adoniram Judson to the Rev. James L Knowles, letter, February 20, 1832, Box No. AJ 5, Folder 1 and Microfilm Roll 2, Judson Letters, ABHS.

"enlarging and establishing his kingdom throughout the world." In light of this great opportunity and hope of future glory, he called the audience neither to grieve losing the earlier generation of missionaries nor to neglect the call themselves. Rather, he charged, "Follow them who, through faith and patience, inherit the promises [Heb 6:12]." Their heavenly rewards would be in proportion to their earthly works.[73] The works of those who die in Christ will follow them.[74] In addition to his explicit postmillennialism, this address is a good example of Judson's implicit Trinitarianism; he spoke of the Trinity in terms of the will and designs of God the Father, the glory and lordship of God the Son, and the work and power of the Holy Spirit.

At the final meeting of the General Convention at the Pierre-pont Street Church in Brooklyn, in May 1846, Baron Stow read a sermon written by Judson, who was unable to speak clearly. In a lengthy address, Judson tackled the objections made by so many Americans who were increasingly interested in missions, but also increasingly disappointed with the lack of missionary success. Judson said that there had been some progress, though it was not impressive enough to the scrutinizing public. He went on to explain that there are generally three divisions of people: those who are open to the gospel, those who have forsaken the gospel, and those who are resistant to the gospel. The third division comprises those groups who are so hard and hostile that they "will tire out the wavering and faint-hearted" missionaries. This third division, he said, is the majority, which includes the world of Islam, Buddhism, Hinduism, and those animistic tribes where "false religions

---

73. Expressing a similar sentiment in a thank-you card to the American Baptist Magazine on January 1, 1835, Judson wrote of himself in third-person: "He rejoices in the belief that every distant expression and recognition of fraternal affection here below will form an additional tie, binding heart to heart, in the world above; that every cup of cold water given to a disciple will become a perennial stream, flowing on from age to age, and swelling the heavenly tide of life and gladness." Adoniram Judson to the Missionary Magazine, letter, Moulmein, January 1, 1835, Box No. AJ 2, Folder 1 and Microfilm Roll 1, Judson Letters, ABHS. See also Wayland, *Memoir*, 2:92; Edward Judson, *The Life of Adoniram Judson*, 323–24.

74. Adoniram Judson, "Parting Address of Mr. Judson," 31–33. See also Adoniram Judson, "Address of Dr. Judson," 267–68; Dowling, *The Judson Offering*, 279–83; and see Middleditch, *Burmah's Great Missionary*, 396–98; Wayland, *Memoir*, 2:254–58. See Rev 14:13. In his last year of life, Judson wrote a letter in August 1849, to George William Anderson (1791–1857), the governor of Mauritius, expressing his optimism of the coming reign of Christ. He said that in his old age he could "hardly expect to see the long-desired and long-prayed-for triumph of the Redeemer's kingdom in Burmah." Nevertheless, he was confident that he would "see it from the windows of paradise." He anticipated that the glorious era of Christ's triumph was at hand. He said, "We live in wonderful times. Every revolution among the kingdoms of the earth seems to be designed to prepare the way for the universal establishment of the kingdom of Christ." Wayland, *Memoir*, 2:325–26.

prevail." He went on to paint a seemingly discouraging picture of how hostile, despotic, resistant, and intolerant are such nations. Judson, nevertheless, rebuked the critics of slow missionary labor, because missionaries were indeed making progress in translating the Bible, in creating seminaries, and even in converting some souls, though maybe not in the thousands. He contended that such places, though not teeming with revival, contain "the first-fruits" of the coming eschatological harvest. Judson argued that all criticism and despair should be silenced by the fact that, though the work be slow, it was nonetheless "gradually undermining the reigning superstitions, and preparing the way for the triumph of truth, the full ushering in of millennial glory," which demonstrated that in his theology, the millennial glory advanced to the degree that gospel truth prevailed.[75] Judson said that in the face of disparaging progress and quibbling remarks from his native land, his encouragement came from his abiding conviction that Christ's kingdom was indeed covering the world and taking root as a farmer would liberally cover a field with seed and wait for a great harvest. Judson closed his rebuttal to the critics by quoting the motto of his late father after his father became a Baptist later in life (1817). Judson Sr. said, as he was dying, "Keep straight forward, and trust in God."[76]

After they had left for Burma, Emily recorded a conversation that Judson had with a female missionary who was criticizing the meager progress of missions and ridiculing those in America who exuded postmillennial optimism. Not willing to excuse her pessimism, Judson asserted that the time "for millennial hymns" was at hand. He went on to say that a joyful heart in the coming reign of Christ was "a pledge of interest which would lead to future results far more glorious." He said, "To be sure, our oak is a tiny sapling yet; but it is a real live oak, and well out of the ground." He went on to say that when he thought of God bringing the oak to fullness and completion, his heart burst with "joy indescribable." In light of the imminence of heaven coming to earth through the global proclamation of the gospel, he said, "It is base ingratitude to be blind to all these wonders." Judson argued that because the world was more than half-converted, Christians should not

---

75. After having served in Burma for twenty-five years, in a letter on July 20, 1838 to his sister, Abigail, Judson recounted how many churches the missionaries had established and how the gospel seemed to be advancing throughout the land. He indicated in this letter that the hastening millennial glory corresponded to the pervading influence of the gospel. Judson said, "I trust that the good work will go on, until every vestige of idolatry shall be effaced, and millennial glory shall bless the whole land." Wayland, *Memoir*, 2:124.

76. Middleditch, *Burmah's Great Missionary*, 391–94. See also Wayland, *Memoir*, 2:285–88. A month after this message, on June 2, 1846, Judson and Emily Chubbuck (Judson's third and last wife) married at Hamilton.

dissuade any from engaging in the Great Commission. Contrarily, such a prospect should be "spirit-stirring," and it should constrain Christians to embrace any kind of pain and adversity, "so that life itself will seem nothing in the balance."[77]

Related to Judson's urgency for the return of Christ, he was also impatient with temporal trifles and fusses that distracted from eternal matters. After Judson had seceded from the Congregational ecclesiastical body and joined the Baptists, Samuel Worcester of Salem claimed that Samuel Spring of Newburyport had reprimanded Judson for not collecting sufficient details during his trip to London regarding potential cooperation with the London Missionary Society, and for his impetuousness in seeking immediate appointment to missions.[78] Yet, Judson denied awareness of the initial reprimand. Though his character and motives were criticized, his view of life's uncertainty and eternal consequences strengthened his resolve to stay focused on his mission.[79] In 1819, he mentioned the case in a letter to Thomas Baldwin and referred to what truly concerned his heart. He said that he considered it to be "exceedingly insignificant in comparison with . . . the introduction of the Messiah's kingdom into the empire of Burmah." He went on to say that he felt the weight of the looming damnation of the heathen, and if he could only "be instrumental in saving a few precious souls," he wished his name to "live in oblivion or disgrace till the great day."[80]

Like his impatience for minor scuffles, Judson was also irritated with those who were so fearful of worldliness that they cut themselves off from the world and did not engage it for the sake of Christ's coming kingdom. Emily recorded his conversation with a visitor during his dying days. Judson said, "At the risk of being written down a bigot," he condemned the insular nature of the Plymouth Brethren because their doctrine had "ruined" their "usefulness in this world." He said, "Their influence goes to discourage and paralyze all missionary enterprise." He went on to assert that sometimes "when seekers after sanctification attain to a certain degree of spirituality, they are peculiarly liable to fall into errors of form." He charged that "instead of sitting down at the Saviour's feet, and drinking in his words, they go away to furnish themselves with swimming bladders, the work of their own invention." Judson went on to say that when Satan finds Christians so separated from the world that they are not susceptible to its temptations,

---

77. Wayland, *Memoir*, 2:371–72.

78. See Adoniram Judson, *A Letter to the Rev. Adoniram Judson, Sen.*

79. For an apt summary of the context of this situation, see Middleditch, *Burmah's Great Missionary*, 96–98. See also Wills, "From Congregationalist to Baptist," 150–53.

80. Adoniram Judson, "Letter from the Rev. Adoniram Judson, Jun. to Dr. Baldwin, Dated Rangoon, December 9, 1819," 380.

Satan then "dons this sheep's clothing of Plymouth Brethrenism." Unable to woo the Christian to worldliness, Satan "puts a veto on the man's usefulness, to the serious detriment of hundreds of thousands of others."[81]

In an apologetic against Buddhism, Judson concluded with a demonstration of his conviction in the triumphant fulfillment of God's millennial promises. He was confident that the God who planned the cross of Christ also planned the eschatological consummation. Revealing his hope-filled ground for courage in missions, he declared thus:

> The trumpet of the Lord is pealing forth a battle call. We are standing on the vestibule of a resplendently glorious era. The angel "having the everlasting gospel to preach," is already "in the midst of heaven [Rev 14:6]," and we hear the rushing of his mighty wings; the church is shaking off the drowsy dust of ages, polishing her weapons, and spreading her banner to the breeze; the word of command has sounded from the walls of heaven; and there are sure indications that the immutable promises of Jehovah are hastening to their accomplishment . . . Courage, lone laborer! . . . Courage! Every ray shed from thy gospel lamp speeds away as the mountain rill to the ocean, swelling the flood of radiance which is ere long to sweep over the entire earth. Then, at the rising of the Sun of Righteousness, shall the nations clap their hands in gladness, and the redeemed and the renovated race of man burst forth in one universal shout: "*Hallelujah! Hallelujah! The Lord God omnipotent reigneth!*"[82]

Judson's postmillennial optimism not only strengthened his persevering piety, but it also propelled his evangelical activism and his Christocentric ardor. Grounded in the promises of the Bible, his heavenly-minded piety was a product of the juxtaposition of Edwardsean eschatology, Hopkinsian disinterested benevolence, and the national spirit of the "The Rising Glory of America."[83]

---

81. Wayland, *Memoir*, 2:365–66.

82. Ibid., 2:410; emphasis in original. In Wayland's transcription of these emphasized words, he capitalized them to indicate Judson's extra emphasis. For the full apologetic treatise contra Buddhism, see ibid., 2:410–17.

83. Hutchison, *Errand to the World*, 42. Hutchison noted that "this was the title of a commencement poem by Philip Freneau and H. H. Brackenridge for the College of New Jersey (Princeton) in 1771."

Conclusion

Judson's spirituality was neither temporal nor transient. From his early years to his final days, his was a wholehearted heavenly disposition. The reward of heaven's happiness gave hope to Judson in the adversity of submitting to the will of God. His certainty that heaven was a place of love and peace consoled him in loneliness, uncertainty, and risk. Judson believed that the experience of heavenly joy corresponded directly to the love and sacrificial benevolence poured out in this life. Hope in heaven's blessings also influenced how he counseled others through their own trials. He longed for eternal rest more than for temporal relief. Judson ardently longed for heaven because that was where he would see his Redeemer and Friend. His missionary spirituality remained optimistic because he believed that Christ's heavenly glory would fill the earth to the degree that the gospel triumphed through Bible translation and preaching. Christ's millennial glory was at hand, and Judson was devoted to hastening the peaceful and loving reign of Christ. Self-denying sacrifice was the means through which he sought to please his Savior and coming King. With bright optimism, Judson could say all his life,

> —In joy or sorrow, health or pain,
> Our course be onward still;
> We sow on Burmah's barren plain,
> We reap on Zion's hill.[84]

---

84. In Wayland's opinion, Judson's habitual heavenly-minded disposition was never better expressed than in these words that he penciled in a book he used in making the dictionary. See Wayland, *Memoir*, 2:381–82.

6

"O, The Love of Christ": Christocentric Spirituality

IN HIS DYING DAYS after spending hours in meditation and prayer, Adoniram Judson would rejoice with tears of joy in the overwhelming love of Christ. He was Christocentric to the end.[1] One biographer maintained that the Christ-enamored theme of Ephesians 3:18–19 dominated Judson's spirituality from his conversion through the rest of his life:

> *To comprehend the breadth and length and depth and height and to know the love of Christ which passeth knowledge*—this became, at the dawn of his manhood, his one supreme and passionate aspiration. It is the climax of all that has gone before; it is the key of all that follows.[2]

From his early days at Andover until his final days in Burma, Judson sought to know Christ and to please him as his all-consuming holy ambition. Judson's spirituality was one of submissive self-denial in the service of the sovereign Christ, whose Scriptural example of benevolence Judson was motivated to imitate, whose final command he was passionate to obey, whose love he was earnest to enjoy through religion, and whose glory he was importunate to seek through prayer. This chapter will establish that the unifying feature of Judson's spirituality was an affectionate ardor to please the Lord Christ. The love of Christ and a supreme, self-denying devotion to the will of Christ were Judson's controlling themes.[3]

1. See Emily Chubbuck Judson, "Closing Scenes in Dr. Judson's Life," 36.
2. Boreham, *A Temple of Topaz*, 134.
3. The Southern Baptist preacher, Basil Manly, Jr. (1825–1892), preached a sermon called, "The Christian Motive," from 2 Corinthians 5:14. At the outset, he referenced

In seeking to please Christ, Judson sought to imitate the example of Christ by going and doing good, with benevolent self-sacrifice. Judson sought above all to please Christ by obeying that final command that he deemed so dear to Christ's heart—the command to preach the gospel to every creature.[4] He derived evangelical assurance from the fact that he was seeking to heed Christ's commission, and he awaited that Day of Judgment when the proof of his true religion would be manifest. If Judson were not to keep Christ's command to proclaim the gospel, he feared for the legitimacy of his salvation. Nevertheless, his spirituality was not one of cold duty; rather, his duty to follow and please Christ as a missionary emerged out of the roots of his true religion and enjoyment of God in Christ. Judson employed his spirituality with great concern for demonstrating true religion. Prayer, like breathing, gave life to his heart religion. He urged others to be concerned for the same, including his family and children. Judson carried a great burden for his children and, through fervent prayer, letters, and even poetry, he sought to arouse in them a desire for religion. He upheld the value of importunate praying, because he believed that God would bless such dependency. He yearned for that day when the glory and love of Christ, which he knew in part, would fill the world through the proclamation of the gospel. Thus, Judson went forward, the love of Christ sustaining him, with a supreme desire to please his Savior.

Pleasing Christ

In order to honor Christ, Judson sought to obey the final and dearest command of Christ. Judson's affection for Christ impelled his abandonment of the world's pleasures for the sake of imitating Christ and proclaiming the good news of Christ's dying love to the unreached. Following his Exemplar, Judson practiced disinterested benevolence, and he sought to bring as many as possible into Christ's loving and happy kingdom.

During his furlough in America, Judson often preached to rouse his hearers to love and please Christ through a life of self-denial. One pastor, D. W. Faunce (1829–1911),[5] was a young man in Plymouth, in 1846, when he

---

Judson's "missionary spirit" and "emphatic Christianity" to illustrate "the great principle that the love of Christ is alone the motive which prompts to true Christian obedience, constitutes the theme of the preacher." Manly Jr., "The Christian Motive," 169–72.

4. See Mark 16:15.

5. Daniel Worcester Faunce was the pastor of Baptist Churches in Washington D. C. and in Worcester. He studied at Amherst College and Newton Theological Institute. He served as a member of the Board of Managers of the American Baptist Missionary Union. One of his well-known works was Faunce, *A Young Man's Difficulties with*

heard Judson preach. Later in life, Faunce reminisced about the piety manifested in Judson's great Christ-enamored preaching. Initially unimpressed with Judson's haggard appearance and weak voice, his opinion changed as Judson unfolded the biblical text: "These are they that follow the Lamb [Rev 14:4]." Faunce recalled that Judson repeatedly declared "pleasing Jesus" as his highest aim. He said that Judson's "great tenderness" arrested his attention, and Faunce went on to say, "Was this venerated man influenced in all he had done by the simple thought of 'pleasing Jesus'? Well, then, might not I, boy as I was, strive to please Jesus also?" He said that throughout his life, his memories of Judson's love for pleasing Christ often inspired him to do the same.[6]

Christ's Benevolent Example

Judson believed that Christ's example of benevolent self-sacrifice was an essential feature of evangelical spirituality. This demanding path of love, in imitation of Christ, was one of doing good. For his missionary spirituality, he could not justify practicing self-denial isolated from the world and the lost. The devotional practices of Judson's ascetic spirituality corresponded directly to the affection and ardor of his Christocentric spirituality.

Christ's self-denying service to the Father inspired Judson to follow Christ in the same way. His widow, Emily C. Judson, recorded a conversation she had with him about people in America elevating him to the status of the Apostle Paul and the Apostle John. Judson did not desire such flattery, and he retorted, "I want to be like Christ . . . [the] only one perfectly safe Exemplar—only One who, tempted like as [sic] we are in every point, is still without sin. I want to follow *him* only . . . O, to be more like Christ!"[7]

Judson spoke at a gathering in March 1846, in Philadelphia at the First Baptist Church of Abram Dunn Gillette, the manager of the American Baptist publication society. Judson's address called the people to meditate on Christ's agony and thus to follow Christ's call even into suffering. Judson urged them to "look unto Jesus" on the cross and listen to the three prayers Christ prayed in his agony. In a long explanation of these three prayers, Judson showed that Christ's first prayer was for forgiveness for his persecutors,

---

His Bible. He was also the father of W. P. Faunce (1859–1930), president of Brown University.

6. Edward Judson, *The Life of Adoniram Judson*, 460–61. One biographer commented on Judson's influence on Faunce to please Christ; see Warburton, *Eastward*, 195.

7. Wayland, *Memoir*, 2:369; emphasis in original.

which includes everyone; Christ's second prayer came from feeling forsaken by the Father; at this point in the sermon, Judson interjected: "Where would we all be, if Jesus had yielded then? But he did not yield; he suffered on for three more awful hours." Judson's exclamation here illustrated how vivid Christ's disinterested benevolence was to him. And, then he said that Christ's third prayer was to offer up his spirit. After painting a picture of Christ's example of ultimate disinterested benevolence, Judson made an application for self-denial: "It was for us that this agony was endured; let us remember this, and though we cannot repay his love, let us give our hearts to him—let us devote our lives to his service." He concluded by urging them to live in such a way that when death comes, they could fearlessly pray as Christ did: "Father, into thy hands I commit my spirit [Luke 23:46]."[8]

In May 1836, Judson preached for the ordination of the missionary printer, S. M. Osgood. This lengthy sermon is a definitive presentation of the inherent relationship in Judson's spirituality between the example of

---

8. Middleditch, *Burmah's Great Missionary*, 385-87. In 1845, Judson addressed the students at Madison University in Hamilton, New York, about the struggles of missionary labor. At the conclusion of his address, he implored them to "look to Jesus," which would be their source of "the greatest consolation and delight." He directed them to look to the manifestations of Christ's love on the cross and of Christ's happiness in heaven. By looking to Christ, they would find strength in affliction, comfort in trial, security in death, and salvation at the Judgment. Then he closed his appeal, grounding his call to their benevolent self-denial in the love of Christ for them. Judson asserted, "Jesus loves you, how can you avoid loving him with all your heart, and mind, and strength? You cannot then hesitate to be and to do all that he requires at any and every conceivable cost." Edward Judson, *The Life of Adoniram Judson*, 474. See also Middleditch, *Burmah's Great Missionary*, 373-74. After this address at Madison University, Josiah Hatt (1821-1857), a student at the time but later the pastor of the Baptist Church in Hoboken, New Jersey, said, "It is useless to attempt a description of the electric effect of these compendious sentences. Dr. Maginnis [that is, John Sharp Maginnis (1805-1852), the Professor of Biblical Theology] was himself deeply moved . . . Dr. Conant [that is, T. J. Conant (1802-1891), the Professor of Hebrew] followed with the concluding prayer, and, notwithstanding the concise and classical style which marks all his performances, it was so full of heavenly unction that it was evident that he had drunk deeply into the spirit of the occasion. As for Dr. Eaton [that is, George W. Eaton (1804-1872), the President of Madison University], his emotional soul literally *rocked* with intensity." Middleditch, *Burmah's Great Missionary*, 372-73; emphasis in original. Also, Judson illustrated his convictions from this address nineteen years earlier after his release from his tortuous prison sentence in Ava. Judson wrote a letter, which remained unpublished, to Francis Wayland, then the pastor of the First Baptist Church in Boston. In the letter, Judson said, "When I look back upon those scenes of horror, through which we passed, I can hardly realize that I am now free and happy. Our lives were spared and our deliverance finally effected in answer, I believe, to the prayers of our dear friends at home. I desire to devote the remainder of my days to His service, who in wrath remembered mercy." Adoniram Judson to Rev Francis Wayland, letter, May 13, 1826, Box No. AJ 6, Folder 2 and Microfilm Roll 2, Judson Letters, ABHS.

Christ and the Christian minister's mandatory self-denial in imitation of Christ. Preaching from John 10:1–18 about Christ as the Good Shepherd, Judson began by saying that though Christ is the "Exemplar" of all his people, he is especially the "Exemplar" of his "subordinate shepherds." He urged Osgood to "look continually to the chief Shepherd" for emulation. First, Judson said, the minister ought to imitate Christ's wholesale denial of worldly desires. Christ gave up his life for the good of his flock, and in the language of disinterested benevolence, Judson said the minister ought to imitate Christ by surrendering all worldly ambitions, pleasures, and gains "that he may, by all means, save some." Second, Judson went on to say, the minister ought to imitate Christ by showing affection and brotherly love to the flock. And third, the chief duty of a minister in imitation of Christ is to indiscriminately call out Christ's elect. Judson explained that once they come in through the universal preaching of the gospel, the minister ought to make disciples through teaching them to observe Christ's commands, of which the minister should strive to be the greatest example of obedience. Though the minister's chief duty should be doing good, Judson went on to elaborate on the dominant motivation of such duty: Christ's "supreme regard to his Father's will" and "the love of God" were the controlling themes of Christ's life. Judson tied Christ's example of supreme love to the Father and a supreme desire to please the Father to the responsibility of the minister to esteem the will of God above all other good things. He said no good works of self-denial or charity "are truly estimable, but just so far as they spring from regard to the will of God." He went on to explain that "all true virtue has its root in the love of God. Every holy affection looks beyond self . . . and finds its resting place in God alone." Then Judson eloquently described God's God-centeredness and righteous love for himself above everything else. In light of God's supreme happiness in God, Judson said it was fitting that Christ would "have supreme regard to the will of the Father," greater than his regard for perishing souls. Judson maintained, therefore, that every minister must submit to the will of God, and all evangelical love for souls must be subordinate to an all-consuming love for God in Christ. In light of Christ's example of supreme submission to the infinitely wise and loving will of the Father, the most God-centered Being in the universe, Judson issued a decisive verdict for his spirituality of self-denial:

> On this ground we rest the doctrine of self-denial, renunciation of self-interest, abandonment of self. Still further, even our compassion for souls and our zeal for their salvation must be kept in subordination to the supreme will of God.[9]

9. Wayland, *Memoir*, 2:486–94. In Judson's self-denying imitation of Christ, the

Furthermore, this spirituality of self-denying submission to the will of God in Christ was not only Judson's conviction for the Christian minister; it was also his conviction for the truly renewed man. In his first tract, *A View of the Christian Religion*, Judson said that by looking to Christ for his expiation of guilt and imputation of righteousness, the true Christian, "therefore, through supreme love to Jesus Christ, and a desire to do his will, endeavors to avoid evil deeds, and to perform good deeds only, according to the divine commands." In the third part of his tract, Judson outlined all the commands of Christ, of which the first four are: repent, believe in Christ, love God supremely, and love people as oneself.[10]

In December 1845, Judson preached at an assembly in Philadelphia about the cost of following Christ to the mission field. At the beginning he quoted, "Be ye imitators of me, as I am of Christ [1 Cor 11:1]," which he asserted "is a divine command." Judson went on to propose: "There is one Being in the universe who unites in himself all the excellences of human and divine nature—that being is Jesus Christ." In order "to become like Jesus Christ," Judson said that Christians must seek to imitate Christ, not only in "character," but also in his "whole course and conduct of life." Judson went on to say that becoming like Christ "ought to be our whole aim." Asking how it is that Christians become like Christ, he answered that Christ "went about doing good [Acts 10:38]." Therefore, in order to imitate Christ, Christians ought to "not merely stay and do good, but go and do good." Because Christ "led the life of a missionary," Judson suggested that Christians should "endeavor, as far as possible, to lead the life of missionaries." Toward the end of his message, Judson said that he regarded the missionary vocation as "a most glorious occupation." Nevertheless, he said he did not wish to coerce people to become missionaries without a heavenly calling, so he also explained that Christ is no longer a missionary; rather, he sustains missionaries by "his prayers . . . his influence . . . and his property." Then, Judson said that all Christians ought to "go about doing good," by committing their prayers, influence, and property for missions "in order, therefore, to be like Christ."[11]

---

church historian John Woolman Brush (1899–1990) well said, "Judson was indeed a Gethsemane soul." Brush, "The Magnetism of Adoniram Judson," 3.

10. Adoniram Judson, *A View of the Christian Religion*, 1–3; Adoniram Judson, "A View of the Christian Religion," in *Septenary*, 13–21. For an easily accessible version, see also McElroy, *Adoniram Judson's Soul Winning Secrets Revealed*, 27–29. See also Edward Judson, *The Life of Adoniram Judson*, 568–72.

11. Edward Judson, *The Life of Adoniram Judson*, 469–70; Middleditch, *Burmah's Great Missionary*, 374–76. In January 1846, while traveling through Washington after giving this address in Philadelphia in December 1845 and before his address in Richmond in February 1846, Judson concluded a letter to Emily Chubbuck, thus: "Christ

Forty-six days later, on February 8, 1846 in Richmond, Virginia,[12] he again referred in identical terms to Christ as the "one Being in the universe that unites in himself all the perfections of Deity with all the purest and tenderest of human nature." Yet, in this address he did not argue for "doing good" as the necessary self-denying conduct of imitating Christ. Instead, he contended that the missionary's motive for such self-sacrifice should be a passion to please Christ.[13] This statement of motivation did not rule out what he said forty-six days earlier; it simply revealed how Judson's Christ-centered spirituality motivated his self-denying activity.

Judson also had much to say throughout his life about the spiritual necessity of imitating Christ by doing good. In *A Digest of Scripture*, Judson delineated the biblical duties that the Christian owed to men. One of the basic duties owed to mankind was "do good to all."[14] Additionally, in the third section, "Doing Good," of *The Threefold Cord*,[15] he said,

> Doing good imparts beauty and utility to the rest. It is written of the Lord Jesus that he went about doing good.[16] Art thou his disciple? Imitate his example, and go about doing good. *Do good.* Let this be thy motto.[17]

---

went about doing good—May it be our glory to imitate his example!" According to Rosalie Hall Hunt, this letter from Judson to Emily on January 26, 1846 is "in possession of a Judson descendant." See Hunt, *Bless God and Take Courage*, 211, 370.

12. Judson was speaking at the Foreign Mission Board of the Southern Baptist Convention.

13. Middledicth, *Burmah's Great Missionary*, 384–85.

14. See Adoniram Judson, *A Digest of Scripture*, 79–107.

15. Adoniram Judson, *The Threefold Cord*.

16. See Acts 10:38.

17. Adoniram Judson, *The Threefold Cord*, 5; see also Edward Judson, *The Life of Adoniram Judson*, 575; Wayland, *Memoir*, 2:464; emphasis in original. In the original tract, the italicized words were capitalized for added emphasis. For examples of Judson's self-described devotion to doing good according to each person specific path for the glory of Christ, see his lecture in 1845 at Brown University in Middleditch, *Burmah's Great Missionary*, 362–64; and Wayland, *Memoir*, 2:227–28. Also for a similar example, see his letter to the Corresponding Secretary of the American Baptist Board, Lucius Bolles, in March 1826. In that letter Judson illustrated his belief that, though there may be good alternative paths of doing good, there is one path of duty on which Christians would be most fruitful. He went on to outline what he believed was his specific path of glorifying Christ through preaching the gospel. See Middleditch, *Burmah's Great Missionary*, 215; and see Wayland, *Memoir*, 2:421.

Christ's Great Commission

Judson was eminently devoted to the final command of Christ to preach the gospel to every creature. This was Christ's final, dearest word to his followers, and Judson spent his life heeding it at all costs in order to please Christ. Indeed, to the degree that he obeyed that command, to the same degree was he assured of his genuine love to Christ and the authenticity of his spirituality. He feared neglecting Christ's final command through negligence and indifference due to the distractions of the world and the weight of his sin; Judson believed such disregard would certainly threaten his prospects in eternity. As the pastor of Madison Avenue Baptist Church, William Hague, well said, "The Great Commission gained the homage of his conscience."[18]

In 1819, as has been noted, Judson first took up the practice of writing rules of life to follow daily for his improvement in holiness and religion.[19] Among his rules, he consistently focused on not doing anything that would displease his Lord; and he equally sought to do everything in order to please Christ.[20] In 1842, he shortened his rules and summarized them under one final all-consuming resolution: "Resolved to make the desire to please Christ the grand motive of all my actions."[21]

From the very beginning of his missionary venture, Judson sought to know and keep the Scriptures. After his change of sentiments from Congregationalist to Baptist, in his sermon, *Christian Baptism* (1813), Judson concluded with an appeal to consider the truth of Christ's Word; his plea for obedience to the Scripture revealed his utmost desire to please Christ:

> If you love Christ, you cannot consider this question [of the biblical mode of baptism] unimportant. You will be desirous of discovering the will of him whom you love, and of testifying your love, by joyfully obeying. "*If ye love me,*" said Jesus, "*keep my commandments* [John 14:15]." "*Ye are my friends, if ye do whatsoever I command you* [John 15:14]."[22]

Toward the end of his life, Judson's passion to please Christ by obeying the Bible remained just as prominent in his heart. Moreover, he believed that obedience to Christ's commands, and especially Christ's ultimate and

---

18. Hague, *The Life and Character of Adoniram Judson*, 7.

19. To read all his Rules of Life, see Edward Judson, *The Life of Adoniram Judson*, 315–16; Wayland, *Memoir*, 1:322–23; Wayland, *Memoir*, 2:61, 103, 190.

20. Edward Judson, *The Life of Adoniram Judson*, 315. See also Wayland, *Memoir*, 1:322.

21. Wayland, *Memoir*, 2:190.

22. Adoniram Judson, *Christian Baptism*, 93; emphasis in original.

final command, was preeminently pleasing to Christ. Before the Boardman Missionary Society at Waterville College, in 1846, he spoke about pleasing Christ, as the foundation of mission work:

> If any of you enter the Gospel ministry in this or other lands, let not your object be so much to "do your duty," or even to "save souls," though these should have a place in your motives, as to *please the Lord Jesus*. Let this be your ruling motive in all that you do. Now, do you ask, *how* you shall please Him? How, indeed, shall we know what will please Him but by *His commands*? Obey these commands and you will not fail to please Him. And there is that "last command," given just before He ascended to the Father, "Go ye into all the World, and preach the Gospel to every creature [Mark 16:15]." It is not yet obeyed as it should be. Fulfill that, and you will please the Saviour.[23]

His ideas expressed in this portion of his address do not nullify his consecration to the duty of missionary activism; rather, his words here put in perspective and prioritize how his dominant motive to please Christ impelled and sustained his devotion to duty and his desire to convert the lost. Commenting on this particular address, William R. Hutchison aptly observed,

> [Disinterested benevolence] was grounded not upon terror but upon divine and human compassion. Adoniram Judson . . . preached duty and obedience in voluntaristic and very personal terms . . . Judson thought that simple admonitions to do one's duty, or to obey the Great Commission, were usually cold and inappropriate. The idea, instead, is that in exercising benevolence one is responding to the benevolence of God. And obedience to Jesus' explicit commands should be motivated not by terror or even by the stern requirements of conscience but by the opportunity, as Judson put it, of "pleasing Christ."[24]

Akin to his discourse at Waterville College in 1846, Judson also addressed the Foreign Mission Board of the Southern Baptist Convention in Richmond in 1846 and explained the different levels of motives for the missionary. He said that "evangelical motives" should compel missionary labor, and love for fame is "worse than useless." He went on to say that even engaging in missions primarily to realize assurance of salvation, though desirable, is insufficient; the salvation of the heathen, which should be a great concern,

---

23. Edward Judson, *The Life of Adoniram Judson*, 473–74. See also Wayland, *Memoir*, 2:234–35; emphasis in original.

24. Hutchison, *Errand to the World*, 49; quoting from Edward Judson, *The Life of Adoniram Judson*, 473.

must not be the controlling motive. He then asked the question that would divulge the secret to his life of self-denial in Christ's service: "What, then, is the prominent, all-constraining impulse that should urge us to make sacrifices in this cause?"[25] Judson went on to set up his answer by describing the excellency of the union of Christ's divinity and humanity and that this God-Man has "at great expense" established his kingdom and "has set his heart on the enlargement of that kingdom." Therefore, in view of such a King and the prospects of such a kingdom, he answered his own question: "A supreme desire to please him is the grand motive that should animate Christians in their missionary efforts."[26]

This affectionate desire to please Christ indeed had been his consuming motive ever since his days at Andover Theological Seminary. About his solemn dedication to Christ's service during a walk in the woods behind Andover in December 1808, Judson said, "All at once that 'last command' seemed to come to my heart directly from heaven. I could doubt no longer, but determined on the spot to obey it at all hazards, for the sake of pleasing the Lord Jesus Christ."[27] Indeed, he said he devoted his life to missions for the sake of Christ.[28] Moreover, as Judson said to his fiancée and later his first wife, Ann, in order to "avoid every thing displeasing to God," he would consequently ask himself regularly, "Is it pleasing to God?"[29] This question is remarkably similar to the question with which he concluded his address

---

25. In the foreword of *To the Golden Shore*, Courtney Anderson asked a similar but truncated version of Judson's question here; see Anderson, *To the Golden Shore*, ix.

26. Middleditch, *Burmah's Great Missionary*, 384–85. As previously mentioned, forty-six days earlier on December 24, 1845, Judson preached at an assembly in Philadelphia about the cost of following Christ to the mission field. He made the identical assertion about the excellence of Christ's union of divine and human natures. Yet, Judson argued, in view of the beauty of Christ, the Christian's necessary duty is to imitate him and "go and do good." Therefore, comparing these two similar sermons, Judson demonstrated that in light of the magnificence of Christ, his duty was to deny himself and imitate Christ by going as a missionary and doing good through gospel proclamation; and, his motivation for such Christ-imitating activism was an all-consuming desire to please his Master. See Edward Judson, *The Life of Adoniram Judson*, 469–70. See also Middleditch, *Burmah's Great Missionary*, 374–76.

27. Edward Judson, *The Life of Adoniram Judson*, 474. See also Wayland, *Memoir*, 2:235. For similar statements in various letters regarding when Christ's Spirit called Judson to missions through his prayers and meditation on Mark 16:15, see Middleditch, *Burmah's Great Missionary*, 22; Wayland, *Memoir*, 1:51–52; and also, see Conant, *The Earnest Man*, 42–44.

28. See his letter on December 18, 1837, to Stephen Chapin, in Conant, *Earnest Man*, 49–50. See also Middleditch, *Burmah's Great Missionary*, 25–26; and Wayland, *Memoir*, 1:51–53.

29. This was from a letter on December 30, 1810 to Ann. See Wayland, *Memoir*, 1:32.

"O, The Love of Christ": Christocentric Spirituality

in 1846 at the Foreign Mission Board of the Southern Baptist Convention: "In every concern of life we should often look up to that lovely Being and inquire, 'Does this please him?'"[30] One biographer aptly observed his lifelong piety: "Through all these years to please Christ was his unfaltering purpose."[31]

After being in Burma for eighteen years, Judson grew weary of the mounting pressure to translate, publish, and distribute gospel literature. In March 1831, after a long week of handing out ten thousand tracts at the Shway Dagon festival, Judson had run out of tracts and still had to turn away thousands of inquirers for lack of literature resources. In his journal, he attributed the lack of supplies and materials to those churches in America that had wavered and waned in their support of the mission. He said that their unresponsiveness to Christ's Great Commission resulted in insufficient missionary personnel that he so badly needed. Judson said that such lack of support from the churches revealed that they considered the Great Commission as optional or inconsequential. This neglect of supporting the global proclamation of the gospel, he asserted, would certainly be the source of "irremediable, everlasting despair" on the day of judgment. In revealing what would be the cause of one's great remorse, Judson went on to say,

> Surely, if any sin will lie with crushing weight on the trembling, shrinking soul, when grim death draws near, if any sin will clothe the face of the final Judge with an angry frown, . . . it is the sin of turning a deaf ear to the plaintive cry of ten millions of immortal beings, who by their darkness and misery cry day and night, *Come to our rescue, ye bright sons and daughters of America, come and save us, for we are sinking into hell!*[32]

---

30. Middleditch, *Burmah's Great Missionary*, 384–85.

31. Warburton, *Eastward*, 119. Compare the sermon by Leonard Woods at Judson's ordination in 1812 to Judson's motives for showing benevolence to the lost, for obeying the Great Commission (see Mark 16:15), and for Christ to be ultimately glorified. There are many similarities. See Woods, *A Sermon Delivered at the Tabernacle in Salem*, 11–29.

32. Adoniram Judson, journal, February 28, 1831 to March 4, 1831, Box No. AJ 4, Folder 2 and Microfilm Roll 1, Judson Letters, ABHS. In order to emphasize his ardor in his letters, Judson often underscored salient points. For instance, in this letter, he wrote in the original, "[C]ome to our rescue, ye bright sons and daughters of America [which he underlined one time for emphasis]; come and save us, for we are sinking into hell [which he underlined twice for extra emphasis]." *The Baptist Missionary Magazine* transcribed and published it with italics and capitals. Often when Judson underlined something in his hand-written letters, the transcription italicized it. And when he double-underlined something, the transcription capitalized it. See Adoniram Judson, "Extracts from Mr. Judson's Journal, to Rev. Dr. Bolles, Rangoon, Feb. 28, 1831 [to March 4, 1831]," 374; and see Middleditch, *Burmah's Great Missionary*, 273–74;

In a letter on the same day, March 4, 1831, Judson further rebuked those unfeeling Christians in America, "as hard and immovable as rocks; just as cold and repulsive as the mountains of ice in the Polar seas." Judson was optimistic that the mass distribution of gospel literature directly corresponded to the imminent "great renovation of Burma." Yet, the revival of religion's main barriers, he charged, were "those rocks and those icy mountains."[33]

Fifteen years later, Judson addressed some would-be missionaries, and he explained that Christ's final command, to preach the gospel to all creatures, was what stirred him to be a missionary. He urged them to obey that command at all costs if that were what Christ had truly impressed upon them. Judson warned them of being indifferent to Christ's final command, even though they might do other good activities; he said, "If the Lord wants you for missionaries, He will set that command home to your hearts. If He does so, *you neglect it at your peril.*"[34]

Judson argued that the Great Commission is equally binding on every true believer who claims love for Christ. Though maintaining that not all can or should leave their homeland to the mission field, he believed that God has called all Christians to obey the Scripture in spreading the gospel so that the nations would submit to Christ. At a united missionary gathering held by the Baptist churches in Boston in July 1846, Judson attended the final service before returning to Burma. In his remarks, he spoke plainly. He said that the highest aim of Christ's heart was the Great Commission, which the Church could only accomplish through indiscriminately preaching the gospel to the whole world. Then he asked,

---

Wayland, *Memoir*, 1:525–26. Emphasis in original.

33. Adoniram Judson, "Mr. Judson's Letter to Rev. Mr. Grow," 32. See also Middleditch, *Burmah's Great Missionary*, 273–74. This was a letter of thanks to James Grow in Thompson, Connecticut who donated fifty dollars for publication materials. See Bayles, *History of Windham County*, 677. In that letter Judson lamented the overwhelming needs and the meager supply of missionaries and materials. Also, on this same day, Judson wrote a letter of sympathy and encouragement to Sarah Boardman, whose husband, George Boardman, had just died on February 11, 1831. When writing these letters, Judson was grieving the loss of Boardman, his coworker. See Edward Judson, *The Life of Adoniram Judson*, 374–75.

34. Wayland, *Memoir*, 2:235; Edward Judson, *The Life of Adoniram Judson*, 474; emphasis in original. He was speaking here to the Boardman Missionary Society at Waterville College, in 1846. Related to unashamed dedication to heeding the Great Commission, in some sketches and anecdotes of her marriage to Judson, Emily, his widow, recorded his single-minded devotion to preaching Christ as a missionary and his refusal to entertain people with stories of his labors. See Wayland, *Memoir*, 2:368–70; and Edward Judson, *The Life of Adoniram Judson*, 459–60. One of Judson's colleagues described him as uncommonly disinclined to talking of himself and his notable experiences, but he was happy to talk about Christ. See Stevens, *A Half-Century in Burma*, 12–17.

> Do you, a professor of religion, love the Lord Jesus Christ in sincerity? Have you set your heart on that object which is dearest to his heart? Are you endeavoring to obey his great parting command?[35]

Responding to supposed objections that the command was not binding for all Christians because it is impossible for all Christians to obey, he countered that all are obliged to obey it. He explained that "no profession ought to be regarded as sincere, no love to the Saviour genuine, unless it be attended with a sincere endeavor to obey [Christ's final command]." He went on to say that all Christians can and must invest in prayer, financial support, sending, or going to the mission field; all can be equally engaged in the Great Commission regardless of actual roles and vocations.[36] To those who never had never seriously kept the Great Commission in some way, he queried,

> How can you hope that your love to the Saviour is anything more than an empty profession? . . . What, love the Saviour, who bled and died for this cause, and yet spend your whole existence on earth in toiling for your personal sustenance, and gratification, and vainglory! O, that dread tribunal to which we are hastening! Souls stripped of all disguise there! The final Judge, a consuming fire![37]

---

35. Wayland, Memoir, 2:519.

36. In connection with Judson's contention that all Christians should endeavor to obey Christ's Great Commission, his third wife, Emily, recorded Judson saying that though most Christians could not go, they could pray and send others. He said there are many unknown Christians in America who pray for the advance of the gospel and so participate truly in the Great Commission. He said, "There is many a martyr spirit at the kitchen fire, over the wash tub, and in the plough field." Yet, he admitted that many others do not even heed the Great Commission through the simple act of prayer, and they thus prove that they regard Christ's final command "with slumberous indifference." Wayland, Memoir, 2:372.

37. Middleditch, Burmah's Great Missionary, 398–400. See also Wayland, Memoir, 2:519–21. Addressing the ninth annual meeting of the American and Foreign Bible Society in New York, held two months earlier, in May of 1846, Judson issued a series of woes to those who withhold the treasure of God's translated and preached Word from their neighbors, and presumably he meant the nations in particular. He said it was difficult to imagine anyone experiencing genuine assurance of heaven without spending oneself for the translation and proclamation of the Bible. In light of the explosion of missionary societies and missions mobilization, Judson asked stridently, "Can any believer in the Christian religion hope to lie down in the grave, and pass quietly to paradise, without having made some effort to diffuse the light of the Bible throughout the world?" Judson went on to warn professing Christians against entertaining false assurance of their conversion if they did nothing to help reach those "who have never . . . tasted so much as one drop of the water of that well from which [they were] drawing and drinking every day." Judson went on to say that such Christians should ask

In sum, Judson affectionately longed to please Christ more than any other duty. His spirituality was oriented around his consuming devotion to obey Christ's command, in order that he might please Christ and enjoy eternity in Christ's happy presence. Obedience to the Great Commission was not an option for any Christian, and especially for those Christians whom God had called specifically to go as missionaries. He argued that it is virtually unthinkable that any believer would go to heaven without manifesting the fruit of caring about and laboring for the fulfillment of the Great Commission. For Judson, the ultimate test of true religion and devotion to Christ was glad obedience to Christ's final command. To not obey the Great Commission was to prove indifference to Christ and to scoff at the dreadful eschatological Judgment. Judson, among such a number, counted it a high honor and a high duty to lovingly deny himself and go, doing good, in

themselves what they have done in light of the financial investment, the years of toil, and the actual lives sacrificed in order to translate, print, publish, and disseminate the Bible. He said if such people were honest with their consciences they would flee to God and plead for mercy for their indifference to sharing the Word of God with the perishing millions. Such repentance would cause them to enthusiastically, resolutely, and devoutly embrace the work, and such effort would "secure the approving smile of the Saviour" and thus evidence fruit in keeping with repentance. Adoniram Judson to the American and Foreign Bible Society, address, May 15, 1846, Papers, 1811–1888, Trask Library Special Collections, Newton Centre, Massachusetts; see also Middleditch, *Burmah's Great Missionary*, 388–91; and Wayland, *Memoir*, 2:235–38. Moreover, Judson wrote a letter to the American Baptist Board eight years earlier on December 21, 1838, which sounds strikingly similar to the manuscript of his address at the American and Foreign Bible Society, held May 15, 1846, in New York. See Middleditch, *Burmah's Great Missionary*, 318–19. See also Wayland, *Memoir*, 2:126–27. With similar forwardness, in a letter fourteen years earlier on November 21, 1832, Judson pleaded with the "numerous and flourishing" Baptist churches of the United States, "sitting every man under his vine and under his fig tree, laden with the richest fruit," to send their young men as servants of the cross to assist in his tireless labor for the conversion of souls. Adoniram Judson to Baptist Churches in America, letter, November 21, 1832, Box No. AJ 2, Folder 2 and Microfilm Roll 1, Judson Letters, ABHS; Adoniram Judson, "Letter of Rev. Mr. Judson, to the Baptist Churches in the United States of America, Maulmein, Nov. 21, 1832," 245–46. See also Middleditch, *Burmah's Great Missionary*, 303; and Wayland, *Memoir*, 2:56–57. Likewise, Judson wrote a similar letter in 1817, fifteen years before the aforementioned letter in 1832 and thirty-one years before his address in 1846 to the American and Foreign Bible Society in New York. In the letter from 1817 he said, "O that all the members of the Baptist convention could live in Rangoon one month! Will the Christian world ever awake? Will means ever be used adequate to the necessities of the heathen world? O Lord, send help." Adoniram Judson to Rev Thomas Baldwin, letter, February 10, 1817, Box No. AJ 1, Folder 1 and Microfilm Roll 1, Judson Letters, ABHS. See also Wayland, *Memoir*, 1:186–87. Moreover, in 1847, in relation to the decrease of funds, Judson said, "The Baptist churches in America are behind the age in missionary spirit . . . The Baptist missions will probably pass into the hands of other denominations, or be temporarily suspended; and those who have occupied the van will fall back into the rear." Edward Judson, *The Life of Adoniram Judson*, 512–13.

imitation of Christ. Emily said that he often stated, "If we only please Christ, no matter for the rest!"[38]

Loving Christ

Judson loved to enjoy true religion by drawing near to Christ through prayer. He was active in prayer throughout his life and even throughout each day. He saw the regular practice of prayer as a sign of true religion, and indeed, without effort in prayer, there would be no enjoyment of communion with Christ. Judson esteemed the practice of persevering prayer because he believed that God would bless it in bringing about revival of religion and the advance of Christ's kingdom. Judson importunately prayed for the salvation of the heathen, and in addition, he felt a great burden for the conversion and religious enjoyment of his family, especially his children, for whom he prayed unceasingly. He sometimes expressed his prayers to Christ, whether in affliction or in exultation, through the medium of poetry. He also often communicated prayers for his children through poems that they could easily remember because he believed that memorization and repetition of simple poetry and prayers were useful for maintaining religion.

True Religion and Prayer

Judson's spirituality was not merely dry duty.[39] He, indeed, delighted in drawing near to Christ and communing with him. After hearing Judson preach about pleasing Christ, before the Boardman Missionary Society at Waterville College in 1846, Wayland recalled that Judson's prayer after the address was most memorable: "[He] offered a prayer which I can only describe by saying, it was one of *Judson's* prayers."[40]

For Judson, one major proof of a yielded heart and true religion was the practice of private prayer.[41] In a journal entry in May 1828, he described

---

38. Wayland, *Memoir*, 2:372.

39. See ibid., 2:381–82.

40. Ibid., 2:235; emphasis in original. One well-researched biographer said, "His piety was formed in no common model. It sprung intimate nearness and constant fellowship with the Son of God. More than most men, he was a man of prayer. In this respect he lived by rule." Middleditch, *Burmah's Great Missionary*, 437. For a well-written summary of Judson's prayer life, see Warburton, *Eastward*, 119–20.

41. For example, in a report to the Corresponding Secretary, Solomon Peck, on March 28, 1847, Judson identified the growing number of Christian converts throughout Burma as those who were, "penitent, believing, praying souls." Adoniram Judson to Solomon Peck, report, March 28, 1847, Box No. AJ 3, Folder 4 and Microfilm Roll 1,

a Buddhist man, Moung Bo, who was making headway in his pursuit of truth; Moung Bo had rejected Buddhism and had already tried Unitarianism and Deism. Judson said that Moung Bo demonstrated "a disposition to yield," and Moung Bo assured Judson that he was praying in secret, which Judson saw as a necessary sign of a humble heart.[42]

Judson viewed the early part of the conversion process as requiring prayer to God for a new heart. In order to begin to hope for assurance of true religion, the Christian must pray fervently to God for enlightening and awakening of religion. He demonstrated this in a letter to his stepson, George Dana Boardman . In December 1840, Judson implored George Dana to not "neglect the duty of *secret prayer*," and Judson urged him to "pray earnestly that you may have a new heart, and become a child of God, and that you may have satisfactory evidence that such is your happy state."[43] Similarly, in a letter in March 1845, to his daughter, Abby Ann, he instructed her to seek Christ:

> Think of the dear Saviour every day, and frequently lift up your heart in fervent prayer to God, that he will give you converting,

Judson Letters, ABHS. See also Wayland, *Memoir*, 2:284–88.

42. Adoniram Judson, journal, January 25 to May 31, 1828, Box No. AJ 4, Folder 3 and Microfilm Roll 1, Judson Letters, ABHS. See also Adoniram Judson, "Dr. Judson's Journal, Jan. 25, 1828 [to May 31, 1828]," 73–74. For another example of how Judson associated secret prayer with God drawing a sinner, see Adoniram Judson, "Mr. Judson's Letter, to the American Missionaries in Rangoon and Maulmein," 55–58. Additionally, in a similar vein to this account of Judson's scrutiny of the piety of Moung Bo, nine years earlier Judson had started the first Burman prayer meeting in November of 1819 with the first three Burmese converts. He was delighted to find out four days later that they had continued to meet regularly in the *zayat* for prayer meetings "of their own accord." Their personal initiation to pray together gave him hope that their spirituality was real. See Wayland, *Memoir*, 1:240. Furthermore, the following year, after many evangelistic conversations with another Burman man, Moung Shwa-gnong, Judson still held reservations regarding the authenticity of his conversion. However, in July 1820, he said that he finally felt sure that Moung Shwa-gnong was the "subject of the special operations of the Holy Spirit," and that he was "indeed a true disciple." Judson concluded this because of Moung Shwa-gnong's "account of his mental trials, his struggles with sin, his strivings to be holy, his penitence, his faith, his exercises in secret prayer." Wayland, *Memoir*, 1:280. In a letter on May 21, 1848 to Solomon Peck, twenty-eight years later, Judson was encouraged that the Burmans were still going to the "throne of grace" in prayer." Adoniram Judson to Solomon Peck, report, May 21, 1848, Box No. AJ 4, Folder 2 and Microfilm Roll 1, Judson Letters, ABHS. See also Wayland, *Memoir*, 2:306–7.

43. Wayland, *Memoir*, 2:159; emphasis in original. Likewise, when counseling a Burman man, Moung Thah-lah, who was showing signs of being drawn to Christ, Judson said, "I stated to him, as usual, that he must think much on the love of Christ, and pray to God for an enlightened and loving heart, and then gave him a form of prayer suited to his case." Middleditch, *Burmah's Great Missionary*, 128.

sanctifying grace,[44] and make you his own child... In your daily deportment and intercourse with others, remember these two lines: — "Sweet in temper, face, and word, To please an ever-present Lord."[45]

Communion with Christ

For Judson, prayer and the practice of true religion were not merely a means of gaining a sense of assurance and placating fears of eschatological Judgment; rather, drawing near to Christ found its *telos* in knowing and enjoying him. Judson did not believe that enjoyment of religion came easily or half-heartedly. He held that it required earnest effort, but that it would reap indescribable joy in the knowledge of Christ. Delighting in the glory of Christ required a passionate pursuit of holiness.

Even before leaving for the mission field, Judson testified to the joy of communion with God in Christ. In a letter to his parents in July 1810, Judson demonstrated his concern for his fiancée, Ann, being "all alone at Plymouth." Yet, he said, "There is a Friend, whose friendship, if she would secure it, would never leave her alone." And he went on to exult in "the pleasure which a lively Christian must enjoy in communion with God." Even if alone in the remotest part of the world, he said the Christian's "infinite Friend is always at hand." Judson went on to say that though sickness and death come, the Christian should not fear since "his best Friend does all

---

44. One anonymous missionary recorded that Judson used "the word *grace* very frequently, and in a way somewhat peculiar to himself... 'I think he has grace,' 'I fear he is without grace,' were very common expressions with him." Wayland, *Memoir*, 2:332; emphasis in original.

45. Edward Judson, *The Life of Adoniram Judson*, 444. See also Wayland, *Memoir*, 2:193–94. Abby Ann remembered this concluding rhyme. Having mourned the death of so many loved ones in her young life, Abby Ann sought to hold on to those bygone relations and to even communicate with the dead. Consequently, she became a spiritualist in 1887. In a book that she wrote about mediumship, she cited this rhyme from her father in the context of explaining how to "take the initial step in soul-culture." Abby Ann Judson, *The Bridge Between Two Worlds*, 63. In her concluding chapter of that book, she claimed to have had an encounter with her father through a medium, in which he supposedly said that he should not have sacrificed his life for the world and that people "are saved by doing, not by believing." Abby Ann Judson, "Communication from My Father, Adoniram Judson," 206. Also, to see more supposed communications with her father, mother, and even Jonathan Edwards, see Abby Ann Judson, "Personal Communications," 260–63. To read the letter that she wrote for the Judson Centennial Services in 1888, see Abby Ann Judson, "To the First Baptist Church, Malden, Mass.," 50.

things well . . . For death is only a withdrawing of the veil which conceals his dearest Friend."[46]

Judson not only sought to enjoy communion with Christ in the hard, lonely times, but he also sought to translate life's greatest pleasures into occasions of enjoying communion with Christ. For instance, in a letter to his second wife, Sarah, in March 1839, he rejoiced that, in light of the joys of "wedded love on earth," he could not imagine how unparalleled their joy would be in the heavenly presence of the Bridegroom. He said that he viewed marital chastity and consecration in this life as "a type and shadow" of the "joys of heaven" and the "high and transporting intercommunion of souls . . . to all eternity . . . between one another, and between the 'Bridegroom' and 'Bride.'"[47]

In a sermon on Colossians 1:27, entitled, "Christ in you, the hope of glory," Judson said that Christ indwells the hearts of his people by faith in him, by love to him, and by his love conveyed to them. He said that the evidence of Christ's "character stamped on our souls" is love for God and love for people. This indwelling Christ loves his people "to the end," and Christ will fill up his indwelling in their future glorification. The inferences of such truths, Judson maintained, are that "the indwelling of Christ is the greatest of all blessings." Therefore, he said, it is the "first thing . . . to which we ought to attend." If communion with the indwelling Christ is experienced to some degree, he urged, "How careful we ought to be to improve the blessing! It is necessary to peace of mind, usefulness, future eminence."[48]

In a similar vein, Judson preached another sermon on Hebrews 12:14, about pursuing holiness to see the Lord. He articulated that seeing the Lord is "the greatest good," which "comprises all other good." He said, "To see is to enjoy." Judson argued that "the nature of holiness" is comprised of both "purity" and "consecration" to Christ. Faith must show itself in holiness. He said that holiness is required for seeing God, and this holiness "is the object of the plan of redemption."[49] Likewise, in a letter to his sister, Abigail Judson, in December of 1829, only two weeks after his dark season of melancholy began to lift,[50] Judson implored,

---

46. Wayland, *Memoir*, 1:57–58. For more examples of Judson's effort to enjoy Christ in the midst of grief, see his letter on December 4, 1827 to Ann's sisters, in Middleditch, *Burmah's Great Missionary*, 231–32, and see his letter on September 2, 1845 to the Burmese mission, in Wayland, *Memoir*, 2:203–4.

47. Wayland, *Memoir*, 2:139–40.

48. Ibid., 2:498.

49. Ibid., 2:499.

50. The death of Judson's brother Elnathan Judson, in 1829, marked the turning point for Judson. Elnathan had trusted in Christ on his deathbed, and when Judson

> Let me urge you frequently to reexamine the foundation of your hope. O, it is a solemn thing to die—an awful thing to go into eternity, and discover that we have been deceiving ourselves! Let us depend upon it that nothing but real faith in Christ, *proved to be genuine by a holy life*, can support us at last. That faith which consists merely in a correct belief of the doctrines of grace, and prompts to no self-denial,—that faith which allows us to spend all our days in serving self, content with merely refraining from outward sins, and attending to the ordinary duties of religion,—is no faith at all. O, let me beg of you to look well into this matter! And let me beg my dear mother, in her old age, and in view of the near approach of death and eternity, to examine again and again whether her faith is of the right kind. Is it that faith which gives her more enjoyment in Jesus, from day to day, than she finds in any thing else?[51]

Judson believed that the enjoyment of communion with Christ required earnestness and discipline. In a letter to Ann in December 1810, Judson expressed exhaustion from a seasonal cold and from preaching that day. He contended in the letter that the primary reason that Christians do not actually find joy in communion with God in Christ is because they "do not try to enjoy it." He criticized those lazy Christians who are not "resolved" to grow spiritually.[52] He then said that in spite of his sickness and weariness, he devoted himself that morning to refrain from anything "displeasing to God," and he found it useful to force himself to enjoy religion even when his body was worn out. To remind himself to faithfully keep his spiritual resolution, he wrote notes to himself where he would see them routinely. The notes asked if what he was doing pleased God. Such reminders, he said, would be useless, "unless I resolve, in divine strength, instantly to obey the decision of conscience."[53] He wrote to Ann again the next day and described his sweet "enjoyment of God." He went on to say that God would gladly give

---

heard this news, he said in a letter, "When I read this account, I went into my little room, and could only shed tears of joy." Anderson, *To the Golden Shore*, 391.

51. Wayland, *Memoir*, 1:480; emphasis in original.

52. In contrast to his frustration with lethargic Christians, Judson had previously highlighted examples of "deep and ardent piety" expressed in passion for "the kingdom of Christ," and prayer for "revival of religion," which he admired in his late friend and seminary roommate, Lewis Le Count Congar (1787–1810) of Newark, New Jersey. Judson witnessed Congar die slowly from a typhus fever, and after his death on January 6, 1810, Judson wrote a short narrative of his dying days; see Adoniram Judson, "Narrative [of Lewis Le Count Congar]," 155–59. See also Richards, *A Discourse, Delivered 14th January, 1810, at Newark*.

53. Edward Judson, *The Life of Adoniram Judson*, 13–14.

Christians joy in communion with him, if only they would not grieve the Holy Spirit by "little sins" and neglecting to employ the means of enjoying religion. He said that "the secret of living a holy life is to avoid everything which will displease God and grieve the Spirit, and to be strictly attentive to the means of grace." God will draw near to those who "tremble at his Word" and "wait upon him." Judson went on to say that the great hindrance to happiness in God was, "preferring a trifle to God" and putting off religion for a more convenient time.[54]

Judson's pursuit of knowing Christ stimulated his activism. In a letter in October 1830, to encourage Stella Bennett, Judson sought to remind her that life is fleeting and that Christians must improve upon the time God has allotted them. Then, explaining how communion with God in Christ should incite active obedience in service to Christ, he said,

> The first duty of every lover of Christ is to enter constantly within the veil, offering himself a sacrifice to God, to obtain some sensible communion with the great Invisible; and his second, to come forth with a shining face, as Moses, and be ready to speak and do whatever God, by his word, providence, and indwelling Spirit, shall appoint.

Judson went on to say that to reverse these two duties and labor "without an habitual sense of holy unction and divine communion" might receive God's merciful blessing, but it would nevertheless "wear out" the missionary and produce "irreparable loss" in eternity.[55]

Judson's daily effort to pursue Christ and enjoy his presence was clearly manifest in his aforementioned rules of life, in which he promoted routine and frequent meditation and prayers every day for much of his Christian life. From 1819 to 1843, Judson practiced daily rule keeping for the sake of spiritual discipline. Judson would often write out spontaneous thoughts that

---

54. Wayland, *Memoir*, 1:33. He demonstrated this effort to practice the means of enjoying religion throughout his life. For example, in 1821 during Ann's voyage back to America for health concerns, Judson wrote to Daniel Sharp in September 1821. He said that though there was "not a single person" who could cheer him, yet he roused himself to seek his joy in Christ, "committing this forlorn hope into the hands of the Great Captain of our salvation." Judson took heart, knowing that Christ "is able to keep those who are persecuted from being forsaken, and those who are cast down from being destroyed." Adoniram Judson, "Letter from Mr. Judson to Mr. Sharp, Dated Rangoon, September 17, 1821," 344–45. For another example, see Adoniram Judson to the Rev. Thomas Baldwin, letter, February 19, 1824, Box No. AJ 1, Folder 2 and Microfilm Roll 1, Judson Letters, ABHS; for a short extract, see Adoniram Judson, "Letter from Dr. Judson to Rev. Dr. Baldwin, Dated Ava, Feb. 19, 1824," 22–23.

55. Wayland, *Memoir*, 1:507–8. See Ranney, *A Sketch of the Lives and Missionary Work*.

would encourage him to pray. Such topics might include a thought from a devotional book, a Scripture passage, or one of his own resolutions.[56] Both of his eminent biographers, Francis Wayland and Edward Judson, compiled Judson's penciled fragments of "Topics to Encourage Prayer." Some topics that Judson jotted down to remind him to pray were: "wrestling Jacob . . . friend at midnight . . . the unjust judge . . . whatever others do, let my life be a life of prayer[57] . . . self-denial . . . keep the cross of Christ in view."[58] He practiced prayer and meditation in the middle of the night, in the morning, and in the evening. As previously noted, he indicated in his tract, *The Threefold Cord*, that he sought to pray seven times interspersed throughout each day, which would amount to two to three hours of daily prayer.[59] In all his journals and letters since writing this tract in 1829, there are no indications of how many months or years he sustained these seven times of daily prayer. However, there are numerous accounts of his resolve to pray two or three times each day. For instance, in 1840 he wrote a letter to his stepson, George Dana, and encouraged him to rise early every day before the sunrise to take a brisk walk and pray in secret. Judson also instructed him not to neglect praying in secret five to ten minutes every morning and evening along with spending early morning walks in prayer, which he said had been his practice for thirty-five years. Judson went on to say that such disciplined routines of physical and spiritual exercises were his two "pieces of advice" that would lead George Dana to "be virtuous and happy."[60]

By briefly analyzing the ascetic training at Andover, his penchant for routine practices of prayer is understandable. Judson's early years of spiritual formation found their rhythm in the scheduled practices at Andover, which required what one writer called "an ascetic tendency."[61] The faculty and the students would rise early for prayer, and then after morning studies and lunch, they would have another hour of prayer. Then after more studies, they would practice scheduled prayer in the evenings as well. One student

---

56. See Edward Judson, *The Life of Adoniram Judson*, 315–16; Wayland, *Memoir*, 1:322–23; Wayland, *Memoir*, 2:61, 103, 190.

57. These and some others were the "Topics to Encourage Prayer" that Edward Judson compiled. See Edward Judson, *The Life of Adoniram Judson*, 314.

58. Wayland also compiled a list of "Topics to Encourage Prayer," in which he included those that Edward Judson compiled and seven additional points that Wayland found. See Wayland, *Memoir*, 1:533.

59. Adoniram Judson, *The Threefold Cord*, 1–2.

60. Wayland, *Memoir*, 2:158–60.

61. Bendroth, *A School of the Church*, 21.

in the early years described this threefold routine as "rules adopted by the majority" and "the order of the day."[62]

Despite melancholic periods, Judson still sought to draw near to Christ and enjoy his presence. During his most depressed season, on the third anniversary of Ann's death (October 24, 1829), he queried Ann's sisters, Mary Hasseltine and Abigail Hasseltine, and asked them if they discovered how to commune with God because he could not find enjoyment in God.[63] This season of despondency lasted for over two years. And yet, before the depression departed, Judson wrote a long letter, in January 1829, to Archibald Campbell (1769–1846), the conquering hero of the first Burman war with England, who was about to depart for England. This letter reveals much about the tenor of Judson's religion even in his darkest days. Judson promoted true religion and implored Campbell to yield his life to God. Judson said that true religion does not consist in the mere avoidance of wickedness; rather, true religion consists in the enjoyment of God. He went on to say that our fear of God is placated by "vague and indefinite ideas of the mercy of God" and by a false hope that everything will be well in the end. Consciences are dulled by the "fatal machinations of the god of this world," and "the intoxicating draught of pleasure . . . [and] the height of human ambition." He said soon the delusion of this world would dissipate, and unless one is born again, he cannot enter the kingdom of God. As an "ambassador of Christianity," Judson beseeched Campbell to give his heart "to the Friend and Lover of man, who hung and died on the cross to redeem us from eternal woe." There, in Christ's love alone would Campbell find unimaginable "peace and sweetness . . . transcendent beauty . . . [and] true happiness." Judson closed by saying that he prayed regularly for Campbell's conversion.[64] Judson penned all of these devotional sentiments to Campbell in spite of his melancholy. And a year later, writing a letter in 1830 to Stella Bennett after the darkness had lifted, Judson still rejoiced in the "sweet peace in Jesus, which the world can neither give nor take away. O, the freeness, the richness of divine grace, through the blood of the cross!"[65]

As Judson suggested to Ann in 1810, in the aforementioned letters, enjoyment of religion would only come through strictly appropriating the means of grace, making the effort to draw near to God, seeking to never displease him, waiting upon him, and trembling at his Word. All of these

62. Rowe, *History of Andover*, 36–37.

63. See Wayland, *Memoir*, 1:473.

64. The whole letter is quoted in "Adoniram Judson," *The Friend*, 69–70. See also Edward Judson, *The Life of Adoniram Judson*, 311–14

65. Wayland, *Memoir*, 1:512–13.

spiritual exercises remained his priority at the end of his life. Forty years later, in her reminiscences of him, Emily characterized Judson's spirituality with his unique ability to interpret everything, "whether trivial or important," including common incidences, books, and casual conversations, with "a peculiarly spiritual train of thought." Emily said that "Christ was all his theme." She recalled that he exuded an otherworldly piety in his preaching. Judson's practice was to prepare his sermons audibly, and in his preparations, he would be "so much affected as to weep." Overcome with the weightiness of his sermon topic and the presence of Christ, he would sometimes choose another. Emily said she would often listen to him prepare extemporaneously for his sermons. She went on to say that "the fervid, burning eloquence, the deep pathos, the touching tenderness, the elevation of thought, and intense beauty of expression," of his "private teachings" were beyond anything she had ever experienced. Indeed, she said, at times his burning piety "surprised even himself."[66]

In Judson's final months, Emily described his enjoyment of Christ as increasing with his anticipation of meeting Christ face-to-face. Though his health declined, Judson gave himself increasingly to prayer and communion with Christ. He continually meditated on Christ's redemptive indicative, "As I have loved you [John 13:34]." Emily recalled that "he would murmur, as though unconsciously, 'As I have loved you,'—'as I have loved you,'—then burst out with the exclamation, 'O, the love of Christ! the love of Christ!'" Emily said that he referred to himself regularly as a "great sinner, who had been overwhelmed with benefits." The "unfathomable love" of Christ captivated him increasingly in his final months. She said tears would run down his face as he would exult aloud in the love of Christ, of which he said he had all of eternity to evermore enjoy.[67]

---

66. Ibid., 2:336–37. For more about Judson's prayerful and meditative practice for sermon preparation, see Emily's description in ibid., 2:390–91.

67. Emily Chubbuck Judson, "Closing Scenes in Dr. Judson's Life," 36. Similarly, in Judson's concluding appeal to the Society for Missionary Inquiry at Brown University in 1845, he said, "When our work is done on earth, may we all be raised to heaven, where we shall know more of his love to us, and love him more." Wayland, *Memoir*, 2:228. See also Middleditch, *Burmah's Great Missionary*, 364. Judson wrote in his journal in 1834 that he expected that he would know Christ more in this life and that such enjoyment would increase throughout eternity, "consummated in the bright world of love." Adoniram Judson, journal, March 12, 1834 to April 10, 1834, Journal, Box No. AJ 4, Folder 4 and Microfilm Roll 1, Judson Letters, ABHS. See also Wayland, *Memoir*, 2:83.

Importunate Praying

For Judson, the employment of self-denial was a means to being happy in Christ as the final aim of the progress of holiness. His son, Edward, described him as "possessed with a consuming zeal to be made holy . . . He was a man of prayer." Edward described his father's piety as "intense," and though it led him into "extremes of self-denial," Edward said his piety was indeed "a great religious nature, wrestling for Christ-likeness." Edward went on to say he habitually walked "rapidly in the open air" and prayed and meditated. Judson would regularly pace back and forth in his room, and when his children heard his hard pacing, they knew "Papa is praying."[68] From his early days at Andover, Judson made it his habit of walking in the open air and praying and meditating on Scripture, which is what he was doing in the woods behind Andover when he was meditating on Mark 16:15 and sensed his call to missions.[69]

Judson often prayed with passion and persistence, especially for the salvation of sinners. Emily recorded that his prayers

> were marked by an earnest, grateful enthusiasm, and in speaking of missionary operations in general, his tone was one of elevated triumph, almost of exultation; for he . . . felt an unshaken confidence in their final success.[70]

---

68. Edward Judson, *The Life of Adoniram Judson*, 311. Judson would also prepare for preaching by walking, meditating on Scripture, and praying fervently aloud; see Emily's account in Wayland, *Memoir*, 2:389–90.

69. See Conant, *The Earnest Man*, 43. See also Middleditch, *Burmah's Great Missionary*, 22; and see Wayland, *Memoir*, 1:52. Before their marriage in 1812, Judson wrote to Ann in January 1811, and pondered the unknown hazards they would likely face as missionaries. In view of potential suffering and even death, Judson urged her to "pray with earnestness," and then he exclaimed, "O for an overcoming faith." Wayland, *Memoir*, 1:35. Ann recalled later that he would "spend whole days in fasting and prayer, taking no nourishment but a little fruit in the morning." Wayland, *Memoir*, 1:31.

70. Edward Judson, *The Life of Adoniram Judson*, 532. In May 1852, two years after Judson's death, his fellow missionary, the L. Ingalls wrote to Francis Wayland, and described Judson's passionate praying: "The Burmans lay near his heart; he was accustomed to spend a portion of each day in secret prayer for them. I had the privilege of enjoying some of these seasons, and shall never forget those hallowed hours. He not only prayed, but labored." Wayland, *Memoir*, 2:355. Wayland observed that because of Judson's "unshaken confidence in God," Judson continually asked "until he received in his own consciousness an assurance that his requests would be granted." Wayland, *Memoir*, 2:381. Wayland also said that Judson was "always relying with earnest prayer on the power of the Holy Spirit to make the truth effectual for the regeneration of men." Wayland, *Memoir*, 2:388. Ann recorded an evangelistic conversation Judson had with her language teacher on September 30, 1815, in which Judson said he prayed every day for the teacher's salvation. See Wayland, *Memoir*, 1:173. For another illustration of

Judson also combined prayer with Scripture as he passionately interceded for those in his care. For instance, in a letter in May 1833 to Stella Bennett, whose husband and two daughters had returned to America, Judson described his recent intercession for her and her daughters. He said he had a "remarkable instance of divine guidance" where it was as if Christ himself were "pointing out the particular passage, and shedding a flood of light on the sacred page." Judson said he prayed for her daughters, and he said, "It was the only time that I had ever been enabled to *pray* for them, and I had a momentary feeling that they would receive some saving impression before they reached home." He recorded his intense prayer for them in this instance because at other times he said he felt as though he were merely a "prayerless, heartless creature."[71]

Judson believed that revival of true religion was God's appointed means of ushering in Christ's glory, and he believed that it was effected through persevering prayer. In a letter to William Crane (1790–1866)[72] about Crane's attempt to "revive the state of true religion" in Baltimore, Judson praised his "faithful and persevering labors to counteract the overwhelming tide of immorality and false religion." Judson prayed that Crane would see an outpouring of the Holy Spirit and an ingathering of lost souls. Judson said, "'Nothing is impossible to industry,' said one of the seven sages of Greece. Let us change the word *industry* for *persevering prayer*, and the

---

Judson praying for the salvation of an individual, see Judson's journal entry on April 29, 1819 in Wayland, *Memoir*, 1:216, and also see his journal entry on June 23, 1819 in Wayland, *Memoir*, 1:223–24. Judson combined fervent praying with his evangelical activity. While on the ship, *Ramsay*, during his voyage to Port Louis and Maulmain in 1841, Judson "made it a matter of prayer to God that he might be instrumental in turning some of them [that is, the sailors] from the error of their ways; and, before going on board, expressed a conviction that God had heard him." Judson "earnestly prayed," and through much "private instruction," three sailors were converted. When they arrived at Maulmain, Judson baptized the captain (who doubted his infant baptism), the three other sailors, and a Burmese woman. This account was taken from a pamphlet entitled, "A Brief Narrative of the last Voyage of the Ship Ramsay, of Greenock; illustrative [sic] of the Beneficial Effects of Total Abstinence, and the Success of the Gospel in the Conversion of a Number of the Crew, the Formation of a Church on Board, &c., &c.," compiled by John Simpson, published in Greenock; quoted in Wayland, *Memoir*, 2:182–84. In a letter in December 1841, to his mother, Abigail Brown Judson, and sister, Abigail Judson, Judson recorded the event and joyfully spoke of the "pleasure" he felt in seeing the sailors converted and baptized. Wayland, *Memoir*, 2:187.

71. Wayland, *Memoir*, 2:68; emphasis in original.

72. Crane moved from Richmond to Baltimore and helped establish the Maryland Baptist Union Association. A churchman and a proponent of Sunday School and Bible study, Crane also strongly opposed slavery; he helped establish the first African American Baptist church in Maryland on February 20, 1836. For a short introductory biography, see Moore, *William Crane, Layman Extraordinary*.

motto will be more Christian and worthy of universal adoption." Judson went on to argue that Christians are weaker in prayer than any other grace. Seeking to arouse expectancy for receiving the blessing of God through persistent prayer, he said,

> God loves importunate prayer so much that he will not give us much blessing without it; and the reason he loves such prayer is, that he loves us, and knows it is necessary for our receiving the richest blessings which he is waiting and longing to bestow.[73]

Judson believed that God would guide him as a weak child looks to his father to supply his every need and show him the way he should go.[74] He also believed that persevering prayer would not only effect a revival, but that it would also be the means through which missionaries could ascertain wise methods for disseminating the Gospel and evangelization. He said in a letter to Ira Chase (1793–1864), a professor at Andover Theological Seminary, in April 1822, that he did not know then how exactly the Spirit of Christ would lead him to introduce Christianity to Burma, but, he said, "We hope that such a discovery will in due time be granted to humble trust and fervent prayer."[75]

True Religion and Family

Judson may have been busy in his translation efforts, but he, nevertheless, spent time worshiping with his family, seeking the spiritual improvement of his family as he did for himself.[76] From the perspective of the aforementioned unbelieving Anglo-Indian merchant, Henry Gouger, who suffered with Judson in prison, Judson's home exuded the warmth of evangelical

---

73. Wayland, *Memoir*, 2:151; emphasis in original. In Judson's, *A Digest of Scripture*, he outlined the basic biblical teaching on prayer. He concluded the chapter on the essential doctrines of prayer with a section called, "It Must be Earnest and Persevering." Adoniram Judson, *A Digest of Scripture*, 124–30.

74. Emily recorded that Judson would often say things like, "'If God has designed a work for us to do, he will arrange all the little particulars, and we have only to trust in him;' 'If it be the will of God, never fear for the consequences,' &c." And she said that "the way he learned the will of God, was prayerfully to look for manifestations of it; not in any wonderful way, but as an affectionate child almost intuitively seems to know what will please a parent." Wayland, *Memoir*, 2:372.

75. Middleditch, *Burmah's Great Missionary*, 169. Wayland observed that the more he faced discouragements and setbacks, "the more earnestly he fasted and prayed for the coming of the Holy Spirit." Wayland, *Memoir*, 2:387.

76. Wayland, *Memoir*, 2:394–96.

piety. Gouger said that during their family worship times, he was astonished at

> the reverence of demeanour, the propriety of language, and above all the knowledge of the New Testament and its saving doctrines, which some of them manifested in their extempore prayer. No one who heard could doubt their sincerity.[77]

Despite his sacrifice on behalf of the Burmans, Judson's heart yearned for the salvation of his family, especially his children.[78] After his death, Emily wrote to his sister, Abigail, and in the letter, Emily described Judson's dying days as growing in his enjoyment of communion with Christ. From these times of "private devotions," he was motivated to intercede increasingly for "special subjects of prayer," of which he was predominantly burdened for "the conversion of his posterity." She said that he always devoted himself to praying for his children, but he was devoted to praying also for their children and the ensuing generations, "so that he should ultimately meet a long, unbroken line of descendants before the throne of God, where all might join together in ascribing everlasting praises to their Redeemer."[79] His desire for them was that they too would enter his legacy and become ministers of the Gospel.[80] In March 1839, Judson wrote to young George Dana, and said that

---

77. Gouger, *A Personal Narrative*, 177.

78. With evangelical fervency in prayer, similar to his importunate praying for the heathen and for his own children, Judson also prayed perseveringly for the conversion of his brother, Elnathan, who had trusted in Christ about ten minutes before his death. See Wayland, *Memoir*, 1:474–75. For another example of Judson's prayers for his family, see a letter on December 13, 1827 to his mother and sister following his father's death; in it Judson prayed for them to enjoy the "divine presence" in spite of "the repeated strokes of our heavenly Father's hand" in their anticipation of "the high enjoyment of everlasting life." Ibid., 1:443–44.

79. Edward Judson, *The Life of Adoniram Judson*, 530–36. In July 1846, Judson left his daughter, Abby Ann, in Bradford at the old homestead of the Hasseltine family. Judson said that he prayed passionately that she and her siblings would submit to Christ and thus meet him again in heaven in the presence of Christ. See Adoniram Judson, "Adoniram Judson's Letter to His Daughter Abby Ann," 14. See also Edward Judson, *The Life of Adoniram Judson*, 522. In a final letter to Abby Ann, in October 1849, Judson said that he was sad that she had not yet given her "heart to the Saviour." He warned her: "Believe me, that every year; every month, you live without grace, will occasion you a loss that will be irreparable through all eternity." Wayland, *Memoir*, 2:322. Emily also recorded that "he always prayed most fervently, both in [sic] his own behalf and that of his children, for a long life of labor and self-denial." Wayland, *Memoir*, 2:366–68.

80. For some examples, see some letters Judson wrote to George Dana on August 23, 1836, in Edward Judson, *The Life of Adoniram Judson*, 419–20; on January 26, 1846, in Wayland, *Memoir*, 2:241–42; and on December 24, 1840, in Wayland, *Memoir*, 2:158–60.

he and George Dana's mother, Sarah B. Judson, prayed for him every day in their family devotions. In the letter, Judson outlined for him the reality of the depraved heart, being "full of self-love, and wholly under the influence of self-will." Judson charged him to "depend on the Word of God," trusting in Christ. Judson said that the signs of a new heart are repentance and faith, without which George Dana would never go to heaven and see his parents again.[81]

Likewise, illustrating his deep concern for his children's religion, in May 1848, Judson wrote a letter to his sons, Elnathan and Adoniram Brown, who were studying in Worcester, and he called them to a relentless love for Christ. He said that he rejoiced to hear that his son, Elnathan, was beginning "to entertain a hope in Christ." He said that he believed that Abby Ann and they would "become true Christians, and meet [him] in heaven." The reason he gave for his confidence of their conversions was that he was persevering in prayer for them. He believed his persistence was evidence of the strength of his faith. With the evangelical urgency of a missionary father, he implored them to seek Christ:

> O, heaven is all. Life, life, eternal life! Without this, without an interest in the Lord of life, you are lost, lost forever . . . Give your heart at once to the Saviour. Don't go to sleep without doing it. Try, try for your life. Don't mind what anybody may say to the contrary, nor how much foolish boys may laugh at you. Love the dear Saviour, who has loved you unto death. Dear sons, so soon as you have a good hope in Christ that your sins are pardoned, and that Christ loves you, urge your pastor and the church to baptize and receive you into communion. They will hold back, thinking you are too young, and must give more evidence. But don't be discouraged. Push on. Determine to do it. Determine to stand by Christ, come what will. That is the way to get to heaven.[82]

---

81. Wayland, *Memoir*, 2:135–36. Nearly two years later, Judson wrote again to George Dana on December 24, 1840, and said that he and Sarah earnestly prayed every morning during family devotions for the salvation of all their children. Then Judson instructed him to "never neglect the duty of secret prayer. Never let a morning or evening pass without going into some room or place by yourself, kneeling down and spending five or ten minutes at least in praying to God, in the name of Jesus Christ." Judson urged him to "pray earnestly" for a renewed heart and prove with "satisfactory evidence" the validity of his conversion. Ibid., 2:158–60. George Dana subsequently professed faith in Christ in 1843. See Judson's letter to George Dana on April 7, 1843, in Ibid., 2:190.

82. Edward Judson, *The Life of Adoniram Judson*, 523. See also Wayland, *Memoir*, 2:307–8. At the time of writing Judson's memoir, Wayland said, "[Judson] ever prayed for the early conversion of his children; and it is worthy of remark that, since his death, three of them have, as we hope, become heirs of eternal life." Wayland, *Memoir*, 2:381.

Around that same time, Judson wrote to his sons again and told them, "I pray for you every time I pray for myself." He said that he had heard of revivals in different parts of the country, and he encouraged them to not only seek to experience one but to even begin one in Worcester. He then urged them to "cherish this desire in your hearts, and pray in faith that the blessing may come." He went on to instruct them how to discern if the work of renewal in their souls was beginning. He said they would feel contrition for sins, fear of God's wrath, love for Christ, and a devotion to him.[83] In his farewell letter to his sons, in July of 1846, before setting sail for Burma, Judson wrote a short note, which he concluded, exhorting them: "Pray every morning and evening."[84]

Poetry and Piety

In his letters and journals, Judson articulated both the heights of optimism and the depths of despondency, and occasionally he conveyed his piety through poetry.[85] Judson found it difficult sometimes to express the degree of his intensity in straightforward prose. Truncated ministry reports at times turned into exclamations of either celebration or lamentation. The spiritual state of the Burmans often triggered his poetic expressions. He was not an unemotional, placid translator who only operated in the socially aloof mechanics of contextual and linguistic theory; rather, his conversionist piety expressed both joy over the conversion and baptism of even one Burman and sadness over the multitudes without a gospel witness. Moreover, he often composed his poems as prayers or praise directed to God. One way to identify his heightened level of emotion in his journals and letters is to note those circumstances that prompted him to compose or to quote poetry.

---

83. Wayland, *Memoir*, 2:241. See also another letter in 1846 to Adoniram Brown and Elnathan expressing Judson's desire for their conversion, in ibid., 2:242.

84. Ibid., 2:259.

85. After studying the whole Judson corpus, Wayland said that Judson's poetry manifested "a talent for versification, sometimes called into action by the humorous, and at other times by the devout or the pathetic." Ibid., 2:375. One account recorded Judson's poetic skills even in Burmese: "Dr. Judson composed that first hymn more nearly in accordance with the complicated style of Burmese poetry than any other now in our collections." Stevens, *A Half-Century in Burma*, 12. Commenting on the dominance of poetry and literary elegance in Judson's letters, Kendrick said, "Dr. Judson was unquestionably one of the finest epistolary writers in our language—chaste, simple, elegant, every word selected with felicitous yet unconscious precision, and passing spontaneously from delicate playfulness into those regions of sacred thought in which he habitually dwelt." Kendrick, *The Life and Letters of Mrs. Emily C. Judson*, 154. See also Rosalie Hall Hunt's comments in Hunt, *Bless God and Take Courage*, 210–11.

For example, after witnessing an old Karen chief "make a proper surrender of himself to Christ" and then receive baptism right before his death, Judson wrote of his joy in the salvation of souls. Judson was so relieved that God had mercifully delivered the man from the flames of hell. He exuberantly reflected on the man's dying words, "The best of all is, God is with us," and Judson composed a short poem to express his praise of God:

> In these deserts let me labor,
> On these mountains let me tell
> How he died—the blessed Saviour,
> To redeem a world from hell.[86]

This poem shows both how Judson viewed the purpose of Christ's death and Judson's reasonable response. Having reflected on the dying chief's joy in God's gracious, steadfast presence procured by Christ, Judson rejoiced that Christ died to deliver sinners from hell. And he started the poem by indicating what he believed to be his duty in light of such good news: to labor in remote lands to tell sinners of the gospel.

Furthermore, his more painful emotions often times elicited longer, more solemn poetry. A good example of this is his famous hymn that he likely wrote in 1829 during his dark season of despondency: "Come, Holy Spirit, Dove Divine." It is helpful to understand the historical and spiritual contexts in which Judson wrote this hymn. The last three stanzas say,

> We love Your name, we love Your laws,
> And joyfully embrace Your cause;
> We love Your cross, the shame, the pain,
> O Lamb of God for sinners slain.
>
> We sink beneath the water's face,
> And thank You for Your saving grace;
> We die to sin and seek a grave
> With You, beneath the yielding wave.
>
> And as we rise with You to live,
> O let the Holy Spirit give
> The sealing unction from above,
> The joy of life, the fire of love.[87]

---

86. Adoniram Judson, journal, February 29, 1832 to June 25, 1832, Box No. AJ 4, Folder 8 and Microfilm Roll 1, Judson Letters, ABHS; Adoniram Judson, "Mr. Judson's Journal, Feb. 29th, 1832 [to May 16, 1832]," 41–45. See also Wayland, *Memoir*, 2:44–45; and Middleditch, *Burmah's Great Missionary*, 294.

87. Adoniram Judson, "Come, Holy Spirit, Dove Divine," 586. Judson is also wrote the following hymns: "Our Father God, Who Art in Heaven" and "Our Saviour Bowed Beneath the Wave." See Julian, *A Dictionary of Hymnology*, 609.

This hymn seems to indicate a few things about how Judson viewed the struggles of the Christian life. Part of loving Christ, in Judson's mind, entailed esteeming Christ's cause, which Judson regularly considered to be the Great Commission. Devotion to glorifying the name of Christ involved enduring pain and dying to sin. And it also indicates how Judson upheld the role of believer's baptism in marking the Christian as one set apart, united with Christ. In the final analysis, this hymn demonstrates his strong Christocentrism, with each stanza either addressing Christ or pleading with the Holy Spirit to stimulate more love to Christ in the Christian's heart.

Having beheld much fruit among the Karen people, Judson wrote a letter to the American Baptist Board in June 1832, which the others at his mission station signed. He earnestly implored them to send more missionaries. For much of the second half of this very long letter, Judson prayed and appealed for God's mercy upon both small villages and large cities alike throughout the Southeast Asia region. By the end of his prayer, the impression he gave is one of great urgency because of the hopelessness of so many unreached peoples. He concluded the letter pleading with God to pour out the Holy Spirit to help the missionaries "in the solemn and laborious work of translating and printing thine holy, inspired Word in the languages of these heathen. O, keep our faith from failing, our spirits from sinking."[88] But Judson did not sign off there; he wrote a poem to accentuate his aforementioned appeal. These famous extracts disclose his intense activistic spirituality:

> A cry—a cry—is in the air!
> It comes from Asia's peopled plain;
> A voice of grief, of love, and prayer—
> O Christian, shall it come in vain?
>
> To see, to hear, to think, to know,
> All this—for deathless souls are there!
> And yet have none for us to go—
> This, this is more than we can bear!
>
> O Christians! in the land we love,
> And only left these souls to save—
> Have ye no feeling hearts to move,
> When pity pleads across the wave?[89]

In the context of his entire letter, these stanzas are short poetic expressions of how he viewed the weighty responsibility of the church to rescue

88. Dowling, *The Judson Offering*, 175–81.
89. Ibid., 181–82.

perishing sinners from hell. Yet, he was skeptical that the American churches were burdened enough to send necessary support and laborers to reach the nations. Throughout this letter and poem, he contrasted the dire need of those languishing in spiritual barrenness against the comfortable churches of his native country that were hoarding plenteous resources that they could have used to influence the nations for Christ. This poem, in its longer form, illustrates how the heathen's prospect of eternal suffering energized his Christ-centered activistic piety. This poem also reveals Judson's strong conversionistic spirituality.

In January 1825, Ann gave birth to Maria. During this time, Judson was in prison, and though he was innocent and though Ann pleaded relentlessly for his release, the jailers would not let him out. During his long imprisonment, to convey his piety and hope in spite of his agony, he composed a prayerful poem for his newborn daughter, which was entitled, "Lines addressed to an infant daughter, twenty days old in the condemned prison of Ava." The following lines are a few short extracts from the end of his very long lullaby, which he composed in March of 1825:

> There is a God on high,
> The glorious King of kings,
> 'Tis He, to whom thy mother prays.
> Whose love she sits and sings.
>
> That glorious God, so kind,
> Has sent his Son to save
> Our ruined race from sin and death,
> And raise them from the grave.
>
> And to that covenant God,
> My darling I commend;
> Be thou the helpless orphan's guide,
> Her father and her friend.[90]

These few extracts reveal Judson's reflections on the tenderness of God. He extolled God as exalted and glorious, but who, nevertheless, is loving and kind. He saw God's kindness as supremely demonstrated in sending Christ to redeem sinners, and if God loved thus, certainly God would never forsake those whom Christ died to save. This poem shows that even in Judson's absence, he trusted that his covenant-keeping God would aid little Maria as her enduring father and friend.[91]

---

90. Ibid., 89–91. See also Wayland, *Memoir*, 1:380–83. The poem's last five stanzas are in Middleditch, *Burmah's Great Missionary*, 193.

91. After writing this poem, Judson composed a versification of the Lord's Prayer

In 1826, Ann died and Judson was left to mourn and persevere in his missionary labor. In a letter that December, to Ann's mother, Judson described his resolve to exercise religion and find fresh communion through "the Gospel of Jesus Christ, which brings life and immortality to light." He rejoiced in the "blessed assurance" that Ann was "rejoicing in the heavenly paradise," and he expressed his joy in quoting a hymn:

> Where glories shine, and pleasures roll
> That charm, delight, transport the soul,
> And every panting wish shall be
> Possessed of boundless bliss in Thee.[92]

His quotation of this hymn underscores how his meditation on heavenly happiness sustained him. This poetic extract is illustrative of how often he composed poetry or quoted hymns that turned his meditations heavenward. Throughout his letters and journals, due to his Christ-centered orientation, there is a recurring pattern of eternity-minded poetry.

Judson also created poems and rhymes to encourage simple religion in his children. He wrote poetry for his children to help them pray to Jesus in a memorable way. For instance, he composed two separate stanzas, called, "Prayer to Jesus":

> Dear Jesus, hear me when I pray,
> And take this naughty heart away;
> Teach me to love thee, gracious Lord,
> And learn to read thy holy word.
>
> Come, dearest Saviour, take my heart,
> And let me ne'er from thee depart;
> From every evil set me free,
> And all the glory be to thee.[93]

One other example of a simple prayer poem that he wrote for his children, called, "A Morning Prayer," says,

---

for the purpose of meditation and prayer to sustain his mind through the unremitting agonies of prison. See Adoniram Judson, "The Lord's Prayer," poem, March 1, 1825, Box No. AJ 4, Folder 3 and Microfilm Roll 1, Judson Letters, ABHS; Adoniram Judson, "The Lord's Prayer Versified in the Shortest Compass," poem, March 1, 1825, Box No. AJ 1, Folder 1 and Microfilm Roll 1, ABHS. See also Wayland, *Memoir*, 1:384–85.

92. Middleditch, *Burmah's Great Missionary*, 222. See also Wayland, *Memoir*, 1:420–21. From a hymn by Isaac Watts; see Watts and Rippon, *The Psalms and Hymns of Dr. Watts*, 215.

93. Edward Judson, *The Life of Adoniram Judson*, 427. See also Wayland, *Memoir*, 2:136.

> My waking thoughts I raise to thee,
> Who through the night hast guarded me;
> Keep me this day from every ill,
> And help me, Lord, to do thy will.[94]

His son, Adoniram B. Judson, also recalled a short rhyme that Judson wrote to remind his children to take delight in knowing God. Judson would quote this to his children for their comfort and guidance: "Be the living God my friend, then my joys shall never end."[95] Common in the poetry that he taught his children were themes such as Christ's nearness, kindness, everlasting love, secure protection, and the need to seek Christ more through prayer and the Scriptures. By briefly surveying the poetry that he wrote for his children, it seems that Judson wished to impress upon their hearts and minds that Jesus was near and ready to help them. By analyzing other portions of his poetry throughout his journals and letters, the general themes of his frequent meditation come into view, which the above thematic samples all exemplify.

In sum, Judson sometimes found satisfying expression of his prayers through poetry. During times of great despair or great thanksgiving, he would often use poetry in his written prayers. Overall, his poetry included general themes such as Christ's redeeming power and unending love, God's great kindness and sustaining grace, the desperate plight of the perishing and the urgent need for gospel proclamation, and the pain of death and the happy hope of eternal bliss in Christ's presence. Often he penned his prayerful poems for his family to meditate on and even to use for their own prayer times. Judson believed that prayer was essential for enjoying communion with Christ, and he saw poetry as subservient to that great end.

Conclusion

All of his Christian life, Adoniram Judson eagerly sought to know Christ and love him more. This was his controlling ambition. He desired to imitate and please his Master through benevolent self-denial in submission to the will of God. Judson aimed to obey Christ's final command through gospel

---

94. Edward Judson, *The Life of Adoniram Judson*, 427. See also Wayland, *Memoir*, 2:137; for more short poems of prayers that he composed for his children to use, see Edward Judson, *The Life of Adoniram Judson*, 427; and Wayland, *Memoir*, 2:136–37. He even found the prayerful poetry of others to be helpful in his meditation and praying. For instance, see his journal entry on March 20, 1839 in Wayland, *Memoir*, 2:141. For a number of poems that Judson wrote for his stepson, George Dana, see Edward Judson, *The Life of Adoniram Judson*, 419–20; and see Wayland, *Memoir*, 2:111.

95. Adoniram Brown Judson, *How Judson Became a Baptist Missionary*, 3.

proclamation and persevering prayer. His evangelical assurance grounded itself in the reality of his obedience to Christ's command. The great judgment, and the prospects of eternal misery and eternal happiness, compelled him to keep onward, no matter the cost, to please Christ.

Though evangelical activism permeated his Christocentric spirituality, Judson also treasured the joy of drawing near to Christ through meditation and prayer. Practicing true religion was not supplemental to his missionary spirituality; it was essential. Because he valued the enjoyment of true religion so much, he prayed for and called others to seek the pleasure of religion as well. His children's piety was of special concern for him. Judson prayed daily for their salvation and that they would heed Christ's command. He sometimes found release in moments of strong emotion through poetry, whether that emotion be joy or despondency. Because of the glory of Christ's indescribable love, Judson longed for that day when Christ's glory would fill the earth and usher in perfect peace and love. To that end, he prayed perseveringly. Thus, Judson followed his Savior to Burma, the love of Christ satisfying him, with a supreme desire to please him. Awaiting his happy reward, on his death bed, he declared, "O, the love of Christ! the love of Christ! . . . We cannot understand it now—but what a beautiful study for eternity!"[96]

---

96. Emily Chubbuck Judson, "Closing Scenes in Dr. Judson's Life," 36.

7

Conclusion

THIS BOOK BEGAN BY asking, "in what ways and to what extent did Adoniram Judson's spirituality affect the endurance and effect of his missionary labor?" In order to answer this inquiry, additional questions sought answers to (1) how the Scriptures influenced Judson's missionary spirituality, (2) how his self-denying submission to the will of God reinforced his spiritual life, (3) the extent to which the promises of eternity focused Judson's vision of reality, (4) and how Judson's affectionate desire to know Christ and his consecration to Christ's final command in order to please him controlled Judson's missionary spirituality.

This book has demonstrated that Adoniram Judson was not only an historic figurehead in the first wave of foreign missionaries from the United States, a "Christian Hero of the Nineteenth Century"[1] whose name became a "household word throughout the length and breadth of Christendom,"[2] but furthermore, Judson's renowned fortitude emerged out of a peculiar missionary spirituality, which was bibliocentric, ascetic, heavenly-minded, and Christocentric. The center of Adoniram Judson's spirituality was a heavenly-minded, self-denying submission to the sovereign will of God, motivated by an affectionate desire to please Christ through obedience to his final command revealed in the Scriptures.[3] Moreover, Judson's ascetic

1. Gray, *The Christian Hero of the Nineteenth Century*, 2.
2. Richards, *The Apostle of Burma*, vi.
3. For some prominent examples of Judson's own words that capture the essence of his missionary spirituality, see his address to the Foreign Mission Board of the Southern Baptist Convention in Richmond on February 8, 1846, in Middleditch, *Burmah's Great Missionary*, 384–85. See also his sermon before the Boardman Missionary Society at Waterville College, in 1846, in Edward Judson, *The Life of Adoniram Judson*, 473–74;

spirituality went beyond the traditional expressions of classic evangelical piety. Unveiling the heart of his missionary spirituality, Judson himself asked, "What, then, is the prominent, all-constraining impulse that should urge us to make sacrifices in this cause?" And he answered thus: "A supreme desire to please him is the grand motive that should animate Christians in their missionary efforts."[4]

The introductory chapter grounded the significance of this study. It established the research question, thesis, methodology of research, and it outlined the significance of studying Judson's spirituality for contemporary theology and ministry.

The second chapter explored Judson's historical context of the eighteenth century, especially in relation to the modern missionary movement, New Divinity theology, and the religious zeal of Andover Seminary. These all stamped their religious impress on his spirituality, theology, and missionary activism. This chapter also surveyed his life and ministry.

The third chapter demonstrated that the foundation for Judson's missionary activism was the supreme and sufficient Scripture. He earnestly sought to obey, translate, preach, and build up the church of Burma with the Bible. He bound together his activistic piety and bibliocentrism.

The fourth chapter revealed that Judson submitted himself to God's divine authority. Judson undoubtedly employed asceticism as a dominant feature of his God-centered piety. Judson's spirituality drew chiefly from his admiration for the devotion of Roman Catholic asceticism and his formational training in New Divinity theology. His spirituality was one of quiet submission to the infinitely wise and loving will of God. Judson's consecrated self-denial sought the good of God's glory and the salvation of sinners above his own pleasure.

The fifth chapter illustrated how Judson's heavenly-mindedness saturated his spirituality. His fixation on heaven was useful for his hopeful endurance through tremendous adversity. Judson's optimism in the coming millennial reign of Christ proved indomitable in the face of much

---

and Wayland, *Memoir*, 2:234–35. Consider also his address to the American and Foreign Bible Society on May 15, 1846 about preaching and translating; see Adoniram Judson to the American and Foreign Bible Society, address, May 15, 1846, Papers, 1811–1888, Trask Library Special Collections, Newton Centre, Massachusetts. See also Wayland, *Memoir*, 2:235–38, and Middleditch, *Burmah's Great Missionary*, 388–91. And see his only English sermon in Burma, on May 10, 1836, for the ordination of S. M. Osgood in Wayland, *Memoir*, 2:490–93.

4. This was from an address to the Foreign Mission Board of the Southern Baptist Convention in Richmond on February 8, 1846. See Middleditch, *Burmah's Great Missionary*, 384–85.

discouragement. Because of his heavenly preoccupation and postmillennial confidence, he could persevere through the most arduous labor and sorrow.

The sixth chapter established the unifying feature of Judson's piety as an affectionate desire to please his Savior and Lord. Christ's Great Commission held supreme import in Judson's missionary spirituality. Because of Christ's self-denying love on the cross, Judson sought to please him by imitating him through doing good and obeying Christ's final command. His love for Christ was evident in his desire to commune with Christ and pray fervently for the salvation of sinners and for the triumph of Christ's glorious gospel throughout the earth. Themes from the previous chapters coalesce in this unifying theme of Judson's affection for Christ. This chapter makes sense of all the unique strands of Judson's piety.

Analysis

Having considered Judson's life and thought, and his ministry and inspiration, this study underscores several factors. David W. Bebbington's authoritative description of evangelicalism in Britain included four features: biblicism, crucicentrism, conversionism, and activism.[5] The spirituality of Adoniram Judson definitely included this fourfold synthesis of evangelicalism. Judson's Baptistic theology affected his conversion-oriented evangelism and discipleship. His confidence in the supremacy and sufficiency of the proclaimed Scripture incited his indefatigable preaching and translation activism. Affectionately responding to Christ's dying love for sinners, Judson sought to imitate Christ's example through self-denial and to proclaim the gospel of Christ for the conversion of the heathen. Nevertheless, acknowledging that the Bebbington quadrilateral is not an exhaustive description of evangelical spirituality,[6] Judson's spirituality contained its own distinctions. Judson's piety must speak for itself in its own terms, in its own way. Considering the whole Judson corpus, his vision of spirituality and religion certainly included degrees of the quadrilateral of evangelical piety, but his spirituality was fundamentally rooted in and ruled by a mixture of New Divinity theology and Roman Catholic asceticism. Some unique features of New Divinity theology that directed Judson's spiritual life and missionary piety were: disinterested benevolence, postmillennial optimism, true religion, and the infinitely wise and loving sovereignty of God. The combination of Roman Catholic asceticism, rule-keeping, disinterested benevolence,

---

5. Bebbington, *Evangelicalism in Modern Britain*, 20.

6. For example, see Gillett, *Trust and Obey*, 34–39; Sheldrake, *Spirituality and History*, 52; Randall, *What a Friend*, 20; and McGrath, *Christian Spirituality*, 4.

and Judson's own eccentric personality demonstrated a unique expression of spirituality that only he could withstand. Indeed, his contemporaries and fellow missionaries even acknowledged that his piety was exclusively his own, which was over and above typical evangelical piety. Few evangelicals today would likely find all the expressions of his spirituality to be instructive and imitable, yet for those missionaries who have chosen fields that require incredible degrees of self-denial and sacrifice, Judson's own example might prove helpful. Judson's ascetic spirituality may have proven useful for his context where the uncertainty of life and the nearness of death were cause of great concern; if he had to take a ship back to America to get well or if he died of sickness, the whole translation project would have likely faded with him. But for those contemporary Christians who do not labor in an isolated pre-modern Asian context, who have families, who did not train in a staunch Hopkinsian school, and who are beneficiaries of modern medicine, vaccinations, jet-travel, and instant communication, Judson's ascetic missionary spirituality might seem as foreign as nineteenth-century Burma.

Judson was a Great-Commission activist, a devout man of prayer, a Christ-loving laborer, a self-sacrificing family man and friend, and a self-denying servant submitted to the sovereign rule of God. That very little remains of his sermons can be credited to the fact that he predominantly preached extemporaneously in Burmese, which limits access to the content of his regular preaching ministry. The fact that he never wrote a massive systematic theology or any volumes of doctrine restricts the study of his theological developments. However, he committed himself to mastering a very difficult language[7] and to producing a Bible translation still used and admired today, which demonstrates that his knowledge of the Bible was robust.[8] Though unable to research formal volumes of Judson's unique theological formulations, his uncommon spirituality scattered throughout his letters, journals, tracts, and sermons warrants exploration. Because the synthesis of his spirituality is limited predominantly to his letters and journals that survived multiple occasions of loss and destruction, it is necessary to note the frequency of his dominant spiritual themes throughout his life. Due to the insufficiency of highlighting an occasional theme that occurred once in a single letter or journal, this book has synthesized and analyzed those themes that were pervasive in his letters, journals, tracts, and sermons throughout his whole Christian life.

7. See Adoniram Judson to Rev Lucius Bolles, letter, January 16, 1816, Box No. AJ 1, Folder 2 and Microfilm Roll 1, Judson Letters, ABHS. See also Wayland, *Memoir*, 1:176–78.

8. See Brown, "The Life and Work of Adoniram Judson," 24. See also Hunt, *Bless God and Take Courage*, 254–55.

The numerous references he made to Mark 16:15[9] from the beginning of his missionary venture to the end of his life demonstrate that Christ's commission to preach the gospel to the whole world dominated his missionary religion. What is more, his prayerful meditation on and frequent use of ideas from Bible verses such as Acts 10:38,[10] Romans 12:10,[11] 1 Corinthians 11:1,[12] Revelation 14:13,[13] John 13:34 and 15:12,[14] and John 14:15 and 15:14[15] reveal those biblical passages that deeply affected him.[16] And as F. W. Boreham well observed, the language Judson used throughout his corpus illustrated his devotion to the theme of the Christ-enamored prayer of Ephesians 3:18–19.[17]

No single volume can exhaust its object of study. While the scope of this book is limited primarily to an overall synthesis of Judson's spirituality, many aspects of Judson's life, thought, and influence remain unexamined. For instance, much more work needs to be done in tracing the dominant themes and influences of Hopkinsianism and Roman Catholic mysticism. There needs to be much more research to identify Judson's expressions of theology and spirituality that he borrowed from his New Divinity training, especially from the writings of Samuel Hopkins. Judson's early training in ascetic spiritual formation practices at Andover needs much more analysis. Moreover, his collegiate bonds and the theological and spiritual influences of professors, Moses Stuart, Leonard Woods, and Edward Dorr Griffin need greater study. Throughout his letters and journals, there is no indication as to why and when exactly he first started reading the mystics. Among all

---

9. For examples, see Wayland, *Memoir*, 1:51–52; ibid., 2:234–35, 519–21; Middleditch, *Burmah's Great Missionary*, 22, 398–400; Edward Judson, *The Life of Adoniram Judson*, 473–74; and Conant, *The Earnest Man*, 42–44.

10. For examples, see Middleditch, *Burmah's Great Missionary*, 374–76; Edward Judson, *The Life of Adoniram Judson*, 469–70, 475; and Wayland, *Memoir*, 2:486–94.

11. For example, see Emily Chubbuck Judson, "Closing Scenes in Dr. Judson's Life," 36.

12. For examples, see Edward Judson, *The Life of Adoniram Judson*, 469–70; and Middleditch, *Burmah's Great Missionary*, 374–76.

13. For examples, see Adoniram Judson, "Parting Address of Mr. Judson," 31–33; Adoniram Judson, "Address of Dr. Judson," 267–68; Dowling, *The Judson Offering*, 279–83; Wayland, *Memoir*, 2:254–58; and Middleditch, *Burmah's Great Missionary*, 396–98.

14. For examples, see Wayland, *Memoir*, 2:338; and Emily Chubbuck Judson, "Closing Scenes in Dr. Judson's Life," 36.

15. For example, see Adoniram Judson, *Christian Baptism*, 93.

16. Judson also preached from the proceeding passages, but their themes and references do not appear as often as the aforementioned verses: Colossians 1:27; Hebrews 12:14; and John 10:1–18. For examples, see Wayland, *Memoir*, 2:486–94, 98–99.

17. Boreham, *A Temple of Topaz*, 134.

CONCLUSION

his letters in which he requested books, he always asked for critical commentaries and other theological works to assist him in his translation.[18] Whether he first began reading the writings of Roman Catholic mystics at Andover or later in Burma is open for speculation; but it is clear that once he finished formal language study in 1819, he first started writing his ascetic rules of life as he commenced his preaching ministry. Much more study needs to be given to the historical events, influences, and persons that might correspond to when he started applying more ascetic practices. Also, the legacy of Judson's spiritual influence, both positively and negatively, on his children deserves more attention.[19] The widespread and profound religious influence of the Judson drama for young Christians deserves significant treatment.[20] Moreover, the impact of Judson's legendary piety propounded by his sons, Edward and George Dana, needs further consideration, and the life and thought of Judson's Congregationalist father needs thorough analysis.[21] Because Judson was not alone and had religious colleagues, the likeminded spirituality expressed by his fellow missionaries in records such as *The Baptist Missionary Magazine*[22] is worthy of greater analysis.

The life and labor of Adoniram Judson has been eminently influential from his own era to the present. His spirituality was peculiar because of his historical, educational, familial, and theological contexts. Furthermore, his own personality and God-given abilities predisposed his spiritual formation. It is unnecessary to try retrofitting his spirituality into contemporary evangelicalism; he was remarkable even in his own day and context. Nevertheless, Judson served the God of the Bible, and his self-denying passion of knowing and pleasing Christ as a missionary can serve as an excellent

18. For examples, see Adoniram Judson to Lucius Bolles, letter, December 20, 1830, Box No. AJ 2, Folder 2 and Microfilm Roll 1, ABHS; Adoniram Judson to Lucius Bolles, correspondence, February 5, 1831, Box No. AJ 2, Folder 2 and Microfilm Roll 1, ABHS; Adoniram Judson, "Mission Books," correspondence, January 31, 1835, Box No. AJ 2, Folder 1 and Microfilm Roll 1, ABHS; Adoniram Judson to Lucius Bolles, letter, August 29, 1836, Box No. AJ 2, Folder 1 and Microfilm Roll 1, ABHS; Adoniram Judson to Solomon Peck, letter, January 21, 1839, Box No. AJ 3, Folder 1 and Microfilm Roll 1, ABHS; and Adoniram Judson to Solomon Peck, correspondence, December 22, 1839, Box No. AJ 3, Folder 2 and Microfilm Roll 1, ABHS.

19. Rosalie Hall Hunt has masterfully chronicled Judson's familial lineage, but the connection between the life, thought, and ministry of each of Judson's adult children remains unexplored in depth. See Hunt, *Bless God and Take Courage*, 241–348.

20. For a scholarly resource to begin understanding Judson's broad impact on youth voluntarism in the nineteenth century, see Brumberg, *Mission for Life*.

21. The Director of Acadia Centre for Baptist and Anabaptist Studies, William H. Brackney, suggested this in an email to the author; see Brackney, "Re: Questions about Archives and Adoniram Judson Research," October 16, 2013.

22. *The Baptist Missionary Magazine* 1–89 (1817–1909).

example to which contemporary evangelicals, especially missionaries and ministers, should aspire. His Bible-saturated, God-honoring, self-denying, heavenly-minded, Christ-enamored piety, expressed in his fervent-praying, Bible-translating, and gospel-proclaiming missionary activity, remain distinct still today. Yet, Judson would not wish to distract his admirers from the glory of his great God and Savior. He insisted that his name should "live in oblivion or disgrace till the great day."[23] Hence, Judson would assert that all study and admiration of his missionary spirituality should look finally to the glory of Christ himself, whose redeeming love is "a beautiful study for eternity!"[24] Though dead, the missionary still speaks, making his appeal:

> Brethren, look to Jesus. This sight will fill you with the greatest consolation and delight. Look to Him on the cross; so great is His love that, if He had a thousand lives, He would lay them all down for your redemption. Look to Him on the throne; His blessed countenance fills all heaven with delight and felicity. Look to Him in affliction; He will succor you. Look to Him in death; He will sustain you. Look to Him in the judgment; He will save you.[25]

---

23. Adoniram Judson, "Letter from the Rev. Adoniram Judson, Jun. to Dr. Baldwin, Dated Rangoon, December 9, 1819," 380. See also Middleditch, *Burmah's Great Missionary*, 97–98.

24. Emily Chubbuck Judson, "Closing Scenes in Dr. Judson's Life," 36.

25. Judson was speaking to students at Madison University in Hamilton, New York, in 1846. Edward Judson, *The Life of Adoniram Judson*, 474. See also Middleditch, *Burmah's Great Missionary*, 373.

Bibliography

à Kempis, Thomas. *Imitation of Christ*. Translated by Robert Jeffrey. London: Penguin, 2013.
Aberly, John. "Bartholomew Ziegenbalg: The First Protestant Missionary to the Gentiles." In *Missionary Heroes of the Lutheran Church*, edited by L. B. Wolf, 39–65. Columbia, SC: Lutheran Board, 1911.
Adam, Peter. *Hearing God's Words*. Edited by D. A. Carson. New Studies in Biblical Theology. Downers Grove, IL: InterVarsity, 2004.
Adams, Hannah. "The View of Religions." In *History of the Andover Theological Seminary*, by Leonard Woods, 32–34. Boston: Osgood, 1885.
Adamson, H. Sir. "Address." In *The Judson Centennial Celebrations in Burma: 1813–1913*, edited by F. D. Phinney, 71–73. Rangoon: American Baptist Mission, 1914.
———. "The Baptist Mission and Burma." In *The Judson Centennial, 1813–1913: Scrapbook*, edited by Melvin Jameson, n.p., n.p., n.d.
"Adoniram Judson." *Christian Watchman and Reflector* 34, no. 40 (1853) 158.
"Adoniram Judson." *The Friend: A Religious and Literary Journal* 64 (1891) 69–70.
American Baptist Foreign Mission Society records, #4424. Division of Rare and Manuscript Collections. Cornell University Library, Ithaca, NY.
American Baptist Missionary Union. *Seventy-Seventh Annual Report with the Proceedings of the Annual Meeting, Held in Cincinnati, Ohio, May 25 and 26, 1891*. Boston: Missionary Rooms, Tremont Temple, 1891.
American Board of Commissioners for Foreign Missions. *First Ten Annual Reports of the American Board of Commissioners for Foreign Missions*. Boston: Crocker and Brewster, 1834.
American Board of Commissioners for Foreign Missions Archives, 1810–1961 (ABC 1–91). Houghton Library, Harvard University, Cambridge, MA.
Anderson, Courtney. *To the Golden Shore: The Life of Adoniram Judson*. 2nd ed. Valley Forge, PA: Judson, 1987.
Anderson, Gerald H. "Amos Sutton." In *Biographical Dictionary of Christian Missions*, 652. Grand Rapids: Eerdmans, 1999.
Augustine. *Confessions*. Translated by R. S. Pine-Coffin. London: Penguin, 1961.
Austin, Samuel. *A View of the Economy of the Church of God, as It Existed Primitively, under the Abrahamic Dispensation and the Sinai Law : And as It Is Perpetuated under the More Luminous Dispensation of the Gospel : Particularly in Regard to the Covenants*. Worcester, MA: Thomas & Sturtevant, 1807.

Babcock, Rufus. *God Glorified in His Servants, A Discourse Commemorative of the Life and Labors of the Rev. Adoniram Judson, D. D.: Specially as a Translator of the Holy Scriptures: Delivered at the Request of the Board of Managers of the American and Foreign Bible Society, in the Tabernacle Baptist Church, Second Avenue, New York, on Sunday Evening, May 11, 1851.* New York: Fletcher, 1851.

———. *Manual for Christian Psalmody: A Collection of Psalms and Hymns for Public Worship.* Boston: Perkins and Marvin, 1832.

Balderston, Lloyd. "Adoniram Judson." *The Friend: A Religious and Literary Journal* 72 (1899) 180, 189–90, 94–95.

Baptist Collection. University Archives, John Hay Library, Brown University, Providence, RI.

The Baptist Missionary Magazine. 89 vols. Boston: American Baptist Missionary Union, 1817–1909.

Barnes, Lemuel Hall. *Pioneers of Light: The First Century of the American Baptist Publication Society, 1824–1924.* Philadelphia: American Baptist, 1924.

Bayles, Richard M. *History of Windham County, Connecticut.* New York: Preston, 1889.

Bebbington, David W. *Evangelicalism in Modern Britain: A History from the 1730s to the 1980s.* London: Routledge, 1995.

Beeke, Joel. "Puritan Meditation." In *Reformed Spirituality,* edited by Joseph A Pipa Jr. and J. Andrew Wortman, 73–100. Taylors, SC: Southern Presbyterian, 2003.

Bellamy, Joseph. "True Religion Delineated, in Two Discourses." In *The Works of Joseph Bellamy, D. D., First Pastor of the Church in Bethlehem, Conn., with a Memoir of His Life and Character,* 1:3–363. Boston: Doctrinal Tract and Book Society, 1853.

———. "The Wisdom of God in the Permission of Sin." In *The Works of Joseph Bellamy, D. D., First Pastor of the Church in Bethlehem, Conn., with a Memoir of His Life and Character,* 2:3–270. Boston: Doctrinal Tract and Book Society, 1853.

———. *The Works of Joseph Bellamy, D. D., First Pastor of the Church in Bethlehem, Conn., with a Memoir of His Life and Character.* 2 vols. Boston: Doctrinal Tract and Book Society, 1853.

Bendroth, Margaret L. *A School of the Church: Andover Newton Across Two Centuries.* Grand Rapids: Eerdmans, 2008.

Benedict, Abbot of Monte Cassino. *RB 1980: The Rule of St. Benedict in Latin and English with Notes.* Translated by Timothy Fry. Collegeville, MN: Liturgical, 1981.

Bennett, Cephas, ed. *Tracts, In Burmese: Containing, The Creation, the Catechism, View of the Christian Religion, Way of Heaven, How Do We Know There Is a God?, The Atonement, Tree of Life, Glad Tidings, Golden Balance, The Awakener, The Investigator, Heaven and Hell, The Ship of Grace, Father's Advice, The Examiner, The Ten Commandments, On Idolatry.* Vol. 1. Maulmain, Burma: American Mission, 1860.

———. *Vocabulary and Phrase Book in English and Burmese.* Rangoon: American Baptist Mission, 1886.

Blaikie, W. G. *Preachers of Scotland.* Edinburgh: T. & T. Clark, 1888.

Boardman, George Dana. "Extracts from Mr. Boardman's Journal, Kept at Calcutta from May 18, to July 30, 1826." *The Baptist Missionary Magazine* 7 (1827) 44.

Booth, Abraham. *Paedobaptism Examined, on the Principles, Concessions, and Reasonings of the Most Learned Paedobaptists.* Newark, NJ: Tuttle, 1805.

Boreham, F. W. *A Temple of Topaz.* New York: Abingdon, 1928.

Boston, Thomas. *Human Nature in Its Fourfold State: Of Primitive Integrity, Entire Depravity, Begun Recovery, and Consummate Happiness or Misery*. London: Banner of Truth Trust, 1964.

Bowden, Henry Warner. "Worcester, Samuel Austin." In *Biographical Dictionary of Christian Missions*, edited by Gerald H. Anderson, 748. New York: Macmillan, 1998.

Brackney, William H. *A Genetic History of Baptist Thought: With Special Reference to Baptists in Britain and North America*. Macon, GA: Mercer University Press, 2004.

———. "Judson, Adoniram." In *Biographical Dictionary of Christian Missions*, edited by Gerald H. Anderson, 345–46. New York: Simon & Schuster, 1998.

———. "The Legacy of Adoniram Judson." *International Bulletin of Missionary Research* 22, no. 3 (1998) 122–27.

Brewster, Paul. *Andrew Fuller: Model Pastor and Theologian*. Nashville: B. & H. Academic, 2010.

Brown, Max H. "The New Divinity: The Theological Context for Adoniram Judson, Jr." MTS thesis, Emory University, 1993.

Brown, Russell E. "The Life and Work of Adoniram Judson." *Andover Newton Quarterly* 2, no. 3 (1962) 9–33.

Brumberg, Joan Jacobs. *Mission for Life: The Judson Family and American Evangelical Culture*. New York: New York University Press, 1984.

Brush, John W. "The Magnetism of Adoniram Judson." *Andover Newton Quarterly* 2, no. 3 (1962) 3–4.

Buchanan, Claudius. *The Star in the East: A Sermon Preached in the Parish Church of St. James, Bristol, on Sunday February 26, 1809, for the Benefit of the Society for Missions to Africa and the East*. Philadelphia: Bradford and Inskeep, 1809.

Burns, E. D. "Moravian Missionary Piety and the Influence of Count Zinzendorf." *Journal of Global Christianity* 1, no. 2 (2015) 19–34.

Butler, Jon, et al. *Religion in American Life: A Short History*. 2nd ed. New York: Oxford University Press, 2011.

Calamy, Edmund. *The Art of Divine Meditation*. London: printed for Tho. Parkhurst, 1634.

Caldwell, Robert. "New England's New Divinity and the Age of Judson's Preparation." In *Adoniram Judson: A Bicentennial Appreciation of the Pioneer American Missionary*, edited by Jason G. Duesing, 31–54. Studies in Baptist Life and Thought. Nashville: B. & H. Academic, 2012.

Carey, William. *An Enquiry into the Obligations of Christians to Use Means for the Conversion of the Heathens*. Leicester, UK: Ireland, 1791.

———. "Letter of Dr. Carey." *The Baptist Missionary Magazine* 26 (1846) 149–50.

———. "Miscellany:—Messrs. Judson and Rice." *The Baptist Missionary Magazine* 26 (1846) 149.

Carpenter, John. "New England Puritans: The Grandparents of Modern Protestant Missions." *Missiology: An International Review* 30, no. 4 (2002) 519–32.

Carver, W. O. "The Significance of Adoniram Judson." *Baptist Review and Expositor* 10, no. 4 (1913) 475–84.

Case, Jay Riley. *An Unpredictable Gospel: American Evangelicals and World Christianity, 1812–1920*. New York: Oxford University Press, 2012.

Cheever, George Barrell. *The Select Works of Archbishop Leighton, Prepared for the Practical Use of Private Christians, with an Introductory View of the Life, Character, and Writings of the Author*. Boston: Peirce and Parker, 1832.

Chessman, Daniel. *Memoir of Rev. Thomas Baldwin, D. D., Late Pastor of the Second Baptist Church in Boston, Who Died at Waterville, ME, August 20, 1825*. Boston: True & Greene, 1826.

Chun, Chris. "Sense of the Heart: Jonathan Edwards' Legacy in the Writings of Andrew Fuller." *Eusebia: The Bulletin of The Andrew Fuller Center for Baptist Studies* 9 (2008) 127.

Chun, Chris, and Allen Yeh, eds. *Expect Great Things, Attempt Great Things: William Carey and Adoniram Judson, Missionary Pioneers*. Studies in World Christianity. Eugene, OR: Wipf and Stock, 2013.

Clemént, Jesse. *Memoir of Adoniram Judson, Being a Sketch of His Life and Missionary Labors*. Auburn, NY: Derby and Miller, 1851.

Clipsham, E. F. "Andrew Fuller and Fullerism: A Study in Evangelical Calvinism." *Baptist Quarterly* 20, no. 3 (1963) 269.

Colley, Linda. *Britons: Forging the Nation 1707–1837*. London: Vintage, 1996.

Collier, Mary Ann. *Colman and Wheelock, Or, The Early Called of the Burman Mission*. Philadelphia: American Baptist, 1853.

Comstock, Grover S. "Journal of Mr. Comstock, Dated Kyouk Phyoo, 1835." *The Baptist Missionary Magazine* 16 (1836) 42–70.

———. "The Way to Heaven." In *Tracts, In Burmese: Containing, The Creation, the Catechism, View of the Christian Religion, Way of Heaven, How Do We Know There Is a God?, The Atonement, Tree of Life, Glad Tidings, Golden Balance, The Awakener, The Investigator, Heaven and Hell, The Ship of Grace, Father's Advice, The Examiner, The Ten Commandments, On Idolatry*, edited by Cephas Bennett, 1:55–77. Maulmain, Burma: American Mission, 1860.

Conant, Hannah Chaplin. *The Earnest Man, A Sketch of the Character and Labors of Adoniram Judson, First Missionary to Burmah*. Boston: Phillips, Samson, 1856.

Conforti, Joseph A. *Jonathan Edwards, Religious Tradition and American Culture*. Chapel Hill: University of North Carolina Press, 1995.

———. *Samuel Hopkins and the New Divinity Movement: Calvinism and Reform in New England Between the Great Awakenings*. Jonathan Edwards Classic Studies. Eugene, OR: Wipf and Stock, 2008.

Cragg, Gerald R. *The Church and the Age of Reason, 1648–1789*. Penguin History of the Church 4. Harmondsworth, UK: Penguin, 1990.

Crisp, Oliver D., and Douglas A. Sweeney, eds. *After Jonathan Edwards: The Courses of the New England Theology*. New York: Oxford University Press, 2012.

Crowell, W. M. "Reception in Boston." In *The Judson Offering, Intended as a Token of Christian Sympathy with the Living, and a Memento of Christian Affection for the Dead*, 236–37. New York: Colby, 1847.

Danvers, Henry. *A Treatise of Baptism*. 2nd ed. London: Francis Smith, 1675.

De Jong, James A. *As the Waters Cover the Sea: Millennial Expectations in the Rise of Anglo-American Missions, 1640–1810*. Laurel, MS: Audubon, 2006.

Dingrin, La Seng. "A Missiological and Theological Critique of Lamin Sanneh's 'Destigmatization' Thesis in the Context of Burma at the Time of Adoniram Judson with Special Reference to Judson's Tracts in Burmese." PhD diss., Princeton Theological Seminary, 2006.

Dowling, John, ed. *The Judson Offering, Intended as a Token of Christian Sympathy with the Living, and a Memento of Christian Affection for the Dead.* New York: Colby, 1847.

Duesing, Jason G., ed. *Adoniram Judson: A Bicentennial Appreciation of the Pioneer American Missionary.* Studies in Baptist Life and Thought. Nashville: B. & H. Academic, 2012.

———. "Breaking the Strong Attachment to Home and Country: The Influence of a Friend of Fuller's Friends on Adoniram Judson." *The Southern Baptist Journal of Missions and Evangelism* 1, no. 2 (2012) 6–13.

Duncan, R. S. *A History of Baptists in Missouri.* Kansas City: Western Baptist, 1934.

Eddy, Daniel Clarke. *A Sketch of Adoniram Judson, D. D., the Burman Apostle.* Lowell, MA: Dayton, 1850.

Edwards, Jonathan. "A Dissertation on the Nature of True Virtue." In *The Works of Jonathan Edwards*, 1:122–42. Peabody, MA: Hendrickson, 2004.

———. "Distinguishing Marks of a Work of the Spirit of God." In *The Works of Jonathan Edwards*, 2:257–77. Peabody, MA: Hendrickson, 2004.

———. "Freedom of the Will." In *The Works of Jonathan Edwards*, 1:3–89. Peabody, MA: Hendrickson, 2004.

———. "God Glorified in Man's Dependence." In *The Works of Jonathan Edwards*, 2:3–6. Peabody, MA: Hendrickson, 2004.

———. "A History of the Work of Redemption." In *The Works of Jonathan Edwards*, 1:532–619. Peabody, MA: Hendrickson, 2004.

———. *An Humble Attempt to Promote Explicit Agreement and Visible Union of God's People in Extraordinary Prayer.* Northampton, England: T. Dicey and Co., 1789.

———. "An Humble Attempt to Promote Explicit Agreement, &c." In *The Works of Jonathan Edwards*, 2:280–312. Peabody, MA: Hendrickson, 2004.

———. "Life and Diary of the Rev. David Brainerd." In *The Works of Jonathan Edwards*, 2:313–458. Peabody, MA: Hendrickson, 2004.

———. "A Treatise Concerning Religious Affections, in Three Parts." In *The Works of Jonathan Edwards*, 1:234–434. Peabody, MA: Hendrickson, 2004.

———. "The True Excellency of a Gospel Minister." In *The Works of Jonathan Edwards*, 2:955–60. Peabody, MA: Hendrickson, 2004.

———. *The Works of Jonathan Edwards.* 2 vols. Peabody, MA: Hendrickson, 2004.

———. *Works of Jonathan Edwards (with a Memoir by Sereno E. Dwight).* Edited by Edward Hickman. 2 vols. Edinburgh: Banner of Truth Trust, 1974.

Edwards, Peter. *Candid Reasons, for Renouncing the Principles of Antipaedobaptism.* London: Gillet, 1799.

Eitel, Keith E. "The Enduring Legacy of Adoniram Judson's Missiological Precepts and Practices." In *Adoniram Judson: A Bicentennial Appreciation of the Pioneer American Missionary*, edited by Jason G. Duesing, 129–48. Studies in Baptist Life and Thought. Nashville: B. & H. Academic, 2012.

Elsbree, Oliver Wendell. *The Rise of the Missionary Spirit in America, 1790–1815.* Eugene, OR: Wipf and Stock, 2013.

Faunce, D. W. *A Young Man's Difficulties with His Bible.* Philadelphia: American Baptist, 1898.

Fénelon, François de Salignac de La Mothe. *The Adventures of Telemachus, the Son of Ulysses in Five Parts.* London: A. and J. Churchil, 1703.

Fletcher, Edward H. *Records of the Life, Character, and Achievements of Adoniram Judson*. New York: Fletcher, 1854.
Forester, Fanny. *Memoir of Sarah B. Judson, of the American Mission to Burmah*. New York: Nelson and Sons, 1860.
Foster, Frank Hugh. *A Genetic History of the New England Theology*. Chicago: University of Chicago Press, 1907.
Froom, LeRoy E. *The Prophetic Faith of Our Fathers*. Vol. 3. Washington, DC: Review and Herald, 1946.
Fuller, Andrew. "An Apology for the Late Christian Missions to India." In *The Complete Works of the Rev. Andrew Fuller*, edited by Joseph Belcher, 2:769-96. London: Sprinkle, 1988.
———. *The Complete Works of the Rev. Andrew Fuller*. Edited by Joseph Belcher. 3 vols. London: Sprinkle, 1988.
———. "The Gospel Worthy of All Acceptation, or the Duty of Sinners to Believe in Jesus Christ, with Corrections and Additions; to which is Added an Appendix, on the Necessity of a Holy Disposition in Order to Believing in Christ." In *The Complete Works of the Rev. Andrew Fuller*, edited by Joseph Belcher, 2:328-416. London: Sprinkle, 1988.
———. "Strictures on Sandemanianism, in Twelve Letters to a Friend." In *The Complete Works of the Rev. Andrew Fuller*, edited by Joseph Belcher, 2:561-646. London: Sprinkle, 1988.
Gifford, O. P. *Adoniram Judson: An Address Delivered by Rev. O. P. Gifford, D. D. on the Occasion of the Judson Centennial Celebration in Tremont Temple, Boston, Mass., June 24, 1914*. Boston: American Baptist Foreign Missionary Society, 1914.
Gillett, David. *Trust and Obey: Explorations in Evangelical Spirituality*. London: DLT, 1993.
Gillette, A. D. *A Sketch of the Labors, Sufferings and Death of the Rev. Adoniram Judson, D.D.* Philadelphia: Daniels and Smith, 1851.
———. *God Seen above All National Calamities: A Sermon on the Death of President Lincoln, April 23, 1865*. Washington, DC: McGill & Witherow, 1865.
Gordon, James M. *Evangelical Spirituality*. Eugene, OR: Wipf and Stock, 1991.
Gouger, Henry. *A Personal Narrative of Two Years' Imprisonment in Burmah, 1824-26*. London: Murray, 1862.
Gray, E. H. *The Christian Hero of the Nineteenth Century*. 2nd ed. Cambridge: Robbins & Ford, 1852.
Grudem, Wayne. *Systematic Theology: An Introduction to Biblical Doctrine*. Grand Rapids: Zondervan, 2000.
Guyon, Jeanne Marie Bouvier de La Motte. *Poems, Translated from the French of Madame De La Mothe Guion by the Late William Cowper, to Which Are Added Some Original Poems of Mr. Cowper Not Inserted in His Works*. 4th ed. London: Johnson, 1811.
———. *A Short and Easy Method of Prayer: Translated from the French of Madam J. M. B. de La Mothe Guion, by Thomas Digby Brooke*. Translated by Thomas Digby Brooke. London: Carnegy, 1775.
Hague, William. *The Life and Character of Adoniram Judson, Late Missionary to Burmah: A Commemorative Discourse Delivered Before the American Baptist Missionary Union, in Boston, May 15, 1851*. Boston: Gould & Lincoln, 1851.

Hankins, Barry. *The Second Great Awakening and the Transcendentalists*. Westport, CT: Greenwood, 2004.

Hanna, T. Carson. "What Price Missions?" *Watchman-Examiner* (1930) 811–12.

Hatfield, Edwin F. *St. Helena and The Cape of Good Hope: Or, Incidents in the Missionary Life of the Rev. James M'Gregor Bertram, of St. Helena*. New York: Fletcher, 1852.

Haykin, Michael A. G. "Evangelicalism and the Enlightenment: A Reassessment." In *The Advent of Evangelicalism*, edited by Michael A. G. Haykin and Kenneth J. Stewart, 37–62. Nashville: B. & H. Academic, 2008.

———. "Just before Judson: The Significance of William Carey's Life, Thought, and Ministry." In *Adoniram Judson: A Bicentennial Appreciation of the Pioneer American Missionary*, edited by Jason G. Duesing, 9–30. Studies in Baptist Life and Thought, edited by Michael A. G. Haykin. Nashville: B. & H. Academic, 2012.

———. "'We Are Confirmed Baptists': The Judsons and Their Meeting with the Serampore Trio in 1812." *The Southern Baptist Journal of Missions and Evangelism* 1, no. 2 (2012) 14–21.

———. "'We Are Confirmed Baptists': The Judsons and Their Meeting with the Serampore Trio." In *Expect Great Things, Attempt Great Things: William Carey and Adoniram Judson, Missionary Pioneers*, edited by Allen Yeh and Chris Chun, 103–12. Eugene, OR: Wipf and Stock, 2013.

Haykin, Michael A. G., and Kenneth J. Stewart, eds. *The Advent of Evangelicalism*. Nashville: B. & H. Academic, 2008.

Hill, James L. *The Immortal Seven*. Philadelphia: American Baptist, 1913.

Hindmarsh, D. Bruce. *The Evangelical Conversion Narrative: Spiritual Autobiography in Early Modern England*. Oxford: Oxford University Press, 2005.

Hitchcock, Edward. *Reminiscences of Amherst College: Historical Scientific, Biographical and Autobiographical*. Applewood's Education Series. Carlisle, MA: Applewood, 1863.

Holifield, E. Brooks. *Theology in America: Christian Thought from the Age of the Puritans to the Civil War*. New Haven, CT: Yale University, 2003.

Hopkins, Samuel. "A Dialogue between a Calvinist and a Semi-Calvinist." In *Works of Samuel Hopkins, D. D., First Pastor of the Church in Great Barrington, Mass., Afterwards Pastor of the First Congregational Church in Newport, R. I., with a Memoir of His Life and Character*, 3:143–57. Boston: Doctrinal Tract and Book Society, 1854.

———. *The Life and Character of the Late Reverend, Learned, and Pious Mr. Jonathan Edwards*. Boston: Kneeland, 1765.

———. "Sin, through Divine Interposition, an Advantage to the Universe, and yet This No Excuse for Sin, or Encouragement to It, Illustrated and Proved; and God's Wisdom and Holiness in the Permission of Sin, and That His Will Herein Is the Same with His Revealed Will, Shown and Confirmed, in Three Sermons, from Romans Iii. 5–8." In *Works of Samuel Hopkins, D. D., First Pastor of the Church in Great Barrington, Mass., Afterwards Pastor of the First Congregational Church in Newport, R. I., with a Memoir of His Life and Character*, 2:493–528. Boston: Doctrinal Tract and Book Society, 1854.

———. *The System of Doctrines: Contained in Divine Revelation, Explained and Defended, Shewing Their Consistence and Connexion with Each Other, to Which Is Added a Treatise on the Millennium*. 2nd ed. 2 vols. Boston: Lincoln & Edmunds, 1811.

———. *Works of Samuel Hopkins, D. D., First Pastor of the Church in Great Barrington, Mass., Afterwards Pastor of the First Congregational Church in Newport, R. I. with a Memoir of His Life and Character*. 3 vols. Boston: Doctrinal Tract and Book Society, 1854.

Hull, J. Mervin. *Judson the Pioneer*. Philadelphia: American Baptist, 1913.

Hulse, Erroll. *Adoniram Judson and the Missionary Call*. Pensacola, FL: Chapel Library, 1996.

———. "Adoniram Judson: Devoted for Life." In *Building on a Sure Foundation: Papers Read at the 1994 Westminster Conference*, 123–56. Mirfield, West Yorkshire, UK: Westminster Conference, 1994.

Hunt, Rosalie Hall. *Bless God and Take Courage*. Valley Forge, PA: Judson, 2005.

———. "The Judson Family Tree." In *Bless God and Take Courage: The Judson History and Legacy*, 404. Valley Forge, PA: Judson, 2005.

Hutchison, William R. *Errand to the World: American Protestant Thought and Foreign Missions*. Chicago: University of Chicago Press, 1987.

"Intelligence from the Missions, Theological Training of Native Pastors." *The Baptist Missionary Magazine* 34 (1854) 6–15.

James, Sharon. *My Heart in His Hands: Ann Judson of Burma*. Grand Rapids: Evangelical, 1999.

Jameson, Melvin, ed. *The Judson Centennial, 1813–1913: Scrapbook*, n.p., n.p., n.d.

———. *Sketch of the Life of Dr. Judson*. 2nd ed. Rangoon: American Baptist Mission, 1907.

Jauhiainen, Peter. "Samuel Hopkins and Hopkinsianism." In *After Jonathan Edwards: The Courses of the New England Theology*, edited by Oliver D. Crisp and Douglas A. Sweeney, 107–17. New York: Oxford University Press, 2012.

Johnson, Maxwell E., ed. *Benedictine Daily Prayer: A Short Breviary*. Collegeville, MN: Liturgical, 2005.

Judson, Abby Ann. *The Bridge Between Two Worlds*. Minneapolis: Alfred Roper, 1894.

———. "Communication from My Father, Adoniram Judson." In *The Bridge between Two Worlds*, 206–10. Minneapolis: Roper, 1894.

———. "Personal Communications." In *Why She Became a Spiritualist: Twelve Lectures Delivered before the Minneapolis Association of Spiritualists*, 260–63. Minneapolis: Roper, 1891.

———. "To the First Baptist Church, Malden, Mass." In *Judson Centennial Services: A Compilation of the Addresses, Papers, and Remarks, Given at These Services, Together with Extracts from Letters Received by the Committee, Etc. (1888)*, edited by James Nelson Lewis, 50. Malden, MA: Mystic Side, 1888.

———. *Why She Became a Spiritualist: Twelve Lectures Delivered before the Minneapolis Association of Spiritualists*. Minneapolis: Roper, 1891.

Judson, Abigail. Judson Letters. American Baptist Historical Society, Atlanta.

Judson, Adoniram. *An Account of Meh Shway-Ee, a Burman Slave Girl*. Philadelphia: Baptist General Tract Society, 1829.

———. "Address of Dr. Judson." *The Baptist Missionary Magazine* 26 (1846) 267–68.

———. "Adoniram Judson's Letter to His Daughter Abby Ann." In *Judson Treasures of The First Baptist Church, Malden, with a Short Biography of the Life of Emily Chubbuck Judson*, edited by George H. Tooze, 14. Malden, MA: First Baptist Church, 1979.

BIBLIOGRAPHY

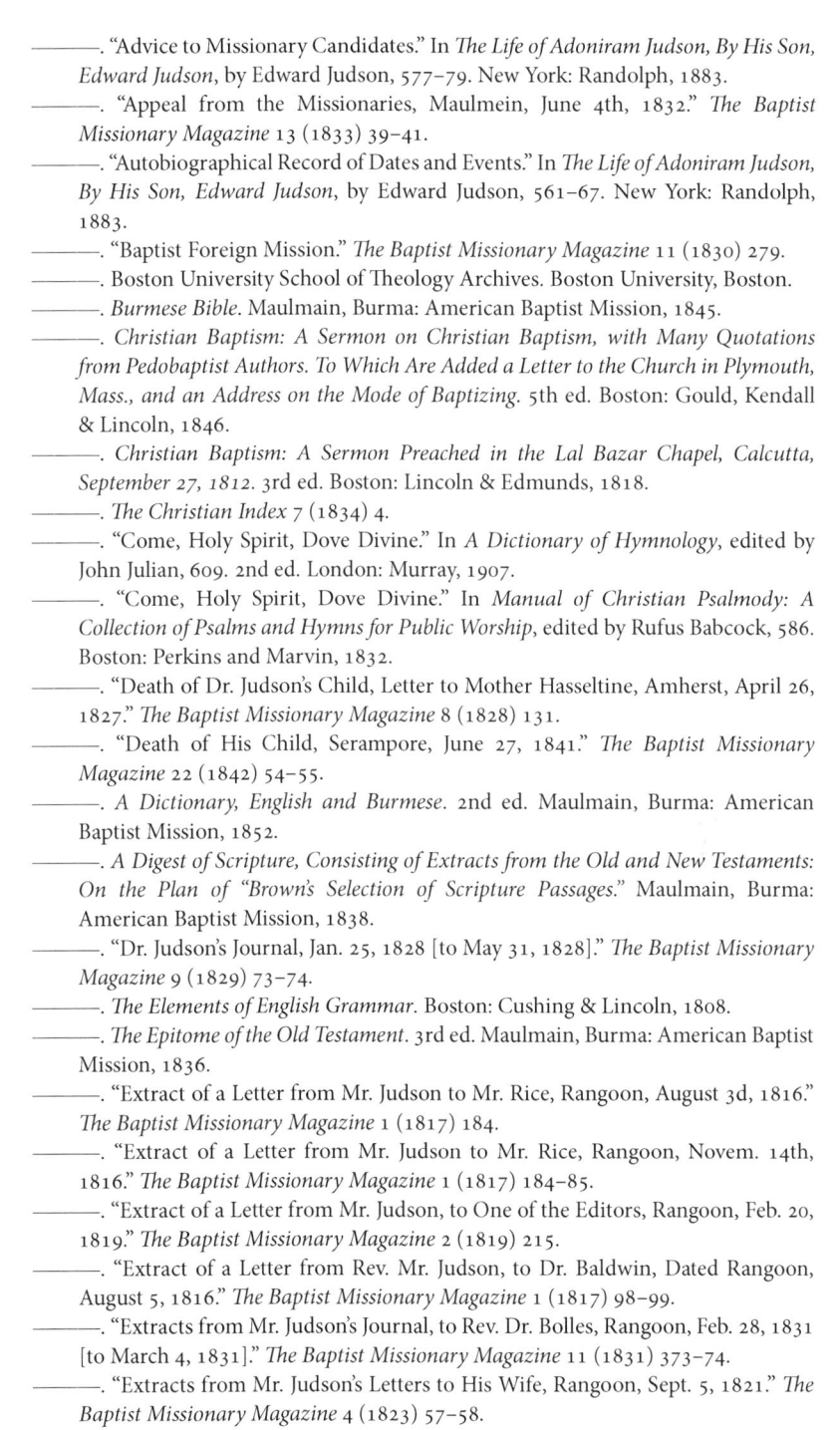

———. "Advice to Missionary Candidates." In *The Life of Adoniram Judson, By His Son, Edward Judson*, by Edward Judson, 577–79. New York: Randolph, 1883.

———. "Appeal from the Missionaries, Maulmein, June 4th, 1832." *The Baptist Missionary Magazine* 13 (1833) 39–41.

———. "Autobiographical Record of Dates and Events." In *The Life of Adoniram Judson, By His Son, Edward Judson*, by Edward Judson, 561–67. New York: Randolph, 1883.

———. "Baptist Foreign Mission." *The Baptist Missionary Magazine* 11 (1830) 279.

———. Boston University School of Theology Archives. Boston University, Boston.

———. *Burmese Bible*. Maulmain, Burma: American Baptist Mission, 1845.

———. *Christian Baptism: A Sermon on Christian Baptism, with Many Quotations from Pedobaptist Authors. To Which Are Added a Letter to the Church in Plymouth, Mass., and an Address on the Mode of Baptizing*. 5th ed. Boston: Gould, Kendall & Lincoln, 1846.

———. *Christian Baptism: A Sermon Preached in the Lal Bazar Chapel, Calcutta, September 27, 1812*. 3rd ed. Boston: Lincoln & Edmunds, 1818.

———. *The Christian Index* 7 (1834) 4.

———. "Come, Holy Spirit, Dove Divine." In *A Dictionary of Hymnology*, edited by John Julian, 609. 2nd ed. London: Murray, 1907.

———. "Come, Holy Spirit, Dove Divine." In *Manual of Christian Psalmody: A Collection of Psalms and Hymns for Public Worship*, edited by Rufus Babcock, 586. Boston: Perkins and Marvin, 1832.

———. "Death of Dr. Judson's Child, Letter to Mother Hasseltine, Amherst, April 26, 1827." *The Baptist Missionary Magazine* 8 (1828) 131.

———. "Death of His Child, Serampore, June 27, 1841." *The Baptist Missionary Magazine* 22 (1842) 54–55.

———. *A Dictionary, English and Burmese*. 2nd ed. Maulmain, Burma: American Baptist Mission, 1852.

———. *A Digest of Scripture, Consisting of Extracts from the Old and New Testaments: On the Plan of "Brown's Selection of Scripture Passages."* Maulmain, Burma: American Baptist Mission, 1838.

———. "Dr. Judson's Journal, Jan. 25, 1828 [to May 31, 1828]." *The Baptist Missionary Magazine* 9 (1829) 73–74.

———. *The Elements of English Grammar*. Boston: Cushing & Lincoln, 1808.

———. *The Epitome of the Old Testament*. 3rd ed. Maulmain, Burma: American Baptist Mission, 1836.

———. "Extract of a Letter from Mr. Judson to Mr. Rice, Rangoon, August 3d, 1816." *The Baptist Missionary Magazine* 1 (1817) 184.

———. "Extract of a Letter from Mr. Judson to Mr. Rice, Rangoon, Novem. 14th, 1816." *The Baptist Missionary Magazine* 1 (1817) 184–85.

———. "Extract of a Letter from Mr. Judson, to One of the Editors, Rangoon, Feb. 20, 1819." *The Baptist Missionary Magazine* 2 (1819) 215.

———. "Extract of a Letter from Rev. Mr. Judson, to Dr. Baldwin, Dated Rangoon, August 5, 1816." *The Baptist Missionary Magazine* 1 (1817) 98–99.

———. "Extracts from Mr. Judson's Journal, to Rev. Dr. Bolles, Rangoon, Feb. 28, 1831 [to March 4, 1831]." *The Baptist Missionary Magazine* 11 (1831) 373–74.

———. "Extracts from Mr. Judson's Letters to His Wife, Rangoon, Sept. 5, 1821." *The Baptist Missionary Magazine* 4 (1823) 57–58.

———. *The Golden Balance*. 6th ed. Maulmain, Burma: American Baptist Mission, 1836.

———. "The Golden Balance." In *Tracts, In Burmese: Containing, The Creation, the Catechism, View of the Christian Religion, Way of Heaven, How Do We Know There Is a God?, The Atonement, Tree of Life, Glad Tidings, Golden Balance, The Awakener, The Investigator, Heaven and Hell, The Ship of Grace, Father's Advice, The Examiner, The Ten Commandments, On Idolatry*, edited by C. Bennett, 1:191–214. Maulmain, Burma: American Mission, 1860.

———. *Grammatical Notices of the Burmese Language*. Maulmain, Burma: American Baptist Mission, 1842.

———. *The Holy Bible, Containing Old and New Testament*. 3rd ed. Rangoon: American Baptist Missionary Union, 1890.

———. Judson Letters. American Baptist Historical Society, Atlanta.

———. *Judson's Letter on Dress: A Letter from Adoniram Judson, Missionary in Burmah to the Christian Women of America*. Boston: Scriptural Tract Repository, 1889.

———. "Letter from Dr. Judson to Mr. Sharp, of Boston, Ava, Nov. 30, 1822." *The Baptist Missionary Magazine* 4 (1823) 209–10.

———. "Letter from Dr. Judson to Rev. Dr. Baldwin, Dated Ava, Feb. 19, 1824." *The Baptist Missionary Magazine* 5 (1825) 22–23.

———. "Letter from Mr. Judson to Dr. Baldwin, Rangoon, Feb. 6, 1822." *The Baptist Missionary Magazine* 3 (1821) 458.

———. "Letter from Mr. Judson to Mr. Sharp, Dated Rangoon, September 17, 1821." *The Baptist Missionary Magazine* 3 (1821) 344–45.

———. "Letter from the Rev. Adoniram Judson, Jun. to Dr. Baldwin, Dated Rangoon, December 9, 1819." *The Baptist Missionary Magazine* 2 (1819) 379–80.

———. "Letter of Mr. Judson, Dated Maulmein, Dec. 21, 1837." *The Baptist Missionary Magazine* 18 (1838) 300–301.

———. "Letter of Mr. Judson, Maulmein, April 13, 1845: Sickness of Mrs. Judson, Expected Departure for American." *The Baptist Missionary Magazine* 25 (1845) 247–48.

———. "Letter of Rev. Mr. Judson, to the Baptist Churches in the United States of America, Maulmein, Nov. 21, 1832." *The Baptist Missionary Magazine* 13 (1833) 245–46.

———. *A Letter to the Rev. Adoniram Judson, Sen., Relative to the "Formal and Solemn Reprimand": To Which Is Added, a Letter to the Third Church in Plymouth, Mass., on the Subject of Baptism*. Boston: Lincoln & Edmunds, 1820.

———. "Mr. Judson's Journal, Feb. 29th, 1832 [to May 16, 1832]." *The Baptist Missionary Magazine* 13 (1833) 41–45.

———. "Mr. Judson's Journal, Maulmein, Aug. 14th, 1831 [to Dec. 29th, 1831]." *The Baptist Missionary Magazine* 12 (1832) 322–25.

———. "Mr. Judson's Journal, Nov. 29th, 1829." *The Baptist Missionary Magazine* 9 (1829) 245–46.

———. "Mr. Judson's Letter, to the American Missionaries in Rangoon and Maulmein, and the Cor. Sec. of the American Baptist Board of Foreign Missions, Prome, June 15, 1830." *The Baptist Missionary Magazine* 11 (1831) 55–58.

———. "Mr. Judson's Letter to Rev. Mr. Grow." *The Baptist Missionary Magazine* 12 (1832) 31–32.

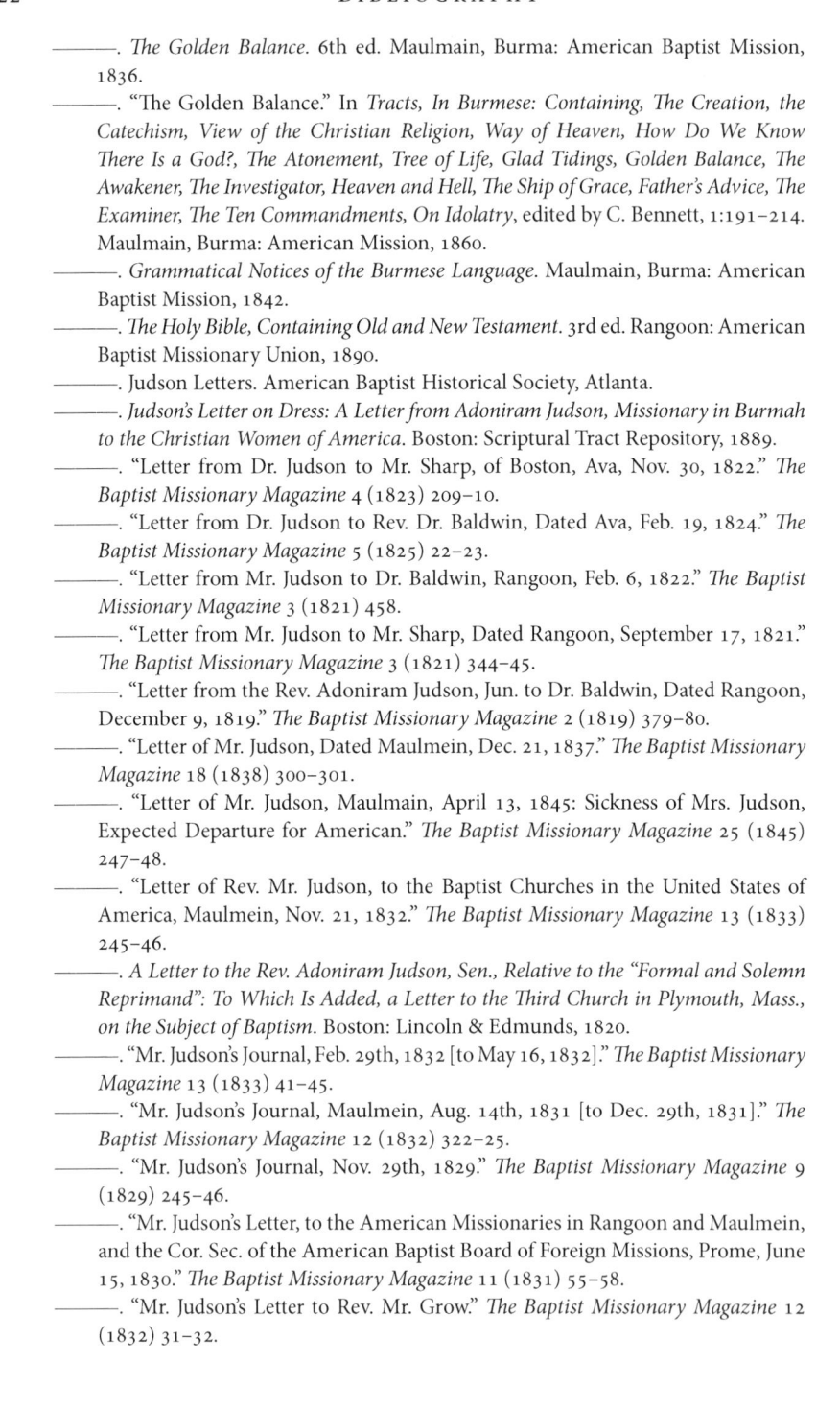

Bibliography

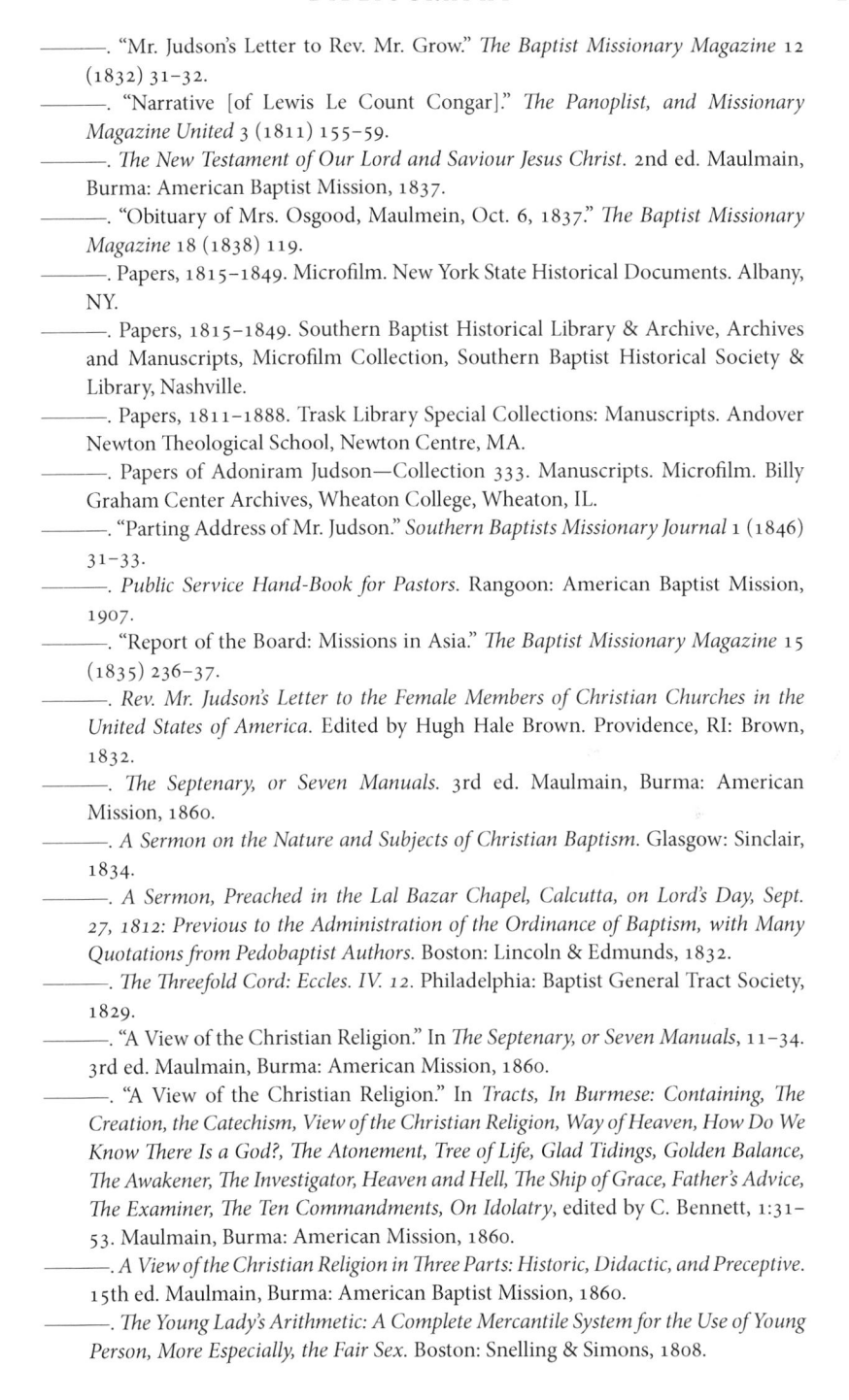

———. "Mr. Judson's Letter to Rev. Mr. Grow." *The Baptist Missionary Magazine* 12 (1832) 31–32.

———. "Narrative [of Lewis Le Count Congar]." *The Panoplist, and Missionary Magazine United* 3 (1811) 155–59.

———. *The New Testament of Our Lord and Saviour Jesus Christ*. 2nd ed. Maulmain, Burma: American Baptist Mission, 1837.

———. "Obituary of Mrs. Osgood, Maulmein, Oct. 6, 1837." *The Baptist Missionary Magazine* 18 (1838) 119.

———. Papers, 1815–1849. Microfilm. New York State Historical Documents. Albany, NY.

———. Papers, 1815–1849. Southern Baptist Historical Library & Archive, Archives and Manuscripts, Microfilm Collection, Southern Baptist Historical Society & Library, Nashville.

———. Papers, 1811–1888. Trask Library Special Collections: Manuscripts. Andover Newton Theological School, Newton Centre, MA.

———. Papers of Adoniram Judson—Collection 333. Manuscripts. Microfilm. Billy Graham Center Archives, Wheaton College, Wheaton, IL.

———. "Parting Address of Mr. Judson." *Southern Baptists Missionary Journal* 1 (1846) 31–33.

———. *Public Service Hand-Book for Pastors*. Rangoon: American Baptist Mission, 1907.

———. "Report of the Board: Missions in Asia." *The Baptist Missionary Magazine* 15 (1835) 236–37.

———. *Rev. Mr. Judson's Letter to the Female Members of Christian Churches in the United States of America*. Edited by Hugh Hale Brown. Providence, RI: Brown, 1832.

———. *The Septenary, or Seven Manuals*. 3rd ed. Maulmain, Burma: American Mission, 1860.

———. *A Sermon on the Nature and Subjects of Christian Baptism*. Glasgow: Sinclair, 1834.

———. *A Sermon, Preached in the Lal Bazar Chapel, Calcutta, on Lord's Day, Sept. 27, 1812: Previous to the Administration of the Ordinance of Baptism, with Many Quotations from Pedobaptist Authors*. Boston: Lincoln & Edmunds, 1832.

———. *The Threefold Cord: Eccles. IV. 12*. Philadelphia: Baptist General Tract Society, 1829.

———. "A View of the Christian Religion." In *The Septenary, or Seven Manuals*, 11–34. 3rd ed. Maulmain, Burma: American Mission, 1860.

———. "A View of the Christian Religion." In *Tracts, In Burmese: Containing, The Creation, the Catechism, View of the Christian Religion, Way of Heaven, How Do We Know There Is a God?, The Atonement, Tree of Life, Glad Tidings, Golden Balance, The Awakener, The Investigator, Heaven and Hell, The Ship of Grace, Father's Advice, The Examiner, The Ten Commandments, On Idolatry*, edited by C. Bennett, 1:31–53. Maulmain, Burma: American Mission, 1860.

———. *A View of the Christian Religion in Three Parts: Historic, Didactic, and Preceptive*. 15th ed. Maulmain, Burma: American Baptist Mission, 1860.

———. *The Young Lady's Arithmetic: A Complete Mercantile System for the Use of Young Person, More Especially, the Fair Sex*. Boston: Snelling & Simons, 1808.

Bibliography

Judson, Adoniram, and George H. Hough. "Articles of Agreement: To Rev. William Staughton, D.D., Cor. Sec. of Baptist Board of Missions, Rangoon, Oct. 21, 1816." *The Baptist Missionary Magazine* 1 (1817) 183–84.

———. "Communication from Rev. Messrs. Judson and Hough, Rangoon, Novem. 7th, 1816." *The Baptist Missionary Magazine* 1 (1817) 182–83.

Judson, Adoniram, Sr. *A Sermon Preached in the New Meeting House, Plymouth, December 22, 1802, in Memory of the Landing of Our Ancestors, December 22, 1620.* Boston: Carlisle, 1803.

Judson, Adoniram Brown. *How Judson Became a Baptist Missionary.* Philadelphia: Griffith & Rowland, 1913.

———. "Letter to Rev. J. Nelson Lewis." In *Judson Centennial Services: A Compilation of the Addresses, Papers, and Remarks, Given at These Services, Together with Extracts from Letters Received by the Committee, &c.*, edited by James Nelson Lewis, 56. Malden, MA: Mystic Side, 1888.

Judson, Ann Hasseltine. *An Account of the American Baptist Mission to the Burman Empire: In a Series of Letters, Addressed to a Gentleman in London.* London: Butterworth & Son and Clark, 1823.

———. "Ann Hasseltine Judson's Letters, 1818–1822." *Baptist Quarterly* 5, no. 8 (1931) 372–75.

———. "The Catechism." In *Tracts, In Burmese: Containing, The Creation, the Catechism, View of the Christian Religion, Way of Heaven, How Do We Know There Is a God?, The Atonement, Tree of Life, Glad Tidings, Golden Balance, The Awakener, The Investigator, Heaven and Hell, The Ship of Grace, Father's Advice, The Examiner, The Ten Commandments, On Idolatry*, edited by C. Bennett, 1:23–30. Maulmain, Burma: American Mission, 1860.

Judson, Edward. *The Life of Adoniram Judson, By His Son, Edward Judson.* New York: Randolph, 1883.

Judson, Emily Chubbuck. "Closing Scenes in Dr. Judson's Life, Maulmain, Sept. 20, 1850." *The Baptist Missionary Magazine* 31 (1851) 33–39.

———. Judson Letters. American Baptist Historical Society, Atlanta.

———. *The Kathayan Slave and Other Papers Connected with Missionary Life.* Boston: Ticknor, Reed, and Fields, 1853.

Julian, John. *A Dictionary of Hymnology.* New York: Scribner's Sons, 1892.

Kam, C. Duh. "Christian Mission to Buddhists in Myanmar: A Study of Past, Present, and Future Approaches by Baptists." DMiss diss., United Theological Seminary, 1997.

Kapic, Kelly M., and Randall C. Gleason, eds. *The Devoted Life: An Introduction to the Puritan Classics.* Downers Grove, IL: InterVarsity, 2004.

———. "Who Were the Puritans?" In *The Devoted Life: An Introduction to the Puritan Classics*, edited by Kelly M. Kapic and Randall C. Gleason, 15–37. Downers Grove, IL: InterVarsity, 2004.

Kendrick, Asahel Clark. *The Life and Letters of Mrs. Emily C. Judson.* London: Nelson and Sons, 1861.

Khai, Ziam Sian. "Barriers in Conversion (Missional and Indigenous Barriers): Identifying the Potential Barriers Contributing to the Stagnant Progress of Evangelistic Works Among the Burman Buddhists." PhD diss., Asbury Theological Seminary, 2010.

King, Alonzo. *Memoir of George Dana Boardman: Late Missionary to Burmah, Containing Much Intelligence Relative to the Burman Mission*. Boston: Lincoln & Edmunds, 1834.

Kling, David W. *A Field of Divine Wonders: The New Divinity and Village Revivals in Northwestern Connecticut, 1792-1822*. University Park: Pennsylvania State University Press, 1993.

———. "The New Divinity and the Origins of the American Board of Commissioners for Foreign Missions." In *North American Foreign Missions, 1810-1914: Theology, Theory, and Policy*, edited by Wilbert R. Shenk, 11-38. Studies in the History of Christian Missions. Grand Rapids: Eerdmans, 2004.

———. "The New Divinity and the Origins of the American Board of Commissioners for Foreign Missions 1." *Church History: Studies in Christianity and Culture* 4 (2003) 791-819.

Knowles, James D. *The Memoir of Mrs. Ann H. Judson, Wife of the Rev. Adoniram Judson, Missionary to Burmah, Including a History of the American Baptist Mission in the Burman Empire*. 2nd ed. London: Wightman and Cramp, 1829.

Laisum, David C. "Naming God in Burma Today." DMin diss., University of Chicago, 1994.

Larsen, Timothy. "The Reception Given *Evangelicalism in Modern Britain* Since Its Publication in 1989." In *The Advent of Evangelicalism*, edited by Michael A. G. Haykin and Kenneth J. Stewart, 21-36. Nashville: B. & H. Academic, 2008.

Law, William. *A Practical Treatise upon Christian Perfection*. 2nd ed. London: W. & J. Innys, 1728.

Leonard, Bill J. *Baptist Ways: A History*. Valley Forge, PA: Judson, 2003.

———. "'Wild and Romantic in the Extreme:' Ann Hasseltine Judson, (Her Husband), and a Duty to Go to the 'Distant and Benighted Heathen.'" *American Baptist Quarterly* 31, no. 1 (2013) 74-95.

Levens, Laura Rodgers. "Reading the Judsons: Recovering the Literary Works of Ann, Sarah, Emily, and Adoniram Judson for a New Baptist Mission History." *American Baptist Quarterly* 31, no. 1 (2013) 37-73.

Lewis, James Nelson, ed. *Judson Centennial Services: A Compilation of the Addresses, Papers, and Remarks, Given at These Services, Together with Extracts from Letters Received by the Committee, &c. (1888)*. Malden, MA: Mystic Side, 1888.

Lincoln, Heman, and Francis Wayland. *A Memoir of the Life and Labors of Francis Wayland*. New York: Sheldon, 1867.

Livingstone, Elizabeth Anne. "Judson, Adoniram." In *The Concise Oxford Dictionary of the Christian Church*, 282. 3rd ed. Oxford: Oxford University Press, 2013.

Lovelace, Richard F. "Afterword: The Puritans and Spiritual Renewal." In *The Devoted Life: An Introduction to the Puritan Classics*, edited by Kelly M. Kapic and Randall C. Gleason, 298-309. Downers Grove, IL: InterVarsity, 2004.

———. *Renewal as a Way of Life: A Guidebook for Spiritual Growth*. Eugene, OR: Wipf and Stock, 2002.

Luther, Calista V. *The Vintons and the Karens: Memorials of Rev. Justus H. Vinton and Calista H. Vinton*. Boston: Corthell, 1880.

Lynd, S. W. *Memoir of the Rev. William Staughton, D. D.* Boston: Lincoln & Edmunds, 1834.

Malcom, Howard. "Journal of Mr. Malcom." *The Baptist Missionary Magazine* 17 (1837) 4-9, 53-59.

Mang, Biak Hlei. "A Chin History of the Encounter with British Colonial Rule and the American Baptist Mission Works in the Chin Hills: A Story of Cultural Adaptation and Transformation in Burma (Myanmar)." PhD diss., Lutheran School of Theology, Chicago, 2010.

Manly, Basil, Jr. "The Christian Motive." *Southern Baptist Missionary Journal* 5 (1851) 169–72.

Marshall, P. J., ed. *The Oxford History of the British Empire: The Eighteenth Century.* Oxford History of the British Empire 2. New York: Oxford University Press, 2002.

Mather, Cotton. *Magnalia Christi Americana: Or, The Ecclesiastical History of New-England: From Its First Planting in the Year 1620, unto the Year of Our Lord, 1698, in Seven Books.* 1st American ed., from the London ed. of 1702. Hartford, CT: Andrus, 1986.

Mauldin, A. Chadwick. *Fullerism as Opposed to Calvinism: A Historical and Theological Comparison of the Missiology of Andrew Fuller and John Calvin.* Eugene, OR: Wipf and Stock, 2011.

McBeth, H. Leon. *The Baptist Heritage: Four Centuries of Baptist Witness.* Nashville: B. & H. Academic, 1987.

McClymond, Michael J., and Gerald R. McDermott. *The Theology of Jonathan Edwards.* New York: Oxford University Press, 2012.

McElroy, Jack. *Adoniram Judson's Soul Winning Secrets Revealed: An Inspiring Look at the Tools Used by "Jesus Christ's Man" in Burma.* Shirley, MA: McElroy, 2013.

McGinnley, William Anderson, ed. "Samuel Spring." In *A Record of Proceedings in the North Congregational Church, Newburyport, January 24, 1868,* 15–28. Newburyport, MA: Clark, 1868.

McGrath, Alister E. *Christian Spirituality.* Malden, MA: Blackwell, 1999.

Middleditch, Robert T. *Burmah's Great Missionary: Records of the Life, Character, and Achievements of Adoniram Judson.* New York: Fletcher, 1854.

Mild, Warren P. *Howard Malcom and the Great Mission Advance.* Valley Forge, PA: American Baptist Churches U.S.A., 1988.

Milton, John. *Paradise Lost, A Poem in Twelve Books.* Glasgow: R. & A. Foulis, 1750.

"Minutes of the First Annual Meeting of the American Board of Commissioners for Foreign Missions." In *First Ten Annual Reports of the American Board of Commissioners for Foreign Missions,* by American Board of Commissioners for Foreign Missions, 9–10. Boston: Crocker and Brewster, 1834.

Mobley, K. P. "Judson, Adoniram, Jr." In *Biographical Dictionary of Evangelicals,* edited by Timothy Larsen, Mark Noll, and David Bebbington, 337–40. Leicester, England: Intervarsity, 2003.

Moore, W. T. *William Crane, Layman Extraordinary: 1790–1866.* Falls of Rough, KY: Sandefur, 1989.

Morden, Peter J. *Offering Christ to the World: Andrew Fuller (1754–1815) and the Revival of Eighteenth-Century Particular Baptist Life.* Studies in Baptist History and Thought 8. Waynesboro, GA: Paternoster, 2003.

Morrow, Honoré Willsie. *Splendor of God.* New York: Grosset & Dunlap, 1929.

Moyer, Elgin. "Judson, Adoniram." In *Wycliffe Biographical Dictionary of the Church,* edited by Earle E. Cairns, 219. Chicago: Moody, 1982.

Mulholland, Kenneth B. "From Luther to Carey: Pietism and the Modern Missionary Movement." *Bibliotheca Sacra* 156 (1999) 85–95.

Bibliography

―――. "Moravians, Puritans, and the Modern Missionary Movement." *Bibliotheca Sacra* 156 (1999) 221–32.

Murdock, John N. "Memorial Address." In *Judson Centennial Services: A Compilation of the Addresses, Papers, and Remarks, Given at These Services, Together with Extracts from Letters Received by the Committee, &c.*, edited by James Nelson Lewis, 10–22. Malden, MA: Mystic Side, 1888.

―――. *Our Civil War: Its Causes and Its Issues: A Discourse Delivered in the Baptist Church, Brookline, on the Occasion of the National Thanksgiving, August 6, 1863*. Boston: Wright & Potter, 1863.

Neely, Alan. "Liele, George." In *Biographical Dictionary of Christian Missions*, edited by Gerald H. Anderson, 400–01. New York: Macmillan Reference USA, 1998.

Neill, Stephen. *A History of Christianity in India, 1707–1858*. Cambridge: Cambridge University Press, 1985.

―――. *A History of Christian Missions*. 2nd ed. The Penguin History of the Church. Vol. 6. Harmondsworth, England: Penguin, 1986.

Nettles, Thomas J. *By His Grace and for His Glory: A Historical, Theological, and Practical Study of the Doctrines of Grace in Baptist Life*. Grand Rapids: Baker, 1986.

Nicole, Roger. "Post Script on Penal Substitution." In *The Glory of the Atonement*, edited by Charles E. Hill and Frank A. James III, 445–52. Downers Grove, IL: IVP Academic, 2004.

Nott, Samuel. *A Letter Addressed to Rev. Enoch Pond of Ward, Mass: On the Insinuations and Charges Contained in His Reply to Mr. Judson's Sermon on Baptism*. Boston: Lincoln & Edmunds, 1819.

Packer, J. I. "Puritan Spirituality." In *The Dictionary of Christian Spirituality*, edited by Glen Scorgie, 702–4. Grand Rapids: Zondervan, 2011.

―――. *A Quest for Godliness: The Puritan Vision of the Christian Life*. Wheaton, IL: Crossway, 1990.

Park, Edwards Amasa. *Memoir of the Life and Character of Samuel Hopkins, D. D.* 2nd ed. Boston: Doctrinal Tract and Book Society, 1854.

Phinney, F. D., ed. *The Judson Centennial Celebrations in Burma: 1813–1913*. Rangoon: American Baptist Mission, 1914.

Pipa Jr., Joseph A., and J. Andrew Wortman, eds. *Reformed Spirituality*. Taylors, SC: Southern Presbyterian, 2003.

Pond, Enoch. *A Treatise on the Mode and Subjects of Christian Baptism: In Two Parts, Designed as a Reply to the Statements and Reasonings of the Rev. Adoniram Judson, Jr., as Exhibited in His "Sermon, Preached in the Lal Bazar Chapel, Calcutta, on Lord's Day, September 27, 1812," and Recently Republished in This Country*. Worcester, MA: Manning, 1818.

Pope, Alexander. *The Works of Alexander Pope*. Vol. 2. London: Murray, 1871.

Randall, Ian. *What a Friend We Have in Jesus*. Maryknoll, NY: Orbis, 2005.

Ranney, Ruth Whitaker. *A Sketch of the Lives and Missionary Work of Rev. Cephas Bennett and His Wife Stella Kneeland Bennett, 1829–1891*. New York: Silver, Burdett, 1892.

Rice, Luther. *Dispensations of Providence: The Journal and Selected Letters of Luther Rice: With an Introduction and Appendices*. Edited by William H. Brackney. Rochester, NY: American Baptist Historical Society, 1984.

Richards, James. *A Discourse, Delivered 14th January, 1810, at Newark: Occasioned by the Death of Lewis Le Count Congar, a Member of the Theological Seminary at Andover: Who Died at That Place 6th January, 1810.* Newark: Gould, 1810.

Richards, Thomas C. *The Haystack Prayer Meeting: An Account of Its Origins and Spirit.* New York: De Vinne, 1906.

———. *Samuel J. Mills, Missionary Pathfinder, Pioneer and Promoter.* Boston: Pilgrim, 1906.

Richards, William C. *The Apostle of Burma: A Missionary Epic, in Commemoration of the Centennial of the Birth of Adoniram Judson.* Boston: Lee and Shepard, 1889.

Rippon, John. *A Brief Memoir of the Life and Writings of the Late Rev. John Gill, D.D.* 1838. Repr., Harrisonburg, VA: Gano, 1992.

Robbins, Joseph Chandler. *Boardman of Burma.* Philadelphia: Judson, 1940.

Roebuck, Claude V. "Adoniram Judson: A Study in Church History." *Journal of Bible and Religion* 20, no. 4 (1952) 239–44.

Rooy, Sidney H. *The Theology of Missions in the Puritan Tradition.* 1965. Repr., Laurel, MS: Audubon, 2006.

Rowe, Henry K. *History of Andover Theological Seminary.* Boston: Todd, 1933.

Samson, G. W. *The Atonement Viewed as Assumed Divine Responsibility: Traced as the Fact Attested in Divine Revelation; Shown to Be the Truth Uniting Christian Theories; and Recognized as the Grace Realized in Human Experience.* Philadelphia: Lippincott, 1878.

Scacewater, Todd. "Adoniram Judson's Understanding and Appropriation of Buddhism." *Churchman* 130, no. 3 (2016) 201–11.

Schaff, D. S. "Judson, Adoniram." In *The New Schaff-Herzog Encyclopedia of Religious Knowledge,* edited by Samuel M. Jackson, 6:257–58. Grand Rapids: Baker, 1977.

Schattschneider, David A. "Pioneers in Mission: Zinzendorf and the Moravians." *International Bulletin of Missionary Research* 8, no. 2 (1984) 63–67.

———. "William Carey, Modern Missions, and the Moravian Influence." *International Bulletin of Missionary Research* 22, no. 1 (1998) 8–10.

Scorgie, Glen, ed. *The Dictionary of Christian Spirituality.* Grand Rapids: Zondervan, 2011.

Sharp, Daniel. *Christian Mourning: A Discourse Delivered at the Funeral of Rev. Lucius Bolles, D.D., Late Secretary of the Baptist Board of Foreign Missions.* Boston: Gould, Kendall & Lincoln, 1844.

———. *Recognition of Friends in Heaven.* Boston: French, 1857.

———. *Services at the Fortieth Anniversary of the Installation of the Rev. Daniel Sharp, D.D.: As Pastor of the Charles Street Baptist Church and Society, Boston, April 29, 1852.* Boston: Ticknor, Reed, and Fields, 1852.

Sheldrake, Philip. *Spirituality and History.* London: SPCK, 1991.

Shenk, Wilbert R., ed. *North American Foreign Missions, 1810–1914: Theology, Theory, and Policy.* Studies in the History of Christian Missions. Grand Rapids: Eerdmans, 2004.

Shwe Wa, Maung. *Burma Baptist Chronicle.* Edited by Genevieve Sowards and Erville Sowards. Rangoon: Burma Baptist Convention, 1963.

Smith, Andrew C. Review of *William Owen Carver's Controversies in the Baptist South* by Mark R. Wilson. *Journal of Southern Religion* 12 (2010). http://jsr.fsu.edu/Volume12/Smith%20on%20Wilson.html. Accessed September 28, 2016.

Smith, Arthur Warren. *Sewall Mason Osgood, D. D., in Missionary Service for Forty-One Years, 1834–1875.* Boston: Backus Historical Society, 1907.
Smith, George. *The Life of William Carey.* New York: Dutton, 1909.
Smith, S. F. *Missionary Sketches: A Concise History of the Work of the American Baptist Missionary Union.* Boston: Corthell, 1879.
Southern Baptist Missionary Journal. 5 vols. Richmond: Board of Foreign and Domestic Missions of the Southern Baptist Convention, 1846–1851.
Spangenberg, August Gottlieb. *The Life of Count Zinzendorf.* Translated by Samuel Jackson. London: Holdsworth, 1838.
Special Collections. University Archives, John Hay Library, Brown University, Providence, RI.
Spener, Philipp Jakob. *Pia Desideria.* Edited and translated by Theodore G. Tappert. Minneapolis: Fortress, 1964.
Spring, Samuel. *Moral Disquisitions: And Strictures on the Rev. David Tappan's Letters to Philalethes.* 2nd ed. Exeter, NH: Norris, 1815.
———. *A Sermon, Delivered before the Massachusetts Missionary Society, at Their Annual Meeting May 25, 1802.* Newburyport, MA: Blunt, 1802.
Spurgeon, Charles H. *Autobiography.* Vol. 2. Edinburgh: The Banner of Truth Trust, 1973.
Stanley, Brian. *The Bible and the Flag: Protestant Missions and British Imperialism in the Nineteenth and Twentieth Centuries.* Leicester, UK: Apollos, 1990.
———. *Christian Missions and the Enlightenment.* Grand Rapids: Eerdmans, 2001.
———. "Christian Missions and the Enlightenment: A Reevaluation." In *Christian Missions and the Enlightenment*, edited by Brian Stanley, 1–21. Grand Rapids: Eerdmans, 2001.
———. "Christianity and Civilization in English Evangelical Mission Thought, 1792–1857." In *Christian Missions and the Enlightenment*, edited by Brian Stanley, 169–97. Grand Rapids: Eerdmans, 2001.
———. *The History of the Baptist Missionary Society, 1792–1992.* Edinburgh: T. & T. Clark, 1992.
Starr, Edward C. *A Baptist Bibliography: Being a Register of Printed Material by and about Baptists; Including Works Written against the Baptists (Section J).* Vol. 12. Chester, PA: American Baptist Historical Society, 1967.
Stennett, Joseph. *An Answer to Mr. David Russen's Book, Entitul'd, Fundamentals without a Foundation, or a True Picture of the Anabaptists, &c. Together with Some Brief Remarks on Mr. James Broome's Letter Annex'd to That Treatise.* London: Brown, Crouch, and Baker, 1704.
———. *The Works of the Late Reverend and Learned Mr. Joseph Stennett.* London, 1731.
Stevens, Edward Oliver. *A Vocabulary, English and Peguan: To Which Are Added a Few Pages of Geographical Names.* Rangoon: American Baptist Mission, 1896.
Stevens, Sarah. "Extracts from Letters of Mrs. Stevens." *The Baptist Missionary Magazine* 19 (1839) 83–85.
Stevens, Sumner Wynne. *A Half-Century in Burma: A Memorial Sketch of Edward Abiel Stevens.* Philadelphia: American Baptist, 1897.
Stillman, Samuel. *A Sermon, Preached January 9, 1805, in the Tabernacle, Salem: At the Ordination of the Rev. Lucius Bolles to the Pastoral Care of the Baptist Church and Society in That Town.* Boston: Manning and Loring, 1805.
Stott, John. *Christ the Controversialist.* Downers Grove, IL: InterVarsity, 1996.

Stow, Baron, and S. F. Smith. *The Psalmist: A Collection of Hymns for the Use of the Baptist Churches*. Philadelphia: American Baptist, 1844.

Sweeney, Douglas A., and Allen C. Guelzo, eds. *The New England Theology: From Jonathan Edwards to Edwards Amasa Park*. Grand Rapids: Baker Academic, 2006.

"A Sweet Surprise." *The Friend: A Religious and Literary Journal* 64 (1891) 174.

Symes, Michael. *An Account of an Embassy to the Kingdom of Ava, in the Year 1795*. Vol. 1. Edinburgh: Constable, 1827.

Taw, Saw Gler. "A Renewal Strategy of the Karen Baptist Church of Myanmar (Burma) for Mission." ThM thesis, Fuller Theological Seminary, 1992.

Taylor, James B. *Memoir of Reverend Luther Rice: One of the First American Missionaries to the East*. 2nd ed. Nashville: Broadman, 1937.

Tooze, George H., ed. *Judson Treasures of The First Baptist Church, Malden, with a Short Biography of the Life of Emily Chubbuck Judson*. Malden, MA: First Baptist Church, 1979.

———. *The Life and Letters of Emily Chubbuck Judson (Fanny Forester)*. 7 vols. Macon, GA: Mercer University Press, 2013.

Torbet, Robert G. *A History of the Baptists*. 3rd ed. Valley Forge, PA: Judson, 1963.

———. *Venture of Faith: The Story of the American Baptist Foreign Mission Society and the Woman's American Baptist Foreign Mission Society, 1814-1954*. Philadelphia: Judson, 1955.

Tracy, Joseph. *History of the American Board of Commissioners for Foreign Missions*. 2nd ed. Boston: Dodd, 1842.

Trevelyan, C. A. *The Application of the Roman Alphabet to All the Oriental Language: Contained in a Series of Papers Written by Messrs. Trevelyan, J. Prinsep, and Tytler, Rev. A. Duff, and H. T. Prinsep and Published in Various Calcutta Periodicals in the Year 1834*. 3rd ed. Calcutta: Serampore, 1858.

Van Til, Cornelius. *A Survey of Christian Epistemology*. 2nd ed. In Defense of Biblical Christianity 2. Phillipsburg, NJ: Presbyterian and Reformed, 1980.

Vidler, Alec R. *The Church in an Age of Revolution*. Penguin History of the Church 5. Harmondsworth, UK: Penguin, 1962.

Vuta, Kawl Thang. "A Brief History of the Planting and Growth of the Church in Burma." DMiss diss., Fuller Theological Seminary, 1983.

Wade, Jonathan. "The Investigator." In *Tracts, In Burmese: Containing, The Creation, the Catechism, View of the Christian Religion, Way of Heaven, How Do We Know There Is a God?, The Atonement, Tree of Life, Glad Tidings, Golden Balance, The Awakener, The Investigator, Heaven and Hell, The Ship of Grace, Father's Advice, The Examiner, The Ten Commandments, On Idolatry*, edited by C. Bennett, 1:239-61. Maulmain, Burma: American Mission, 1860.

Warburton, Stacy R. *Eastward! The Story of Adoniram Judson*. New York: Round Table, 1937.

Washburn, W. H. "The Burial at St. Helena." In *The Judson Offering, Intended as a Token of Christian Sympathy with the Living, and a Memento of Christian Affection for the Dead*, 228-29. New York: Colby, 1847.

———. "Judson Longing for His Burman Home." In *The Judson Offering, Intended as a Token of Christian Sympathy with the Living, and a Memento of Christian Affection for the Dead*, 293-94. New York: Colby, 1847.

Watts, Isaac, and John Rippon. *The Psalms and Hymns of Dr. Watts*. Philadelphia: Clark, 1831.

Wayland, Francis. *A Memoir of the Life and Labors of the Rev. Adoniram Judson, D.D.* 2 vols. Boston: Phillips, Samson, 1853.
Whittemore, Robert C. *The Transformation of the New England Theology.* American University Studies 23. New York: Lang, 1987.
Wills, Gregory A. "From Congregationalist to Baptist: Judson and Baptism." In *Adoniram Judson: A Bicentennial Appreciation of the Pioneer American Missionary*, edited by Jason G. Duesing, 149–63. Studies in Baptist Life and Thought, edited by Michael A. G. Haykin. Nashville: B. & H. Academic, 2012.
———. *Southern Baptist Theological Seminary, 1859–2009.* Oxford: Oxford University, 2009.
Wilson, Arabella M. Stuart. *The Lives of Mrs. Ann H. Judson and Mrs. Sarah B. Judson: With a Biographical Sketch of Mrs. Emily C. Judson, Missionaries to Burmah.* New York: Miller, Orton & Mulligan, 1855.
Winslow, Miron. *A Sketch of Missions: Or, History of the Principal Attempts to Propagate Christianity Among the Heathen.* Andover, MA: Flagg and Gould, 1819.
Woods, Leonard. *History of the Andover Theological Seminary.* Boston: Osgood, 1885.
———. *Memoirs of American Missionaries, Formerly Connected with the Society of Inquiry Respecting Missions, in the Andover Theological Seminary: Embracing a History of the Society, &c., with an Introductory Essay.* Boston: Peirce and Parker, 1833.
———. *A Sermon Delivered at the Tabernacle in Salem, Feb. 6, 1812, on Occasion of the Ordination of the Rev. Messrs. Samuel Newell, A.M. Adoniram Judson, A.M. Samuel Nott, A.M. Gordon Hall, A.M. and Luther Rice, A.B. Missionaries to the Heathen in Asia.* Boston: Armstrong, 1812.
Worcester, Samuel. *A Correction of Erroneous Statements Concerning the Embarkation of the Rev. Messrs. Judson and Newell, at Salem, February 18, 1812. Reprinted from the Christian Review, No. LIV.* Boston: Marvin, 1849.
———. "Minutes of the General Association of Massachusetts Proper." *The Panoplist, and Missionary Magazine United* 3 (1811) 86–90.
———. *A Third Letter to the Rev. William E. Channing, on the Subject of Unitarianism.* Boston: Armstrong, 1815.
———. *Two Discourses on the Perpetuity and Provision of God's Gracious Covenant with Abraham and His Seed.* Salem, MA: Haven Pool, 1805.
Young, Richard Fox. "Making Comparative Missiology More Comparative: Does the Translation Principle Have a Buddhist Corollary?" *Neue Zeitschrift Für Missionswissenschaft* 60, no. 2 (2004) 105–21.

Author Index

à Kempis, Thomas, 59, 138
Aberly, John, 31
Adam, Peter, 25
Adams, Hannah, 34
Adamson, H. Sir, 120
Anderson, Courtney, 2, 8-9, 28, 33, 41, 46-48, 50-53, 55-63, 69, 98, 127-28, 131, 180, 189
Anderson, Gerald H., 56
Augustine, 22
Austin, Samuel, 66

Babcock, Rufus, 48, 51
Balderston, Lloyd, 141
Barnes, Lemuel Hall, 32
Bayles, Richard M., 91, 182
Bebbington, David W., 20, 208
Beeke, Joel, 22
Bellamy, Joseph, 37
Bendroth, Margaret L., 46, 111, 191
Benedict, Abbot of Monte Cassino, 137
Bennett, Cephas, 60-61, 160
Blaikie, W. G., 24
Boardman, George Dana, 61
Booth, Abraham, 66
Boreham, F. W., 50, 171, 210
Boston, Thomas, 49
Bowden, Henry Warner, 41
Brackney, William H., 1-2, 20, 55, 211
Brewster, Paul, 26-27
Brown, Max H., 11, 36, 38, 40, 131
Brown, Russell E., 84, 209
Brumberg, Joan Jacobs, 3, 9, 29, 33, 41-42, 45-46, 50, 56, 211

Brush, John W., 176
Buchanan, Claudius, 11, 51
Burns, E. D., 30
Butler, Jon, 3, 34

Calamy, Edmund, 21-22
Caldwell, Robert, 10, 34-37
Carey, William, 15, 27, 29, 68
Carpenter, John, 29
Carver, W. O., ix, 3, 5, 67, 74
Case, Jay Riley, 87
Cheever, George Barrell, 138
Chessman, Daniel, 69, 98
Chun, Chris, 10, 26
Clemént, Jesse, 7, 15, 91, 97, 107, 145
Clipsham, E. F., 26
Colley, Linda, 19
Collier, Mary Ann, 56-57, 98
Comstock, Grover S., 56, 61, 121
Conant, Hannah Chaplin, 3, 7, 15, 28, 48, 60, 65, 73, 80, 91, 99, 104, 111, 113, 115, 117, 140, 142, 162, 180, 194, 210
Conforti, Joseph A., 33-34, 36, 38-39, 125
Cragg, Gerald R., 18
Crowell, W. M., 2

Danvers, Henry, 66
De Jong, James A., 160-61
Dingrin, La Seng, 11, 82, 160
Dowling, John, 3-4, 7, 15, 82, 147, 164, 166, 201
Duesing, Jason G., 2, 9-10, 51
Duncan, R. S., 111

Author Index

Eddy, Daniel Clarke, 7, 15, 48
Edwards, Jonathan, 24, 36, 38–39, 95, 160
Edwards, Peter, 66
Eitel, Keith E., 28
Elsbree, Oliver Wendell, 161

Faunce, D. W., 172
Fénelon, François de Salignac de La Mothe, 59
Fletcher, Edward H., 6
Forester, Fanny, 7, 15
Foster, Frank Hugh, 34, 37–39
Froom, LeRoy E., 78
Fuller, Andrew, 19, 26

Gifford, O. P., 89
Gillett, David, 20, 208
Gillette, A. D., 3, 7, 15, 121
Gleason, Randall C., 21–22
Gordon, James M., 23–24
Gouger, Henry, 15, 49, 101, 126, 197
Gray, E. H., 3, 206
Grudem, Wayne, 39
Guelzo, Allen C., 34
Guyon, Jeanne Marie Bouvier de La Motte, 59, 101, 125

Hague, William, 3, 7, 15, 120, 178
Hankins, Barry, 34
Hanna, T. Carson, 129
Hatfield, Edwin F., 107
Haykin, Michael A. G., 10, 19–21, 25
Hill, James L., 7, 15
Hindmarsh, D. Bruce, 50
Hitchcock, Edward, 88
Holifield, E. Brooks, 37, 39–40, 90, 125, 161
Hopkins, Samuel, 37, 39–40, 125–26, 139
Hull, J. Mervin, 2
Hulse, Erroll, 7, 12, 28–29, 129
Hunt, Rosalie Hall, 2, 9, 53, 55, 62–63, 69, 84, 98, 115, 129, 149, 177, 199, 209, 211
Hutchison, William R., 160–61, 169, 179

James, Sharon, 2–3, 9
Jameson, Melvin, 14
Jauhiainen, Peter, 40
Johnson, Maxwell E., 137
Judson, Abby Ann, 187
Judson, Abigail, 127
Judson, Adoniram, 4, 10–11, 14–15, 28, 49, 54, 56, 58–63, 66, 68–69, 71–74, 77, 81, 83, 88–90, 92, 96–98, 103, 106–7, 110, 118, 120–21, 127–28, 135–39, 141–42, 145, 147–50, 152–54, 160–61, 163–66, 168, 176–78, 181–82, 184, 186, 189–91, 193, 196–97, 200, 203, 210–12
Judson, Adoniram, Sr., 32–33, 47
Judson, Adoniram Brown, 110, 204
Judson, Ann Hasseltine, 9–10, 15, 55, 87, 98, 118, 145
Judson, Edward, 2–3, 5, 13–15, 48, 50, 52, 54–56, 58–63, 66, 77, 79, 91–92, 96–98, 105–6, 108–9, 126, 130–35, 137–39, 142, 148–49, 152–53, 155–56, 166, 174, 176–80, 182, 184, 191–92, 197, 204, 206, 210, 212
Judson, Emily Chubbuck, 7, 15, 171, 210
Julian, John, 14, 200

Kam, C. Duh, 11
Kapic, Kelly M., 21–22
Kendrick, Asahel Clark, 5, 7, 15, 109, 145, 156, 160, 199
Khai, Ziam Sian, 11
King, Alonzo, 61, 92
Kling, David W., 34, 45, 161
Knowles, James D., 2, 6, 13, 15, 53–54, 56, 61, 65, 68, 98, 100, 111

Laisum, David C., 11, 82, 139–40
Law, William, 138
Leonard, Bill J., 26, 55, 67, 160
Levens, Laura Rodgers, 4
Lewis, James Nelson, 7
Lincoln, Heman, 54, 88
Livingstone, Elizabeth Anne, 1
Lovelace, Richard F., 21, 23

Luther, Calista V., 85
Lynd, S. W., 116

Malcom, Howard, 119
Mang, Biak Hlei, 11
Manly, Basil, Jr., 172
Marshall, P. J., 18
Mather, Cotton, 33
Mauldin, A. Chadwick, 27
McBeth, H. Leon, 46, 54, 111
McClymond, Michael J., 160
McDermott, Gerald R., 160
McElroy, Jack, 14, 97, 136, 160, 176
McGinnley, William Anderson, 113
McGrath, Alister E., 20, 208
Middleditch, Robert T., 2, 4, 13, 15,
    28, 53, 55, 57, 60, 66–68, 73–74,
    78, 80–82, 87, 92, 97–98, 100,
    107–9, 111, 114, 117–21, 130,
    138, 168, 174, 176–77, 180–82,
    184–86, 188, 193–94, 200, 202,
    206–7, 210, 212
Mild, Warren P., 61, 81
Milton, John, 103
Mobley, K. P., 1
Moore, W. T., 195
Morden, Peter J., 26
Morrow, Honoré Willsie, 129
Moyer, Elgin, 1
Mulholland, Kenneth B., 27, 30
Murdock, John N., 94, 110

Neely, Alan, 1
Neill, Stephen, 25, 28–31
Nettles, Thomas J., 34
Nicole, Roger, 40
Nott, Samuel, 69

Packer, J. I., 21–22
Park, Edwards Amasa, 126
Phinney, F. D., 151
Pond, Enoch, 69
Pope, Alexander, 115

Randall, Ian, 20, 208
Ranney, Ruth Whitaker, 60, 152, 190
Rice, Luther, 54
Richards, James, 189

Richards, Thomas C., 45–46
Richards, William C., 7
Rippon, John, 47, 66, 203, 230
Robbins, Joseph Chandler, 92
Roebuck, Claude V., 131
Rooy, Sidney H., 20
Rowe, Henry K., 34, 41–42, 45

Samson, G. W., 123
Scacewater, Todd, 131
Schaff, D. S., 1
Schattschneider, David A., 29
Sharp, Daniel, 88
Sheldrake, Philip, 20, 208
Shwe Wa, Maung, 91
Smith, Andrew C., ix
Smith, Arthur Warren, 61, 153
Smith, George, 25
Smith, S. F., 93, 147
Spangenberg, August Gottlieb, 31
Spener, Philipp Jakob, 29–30
Spring, Samuel, 113
Spurgeon, Charles H., 22
Stanley, Brian, 19–20, 26
Starr, Edward C., 61
Stennett, Joseph, 66
Stevens, Edward Oliver, 63
Stevens, Sarah, 85
Stevens, Sumner Wynne, 5, 14, 105,
    112, 182, 199
Stillman, Samuel, 88
Stott, John, 24
Stow, Baron, 147
Sweeney, Douglas A., 34
Symes, Michael, 51

Taw, Saw Gler, 11
Taylor, James B., 54
Tooze, George H., 7, 15, 109
Torbet, Robert G. 2, 25, 54, 88, 154
Tracy, Joseph, 52, 161
Trevelyan, C. A., 82

Van Til, Cornelius, 90
Vidler, Alec R., 18
Vuta, Kawl Thang, 11

Wade, Jonathan, 10

Warburton, Stacy R., 2, 5, 7–8, 46–47, 49, 60–61, 114, 118, 121, 126, 131, 134, 173, 181, 185
Washburn, W. H., 107
Watts, Isaac, 47, 203
Wayland, Francis, 2, 5–9, 13–15, 28, 49–63, 65–67, 70–71, 73–75, 78–80, 82–92, 94, 96, 98–101, 103–15, 117–24, 126–28, 130–35, 137–39, 141–43, 145–47, 149–59, 162–70, 173, 175, 177–80, 182–200, 202–4, 207, 209–10
Whittemore, Robert C., 34, 38
Wills, Gregory A., ix, 65, 168
Wilson, Arabella M. Stuart., 159
Winslow, Miron, 41
Woods, Leonard, 34, 41–45, 48, 51, 53, 65, 111–12, 125, 138, 181
Worcester, Samuel, 66, 97, 113

Yeh, Allen, 10
Young, Richard Fox, 160

Made in the USA
Monee, IL
23 May 2022